ENGLISH / SPANISH

INGLÉS / ESPAÑOL

OXFORD

PICTURE

DICTIONARY

THIRD EDITION

Jayme Adelson-Goldstein

Norma Shapiro

OXFORD
UNIVERSITY PRESS

198 Madison Avenue
New York, NY 10016 USA

Great Clarendon Street, Oxford OX2 6DP, United Kingdom

Oxford University Press is a department of the University of Oxford.
It furthers the University's objective of excellence in research, scholarship,
and education by publishing worldwide. Oxford is a registered trade
mark of Oxford University Press in the UK and in certain other countries

ACKNOWLEDGMENTS

Translated by: Techno-Graphics & Translations, Inc.

Illustrations by: Lori Anzalone: 13, 70-71, 76-77; Joe "Fearless" Arenella/Will
Sumpter: 196; Argosy Publishing: 66-67 (call-outs), 108-109, 114-115
(call-outs), 156, 196, 205, 206-207, 215; Barbara Bastian: 4, 15, 208; Philip
Batini/AA Reps: 50; Thomas Bayley/Sparks Literary Agency: 162; Sally Bensusen:
217, 220; Peter Bollinger/Shannon Associates: 14-15; Higgens Bond/Anita Grien:
232; Molly Borman-Pullman: 118, 119; Mark Duffin: 7, 37, 61, 94, 238, 239, 240,
241; Jim Fanning/Ravenhill Represents: 80-81; Mike Gardner: 10, 12, 17, 22, 134,
116-117, 145-146, 179, 225, 234-235; Garth Glazier/AA Reps: 106, 111, 120; Dennis
Godfrey/Mike Wepplo: 214; Steve Graham: 126-127, 230; Julia Green/Mendola Art:
231; Glenn Gustafson: 9, 27, 48, 76, 100, 101, 119, 134-135, 138, 159, 165, 197;
Barbara Harmon: 218-219, 221; Ben Hasler/NB Illustration: 94-95, 101, 174, 188,
198-199; Betsy Hayes: 136, 140, 143; Matthew Holmes: 75; Stewart Holmes/
Illustration Ltd.: 204; Janos Jantner/Beehive Illustration: 5, 13, 82-83, 124-125,
132-133, 152-153, 166-167, 168, 169, 174, 175, 182-183, 192, 193; Ken Joudrey/
Munro Campagna: 52, 68-69, 187; Bob Kaganich/Deborah Wolfe: 10, 40-41, 123;
Steve Karp: 237, 238; Mike Kasun/Munro Campagna: 224; Graham Kennedy: 27;
Marcel Laverdet/AA Reps: 23; Jeffrey Lindberg: 33, 42-43, 92-93, 135, 164-165,
176-177, 186; Dennis Lyall/Artworks: 208; Chris Lyons/Lindgren & Smith: 203;
Alan Male/Artworks: 216, 217; Jeff Mangiat/Mendola Art: 53, 54, 55, 56, 57, 58, 59,
66-67; Adrian Mateescu/The Studio: 200-201, 238-239; Karen Minot: 28-29; Paul
Mirocha/The Wiley Group: 206, 222-223; Peter Miserendino/P.T. Pie Illustrations:
208; Lee Montgomery/Illustration Ltd.: 4; OUP Design: 20-21; Roger Motzkus: 235;
Laurie O'Keefe: 112, 222-223; Daniel O'Leary/Illustration Ltd.: 8-9, 26, 34-35, 78, 137,
138-139, 244; Vilma Ortiz-Dillon: 16, 20-21, 60, 98-99, 100, 217; Terry Pazcko: 46-47,
148-149, 156, 194, 233; David Preiss/Munro Campagna: 5; Pronk & Associates: 204-
205; Tony Randazzo/AA Reps: 160, 240-241; Mike Renwick/Creative Eye: 128-129;
Mark Riedy/Scott Hull Associates: 48-49, 79, 142, 157; Jon Rogers/AA Reps: 114; Jeff
Sanson/Schumann & Co.: 84-85, 246-247; Ben Shannon/Magnet Reps: 11, 64-65, 90,
91, 96, 97, 121, 147, 170-171, 172-173, 180-181, 245; Reed Sprunger/Jae Wagoner
Artists Rep.: 18-19, 238-239; Studio Liddell/AA Reps: 27; Angelo Tillary: 108-109;
Samuel Velasco/5W Infographics: 10, 11, 12, 13, 15, 48, 49, 80-81 (design), 110, 112,
113, 138, 143, 146, 156, 159, 210, 211, 212-213; Ralph Voltz/Deborah Wolfe: 50-51,
130-131, 144, 158, 163, 185, 190, 191, 207 (top left), 215 (bot. left), 242-243; Jeff Wack/
Mendola Art: 24, 25, 86-87, 102-103, 136-137, 237; Brad Walker: 104-105, 154-155,
161, 226-227; Wendy Wassink: 112-113; John White/The Neis Group: 209;
Eric Wilkerson: 32, 140; Simon Williams/Illustration Ltd.: 2-3, 6-7, 30-31, 36, 38-39,
44-45, 72-73, 141, 178, 184; Lee Woodgate/Eye Candy Illustration: 228-229; Andy Zito:
62-23; Craig Zuckerman: 14, 88-89, 114-115, 122-123, 206-207.

Cover Design: Studio Montage
Chapter icons designed by Anna Sereda

Commissioned studio photography for Oxford University Press done by Dennis
Kitchen Studio: 37, 61, 72, 73, 74, 75, 95, 96, 100, 189, 194, 195, 232.

*The publishers would like to thank the following for their kind permission to reproduce
photographs:* 20-21 (calender) dikobraziy/Shutterstock; 26 (penny) rsooll/
Shutterstock, (nickel) B.A.E. Inc./Alamy Stock Photo, (dime) Brandon Laufenberg/
istockphoto, (quarter) magicoven/Shutterstock, (half dollar) mattesimages/
Shutterstock, (Sacagawea dollar) Ted Foxx/Alamy Stock Photo; 31 (flowers photo)
Digital Vision/OUP; 48 (apartment interior) Sindre Ellingsen/Alamy Stock Photo;
61 (oven) gerenme/Getty Images; (table) Stefano Mattia/Getty Images, (window)
nexus 7/Shutterstock, (shower) FOTOGRAFIA INC./Getty Images, (dishes) Nika Art/
Shutterstock, (kitchen counter/sink) zstock/Shutterstock; 94 (watch) WM_idea/
Shutterstock; 98 (cotton texture) Saksan Maneechay/123RF, (linen texture)
daizuoxin/Shutterstock, (wool texture) riekephotos/Shutterstock, (cashmere texture)
ovb64/Shutterstock, (silk texture) Anteromite/Shutterstock, (leather texture) Victor
Newman/Shutterstock; 99 (denim) Jaroslaw Grudzinski/123RF, (suede) KPG Payless2/
Shutterstock, (lace) Nataliia Melnychuk/Shutterstock, (velvet) Neirfy/Shutterstock,
(corduroy) Eldad Carin/Shutterstock, (nylon) B Calkins/Shutterstock; 141 (Pentagon)
Don S. Montgomery/Corbis; 208 (civil rights) PhotoQuest/Contributor/Getty
Images, (Civil War) Philip Gould/Corbis, (Great Depression) Rolls Press/Popperfoto/
Contributor/Getty Images, (Industrial Revolution) Mary Evans Picture Library/
Alamy Stock Photo, (Jazz Age) Underwood & Underwood/Underwood & Underwood/
Corbis, (Progressivism) AS400 DB/Corbis, (Reconstruction) MPI/Stringer/Getty
Images, (Spage Age) AFP/Stringer/Getty Images, (Western Expansion) AS400 DB/
Corbis, (WWI) ASSOCIATED PRESS, (WWII) Joe Rosenthal/Associated Press; 212
(thoughtful woman) Di Studio/Shutterstock; 213 (people in uniform) Rawpixel.com/
Shutterstock; 232 (tent) Hurst Photo/Shutterstock, (campfire) wolv/Getty Images;
244 (flute) cowardlion/Shutterstock, (clarinet) Vereshchagin Dmitry/Shutterstock,
(oboe) Matthias G. Ziegler/Shutterstock, (bassoon) Rodrigo Blanco/Getty Images,
(saxophone) Ocean/OUP, (violin) Ocean/OUP, (cello) Stockbyte/Getty Images, (bass)
the palms/Shutterstock, (guitar) Photodisc/OUP, (trombone) seen/Shutterstock,
(trumpet) Photodisc/OUP, (tuba) Ingram/OUP, (French horn) Venus Angel/
Shutterstock, (piano) liangpv/Getty Images, (xylophone) Yuri Kevhiev/Alamy Stock
Photo, (drums) lem/Shutterstock, (tambourine) Vereshchagin Dmitry/Shutterstock,
(keyboard) George Peters/Getty Images, (accordion) Stockbyte/Getty Images, (organ)
C Squared Studios/Getty Images, (harmonica) Goran Bogicevic/Alamy Stock Photo.

*The publisher would like to thank the following for their permission to reproduce
copyrighted material:*
127, 136–137: USPS Corporate Signature, Priority Mail, Express Mail, Media Mail,
Certified Mail, Ready Post, Airmail, Parcel Post, Letter Carrier Uniform, Postal Clerk
Uniform, Flag and Statue of Liberty, Postmark, Post Office Box, Automated Postal
Center, Parcel Drop Box, Round Top Collection Mailbox are trademarks of the United
States Postal Service and are used with permission. Flag and Statue of Liberty © 2006
United States Postal Service. All Rights Reserved. Used with Permission. 156:
MetroCard and the logo "MTA" are registered trademarks of the Metropolitan
Transportation Authority. Used with permission. 156: Metro token image courtesy of
LA Metro ©2016 LACMTA. 156: Amtrak ticket image courtesy of Amtrak. 174: National
Center for O*NET Development. O*NET OnLine. Retrieved November 23, 2015, from
https://www.onetonline.org/. 191: Microsoft Word® is a registered trademark of
Microsoft Corporation. Screen shot reprinted with permission from Microsoft
Corporation. 191: Microsoft Excel® is a registered trademark of Microsoft Corporation.
Screen shot reprinted with permission from Microsoft Corporation. 191: Microsoft
PowerPoint® is a registered trademark of Microsoft Corporation. Screen shot reprinted
with permission from Microsoft Corporation. 210: Microsoft icons reprinted by
permission of Microsoft.

This third edition of the Oxford Picture
Dictionary is lovingly dedicated to the
memory of Norma Shapiro.

Her ideas, her pictures, and her stories
continue to teach, inspire, and delight.

Acknowledgments

The publisher and authors would like to acknowledge the following individuals for their invaluable feedback during the development of this program:

Nawal Abbas, Lawrence Tech University, MI; Dr. Macarena Aguilar, Cy-Fair College, TX; Penny Aldrich, Durham Technical Community College, NC; Deanna Allen, Round Rock ISD, TX; Angela Andrade-Holt, Western Nevada College, NV; Joseph F. Anselme, Atlantic Technical Center, FL; Stacy Antonopoulos, Monterey Trail High School, CA; Carol Antunano, The English Center, FL; Irma Arencibia, Thomas A. Edison School, NJ; Stephanie Austin, CBET Program Moreland School District, CA; Suzi Austin, Alexandria City Public School Adult Program, FL; Carol Beebe, Niagara University, NY; Patricia S. Bell, Lake Technical Center, FL; Derick Bonewitz, College of Lake County, IL; Emily Box, Granite Peaks Learning Center, UT; Diana Brady-Herndon, Western Nevada College, NV; Jim Brice, San Diego Community College District, CA; Theresa Bries, Black Hawk College, IL; Diane Brody, St. John's Lutheran Church; Mindy Bruton, Abilene ISD, TX; Caralyn Bushey, Montgomery College TESOL Certificate Program, MD; Phil Cackley, Arlington Education and Employment Program (REEP), VA; Frieda Caldwell, Metropolitan Adult Education Program, CA; Anne Marie Caney, Chula Vista Adult School, CA; Lynda Cannon, Ashland Community and Technical College, KY; Lenore Cardoza, Brockton Public Schools Adult Learning Center, MA; Victor Castellanos, Covina Public Library, CA; Marjorie Castillo-Farquhar, Community Action/Austin Community College, TX; Patricia Castro, Harvest English Institute, NJ; Paohui Lola Chen, Milpitas Adult School, CA; Alicia Chicas, The Hayward Center for Education & Careers (Adult School), CA; Michelle Chuang, East Side Adult Education, CA; Lori Cisneros, Atlantic Vo-Tech, FL; Joyce Clapp, Hayward Adult School, CA; Stacy Clark, Arlington Education and Employment Program (REEP), VA; Melissa Cohen, Literacy New Jersey - Middlesex Programs, NJ; Dave Coleman, LAUSD District, CA; Edith Cowper, Wake Technical Community College, NC; Leslie Crawley, The Literacy Center; Kelli Crow, City College San Francisco Civic Center, CA; Nancy B. Crowell, Southside Programs for Adults in Continuing Education, VA; Doroti da Cunha, Hialeah-Miami Lakes Adult Education Center, FL; Brenda Custodio, Ohio State University, OH; Dory Dannettell, Community Educational Outreach, CO; Paula Da Silva-Michelin, La Guardia Community College, NY; Peggy Datz, Berkeley Adult School, CA; Cynthia L. Davies, Humble I.S.D., TX; Christopher Davis, Overfelt Adult Center, CA; Laura De Anda, Margaret Aylward Center, CA; Tyler Degener, Drexel University College of Medicine, PA; Jacquelyn Delaney; Mariana De Luca, Charlotte-Mecklenburg Public Schools, NC; Georgia Deming, Johnson County Community College (JCAE), KS; Beverly De Nicola, Capistrano Unified School District, CA; Irena Dewey, US Conversation; Frances Tornabene De Sousa, Pittsburg Adult Education Center, CA; Matthew Diamond, The University of Texas at Austin, TX; Beatriz Diaz, Miami-Dade County Public Schools, FL; Druci Diaz, Program Advisor, Adult & Career Services Center Hillsborough County Public Schools, FL; Natalya Dollar, North Orange County Community College District, CA; Marion Donahue, San Dieguito Adult School, CA; Nick Doorn, International Education Services, MI; Mercedes Douglass, Seminole Community College, FL; Joan Dundas, Brock University, ON (Canada); Jennifer Eick-Magán, Prairie State College, IL; Jenny Elliott, Montgomery College, MD; Paige Endo, Mt. Diablo Adult Education, CA; Megan Ernst, Glendale Community College, CA; Elizabeth Escobar, Robert Waters School, NJ; Joanne Everett, Dave Thomas Education Center, FL; Jennifer Fadden, Arlington Education and Employment Program (REEP), VA; Cinzia Fagan, East Side Adult Education, CA; Jacqui Farrell, Literacy Volunteers on the Green, CT; Ross Feldberg, Tufts University, MA; Sharyl Ferguson, Montwood High School, TX; Emily Finch, FCI Englewood, CO; Dr. Robert Finkelstein, Willamette Dental, OR; Janet Fischer, Lawrence Public Schools - Adult Learning Center, MA; Dr. Monica Fishkin, University of Central Florida, FL; Jan Foley, Wilbur Wright College - City Colleges of Chicago, IL; Tim Foster, Silver Valley Adult Education Center, CA; Nancy Frampton, Reedley College, CA; Lynn A. Freeland, San Dieguito Union High School District, CA; Sally A. Fox, East Side Adult Education, CA; Cathy Gample, San Leandro Adult School, CA; Hillary Gardner, Center for Immigrant Education and Training, NY; Elizabeth Gibb, Castro Valley Adult and Career Education, CA; Martha C. Giffen, Alhambra Unified School District, CA; Elgy Gillespie, City College San Francisco, CA; Lisa Marcelle Gimbel, Community Learning Center, MA; Jill Gluck, Hollywood Community Adult School, CA; Richard Goldberg, Asian American Civic Association, MA; Carolyn Grebe, The Hayward Center for Education & Careers (Adult School), CA; Carolyn Grimaldi, LaGuardia Community College, NY; Cassell Gross, Intercambio, CO; William Gruenholz, USD Adult School, CA; Sandra G. Gutierrez, Hialeah-Miami Lakes Adult Education Center, FL; Conte Gúzman-Hoffman, Triton College, IL; William J. Hall, M.D. FACP/FRSM (UK); Amanda Harllee, Palmetto High School, FL; Kathy Harris, Portland State University, OR; Kay Hartley, Fairfield-Suisun Adult School, CA; Melissa Hassmanm, Northwest Iowa Community College, IA; Mercedes Hearn, Tampa Bay Technical Center, FL; Christyann Helm, Carlos Rosario International Public Charter School, WA; Suzanne Hibbs, East Side Adult Education, CA; Lindsey Himanga, Hiawatha Valley ABE, MN; Marvina Hooper, Lake Technical College, FL; Jill A. Horohoe, Arizona State University, AZ; Roxana Hurtado, Miami Dade Adult, FL; Rachel Johnson, MORE Multicultural School for Empowerment, MN; Randy Johnson, Hartford Public Library, CT; Sherry Joseph, Miami Dade College, FL; Elaine Kanakis, The Hayward Center for Education and Careers, CA; Phoebe Kang, Brock University, ON (Canada); Mary Kaufman, Brewster Technical Center, FL; Jeanne Kearsley, City College San Francisco Chinatown, CA; Sallyann Kovacs, The Hayward Center for Education & Careers (Adult School), CA; Jennifer Latzgo, Lehigh Carbon Community College, PA; Sandy Lawler, East Side Adult Education, CA; Xinhua Li, City College of San Francisco, CA; Renata Lima, TALK International School of Languages, FL; Luz M. Lopez, Sweetwater Union High School District, CA; Osmara Lopez, Bronx Community College, NY; Heather Lozano, North Lake College, TX; Marcia Luptak, Elgin Community College, IL; Betty Lynch, Arlington Education and Employment Program (REEP), VA; Matthew Lyter, Tri-County OIC, PA; Meera Madan, REID Park Elementary School, NC; Julia Maffei, Texas State IEP, TX; Ivanna Mann Thrower, Charlotte Mecklenburg Schools, NC; Anna Mariani, The English Center (TLC Online), FL; Michael R. Mason, Loma Vista Adult Center, CA; Terry Masters, American Schools of Water for Ishmael, OH; Debbie Matsumura, CBET Program Moreland School District, CA; Holley Mayville, Charlotte Mecklenburg Schools, NC; Margaret McCabe, United Methodist Cooperative Ministries, FL; David McCarthy, Stony Brook University, NY; Todd McDonald, Hillsborough Adult Education, FL; Nancy A. McKeand, ESL Consultant, LA; Rebecca L. McLain, Gaston College, NC; John M. Mendoza, Redlands Adult School, CA; Nancy Meredith, Austin Community College, TX; Marcia Merriman, Community College of Baltimore County, MD; Bet Messmer, Santa Clara Adult Education Center, CA; Holly Milkowart, Johnson County Community College, KS; Jose Montes, The English Center M-DCPS, FL; Elaine Moore, Escondido Adult School, CA; Lisa Munoz, Metropolitan Education District, CA; Mary Murphy-Clagett, Sweetwater Union High School District, CA; Jonetta Myles, Rockdale County High School, GA; Marwan Nabi, Troy High School, CA; Dale Nave, San Marcos Academy, TX; Dr. Christine L. Nelsen, Salvation Army Community Center, FL; Michael W. Newman, Arlington Education and Employment Program (REEP), VA; Virginia Nicolai, Colorado Mountain College, CO; Phoebe Nip, East Side Adult Education, CA; Rehana Nusrat, Huntington Beach Adult School, CA; Cindy Oakley-Paulik, Embry-Riddle Aeronautical University, FL; Judy O'Louglin, CATESOL, CA; Brigitte Oltmanns, Triton College, IL; Nora Onayemi, Montgomery College, MD; Lorena Orozco, Catholic Charities, NM; Allison Pickering, Escondido Adult School, CA; Odette Petrini, Huron High School, MI; Eileen Purcell, Clatsop Community College, OR; Teresa Reen, East Side Adult Education, CA; Jean Renoll, Fairfax County Public Schools – ACE, VA; Carmen Rivera-Diaz, Calvary Church; Fatiana Roganova, The Hayward Center for Education & Careers (Adult School), CA; Rosa Rojo, Escondido Adult School, CA; Lorraine Romero, Houston Community College, TX; Phoebe B. Rouse, Louisiana State University, LA; Dr. Susan Rouse, Southern Wesleyan University, SC; Blair Roy, Chapman Education Center, CA; Sharon Saylors, The Hayward Center for Education & Careers (Adult School), CA; Margret Schaefer, Round Rock ISD, TX; Arlene R. Schwartz, Broward Community Schools, FL; Geraldyne Blake Scott, Truman College, IL; Sharada Sekar, Antioch High School Freshman Academy, TN; Denise Selleck, City College San Francisco Civic Center, CA; Dr. Cheryl J. Serrano, Lynn University, FL; Janet Setzekorn, United Methodist Cooperative Ministries, FL; Terry Shearer, EDUCALL Learning Services, TX; Rob Sheppard, Quincy Asian Resources, Inc., MA; Dr. Ira M. Sheskin, University of Miami, FL; Glenda Sinks, Community College of Denver, CO; Elisabeth Sklar, Township High School District 113, IL; Jacqueline Sport, LBWCC Luverne Center, AL; Kathryn Spyksma, The Hayward Center for Education & Careers (Adult School), CA; Linda Steele, Black Hawk College, IL; Robert Stein, BEGIN Managed Programs, NY; Martin Steinman, Canal Alliance, CA; Ruth Sutton, Township High School District 113, IL; Alisa Takeuchi, Chapman Education Center, CA; Grace Tanaka, Santa Ana College School of Continuing Education, CA; Annalisa Te, East Side Adult Education, CA; Oscar Tellez, Daley College, IL; Fotini Terzi, University of Texas at Austin, TX; Geneva Tesh, Houston Community College, TX; Maiko Tomizawa, D.D.S., NY; Don Torluemke, South Bay Adult School, CA; Francisco Torres, Olive-Harvey College, IL; Shawn Tran, East Side Adult Education, CA; Serife Turkol, Literary Council of Northern Virginia, VA; Cristina Urena, CC/Tech Center, FL; Maliheh Vafai, East Side Adult Education, CA; Charlotte van Londen, MCAEL, MD; Tara Vasquez, Robert Waters School, NJ; Nina Velasco, Naples Language Center, FL; Colin Ward, Lone Star College-North Harris, TX; Theresa Warren, East Side Adult Center, CA; Lucie Gates Watel, Truman College, IL; Wendy Weil, Arnold Middle School, TX; Patricia Weist, TALK International School of Languages, FL; Dr. Carole Lynn Weisz, Lehman College, NY; Desiree Wesner, Robert Waters School, NJ; David Wexler, Napa Valley Adult School, CA; Kathy Wierseman, Black Hawk College, IL; Cynthia Wiseman, Borough of Manhattan Community College, NY; Nancy Whitmire, University of Arkansas Community College at Batesville, AR; Debbie Cullinane Wood, Lincoln Education Center, CA; Banu Yaylali, Miami Dade College, FL; Hongyan Zheng, Milpitas Adult Education, Milpitas, CA; Yelena Zimon, Fremont Adult and Continuing Education, CA; Arlene Zivitz, ESOL Teacher, FL

Table of Contents   Índice temático

Introduction Introducción . . . . viii–ix

1.   Everyday Language Lenguaje cotidiano

1.1   Meeting and Greeting Reunirse y saludar 2–3
1.2   Personal Information Información personal 4
1.3   School La escuela 5
1.4   A Classroom Un salón de clase 6–7
1.5   Studying Estudiar 8–9
1.6   Succeeding in School Cómo tener éxito en la escuela 10
1.7   A Day at School Un día en la escuela 11
1.8   Everyday Conversation La conversación diaria 12
1.9   Weather El tiempo 13
1.10 The Telephone El teléfono 14–15
1.11 Numbers Números 16
1.12 Measurements Las medidas 17
1.13 Time La hora 18–19
1.14 The Calendar El calendario 20–21
1.15 Calendar Events Calendario de eventos 22
1.16 Describing Things Descripción de los objetos 23
1.17 Colors Colores 24
1.18 Prepositions Las preposiciones 25
1.19 Money El dinero 26
1.20 Shopping Ir de compras 27
1.21 Same and Different Igual y diferente 28–29

2.   People Gente

2.1   Adults and Children Adultos y niños 30–31
2.2   Describing People Descripción de las personas 32
2.3   Describing Hair Descripción del cabello 33
2.4   Families Las familias 34–35
2.5   Childcare and Parenting Crianza y cuidado de los niños 36–37
2.6   Daily Routines Rutinas diarias 38–39
2.7   Life Events and Documents Sucesos de la vida y documentos 40–41
2.8   Feelings Estados de ánimo y sentimientos 42–43
2.9   A Family Reunion Una reunión familiar 44–45

3.   Housing Vivienda

3.1   The Home El hogar 46–47
3.2   Finding a Home Búsqueda de casa 48–49
3.3   Apartments Los apartamentos 50–51
3.4   Different Places to Live Lugares diferentes para vivir 52
3.5   A House and Yard La casa y el jardín 53
3.6   A Kitchen Una cocina 54
3.7   A Dining Area Un comedor 55
3.8   A Living Room Una sala 56
3.9   A Bathroom Un baño 57
3.10 A Bedroom Un dormitorio 58
3.11 The Kids' Bedroom El dormitorio de los niños 59
3.12 Housework Quehaceres domésticos 60
3.13 Cleaning Supplies Los artículos de limpieza 61
3.14 Household Problems and Repairs Problemas y reparaciones domésticas . 62–63
3.15 The Tenant Meeting La reunión de los inquilinos 64–65

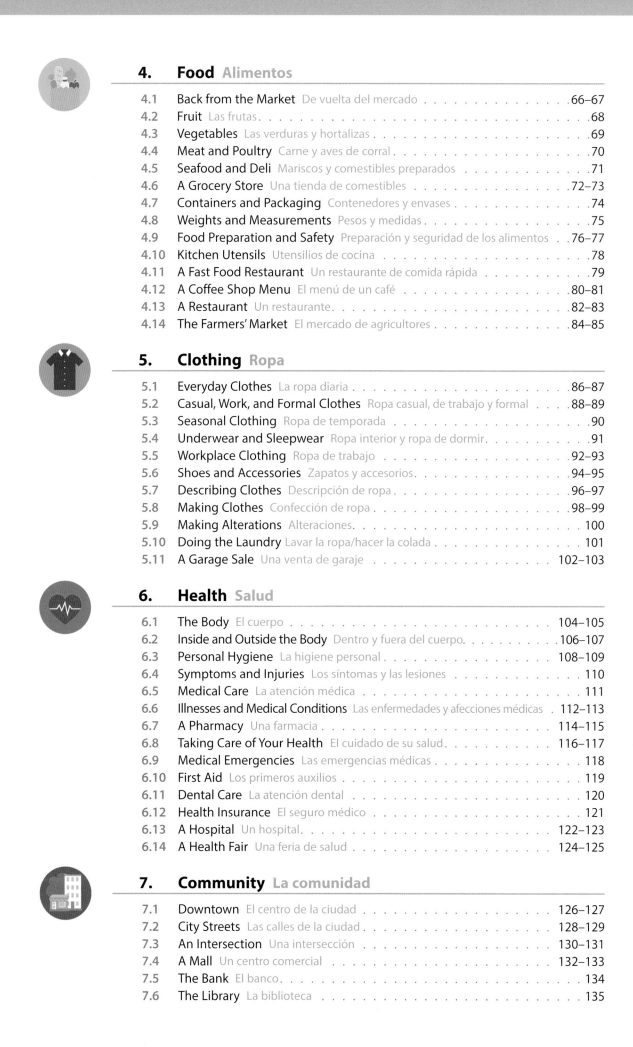

4. Food Alimentos

4.1	Back from the Market De vuelta del mercado	66–67
4.2	Fruit Las frutas	68
4.3	Vegetables Las verduras y hortalizas	69
4.4	Meat and Poultry Carne y aves de corral	70
4.5	Seafood and Deli Mariscos y comestibles preparados	71
4.6	A Grocery Store Una tienda de comestibles	72–73
4.7	Containers and Packaging Contenedores y envases	74
4.8	Weights and Measurements Pesos y medidas	75
4.9	Food Preparation and Safety Preparación y seguridad de los alimentos	76–77
4.10	Kitchen Utensils Utensilios de cocina	78
4.11	A Fast Food Restaurant Un restaurante de comida rápida	79
4.12	A Coffee Shop Menu El menú de un café	80–81
4.13	A Restaurant Un restaurante	82–83
4.14	The Farmers' Market El mercado de agricultores	84–85

5. Clothing Ropa

5.1	Everyday Clothes La ropa diaria	86–87
5.2	Casual, Work, and Formal Clothes Ropa casual, de trabajo y formal	88–89
5.3	Seasonal Clothing Ropa de temporada	90
5.4	Underwear and Sleepwear Ropa interior y ropa de dormir	91
5.5	Workplace Clothing Ropa de trabajo	92–93
5.6	Shoes and Accessories Zapatos y accesorios	94–95
5.7	Describing Clothes Descripción de ropa	96–97
5.8	Making Clothes Confección de ropa	98–99
5.9	Making Alterations Alteraciones	100
5.10	Doing the Laundry Lavar la ropa/hacer la colada	101
5.11	A Garage Sale Una venta de garaje	102–103

6. Health Salud

6.1	The Body El cuerpo	104–105
6.2	Inside and Outside the Body Dentro y fuera del cuerpo	106–107
6.3	Personal Hygiene La higiene personal	108–109
6.4	Symptoms and Injuries Los síntomas y las lesiones	110
6.5	Medical Care La atención médica	111
6.6	Illnesses and Medical Conditions Las enfermedades y afecciones médicas	112–113
6.7	A Pharmacy Una farmacia	114–115
6.8	Taking Care of Your Health El cuidado de su salud	116–117
6.9	Medical Emergencies Las emergencias médicas	118
6.10	First Aid Los primeros auxilios	119
6.11	Dental Care La atención dental	120
6.12	Health Insurance El seguro médico	121
6.13	A Hospital Un hospital	122–123
6.14	A Health Fair Una feria de salud	124–125

7. Community La comunidad

7.1	Downtown El centro de la ciudad	126–127
7.2	City Streets Las calles de la ciudad	128–129
7.3	An Intersection Una intersección	130–131
7.4	A Mall Un centro comercial	132–133
7.5	The Bank El banco	134
7.6	The Library La biblioteca	135

Contents Índice temático

7. Community (continued) La comunidad (continuación)

7.7	The Post Office La oficina de correos.	136–137
7.8	Department of Motor Vehicles (DMV) El Departamento de Vehículos Motorizados (DMV).	138–139
7.9	Government and Military Service El gobierno y el servicio militar	140–141
7.10	Civic Engagement La participación ciudadana	142–143
7.11	The Legal System El sistema legal	144
7.12	Crime La delincuencia	145
7.13	Public Safety La seguridad pública.	146
7.14	Cyber Safety La seguridad cibernética	147
7.15	Emergencies and Natural Disasters Emergencias y desastres naturales	148–149
7.16	Emergency Procedures Procedimientos de emergencia	150–151
7.17	Community Cleanup Limpieza comunitaria	152–153

8. Transportation Transporte

8.1	Basic Transportation El transporte básico	154–155
8.2	Public Transportation El transporte público	156
8.3	Prepositions of Motion Preposiciones de movimiento	157
8.4	Traffic Signs Señales de tráfico	158
8.5	Directions and Maps Direcciones y mapas	159
8.6	Cars and Trucks Automóviles y camiones	160
8.7	Buying and Maintaining a Car Compra y mantenimiento de un automóvil	161
8.8	Parts of a Car Partes de un automóvil	162–163
8.9	An Airport Un aeropuerto	164–165
8.10	A Road Trip Un viaje por carretera	166–167

9. Job Search En busca de trabajo

9.1	Job Search En busca de trabajo	168–169
9.2	Jobs and Occupations A-C Empleos y profesiones A-C.	170
9.3	Jobs and Occupations C-H Empleos y profesiones C-H.	171
9.4	Jobs and Occupations H-P Empleos y profesiones H-P.	172
9.5	Jobs and Occupations P-W Empleos y profesiones P-W	173
9.6	Career Planning Planificación de carreras	174–175
9.7	Job Skills Destrezas laborales	176
9.8	Office Skills Destrezas de oficina	177
9.9	Soft Skills Destrezas no técnicas	178
9.10	Interview Skills Destrezas de entrevista	179
9.11	First Day on the Job El primer día de trabajo.	180–181

10. The Workplace El lugar de trabajo

10.1	The Workplace El lugar de trabajo	182–183
10.2	Inside a Company Dentro de una empresa.	184
10.3	Manufacturing La fabricación	185
10.4	Landscaping and Gardening Paisajismo y jardinería	186
10.5	Farming and Ranching La agricultura y la ganadería	187
10.6	Office Work El trabajo de oficina	188–189
10.7	Information Technology (IT) La tecnología de la información (TI)	190–191
10.8	A Hotel Un hotel.	192
10.9	Food Service Servicio de comidas	193
10.10	Tools and Building Supplies Herramientas y materiales de construcción	194–195
10.11	Construction La construcción	196
10.12	Job Safety La seguridad en el lugar de trabajo	197
10.13	A Bad Day at Work Un mal día en el trabajo	198–199

11. Academic Study La educación formal

11.1   Schools and Subjects Las escuelas y materias 200–201
11.2   English Composition La composición en inglés 202–203
11.3   Mathematics Las matemáticas. 204–205
11.4   Science Las ciencias 206–207
11.5   U.S. History La historia de EE. UU. 208
11.6   World History La historia universal. 209
11.7   Digital Literacy Alfabetización digital 210–211
11.8   Internet Research Búsqueda en Internet. 212–213
11.9   Geography and Habitats La geografía y los hábitats 214
11.10 The Universe El universo 215
11.11 Trees and Plants Árboles y plantas. 216
11.12 Flowers Flores 217
11.13 Marine Life, Amphibians, and Reptiles Vida marina, anfibios y reptiles . . 218–219
11.14 Birds, Insects, and Arachnids Pájaros, insectos y arácnidos. 220
11.15 Domestic Animals and Rodents Animales domésticos y roedores 221
11.16 Mammals Mamíferos 222–223
11.17 Energy and the Environment La energía y el medio ambiente 224–225
11.18 A Graduation Una graduación 226–227

12. Recreation Recreación

12.1   Places to Go Lugares a donde ir 228–229
12.2   The Park and Playground El parque y el patio de recreo 230
12.3   The Beach La playa 231
12.4   Outdoor Recreation Recreación al aire libre 232
12.5   Winter and Water Sports Deportes de invierno y acuáticos. 233
12.6   Individual Sports Deportes individuales 234
12.7   Team Sports Deportes en equipo 235
12.8   Sports Verbs Verbos utilizados en los deportes. 236
12.9   Sports Equipment Equipo deportivo 237
12.10 Hobbies and Games Pasatiempos y juegos 238–239
12.11 Electronics and Photography Electrónica y fotografía 240–241
12.12 Entertainment Entretenimiento 242–243
12.13 Music Música 244
12.14 Holidays Días feriados 245
12.15 A Birthday Party Una fiesta de cumpleaños 246–247

Verb Guide Guía de verbos. 248–250
How to Use the Index Cómo usar este índice. 251
English Index Índice en Inglés 251–287
Spanish Index Índice en Español 288–307
Research Bibliography Bibliografía de investigación 308

The Oxford Picture Dictionary Third Edition provides unparalleled support for vocabulary teaching and language development.

- Illustrations present over 4,000 English words and phrases within **meaningful, real-life contexts**.
- **New and expanded topics** including job search, career planning, and digital literacy prepare students to meet the requirements of their daily lives.
- Updated activities prepare students for **work, academic study, and citizenship**.
- **Oxford 3000 vocabulary** ensures students learn the most useful and important words.

Color coding and icons make it easy to navigate through *OPD*.

Vibrant illustrations and rich contexts improve vocabulary acquisition.

Subtopics present the words in easy-to-learn "chunks."

Revised practice activities help students develop academic and workforce skills.

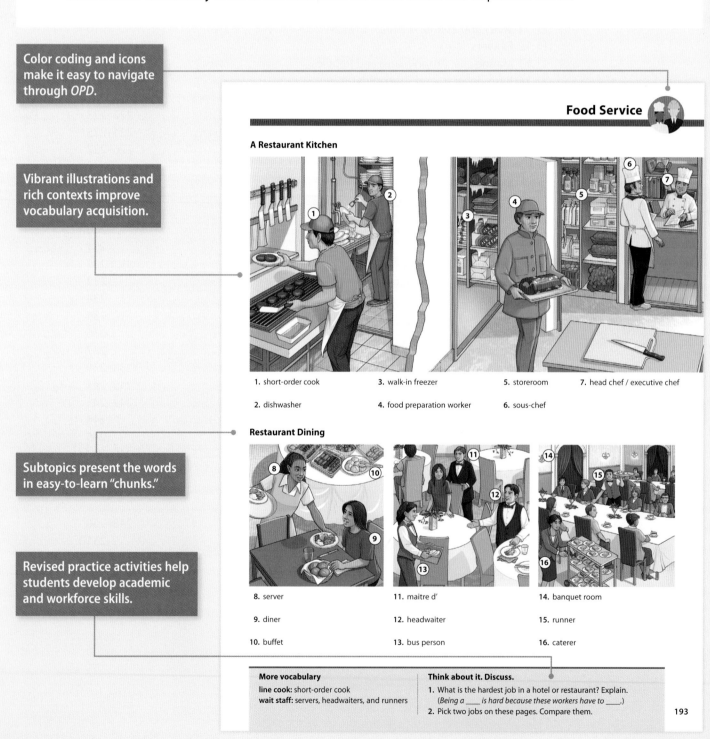

Food Service

A Restaurant Kitchen

1. short-order cook
2. dishwasher
3. walk-in freezer
4. food preparation worker
5. storeroom
6. sous-chef
7. head chef / executive chef

Restaurant Dining

8. server
9. diner
10. buffet
11. maitre d'
12. headwaiter
13. bus person
14. banquet room
15. runner
16. caterer

More vocabulary
line cook: short-order cook
wait staff: servers, headwaiters, and runners

Think about it. Discuss.
1. What is the hardest job in a hotel or restaurant? Explain.
   (*Being a ____ is hard because these workers have to ____.*)
2. Pick two jobs on these pages. Compare them.

193

Intro pages open each unit with key vocabulary related to the unit theme. Clear, engaging artwork promotes questions, conversations, and writing practice for all levels.

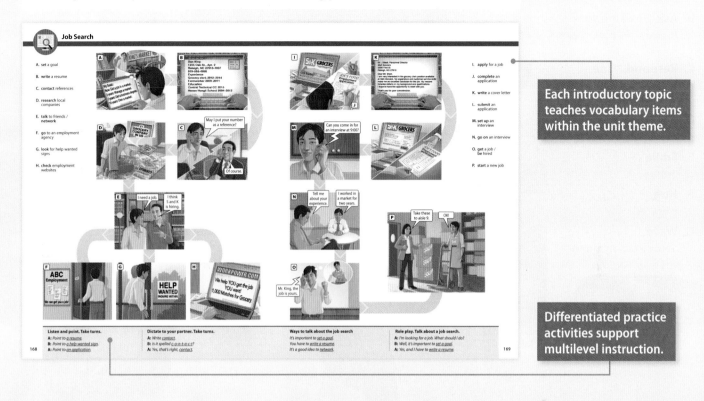

Each introductory topic teaches vocabulary items within the unit theme.

Differentiated practice activities support multilevel instruction.

Story pages close each unit with a lively scene for reviewing vocabulary and teaching additional language. Meanwhile, rich visual contexts recycle words from the unit.

Pre-reading questions build students' previewing and predicting skills.

End-of-unit readings promote literacy skills.

Post-reading questions support critical thinking and textual analysis skills.

The word list previews key vocabulary that students will encounter in the story.

Meeting and Greeting   Reunirse y saludar

A. Say, "Hello."
Diga: "Hola".

B. Ask, "How are you?"
Pregunte: "¿Cómo está usted?".

C. Respond, "Fine, thanks."
Responda: "Bien, gracias".

D. Introduce yourself.
Preséntese.

E. Smile.
Sonría.

F. Hug.
Abrace.

G. Wave.
Salude con la mano.

Tell your partner what to do. Take turns.

1. Say, "Hello."
2. Bow.
3. Smile.
4. Shake hands.
5. Wave.
6. Say, "Goodbye."

Dictate to your partner. Take turns.

A: Write smile.
B: Is it spelled s-m-i-l-e?
A: Yes, that's right.

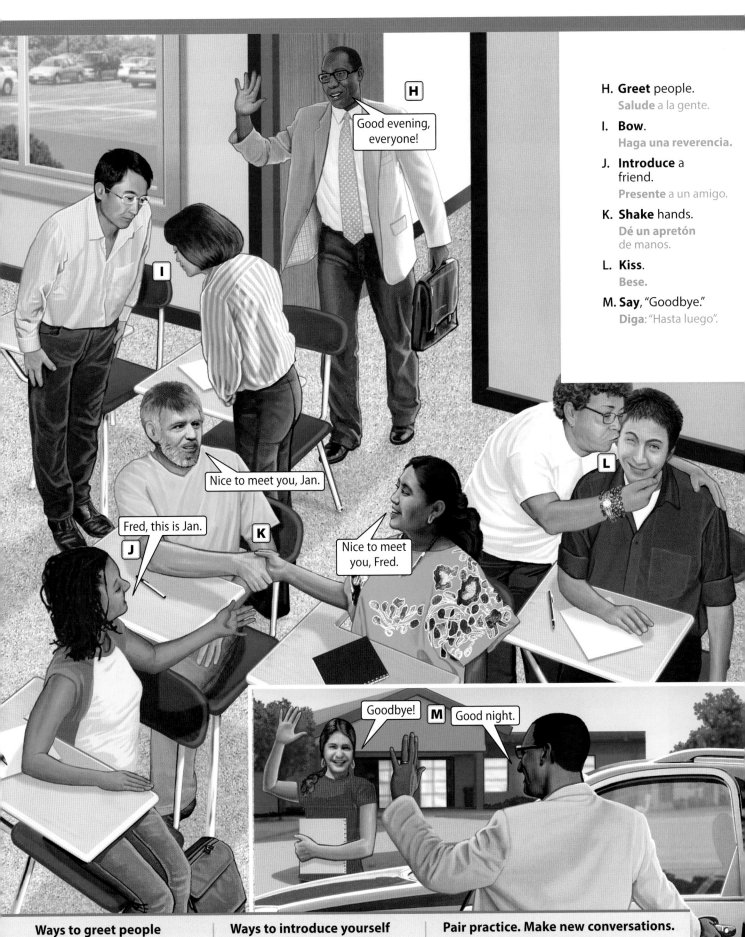

A. **Say** your name.
Diga su nombre.

B. **Spell** your name.
Deletree su nombre.

C. **Print** your name.
Escriba en letra de
imprenta su nombre.

D. **Type** your name.
Teclee su nombre.

E. **Sign** your name.
Firme su nombre.

Filling Out a Form Cómo llenar un formulario

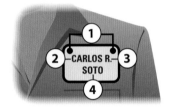

(813) 555-1234
10 11

(813) 555-5005
12

(813) 555-8976
13

COSTA RICA
San Jose
15

17 16 18

SOCIAL SECURITY
19 262-00-0000
CARLOS R. SOTO
Carlos R. Soto

20
Carlos R. Soto

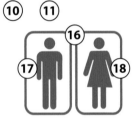

---

https://www.registrationformOPD.com

1. name nombre

2. first name   3. middle initial 4. last name
primer nombre   inicial del   apellido
                    segundo nombre

address dirección

5. street address   6. apartment number 7. city   8. state 9. ZIP code
dirección postal   número de apartamento ciudad   estado   código postal

work phone teléfono de trabajo   **additional numbers** números adicionales

(   )   -   (   )   -   (   )   -
10. area code   11. phone number   12. home phone   13. cell phone
código de área número de teléfono teléfono residencial teléfono celular

                                        17. male
                                        masculino
                          16. gender
                             sexo   18. female
                                        femenino

14. date of birth (DOB) 15. place of birth (POB)   19. Social Security number
fecha de nacimiento   lugar de nacimiento   Número del Seguro Social

20. signature
firma

Pair practice. Make new conversations.

A: *My first name is Carlos.*
B: *Please spell Carlos for me.*
A: *C-a-r-l-o-s.*

Internet Research: popular names

Type "SSA, top names 100 years" in the search bar.
Report: *According to the SSA list, James is the number
1 male name.*

Campus El campus

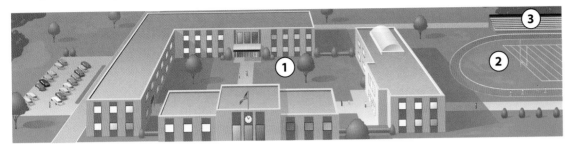

1. quad
   el patio interior
2. field
   el campo
3. bleachers
   las gradas
4. principal
   el director/la directora
5. assistant principal
   el asistente de director
6. counselor
   el consejero/la consejera
7. classroom
   el salón de clase
8. teacher
   el profesor/el maestro
9. restrooms
   los baños
10. hallway
    el pasillo
11. locker
    el armario
12. main office
    la oficina principal
13. clerk
    el empleado/la empleada
14. cafeteria
    la cafetería
15. computer lab
    el laboratorio de computadoras
16. teacher's aide
    el asistente del profesor o maestro
17. library
    la biblioteca
18. auditorium
    el auditorio
19. gym
    el gimnasio
20. coach
    el entrenador
21. track
    la pista

Administrators Los administradores

MARIA GOMEZ PRINCIPAL

STATE COLLEGE

Around Campus Alrededor del campus

Teacher meeting 3 p.m.

SPRING CONCERT

More vocabulary

Students do not pay to attend a **public school**.
Students pay to attend a **private school**.
A church, mosque, or temple school is a **parochial school**.

Use contractions and talk about the pictures.

He **is** = He**'s**   She **is** = She**'s**
It **is** = It**'s**   They **are** = They**'re**
He's a teacher.   *They're* students.

1. **whiteboard**
la pizarra para rotuladores

2. **screen**
la pantalla

3. **chalkboard**
la pizarra

4. **teacher / instructor**
la maestra/la profesora/
la instructora

5. **LCD projector**
el proyector LCD

6. **student**
el estudiante

7. **desk**
el escritorio

8. **headphones**
los audífonos

A. **Raise** your hand.
Levante la mano.

B. **Talk** to the teacher.
Hable con la maestra.

C. **Listen** to a recording.
Escuche una grabación.

D. **Stand up**.
Póngase de pie.

E. **Write** on the board.
Escriba en la pizarra.

F. **Sit down. / Take** a seat.
Siéntese/tome asiento.

G. **Open** your book.
Abra el libro.

H. **Close** your book.
Cierre el libro.

I. **Pick up** the pencil.
Coja el lápiz.

J. **Put down** the pencil.
Suelte el lápiz.

ABCDEFGHIJKLMNOPQRSTUVWXYZ

9. clock
el reloj

10. bookcase
el librero

11. chair
la silla

12. map
el mapa

13. alphabet
el alfabeto

14. bulletin board
la cartelera

15. computer
la computadora

16. document camera
el visualizador digital

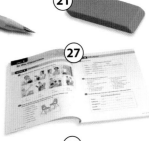

17. dry erase marker
el marcador borrable en seco

18. chalk
la tiza/el gis

19. eraser
el borrador

20. pencil
el lápiz

21. (pencil) eraser
la goma de borrar

22. pen
el bolígrafo/la pluma

23. pencil sharpener
el sacapuntas

24. permanent marker
el marcador indeleble

25. highlighter
el resaltador

26. textbook
el libro de texto

27. workbook
el cuaderno de trabajo

28. 3-ring binder / notebook
la carpeta de 3 anillos/
la libreta

29. notebook paper
el papel para libreta

30. spiral notebook
la libreta de espiral

31. learner's dictionary
el diccionario para estudiantes
de lengua extranjera

32. picture dictionary
el diccionario gráfico

Grammar Point: *there is / there are*

*There **is** a map.*   *There **are** 15 students.*

Describe your classroom. Take turns.

A: *There's <u>a clock</u>.*   B: *There are <u>20 chairs</u>.*

Survey your class. Record the responses.

1. Do you prefer pens or pencils?
2. Do you prefer talking or listening?

Report: *Most of us… Some of us…*

Learning New Words Aprender palabras nuevas

A. Look up the word.
Busque la palabra.

B. Read the definition.
Lea la definición.

C. Translate the word.
Traduzca la palabra.

D. Check the pronunciation.
Verifique la pronunciación.

E. Copy the word.
Copie la palabra.

F. Draw a picture.
Haga un dibujo.

Working with Your Classmates Trabajar con sus compañeros de clase

G. Discuss a problem.
Discuta un problema.

H. Brainstorm solutions / answers.
Elabore soluciones/ respuestas.

I. Work in a group.
Trabaje en grupo.

J. Help a classmate.
Ayude a un compañero.

Working with a Partner Trabajar con un compañero

K. Ask a question.
Haga una pregunta.

L. Answer a question.
Conteste una pregunta.

M. Share a book.
Comparta un libro.

N. Dictate a sentence.
Dicte una oración.

Following Directions Seguir las instrucciones

O. Fill in the blank.
Llene el espacio en blanco.

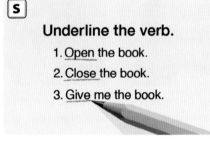

5. How much is the book?
a. $99.99
b. $9.99
c. $0.99

Study Skills For You
$9.99

P. Choose the correct answer.
Escoja la respuesta correcta.

Read the book. pencil.

Q. Circle the answer.
Encierre en un círculo la respuesta.

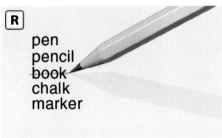

pen
pencil
book
chalk
marker

R. Cross out the word.
Tache la palabra.

Underline the verb.
1. Open the book.
2. Close the book.
3. Give me the book.

S. Underline the word.
Subraye la palabra.

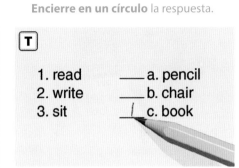

1. read _____ a. pencil
2. write _____ b. chair
3. sit _1_ c. book

T. Match the items.
Empareje los objetos.

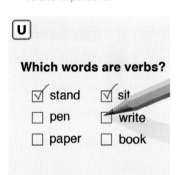

Which words are verbs?
☑ stand ☑ sit
☐ pen ☑ write
☐ paper ☐ book

U. Check the correct boxes.
Marque las casillas correctas.

Study Skills For You
$9.99

book

V. Label the picture.
Identifique la imagen.

1. enp   pen
2. rappe paper
3. okob   book

W. Unscramble the words.
Descifre las palabras.

4 Close the book.
1 Pick up the book.
2 Open the book.
3 Read the book.

X. Put the sentences in order.
Ponga las oraciones en orden.

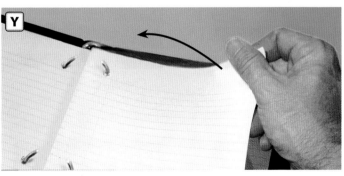

Y. Take out a piece of paper.
Saque una hoja de papel.

Z. Put away your books.
Guarde sus libros.

Survey your class. Record the responses.

1. Do you prefer to study in a group or with a partner?
2. Do you prefer to translate or draw new words?
Report: *Most of us… Some of us…*

Identify Tom's problem. Brainstorm solutions.

Tom wants to study English with a group.
He wants to ask his classmates, "Do you want to study together?" but he's embarrassed.

Ways to Succeed Formas para tener éxito

A. **Set** goals.
Fije metas.

B. **Participate** in class.
Participe en la clase.

C. **Take** notes.
Tome notas.

D. **Study** at home.
Estudie en la casa.

E. **Pass** a test.
Pase una prueba.

F. **Ask** for help. / **Request** help.
Pida ayuda/solicite ayuda.

G. **Make** progress.
Progrese.

H. **Get** good grades.
Obtenga buenas notas.

Taking a Test Cómo tomar una prueba

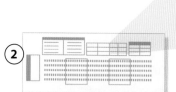

NAME	Lee, Jung
SCORE	35/40

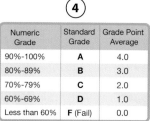

Numeric Grade	Standard Grade	Grade Point Average
90%-100%	A	4.0
80%-89%	B	3.0
70%-79%	C	2.0
60%-69%	D	1.0
Less than 60%	F (Fail)	0.0

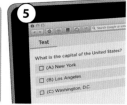

1. test booklet
el folleto de prueba

2. answer sheet
la hoja de respuestas

3. score
el puntaje

4. grades
las calificaciones

5. online test
la prueba en línea

I. **Clear off** your desk.
Limpie su escritorio.

J. **Work** on your own.
Trabaje por sí solo.

K. **Bubble in** the answer.
Ennegrezca el espacio correspondiente a la respuesta.

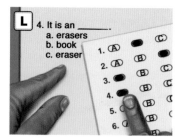

L. **Check** your work.
Revise su trabajo.

M. **Erase** the mistake.
Borre el error.

N. **Correct** the mistake.
Corrija el error.

O. **Hand in** your test.
Entregue la prueba.

P. **Submit** your test.
Envíe la prueba.

A. **Walk** to class.
   Camine a la clase.

B. **Run** to class.
   Corra a la clase.

C. **Enter** the room.
   Ingrese al salón.

D. **Turn on** the lights.
   Encienda las luces.

E. **Lift / Pick up** the books.
   Levante/recoja los libros.

F. **Carry** the books.
   Lleve los libros.

G. **Deliver** the books.
   Entregue los libros.

H. **Take** a break.
   Tome un descanso.

I. **Eat**.
   Coma.

J. **Drink**.
   Beba.

K. **Buy** a snack.
   Cómprese un bocadito.

L. **Have** a conversation.
   Converse con alguien.

M. **Go back** to class.
   Regrese a la clase.

N. **Throw away** trash.
   Tire la basura.

O. **Leave** the room.
   Salga del salón.

P. **Turn off** the lights.
   Apague las luces.

Grammar Point: present continuous

Use **be** + <u>verb</u> + **ing** (*What are they doing?*)
He is walking. They are talking.
Note: **run—runn**ing **leave—leav**ing [**e**]

Look at the pictures. Describe what is happening.

A: *They are entering the room.*
B: *He is walking.*
C: *She's eating.*

11

A. **start** a conversation
   inicie una conversación

B. **make** small talk
   charle

C. **compliment** someone
   elogie a alguien

D. **thank** someone
   agradézcale a alguien

E. **offer** something
   ofrezca algo

F. **refuse** an offer
   rechace una oferta

G. **apologize**
   discúlpese

H. **accept** an apology
   acepte una disculpa

I. **invite** someone
   invite a alguien

J. **accept** an invitation
   acepte una invitación

K. **decline** an invitation
   rechace una invitación

L. **agree**
   asienta

M. **disagree**
   disienta

N. **explain** something
   explique algo

O. **check** your understanding
   verifique lo que oye

More vocabulary

accept a compliment: to thank someone for a compliment

make a request: to ask for something

Pair practice. Follow the directions.

1. Start a conversation with your partner.
2. Make small talk with your partner.
3. Compliment each other.

Temperature Temperatura

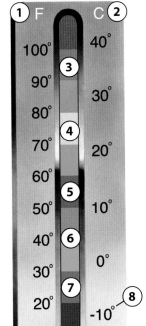

1. Fahrenheit
   Fahrenheit
2. Celsius
   Centígrados
3. hot
   caliente/cálido
4. warm
   tibio
5. cool
   fresco/templado
6. cold
   frío
7. freezing
   bajo cero/muy frío
8. degrees
   grados

A Weather Map Un mapa del tiempo

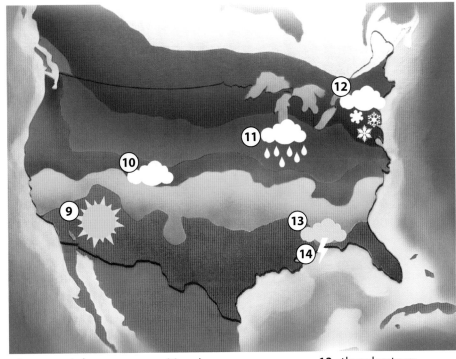

9. sunny / clear
   soleado/despejado
10. cloudy
    nublado
11. rain
    lluvia
12. snow
    nieve
13. thunderstorm
    tormenta
14. lightning
    relámpagos

Weather Conditions Condiciones del tiempo

15. heat wave
    ola de calor
16. smoggy
    con esmog
17. humid
    húmedo
18. hurricane
    huracán
19. windy
    con viento

20. dust storm
    tormenta de polvo
21. foggy
    neblinoso
22. hail
    granizo
23. icy
    helado
24. snowstorm / blizzard
    ventisca/tormenta de nieve

Ways to talk about the weather

It's _sunny_ and _hot_ in _Dallas_.
It's _raining_ in _Chicago_.
Rome is having _thunderstorms_.

Internet Research: weather

Type any city and "weather" in the search bar.
Report: It's _cloudy_ in _L.A._ It's _70 degrees_.

13

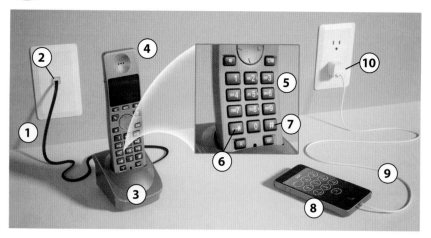

1. **phone line**
la línea de teléfono

2. **phone jack**
el enchufe del teléfono

3. **base**
la base

4. **handset / receiver**
el auricular/el receptor

5. **keypad**
el teclado

6. **star key**
la tecla estrella

7. **pound key**
la tecla numérica

8. **cell phone**
el teléfono celular

9. **charger cord**
el cable de carga

10. **charger plug**
el enchufe de carga

11. **strong signal**
una señal fuerte

12. **weak signal**
una señal débil

13. **headset**
el audífono

14. **Bluetooth headset**
el audífono Bluetooth

15. **contact list**
la lista de contactos

16. **missed call**
la llamada perdida

17. **voice mail**
el mensaje de voz

18. **text message**
el mensaje de texto

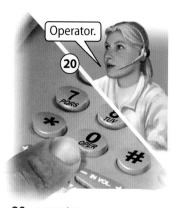

19. **Internet phone call**
la llamada telefónica
por Internet

20. **operator**
el operador

21. **directory assistance**
el servicio de directorio

22. **automated phone
system**
el sistema telefónico
automatizado

14

23. phone card
la tarjeta telefónica

24. access number
el número de acceso

1531-5471-2923-889

25. smartphone
el teléfono inteligente

26. TDD*
el TDD

Reading a Phone Bill Lectura de la factura telefónica

27. carrier
la empresa de telefonía

28. area code
el código de área

29. phone number
el número de teléfono

30. billing period
el período de facturación

31. monthly charges
los cargos mensuales

32. additional charges
los cargos adicionales

HORIZON (27)

BILL SUMMARY
(28) (29)
For **823-555-1357**
From May 15, 2018 to June 14, 2018
(30)

(31) 5/15 - 6/14 charges	$40.00
(32) Other charges	$5.34
Tax	$9.84
TOTAL CHARGES	**$55.18**

Types of Charges Tipos de cargos

33. local call
la llamada local

34. long-distance call
la llamada de larga distancia

35. international call
la llamada internacional

36. data
los datos

Making a Phone Call Para llamar por teléfono

A. Dial the phone number.
Marque el número de teléfono.

B. Press "talk".
Oprima "hablar".

C. Talk on the phone.
Hable por teléfono.
Hi!
Hi!

D. Hang up. / **End** the call.
Cuelgue/finalice la llamada.

Making an Emergency Call Para hacer una llamada de emergencia

E. Dial 911.
Marque 911.
911

F. Give your name.
Dé su nombre.
This is Roy Chu.

G. State the emergency.
Diga cuál es la emergencia.
There's a fire on 5th and Oak.

H. Stay on the line.
Permanezca en la línea.
Please stay on the line.

*telecommunication device for the deaf

Cardinal Numbers Números cardinales

0	zero / cero	20	twenty / veinte
1	one / uno	21	twenty-one / veintiuno
2	two / dos	22	twenty-two / veintidós
3	three / tres	23	twenty-three / veintitrés
4	four / cuatro	24	twenty-four / veinticuatro
5	five / cinco	25	twenty-five / veinticinco
6	six / seis	30	thirty / treinta
7	seven / siete	40	forty / cuarenta
8	eight / ocho	50	fifty / cincuenta
9	nine / nueve	60	sixty / sesenta
10	ten / diez	70	seventy / setenta
11	eleven / once	80	eighty / ochenta
12	twelve / doce	90	ninety / noventa
13	thirteen / trece	100	one hundred / cien
14	fourteen / catorce	101	one hundred one / ciento uno
15	fifteen / quince	1,000	one thousand / mil
16	sixteen / dieciséis	10,000	ten thousand / diez mil
17	seventeen / diecisiete	100,000	one hundred thousand / cien mil
18	eighteen / dieciocho	1,000,000	one million / un millón
19	nineteen / diecinueve	1,000,000,000	one billion / mil millones

Ordinal Numbers Números ordinales

1st / 1º	first / primero	16th / 16º	sixteenth / decimosexto
2nd / 2º	second / segundo	17th / 17º	seventeenth / decimoséptimo
3rd / 3º	third / tercero	18th / 18º	eighteenth / decimoctavo
4th / 4º	fourth / cuarto	19th / 19º	nineteenth / decimonoveno
5th / 5º	fifth / quinto	20th / 20º	twentieth / vigésimo
6th / 6º	sixth / sexto	21st / 21º	twenty-first / vigesimoprimero
7th / 7º	seventh / séptimo	30th / 30º	thirtieth / trigésimo
8th / 8º	eighth / octavo	40th / 40º	fortieth / cuadragésimo
9th / 9º	ninth / noveno	50th / 50º	fiftieth / quincuagésimo
10th / 10º	tenth / décimo	60th / 60º	sixtieth / sexagésimo
11th / 11º	eleventh / undécimo	70th / 70º	seventieth / septuagésimo
12th / 12º	twelfth / duodécimo	80th / 80º	eightieth / octogésimo
13th / 13º	thirteenth / decimotercero	90th / 90º	ninetieth / nonagésimo
14th / 14º	fourteenth / decimocuarto	100th / 100º	one hundredth / centésimo
15th / 15º	fifteenth / decimoquinto	1,000th / 1000º	one thousandth / milésimo

Roman Numerals Números romanos

I = 1	VII = 7	XXX = 30
II = 2	VIII = 8	XL = 40
III = 3	IX = 9	L = 50
IV = 4	X = 10	C = 100
V = 5	XV = 15	D = 500
VI = 6	XX = 20	M = 1,000

A. divide
divida

B. calculate
calcule

75% of 10 = 7.5

C. measure
mida

3 inches

D. convert
convierta

1 mi. = 1.6 km

Fractions and Decimals Fracciones y decimales

1. one whole
1 = 1.00
un entero

2. one half
1/2 = .5
un medio

3. one third
1/3 = .333
un tercio

4. one fourth
1/4 = .25
un cuarto

5. one eighth
1/8 = .125
un octavo

Percents Porcentajes

6. calculator
la calculadora

7. decimal point
el punto o la coma decimal

8 100 percent — 100%

9 75 percent — 75%

10 50 percent — 50%

11 25 percent — 25%

12 10 percent — 10%

0% 10% 20% 30% 40% 50% 60% 70% 80% 90% 100%

8. 100 percent
100 por ciento

10. 50 percent
50 por ciento

12. 10 percent
10 por ciento

9. 75 percent
75 por ciento

11. 25 percent
25 por ciento

Measurement Medidas

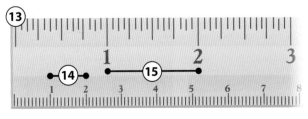

13. ruler
la regla

14. centimeter [cm]
el centímetro [cm]

15. inch [in.]
la pulgada [in]

Dimensions Dimensiones

Equivalencies

12 inches = 1 foot

3 feet = 1 yard

1,760 yards = 1 mile

1 inch = 2.54 centimeters

1 yard = .91 meter

1 mile = 1.6 kilometers

16. height
la altura

18. depth
la profundidad

17. length
la longitud

19. width
el ancho

17

Telling Time Saber la hora

1. hour
la hora

2. minutes
los minutos

3. seconds
los segundos

4. a.m.
a. m.

5. p.m.
p. m.

6. 1:00
one o'clock
la una en punto

7. 1:05
one-oh-five
five after one
la una y cinco

8. 1:10
one-ten
ten after one
la una y diez

9. 1:15
one-fifteen
a quarter after one
la una y quince
la una y cuarto

10. 1:20
one-twenty
twenty after one
la una y veinte

11. 1:30
one-thirty
half past one
la una y treinta
la una y media

12. 1:40
one-forty
twenty to two
la una y cuarenta
veinte para las dos

13. 1:45
one-forty-five
a quarter to two
la una y cuarenta y cinco
un cuarto para las dos

Times of Day Las etapas del día

14. sunrise
la salida del sol/
el amanecer

15. morning
la mañana

16. noon
el mediodía

17. afternoon
la tarde

18. sunset
la puesta del sol/
el atardecer

19. evening
el anochecer

20. night
la noche

21. midnight
la medianoche

Ways to talk about time

I wake up at 6:30 a.m.
I wake up at 6:30 in the morning.
I wake up at 6:30.

Pair practice. Make new conversations.

A: *What time do you wake up on weekdays?*
B: *At 6:30 a.m. How about you?*
A: *I wake up at 7:00.*

22. early
temprano

23. on time
a tiempo

24. late
tarde

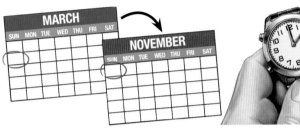

25. daylight saving time
la hora de verano

26. standard time
la hora estándar

Time Zones Zonas horarias

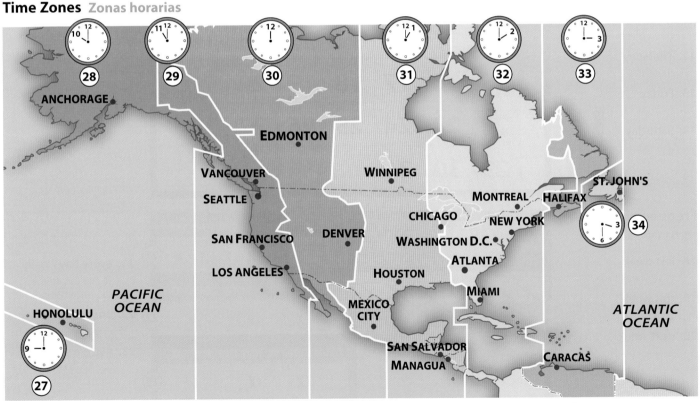

27. Hawaii-Aleutian time
la hora de
Hawai-Aleutianas

28. Alaska time
la hora de Alaska

29. Pacific time
la hora del Pacífico

30. Mountain time
la hora de la montaña

31. Central time
la hora del centro

32. Eastern time
la hora del este

33. Atlantic time
la hora del Atlántico

34. Newfoundland time
la hora de Terranova

Survey your class. Record the responses.

1. When do you watch television? study? relax?
2. Do you like to stay up after midnight?
Report: *Most of us… Some of us…*

Think about it. Discuss.

1. What is your favorite time of day? Why?
2. Do you think daylight saving time is a good idea?
3. What's good about staying up after midnight?

1. date
   la fecha
2. day
   el día
3. month
   el mes
4. year
   el año

5. today
   hoy
6. tomorrow
   mañana
7. yesterday
   ayer

Days of the Week
Los días de la semana

8. Sunday
   domingo
9. Monday
   lunes
10. Tuesday
    martes
11. Wednesday
    miércoles
12. Thursday
    jueves
13. Friday
    viernes
14. Saturday
    sábado

15. week
    la semana
16. weekdays
    los días de la semana
17. weekend
    el fin de semana

MAY

SUN	MON	TUE	WED	THU	FRI	SAT
1	2	3	4	5	6	7
8	9	10	11	12	13	14
15	16	17	18	19	20	21
22	23	24	25	26	27	28
29	30	31				

Frequency
La frecuencia

18. last week
    la semana pasada
19. this week
    esta semana
20. next week
    la semana próxima

21. every day / daily
    todos los días/
    diariamente
22. once a week
    una vez por semana
23. twice a week
    dos veces por
    semana
24. three times a week
    tres veces por
    semana

Ways to say the date

Today is May 10th. It's the tenth.
Yesterday was May 9th.
The party is on May 21st.

Pair practice. Make new conversations.

A: *The test is on Friday, June 14th.*
B: *Did you say Friday, the fourteenth?*
A: *Yes, the fourteenth.*

Months of the Year
Los meses del año

25. January
enero

26. February
febrero

27. March
marzo

28. April
abril

29. May
mayo

30. June
junio

31. July
julio

32. August
agosto

33. September
septiembre

34. October
octubre

35. November
noviembre

36. December
diciembre

Seasons
Las estaciones

37. spring
la primavera

38. summer
el verano

39. fall / autumn
el otoño

40. winter
el invierno

Dictate to your partner. Take turns.

A: *Write Monday.*
B: *Is it spelled M-o-n-d-a-y?*
A: *Yes, that's right.*

Survey your class. Record the responses.

1. What is the busiest day of your week?
2. What is your favorite day?
Report: *Ten of us said Monday is our busiest day.*

21

Calendar Events   Calendario de eventos

1. birthday
el cumpleaños

2. wedding
la boda

3. anniversary
el aniversario

4. appointment
la cita

5. parent-teacher conference
la conferencia de padres
y maestros

6. vacation
las vacaciones

7. religious holiday
la fiesta religiosa

8. legal holiday
el día de fiesta oficial/
el día feriado legal

Legal Holidays Los días feriados legales

Happy New Year!   JAN 1

I have a dream.   JAN

FEB

MAY

JUL 4

SEP

PROUD TO WORK

OCT

DEC 25

NOV

NOV

9. New Year's Day
el Día de Año Nuevo

10. Martin Luther King Jr. Day
el Día de Martin Luther King Jr.

11. Presidents' Day
el Día de los Presidentes

12. Memorial Day
el Día de la Recordación

13. Fourth of July /
Independence Day
el Cuatro de Julio/
el Día de la Independencia

14. Labor Day
el Día del Trabajo

15. Columbus Day
el Día de Colón

16. Veterans Day
el Día de los Veteranos

17. Thanksgiving
el Día de Acción de Gracias

18. Christmas
la Navidad

Pair practice. Make new conversations.

A: *When is your <u>birthday</u>?*
B: *It's on <u>January 31st</u>. How about yours?*
A: *It's on <u>December 22nd</u>.*

Internet Research: independence day

Type "independence day, world" in the search bar.
Report: <u>Peru</u> celebrates its independence on <u>7/28</u>.

1. **little** hand
   la mano **pequeña**
2. **big** hand
   la mano **grande**

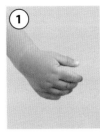
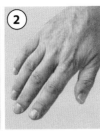

13. **heavy** box
    la caja **pesada**
14. **light** box
    la caja **liviana**

3. **fast** speed
   la velocidad **alta**
4. **slow** speed
   la velocidad **baja**

15. **same** color
    el **mismo** color
16. **different** colors
    colores **diferentes**

5. **hard** chair
   la silla **dura**
6. **soft** chair
   la silla **blanda**

17. **bad** news
    las **malas** noticias
18. **good** news
    las **buenas** noticias

There was an earthquake. Everyone is OK!

7. **thick** book
   el libro **grueso**
8. **thin** book
   el libro **delgado**

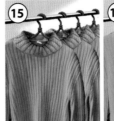
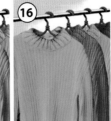

19. **expensive** ring
    el anillo **caro**
20. **cheap** ring
    el anillo **barato**

9. **full** glass
   el vaso **lleno**
10. **empty** glass
    el vaso **vacío**

21. **beautiful** view
    la vista **hermosa**
22. **ugly** view
    la vista **fea**

11. **noisy** children /
    loud children
    los niños **ruidosos**
12. **quiet** children
    los niños **tranquilos**

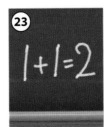
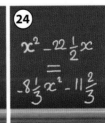

23. **easy** problem
    el problema **fácil**
24. **difficult** problem /
    hard problem
    el problema **difícil**

$1 + 1 = 2$

$x^2 - 22\frac{1}{2}x$
$=$
$-8\frac{1}{3}x^2 - 11\frac{2}{3}$

Survey your class. Record the responses.

1. Are you a slow walker or a fast walker?
2. Do you prefer loud parties or quiet parties?
Report: *Five of us prefer quiet parties.*

Use the new words.
Look at pages 154–155. Describe the things you see.

A: *The subway is full.*
B: *The motorcycle is noisy.*

23

Basic Colors   Los colores básicos

1. red
   rojo

2. yellow
   amarillo

3. blue
   azul

4. orange
   anaranjado

5. green
   verde

6. purple
   morado

7. pink
   rosado

8. violet
   violeta

9. turquoise
   azul turquesa

10. dark blue
    azul oscuro

11. light blue
    azul claro

12. bright blue
    azul brillante

Neutral Colors   Los colores neutros

13. black
    negro

14. white
    blanco

15. gray
    gris

16. cream / ivory
    color crema/color marfil

17. brown
    marrón/café

18. beige / tan
    beige/moreno

Survey your class. Record the responses.

1. What colors are you wearing today?
2. What colors do you like? What colors do you dislike?
Report: *Most of us… Some of us…*

Use the new words. Look at pages 86–87.
Take turns naming the colors you see.

A: *His shirt is* <u>blue</u>.
B: *Her shoes are* <u>white</u>.

1. The yellow sweaters are **on the left**.
   Los suéteres amarillos están **a la izquierda**.

2. The purple sweaters are **in the middle**.
   Los suéteres morados están **en medio**.

3. The brown sweaters are **on the right**.
   Los suéteres marrones están **a la derecha**.

4. The red sweaters are **above** the blue sweaters.
   Los suéteres rojos están **encima** de los suéteres azules.

5. The blue sweaters are **below** the red sweaters.
   Los suéteres azules están **debajo** de los suéteres rojos.

6. The turquoise sweater is **in** the box.
   El suéter azul turquesa está **dentro de** la caja.

7. The white sweater is **in front of** the black sweater.
   El suéter blanco está **en frente del** suéter negro.

8. The black sweater is **behind** the white sweater.
   El suéter negro está **detrás** del suéter blanco.

9. The violet sweater is **next to** the gray sweater.
   El suéter violeta está **al lado del** suéter gris.

10. The gray sweater is **under** the orange sweater.
    El suéter gris está **debajo** del suéter anaranjado.

11. The orange sweater is **on** the gray sweater.
    El suéter anaranjado está **sobre** el suéter gris.

12. The green sweater is **between** the pink sweaters.
    El suéter verde está **entre** los suéteres rosados.

More vocabulary

near: in the same area
far from: not near

Role play. Make new conversations.

A: *Excuse me. Where are the <u>red</u> sweaters?*
B: *They're <u>on the left</u>, <u>above</u> the <u>blue</u> sweaters.*
A: *Thanks very much.*

25

Money   El dinero

Coins   Las monedas

1. $.01 = 1¢
a penny / 1 cent
un centavo

2. $.05 = 5¢
a nickel / 5 cents
cinco centavos

3. $.10 = 10¢
a dime / 10 cents
diez centavos

4. $.25 = 25¢
a quarter / 25 cents
veinticinco centavos

5. $.50 = 50¢
a half dollar
medio dólar

6. $1.00
a dollar coin
una moneda de un dólar

Bills   Los billetes

7. $1.00
a dollar
un dólar

8. $5.00
five dollars
cinco dólares

9. $10.00
ten dollars
diez dólares

10. $20.00
twenty dollars
veinte dólares

11. $50.00
fifty dollars
cincuenta dólares

12. $100.00
one hundred dollars
cien dólares

A. Get change.
Obtener cambio.

B. Borrow money.
Pedir prestado dinero.

C. Lend money.
Prestar dinero.

D. Pay back the money.
Pagar el dinero prestado.

Pair practice. Make new conversations.

A: *Do you have change for a dollar?*
B: *Sure. How about two quarters and five dimes?*
A: *Perfect!*

Identify Mark's problem. Brainstorm solutions.

Mark doesn't like to lend money. His boss, Lia, asks, "Can I borrow $20.00?" What can Mark say? What will Lia say?

26

Ways to Pay Formas de pagar

A. pay cash
pagar en efectivo

B. use a credit card
usar una tarjeta de crédito

C. use a debit card
usar una tarjeta de débito

D. write a (personal) check
escribir un cheque (personal)

E. use a gift card
usar una tarjeta de regalo

F. cash a traveler's check
cambiar un cheque de viajero

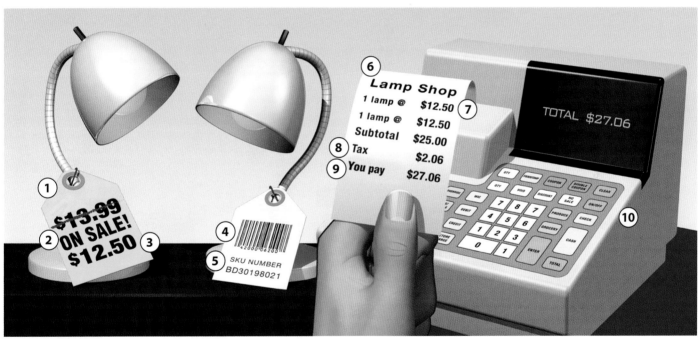

1. price tag	3. sale price	5. SKU number	7. price / cost	9. total
la etiqueta del precio	el precio de oferta	el número SKU	el precio/el costo	el total
2. regular price	4. bar code	6. receipt	8. sales tax	10. cash register
el precio normal	el código de barras	el recibo	el impuesto de ventas	la caja registradora

G. buy / pay for
comprar/pagar

H. return
devolver

I. exchange
cambiar

27

Same and Different   Igual y diferente

1. twins	3. matching	5. navy blue	A. **shop**
las mellizas	iguales	azul marino	buscando para comprar
2. sweater	4. disappointed	6. happy	B. **keep**
el suéter	desilusionada	feliz	quedarse con

What do you see in the pictures?

1. Who is the woman shopping for?
2. Does she buy matching sweaters or different sweaters?
3. How does Anya feel about her green sweater? What does she do?
4. What does Manda do with her sweater?

Read the story.

Same and Different

Mrs. Kumar likes to <u>shop</u> for her <u>twins</u>. Today she's looking at <u>sweaters</u>. There are many different colors on sale. Mrs. Kumar chooses two <u>matching</u> green sweaters.

The next day, Manda and Anya open their gifts. Manda likes the green sweater, but Anya is <u>disappointed</u>. Mrs. Kumar understands the problem. Anya wants to be different.

Manda <u>keeps</u> her sweater, but Anya goes to the store. She exchanges her green sweater for a <u>navy blue</u> sweater. It's an easy answer to Anya's problem. Now the twins can be warm, <u>happy</u>, and different.

Reread the story.

1. Underline the last sentence in each paragraph. Why are these sentences important?
2. Retell the story in your own words.

What do you think?

3. Imagine you are Anya. Would you keep the sweater or exchange it? Why?

29

Adults and Children   Adultos y niños

1. man
   el hombre

2. woman
   la mujer

3. women
   las mujeres

4. men
   los hombres

5. senior citizen
   la anciana

Listen and point. Take turns.

A: *Point to a woman.*

B: *Point to a senior citizen.*

A: *Point to an infant.*

Dictate to your partner. Take turns.

A: *Write woman.*

B: *Is that spelled w-o-m-a-n?*

A: *Yes, that's right, woman.*

6. infant
el bebé

7. baby
el niño

8. toddler
la niña pequeña

9. 6-year-old boy
el niño de 6 años

10. 10-year-old girl
la niña de 10 años

11. teenager / teen
el adolescente

Ways to talk about age

1 month–3 months old = **infant**

18 months–3 years old = **toddler**

3 years old–12 years old = **child**

13–19 years old = **teenager**

18+ years old = **adult**

62+ years old = **senior citizen**

Pair practice. Make new conversations.

A: *How old is* <u>Sandra</u>*?*

B: <u>*She's*</u> <u>*13*</u> *years old.*

A: *Wow,* <u>*she's*</u> <u>*a teenager*</u> *now!*

31

Describing People   Descripción de las personas

Age Edad

1. young
   joven
2. middle-aged
   de mediana edad
3. elderly
   anciano(a)

Height Estatura

4. tall
   alto(a)
5. average height
   de estatura promedio
6. short
   bajo(a)

Weight Peso

7. heavy / fat
   pesado(a)/obeso(a)
8. average weight
   de peso promedio
9. thin / slender
   flaco(a)/delgado(a)

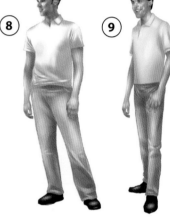

Disabilities Discapacidades

10. physically challenged
    impedido(a) físico
11. sight impaired / blind
    impedido(a) visual/ciego(a)
12. hearing impaired / deaf
    con problemas auditivos/
    sordo(a)

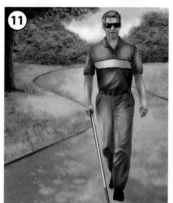

Appearance Aspecto

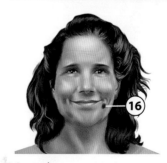

13. attractive
    atractivo(a)
14. cute
    bonito(a)
15. pregnant
    embarazada
16. mole
    lunar
17. pierced ear
    oreja perforada
18. tattoo
    tatuaje

Ways to describe people

He's a <u>heavy</u>, <u>young</u> man.
She's a <u>pregnant</u> woman with <u>a mole</u>.
He's <u>sight impaired</u>.

Use the new words.

Look at pages 44-45. Describe the people you see. Take turns.

A: This <u>elderly</u> woman is <u>short</u> and a little <u>heavy</u>.
B: This <u>young</u> man is <u>physically challenged</u>.

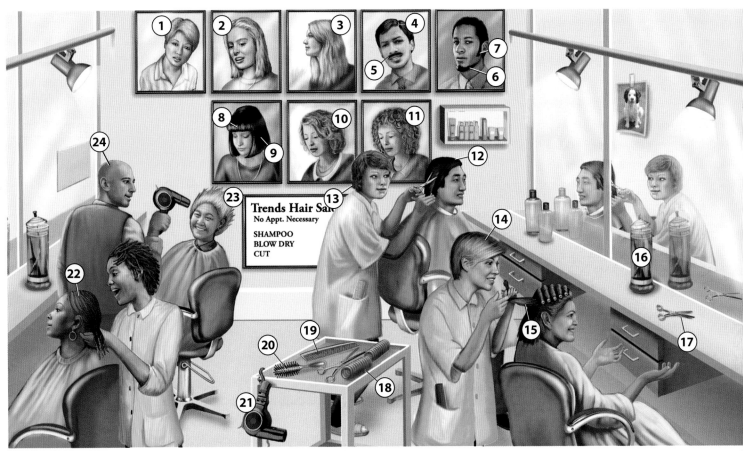

1. **short hair**
   el cabello corto

2. **shoulder-length hair**
   el cabello a la altura de los hombros

3. **long hair**
   el cabello largo

4. **part**
   la raya

5. **mustache**
   el bigote

6. **beard**
   la barba

7. **sideburns**
   las patillas

8. **bangs**
   el flequillo/el fleco

9. **straight hair**
   el cabello liso

10. **wavy hair**
    el cabello ondulado

11. **curly hair**
    el cabello rizado

12. **black hair**
    el cabello negro

13. **red hair**
    pelirrojo(a)

14. **blond hair**
    el cabello rubio

15. **brown hair**
    el cabello castaño

16. **sanitizing jar**
    el recipiente de desinfección

17. **shears**
    las tijeras

18. **rollers**
    los rizadores

19. **comb**
    el peine/la peinilla

20. **brush**
    el cepillo

21. **blow dryer**
    el secador

22. **cornrows**
    con trenzas tejidas en el cabello

23. **gray hair**
    las canas

24. **bald**
    calvo

Style Hair Arreglar el cabello

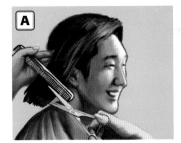

A. **cut** hair
cortar el cabello

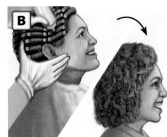

B. **perm** hair
hacer la permanente

C. **add** highlights
hacer mechas

D. **color** hair / **dye** hair
teñir el cabello

Ways to talk about hair

Describe hair in this order: length, style, and then color.
She has <u>long</u>, <u>straight</u>, <u>brown</u> hair.

Role play. Talk to a stylist.

A: *I need a new hairstyle.*
B: *How about <u>short</u> and <u>straight</u>?*
A: *Great. Do you think I should <u>dye</u> it?*

33

1. grandmother
   la abuela

2. grandfather
   el abuelo

3. mother
   la madre

4. father
   el padre

5. sister
   la hermana

6. brother
   el hermano

7. aunt
   la tía

8. uncle
   el tío

9. cousin
   el primo/la prima

Tim Lee's Family

GRANDPARENTS

Immediate Family

PARENTS

CHILDREN

① Min ② Lu

③ Rose ④ Ken ⑦ Lynn ⑧ Dan

Tim ⑤ Lily ⑥ Alex ⑨ Emily

10. mother-in-law
    la suegra

11. father-in-law
    el suegro

12. wife
    la esposa

13. husband
    el esposo

14. daughter
    la hija

15. son
    el hijo

16. sister-in-law
    la cuñada

17. brother-in-law
    el cuñado

18. niece
    la sobrina

19. nephew
    el sobrino

Ana Garcia's Family

Extended Family

⑩ Eva ⑪ Sam

⑫ Ana ⑬ Tito ⑯ Marta ⑰ Carlos

⑭ Sara ⑮ Felix ⑱ Alice ⑲ Eddie

More vocabulary

Tim is Min and Lu's **grandson**.
Lily and Emily are Min and Lu's **granddaughters**.
Alex is Min's youngest **grandchild**.

Ana is Eva and Sam's **daughter-in-law**.
Carlos is Eva and Sam's **son-in-law**.
Note: Ana's married. = Ana **is** married.
Ana's **husband** = the man married to Ana

20. married couple
    la pareja casada
21. divorced couple
    la pareja divorciada
22. single mother
    la madre soltera
23. single father
    el padre soltero

Carol, Bruce, and Lisa

Lisa, Age 4

Lisa Green's Family

Lisa, Age 7

Rick   Carol   Bruce   Sue

Lisa, Today

Mary   David   Kim   Bill

24. remarried
    casados nuevamente
25. stepfather
    el padrastro
26. stepmother
    la madrastra
27. half sister
    la media hermana
28. half brother
    el medio hermano
29. stepsister
    la hermanastra
30. stepbrother
    el hermanastro

More vocabulary

Bruce is Carol's **former husband** or **ex-husband**.
Carol is Bruce's **former wife** or **ex-wife**.
Lisa is the **stepdaughter** of both Rick and Sue.

Use the new words.

Ask and answer questions about Lisa's family.

A: *Who is Lisa's half sister?*
B: *Mary is. Who is Lisa's stepsister?*

A. hold
sostenerlo

B. nurse
amamantarlo

C. feed
alimentarlo

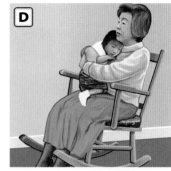

D. rock
mecerlo

E. undress
desvestirlo

F. bathe
bañarlo

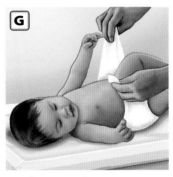

G. change a diaper
cambiarle el pañal

H. dress
vestirlo

I. comfort
consolarlo

Good job!

J. praise
elogiarlo

No!

K. discipline
disciplinarlo

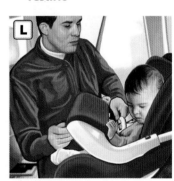

L. buckle up
abrocharle el cinturón

M. play with
jugar con él

N. read to
leerle

O. sing a lullaby
cantarle una canción
de cuna

P. kiss goodnight
besarlo en la noche

Look at the pictures.
Describe what is happening.

A: *She's changing her baby's diaper.*
B: *He's kissing his son goodnight.*

Talk about your experience.

I am great at playing with toddlers.
I have a lot of experience changing diapers.
I know how to hold an infant.

1. **bottle**
   la botella

2. **nipple**
   la mamadera/el chupón

3. **formula**
   la fórmula

4. **baby food**
   el alimento para bebé

5. **bib**
   el babero

6. **high chair**
   la silla alta

7. **diaper pail**
   el cesto para pañales

8. **cloth diaper**
   el pañal de tela

9. **safety pins**
   los prendedores
   de seguridad

10. **disposable diaper**
    el pañal desechable

11. **diaper bag**
    la pañalera

12. **wipes**
    las toallitas húmedas

13. **baby lotion**
    la loción para bebé

14. **baby powder**
    el talco para bebé

15. **potty seat**
    la bacinilla

16. **training pants**
    los calzoncitos de
    entrenamiento

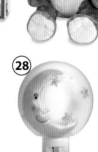

17. **baby carrier**
    el cargador para bebé

18. **stroller**
    el carrito

19. **carriage**
    el cochecito

20. **car safety seat**
    el asiento de seguridad
    para el automóvil

21. **booster car seat**
    el asiento elevador
    para el automóvil

22. **rocking chair**
    la silla mecedora

23. **nursery rhymes**
    las canciones de cuna

24. **teddy bear**
    el osito de peluche

25. **pacifier**
    el chupete/el chupón

26. **teething ring**
    el anillo de dentición

27. **rattle**
    la sonaja/el sonajero

28. **night light**
    la luz de noche

Dictate to your partner. Take turns.

A: *Write pacifier.*
B: *Was that pacifier, p-a-c-i-f-i-e-r?*
A: *Yes, that's right.*

Think about it. Discuss.

1. How can parents discipline toddlers? teens?
2. What are some things you can say to praise a child?
3. Why are nursery rhymes important for young children?

37

A. wake up
despertarse

B. get up
levantarse

C. take a shower
tomar una ducha

D. get dressed
vestirse

E. eat breakfast
desayunar

F. make lunch
preparar el almuerzo

G. take the children to school /
drop off the kids
llevar a los niños al colegio/
dejar a los niños

H. take the bus to school
tomar el autobús para ir al colegio

I. drive to work / **go** to work
conducir al trabajo/ir al trabajo

J. be in class
estar en clase

K. work
trabajar

L. go to the grocery store
ir a la tienda de comestibles

M. pick up the kids
recoger a los niños

N. leave work
salir del trabajo

Grammar Point: third-person singular

For *he* and *she*, add **-s** or **-es** to the verb:
He eat**s** breakfast.   He watch**es** TV.
She make**s** lunch.   She go**es** to the store.

For two-part verbs, put the **-s** on the first part: wake**s** up,
drop**s** off.
Be and **have** are different (irregular).
He **is** in bed at 5 a.m. He **has** breakfast at 7 a.m.

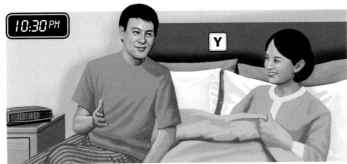

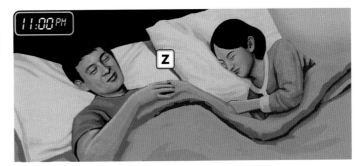

O. clean the house
limpiar la casa

P. exercise
hacer ejercicios

Q. cook dinner / **make** dinner
preparar la cena/**hacer** la cena

R. come home / **get** home
venir a la casa/**llegar** a la casa

S. have dinner / **eat** dinner
cenar/**comer** la cena

T. do homework
hacer la tarea

U. relax
descansar

V. read the paper
leer el periódico

W. check email
revisar el correo electrónico

X. watch TV
ver televisión

Y. go to bed
acostarse

Z. go to sleep
dormirse

Pair practice. Make new conversations.

A: *When does he go to work?*
B: *He goes to work at 8:00 a.m. When does she make dinner?*
A: *She makes dinner at 6:00 p.m.*

Internet Research: housework

Type "time survey, chart, housework" in the search bar.
Report: *According to the survey, men prepare food 17 minutes a day.*

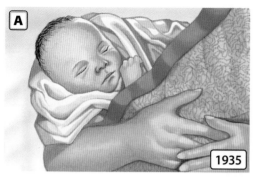

1935

A. be born
nacer

1940

B. start school
empezar a ir al colegio

1. birth certificate
la partida/el acta/
el certificado de nacimiento

DEPARTMENT OF IMMIGRATION

1950

C. immigrate
inmigrar

1953

D. graduate
graduarse

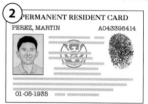

PERMANENT RESIDENT CARD
PEREZ, MARTIN   A043398414
01-08-1935

2. Resident Alien card / green card
la tarjeta de residente permanente

Los Angeles High School
Martin Perez

3. diploma
el diploma

1953

E. learn to drive
aprender a conducir

1954

F. get a job
conseguir empleo

CALIFORNIA
DRIVER LICENSE
M06188
MARTIN PEREZ

4. driver's license
la licencia de conducir

SOCIAL SECURITY
987-65-4321
MARTIN PEREZ

5. Social Security card
la tarjeta del seguro social

1954

G. become a citizen
convertirse en ciudadano

1955

H. fall in love
enamorarse

THE UNITED STATES OF AMERICA
CERTIFICATE OF NATURALIZATION
MARTIN PEREZ DE LEON

6. Certificate of Naturalization
el certificado de naturalización

Grammar Point: past tense

start
learn   } **+ ed**
travel

immigrate   retire
graduate   die   } **+ d**

These verbs are different (irregular):

be – was   go – went   buy – bought
get – got   have – had
become – became   fall – fell

1956

I. go to college
ir a la universidad

1958

J. get engaged
comprometerse para casarse

7. college degree
el diploma universitario

1959

K. get married
casarse

1961

L. have a baby
tener un bebé

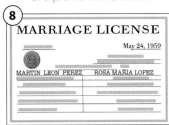

MARRIAGE LICENSE
May 24, 1959

MARTIN LEON PEREZ | ROSA MARIA LOPEZ

8. marriage license
la licencia de matrimonio

1965

M. buy a home
comprar una casa

1986

N. become a grandparent
convertirse en abuelo(a)

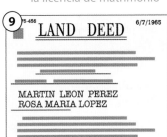

LAND DEED   6/7/1965

MARTIN LEON PEREZ
ROSA MARIA LOPEZ

9. deed
la escritura del terreno

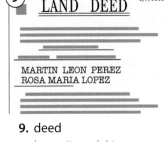

GOODBYE MARTIN AND GOOD LUCK!
2000

O. retire
jubilarse

EGYPT
2005

P. travel
viajar

PASSPORT
United States of America

10. passport
el pasaporte

2006

Q. volunteer
trabajar como voluntario

2008

R. die
morir

CERTIFICATE OF DEATH
MARTIN LEON PEREZ
December 12th, 2008

11. death certificate
el certificado de defunción

More vocabulary

When a husband dies, his wife becomes a **widow**.
When a wife dies, her husband becomes a **widower**.
Someone who is not living is **dead** or **deceased**.

Survey your class. Record the responses.

1. When did you start school? immigrate? learn to drive?
2. Do you want to become a citizen? travel? retire?
Report: *Most of us… Some of us…*

1. hot
   tener calor

2. thirsty
   tener sed

3. sleepy
   tener sueño

4. cold
   tener frío

5. hungry
   tener hambre

6. full / satisfied
   sentirse satisfecho(a)

7. disgusted
   sentirse asqueada

8. calm
   tranquilo(a)

9. uncomfortable
   incómodo(a)

10. nervous
    nervioso(a)

11. in pain
    sentir dolor

12. sick
    enfermo(a)

13. worried
    preocupado(a)

14. well
    bien

15. relieved
    aliviado(a)

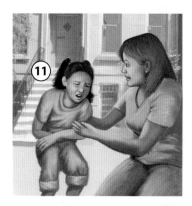
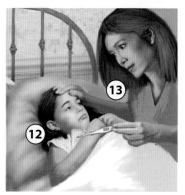

16. hurt
    lastimado(a)

17. lonely
    solo(a)

18. in love
    enamorado(a)

Pair practice. Make new conversations.

A: *How are you doing?*
B: *I'm <u>hungry</u>. How about you?*
A: *I'm <u>hungry</u> and <u>thirsty</u>, too!*

Use the new words.
Look at pages 40–41. Describe what each person is feeling.

A: *Martin is <u>excited</u>.*
B: *Martin's mother is <u>proud</u>.*

19. sad
triste

20. homesick
nostálgico(a)

21. proud
orgulloso(a)

22. excited
emocionado(a)

23. scared / afraid
asustado(a)/
temeroso(a)

24. embarrassed
avergonzado(a)

25. bored
aburrido(a)

26. confused
confundido(a)

27. frustrated
frustrado(a)

28. upset
alterado(a)

29. angry
enojado(a)

30. surprised
sorprendido(a)

31. happy
contento(a)

32. tired
cansado(a)

Identify Kenge's problem. Brainstorm solutions.

Kenge wants to learn English quickly, but it's difficult.
He makes a lot of mistakes and gets frustrated.
And he's homesick, too. What can he do?

More vocabulary

exhausted: very tired
furious: very angry
humiliated: very embarrassed

overjoyed: very happy
starving: very hungry
terrified: very scared

43

A Family Reunion   Una reunión familiar

LU FAMILY REUNION

1. banner
   el anuncio de pancarta

2. baseball game
   el juego de béisbol

3. opinion
   la opinión

4. balloons
   los globos

5. glad
   alegre

6. relatives
   los parientes

A. **laugh**
   reír

B. **misbehave**
   comportarse mal

I think large families are best.

What do you see in the picture?

1. How many relatives are there at this reunion?

2. How many children are there? Which children are misbehaving?

3. What are people doing at this reunion?

Read the story.

A Family Reunion

Ben Lu has a lot of <u>relatives</u> and they're all at his house. Today is the Lu family reunion.

There is a lot of good food. There are also <u>balloons</u> and a <u>banner</u>. And this year there are four new babies!

People are having a good time at the reunion. Ben's grandfather and his aunt are talking about the <u>baseball game</u>. His cousins <u>are laughing</u>. His mother-in-law is giving her <u>opinion</u>. And many of the children <u>are misbehaving</u>.

Ben looks at his family and smiles. He loves his relatives, but he's <u>glad</u> the reunion is once a year.

Reread the story.

1. Find this sentence in the story: "He loves his relatives, but he's glad the reunion is once a year." Explain what this sentence means.

2. Retell the story in your own words.

What do you think?

3. You are at Ben's party. You see a child misbehave. No other guests see him. What do you do? What do you say?

45

The Home   El hogar

1. yard
   el patio

2. roof
   el techo

3. bedroom
   el dormitorio

4. door
   la puerta

5. bathroom
   el baño

6. kitchen
   la cocina

7. floor
   el piso

8. dining area
   el área del comedor

Listen and point. Take turns.

A: *Point to the kitchen.*
B: *Point to the living room.*
A: *Point to the basement.*

Dictate to your partner. Take turns.

A: *Write kitchen.*
B: *Was that k-i-t-c-h-e-n?*
A: *Yes, that's right, kitchen.*

9. attic
el desván

10. kids' bedroom
el dormitorio
de los niños

11. baby's room /
nursery
la habitación
del bebé

12. window
la ventana

13. living room
la sala

14. basement
el sótano

15. garage
el garaje

Ways to give locations

I'm **at** home.
I'm **in** the kitchen.
I'm **on** the roof.

It's **in** the laundry room.
It's **on** the floor.

Pair practice. Ask and answer questions.

A: *Where's the <u>man</u>?*
B: <u>*He's*</u> *in the <u>attic</u>. Where's the <u>mother</u>?*
A: <u>*She's*</u> *in the <u>living room</u>.*

47

Finding a Home   Búsqueda de casa

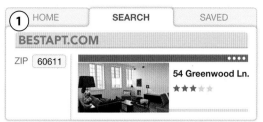

Abbreviations

apt = apartment
bed, br = bedroom
ba, bath = bathroom
kit = kitchen
yd = yard
util = utilities
incl = included
mo = month
furn = furnished
unfurn = unfurnished
mgr = manager
eves = evenings
AC = air conditioning

1. apartment search tool
la herramienta de búsqueda de apartamentos

2. listing / classified ad
los anuncios clasificados

3. furnished apartment
el apartamento amueblado

4. unfurnished apartment
los apartamentos no amueblados

GAS   WATER   ELECTRICITY   TRASH COLLECTION   CABLE   INTERNET ACCESS

5. utilities
los servicios públicos

Renting an Apartment   Alquiler de un apartamento

A. Call the manager.
Llame al administrador.

B. Ask about the features.
Pregúntele sobre las características.

Are utilities included?

No, they aren't.

C. Submit an application.
Presente una solicitud.

D. Sign the rental agreement.
Firme el contrato de alquiler/renta.

E. Pay the first and last month's rent.
Pague el alquiler/la renta del primer y del último mes.

F. Move in.
Múdese al apartamento.

More vocabulary

lease: a monthly or yearly rental agreement
redecorate: to change the paint and furniture in a home
move out: to pack and leave a home

Survey your class. Record the responses.

1. What features do you look for in a home?
2. How did you find your current home?
Report: *Most of us… Some of us…*

Buying a House La compra de una casa

G. Meet with a realtor.
Reúnase con un agente inmobiliario.

H. Look at houses.
Vea casas.

I. Make an offer.
Haga una oferta.

J. Get a loan.
Obtenga un préstamo.

K. Take ownership.
Tome posesión.

L. Make a mortgage payment.
Haga un pago de hipoteca.

Moving In La mudanza

M. Pack.
Empaque.

N. Unpack.
Desempaque.

O. Put the utilities in your name.
Cambie los servicios públicos a su nombre.

P. Paint.
Pinte.

Q. Arrange the furniture.
Acomode los muebles.

R. Meet the neighbors.
Conozca a sus vecinos.

Ways to ask about a home's features

Are *utilities* included?
Is *the kitchen* large and sunny?
Are *the neighbors* quiet?

Role play. Talk to an apartment manager.

A: *Hi. I'm calling about the apartment.*
B: *OK. It's unfurnished and rent is $800 a month.*
A: *Are utilities included?*

Fourth Floor

Third Floor

Second Floor

First Floor

1. apartment building
el edificio de apartamentos

2. fire escape
la salida de incendios

3. playground
el parque

4. roof garden
el jardín aéreo

Entrance   La entrada

5. intercom / speaker
el intercomunicador

6. tenant
el inquilino/el arrendatario

7. vacancy sign
el aviso de "se alquila"

8. manager /
superintendent
el administrador/
el superintendente

Apartment Available
2BR + 2BA
555-4263

Lobby   El vestíbulo

9. elevator
el elevador/el ascensor

10. stairs / stairway
las escaleras

11. mailboxes
los buzones

Basement   El sótano

LAUNDRY ROOM

RECREATION ROOM

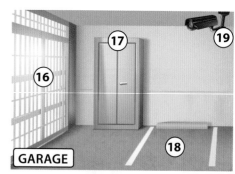

GARAGE

12. washer
la lavadora

13. dryer
la secadora

14. big-screen TV
el televisor de pantalla grande

15. pool table
la mesa de billar

16. security gate
la puerta/la reja de seguridad

17. storage locker
el armario/el depósito
de almacenamiento

18. parking space
el espacio de estacionamiento

19. security camera
la cámara de seguridad

Grammar Point: Is there…? / Are there…?

Is there a rec room?   **Are there** stairs?
Yes, there is.   Yes, there are.
No, there isn't.   No, there aren't.

Look at the pictures.
Describe the apartment building.

A: There's <u>a pool table</u> in <u>the recreation room</u>.
B: There **are** <u>parking spaces</u> in <u>the garage</u>.

APARTMENT COMPLEX

20. balcony
el balcón

21. courtyard
el patio

22. swimming pool
la piscina/la alberca

23. trash bin
el depósito de basura

24. alley
el callejón

Hallway El pasillo

25. emergency exit
la salida de emergencia

26. trash chute
el conducto para basura

Rental Office La oficina de alquiler

27. landlord
el arrendador/el dueño

28. lease / rental agreement
el contrato de alquiler

29. prospective tenant
el posible inquilino

An Apartment Entryway La entrada del apartamento

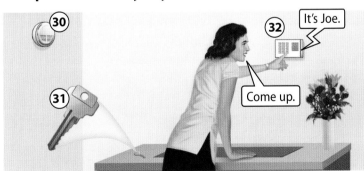

It's Joe.

Come up.

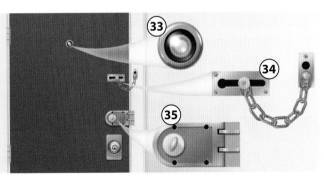

30. smoke detector
el detector de humo

31. key
la llave

32. buzzer
el timbre

33. peephole
el ojo mágico/la mirilla

34. door chain
la cadena para puerta

35. deadbolt lock
el cerrojo de seguridad

More vocabulary

upstairs: the floor(s) above you
downstairs: the floor(s) below you
fire exit: another name for emergency exit

Role play. Talk to a landlord.

A: Is there _a swimming pool_ in this _complex_?
B: Yes, there is. It's near the _courtyard_.
A: Is there…?

51

1. the city / an urban area
la ciudad/un área urbana

2. the suburbs
los suburbios/las afueras

3. a small town / a village
un pueblo pequeño/
una aldea

4. the country / a rural area
el campo/un área rural

5. condominium / condo
el condominio/un condo

6. townhouse
la residencia urbana

7. mobile home
la casa rodante/la casa móvil

8. college dormitory / dorm
la residencia universitaria

9. farm
la granja

10. ranch
la hacienda/el rancho

11. senior housing
las viviendas para ancianos

12. nursing home
el hogar de ancianos

13. shelter
el refugio

More vocabulary

co-op: an apartment building owned by residents
duplex: a house divided into two homes
two-story house: a house with two floors

Think about it. Discuss.

1. Compare life in a city and a small town.
2. Compare life in a city and the country.

Front Yard and House El jardín delantero y la casa

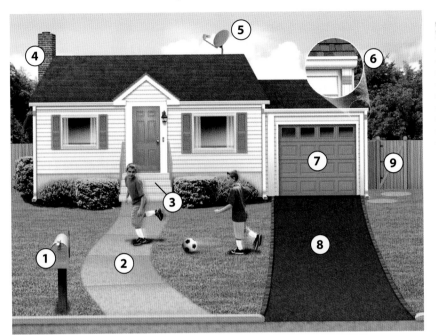

Front Porch El porche frontal

1. mailbox el buzón	**4.** chimney la chimenea	**7.** garage door la puerta del garaje
2. front walk la vereda/el caminito	**5.** satellite dish la antena parabólica	**8.** driveway la entrada del garaje
3. steps los escalones/ los peldaños	**6.** gutter el canal/el canalón	**9.** gate la puerta

10. storm door la contrapuerta	**13.** porch light la luz del porche
11. front door la puerta principal	**14.** doorbell el timbre
12. doorknob la perilla de la puerta	**15.** screen door la puerta mosquitero

Backyard El jardín posterior

16. patio el patio	**19.** patio furniture los muebles del patio	**22.** sprinkler el rociador	**25.** compost pile la pila de abono	**A.** **take** a nap **tomar** una siesta
17. grill la parrilla	**20.** flower bed el lecho de flores	**23.** hammock la hamaca	**26.** lawn el césped	**B.** **garden** **trabajar en el jardín**
18. sliding glass door la puerta de vidrio deslizante	**21.** hose la manguera	**24.** garbage can el cubo de basura	**27.** vegetable garden el jardín de verduras y hortalizas/la huerta/el huerto	

1. **cabinet**
   el gabinete

2. **shelf**
   el estante

3. **paper towels**
   las toallas de papel

4. **sink**
   el fregadero

5. **dish rack**
   el secaplatos/el secador de vajilla

6. **coffee maker**
   la cafetera

7. **garbage disposal**
   el triturador de desperdicios

8. **dishwasher**
   el lavaplatos

9. **refrigerator**
   el refrigerador/la nevera

10. **freezer**
    el congelador

11. **toaster**
    la tostadora

12. **blender**
    la licuadora

13. **microwave**
    el horno microondas

14. **electric can opener**
    el abrelatas eléctrico

15. **toaster oven**
    el horno tostador

16. **pot**
    la olla/la cacerola

17. **teakettle**
    la tetera

18. **stove**
    la estufa/la cocina

19. **burner**
    la hornilla

20. **oven**
    el horno

21. **broiler**
    la parrilla

22. **counter**
    el tope/el mostrador

23. **drawer**
    el cajón/la gaveta

24. **pan**
    la sartén

25. **electric mixer**
    la batidora eléctrica

26. **food processor**
    el procesador de alimentos

27. **cutting board**
    la tabla de cortar/picar

28. **mixing bowl**
    el tazón para mezclar/batir

Ways to talk about location using *on* and *in*

Use **on** for the counter, shelf, burner, stove, and cutting board. *It's on the counter.* Use **in** for the dishwasher, oven, sink, and drawer. *Put it in the sink.*

Pair practice. Make new conversations.

A: *Please move the <u>blender</u>.*
B: *Sure. Do you want it <u>in the cabinet</u>?*
A: *No, put it <u>on the counter</u>.*

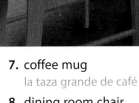

1. **dish / plate**
   el plato

2. **bowl**
   el tazón/el plato hondo

3. **fork**
   el tenedor

4. **knife**
   el cuchillo

5. **spoon**
   la cuchara

6. **teacup**
   la taza de té

7. **coffee mug**
   la taza grande de café

8. **dining room chair**
   la silla del comedor

9. **dining room table**
   la mesa del comedor

10. **napkin**
    la servilleta

11. **placemat**
    el mantel individual

12. **tablecloth**
    el mantel

13. **salt and pepper shakers**
    el salero y el pimentero

14. **sugar bowl**
    la taza de azúcar/
    la azucarera

15. **creamer**
    la lechera

16. **teapot**
    la tetera

17. **tray**
    la bandeja/la charola

18. **light fixture**
    la lámpara

19. **fan**
    el ventilador

20. **platter**
    el platón/el plato grande

21. **serving bowl**
    el plato hondo de servir

22. **hutch**
    el aparador con vitrina

23. **vase**
    el florero

24. **buffet**
    el armario

Ways to make requests at the table

May I have <u>the sugar bowl</u>?
Would you pass <u>the creamer</u>, please?
Could I have <u>a coffee mug</u>?

Role play. Request items at the table.

A: *What do you need?*
B: *Could I have a <u>coffee mug</u>?*
A: *Certainly. And would you…?*

55

1. **love seat**
   el sofá para dos

2. **throw pillow**
   el cojín

3. **basket**
   la cesta

4. **houseplant**
   la planta interior

5. **entertainment center**
   el centro de entretenimiento

6. **TV (television)**
   el televisor/el TV

7. **digital video recorder (DVR)**
   la videograbadora digital

8. **stereo system**
   el sistema estereofónico

9. **painting**
   el cuadro

10. **wall**
    la pared

11. **mantle**
    la repisa de la chimenea

12. **fire screen**
    la pantalla de protección

13. **fireplace**
    el hogar/la chimenea

14. **end table**
    la mesita auxiliar

15. **floor lamp**
    la lámpara de pie

16. **drapes / curtains**
    la cortina

17. **window**
    la ventana

18. **sofa / couch**
    el sofá

19. **coffee table**
    la mesa de centro

20. **candle**
    la vela

21. **candle holder**
    el portavelas

22. **armchair / easy chair**
    la butaca/el sillón

23. **ottoman**
    la otomana

24. **carpet**
    la alfombra

More vocabulary

light bulb: the light inside a lamp
magazine rack: a piece of furniture for magazines
sofa cushions: the pillows that are part of the sofa

Internet Research: furniture prices

Type any furniture item and the word "price" in the search bar.
Report: *I found a sofa for $300.00.*

1. hamper
   la cesta de la ropa sucia

2. bathtub
   la bañera

3. soap dish
   la jabonera

4. soap
   el jabón

5. rubber mat
   la alfombra de goma/
   el tapete de hule

6. washcloth
   la toallita para la cara

7. drain
   el desagüe

8. faucet
   el grifo/la llave

9. hot water
   el agua caliente

10. cold water
    el agua fría

11. grab bar
    la barra de sujeción

12. tile
    la losa/la baldosa/
    el azulejo

13. showerhead
    el cabezal de la ducha

14. shower curtain
    la cortina de la ducha

15. towel rack
    el toallero

16. bath towel
    la toalla de baño

17. hand towel
    la toalla de manos

18. mirror
    el espejo

19. toilet paper
    el papel higiénico

20. toilet brush
    el cepillo para el inodoro

21. toilet
    el inodoro

22. medicine cabinet
    el gabinete de baño/
    el botiquín

23. toothbrush
    el cepillo de dientes

24. toothbrush holder
    el portacepillos

25. sink
    el lavamanos

26. wastebasket
    la papelera

27. scale
    la balanza

28. bath mat
    la alfombrilla de baño

More vocabulary

stall shower: a shower without a bathtub
half bath: a bathroom with no shower or tub
linen closet: a closet for towels and sheets

Survey your class. Record the responses.

1. Is your toothbrush on the sink or in the medicine cabinet?
2. Do you have a bathtub or a shower?
Report: *Most of us… Some of us…*

57

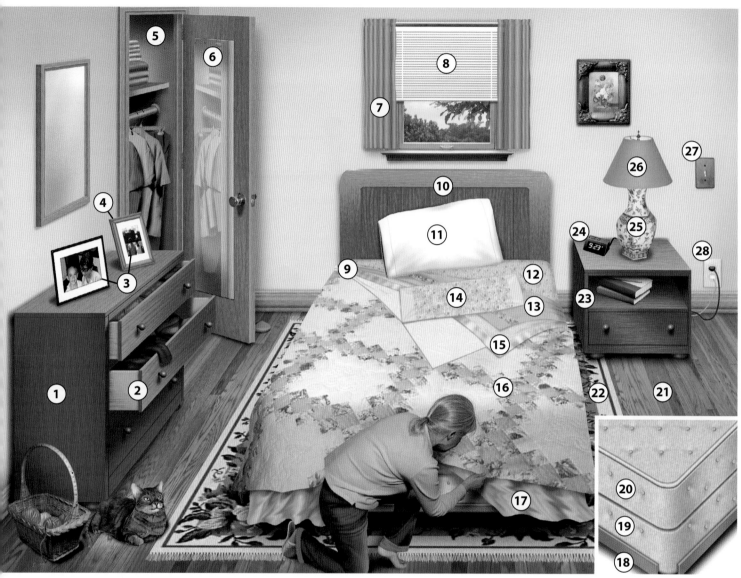

1. **dresser / bureau**
   la cómoda

2. **drawer**
   la gaveta/el cajón

3. **photos**
   las fotografías/las fotos

4. **picture frame**
   el marco de foto

5. **closet**
   el clóset

6. **full-length mirror**
   el espejo largo

7. **curtains**
   las cortinas

8. **mini-blinds**
   las minipersianas

9. **bed**
   la cama

10. **headboard**
    la cabecera

11. **pillow**
    la almohada

12. **fitted sheet**
    la sábana esquinera

13. **flat sheet**
    la sábana

14. **pillowcase**
    la funda de la almohada

15. **blanket**
    la cobija/la manta

16. **quilt**
    la colcha/el cubrecama

17. **dust ruffle**
    el volante

18. **bed frame**
    el marco de la cama

19. **box spring**
    la cama de resortes/
    el somier tapizado

20. **mattress**
    el colchón

21. **wood floor**
    el piso de madera

22. **rug**
    la alfombra

23. **night table / nightstand**
    la mesita de noche

24. **alarm clock**
    el reloj despertador

25. **lamp**
    la lámpara

26. **lampshade**
    la pantalla de la lámpara

27. **light switch**
    el interruptor de la luz

28. **outlet**
    el enchufe/el tomacorriente

Look at the pictures.
Describe the bedroom.

A: *There's a lamp on the nightstand*.
B: *There's a mirror in the closet*.

Survey your class. Record the responses.

1. Do you prefer a hard or a soft mattress?
2. How many pillows do you like on your bed?
Report: *All of us… A few of us…*

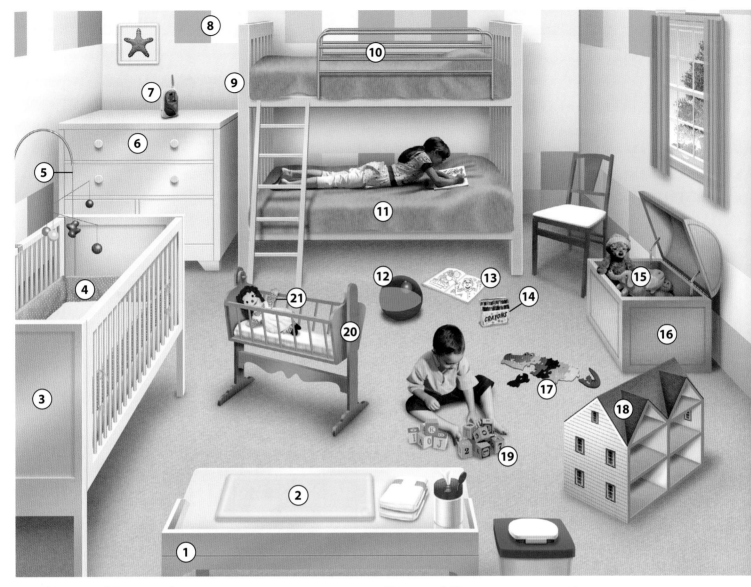

Furniture and Accessories Muebles y accesorios

1. **changing table**
   la mesa para cambiar pañales
2. **changing pad**
   la almohadilla para cambiar pañales
3. **crib**
   la cuna
4. **bumper pad**
   el protector
5. **mobile**
   el móvil

6. **chest of drawers**
   el gavetero/la cómoda
7. **baby monitor**
   el monitor para bebés
8. **wallpaper**
   el papel tapiz
9. **bunk beds**
   la litera
10. **safety rail**
    el riel de seguridad
11. **bedspread**
    el cubrecama/la colcha

Toys and Games Juguetes y juegos

12. **ball**
    la bola
13. **coloring book**
    el libro de pintar
14. **crayons**
    los crayones
15. **stuffed animals**
    los animales de peluche
16. **toy chest**
    el baúl de los juguetes

17. **puzzle**
    el rompecabezas
18. **dollhouse**
    la casa de muñecas
19. **blocks**
    los bloques
20. **cradle**
    la cuna mecedora
21. **doll**
    la muñeca

Pair practice. Make new conversations.

A: *Where's the changing pad?*
B: *It's on the changing table.*

Think about it. Discuss.

1. Which toys help children learn? How?
2. Which toys are good for older and younger children?
3. What safety features does this room need? Why?

A. **dust** the furniture
  sacudir los muebles

B. **recycle** the newspapers
  reciclar los periódicos

C. **clean** the oven
  limpiar el horno

D. **mop** the floor
  trapear/limpiar el piso

E. **polish** the furniture
  pulir los muebles

F. **make** the bed
  hacer la cama

G. **put away** the toys
  guardar los juguetes

H. **vacuum** the carpet
  aspirar la alfombra

I. **wash** the windows
  lavar las ventanas

J. **sweep** the floor
  barrer el piso

K. **scrub** the sink
  fregar el lavamanos

L. **empty** the trash
  vaciar la basura

M. **wash** the dishes
  lavar los platos

N. **dry** the dishes
  secar los platos

O. **wipe** the counter
  limpiar la encimera/el tope

P. **change** the sheets
  cambiar las sábanas

Q. **take out** the garbage
  sacar la basura

Pair practice. Make new conversations.

A: *Let's clean this place. First, I'll* <u>*sweep the floor*</u>*.*
B: *I'll* <u>*mop the floor*</u> *when you finish.*
A: *OK. After that we can…*

Think about it. Discuss.

1. Rank housework tasks from difficult to easy.
2. Categorize housework tasks by age: children, teens, adults.

 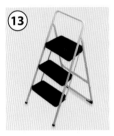    

1. **feather duster**
   el plumero

2. **recycling bin**
   el recipiente de reciclaje

3. **oven cleaner**
   el limpiador de hornos

4. **rubber gloves**
   los guantes de goma

5. **steel-wool soap pads**
   las esponjas de lana de acero

6. **sponge mop**
   la fregona con esponja

7. **bucket / pail**
   el cubo/el balde/la cubeta

8. **furniture polish**
   la cera para muebles

9. **cleaning cloths**
   los trapos de limpieza

10. **vacuum cleaner**
    la aspiradora

11. **vacuum cleaner attachments**
    los accesorios para aspiradora

12. **vacuum cleaner bag**
    la bolsa de la aspiradora

13. **stepladder**
    la escalerilla

14. **glass cleaner**
    el limpiador de vidrios

15. **squeegee**
    el escurridor

16. **broom**
    la escoba

17. **dustpan**
    el recogedor/la pala

18. **multipurpose cleaner**
    el limpiador multiuso

19. **sponge**
    la esponja

20. **scrub brush**
    el cepillo de fregar

21. **dishwashing liquid**
    el líquido lavaplatos

22. **dish towel**
    la toalla para platos

23. **disinfectant wipes**
    las toallitas húmedas desinfectantes

24. **trash bags**
    las bolsas de basura

Ways to ask for something

Please hand me the squeegee.
Can you get me the broom?
I need the sponge mop.

Pair practice. Make new conversations.

A: *Please hand me the sponge mop.*
B: *Here you go. Do you need the bucket?*
A: *Yes, please. Can you get me the rubber gloves, too?*

61

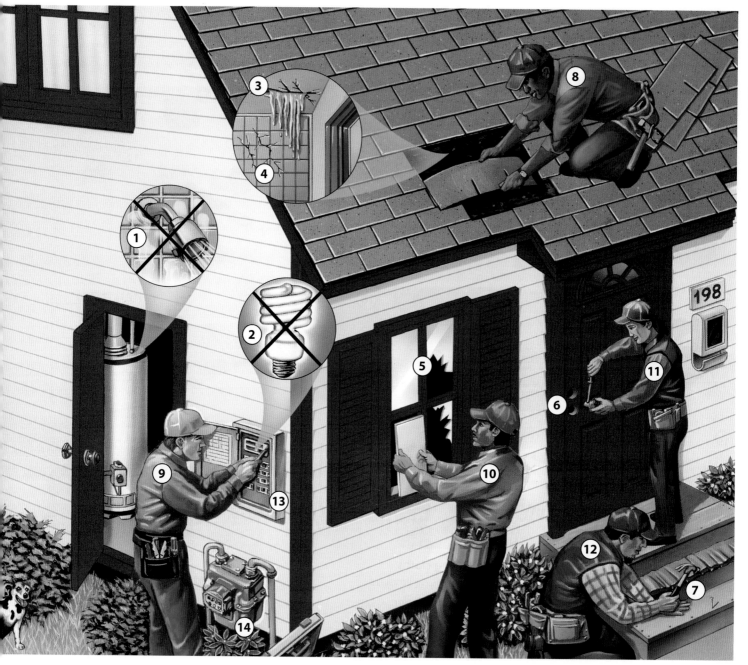

1. The water heater is **not working**.
   El calentador de agua no funciona.

2. The power is **out**.
   No hay electricidad.

3. The roof is **leaking**.
   El techo **gotea**.

4. The tile is **cracked**.
   La losa está **rota**.

5. The window is **broken**.
   La ventana está **rota**.

6. The lock is **broken**.
   La cerradura está **estropeada**.

7. The steps are **broken**.
   Los escalones están **rotos**.

8. roofer
   el reparador de techos

9. electrician
   el electricista

10. repairperson
    el reparador

11. locksmith
    el cerrajero

12. carpenter
    el carpintero

13. fuse box
    la caja de fusibles

14. gas meter
    el medidor de gas

More vocabulary

fix: to repair something that is broken
pests: termites, fleas, rats, etc.
exterminate: to kill household pests

Pair practice. Make new conversations.

A: The _faucet is leaking_.
B: _I think I can fix it._
A: _I think we should call a plumber._

Household Problems and Repairs

15. The furnace is **broken**.
La caldera está **estropeada**.

16. The pipes are **frozen**.
Las tuberías están **congeladas**.

17. The faucet is **dripping**.
El grifo/la llave **gotea**.

18. The sink is **overflowing**.
El lavamanos **se desborda**.

19. The toilet is **stopped up**.
El inodoro está **atorado**.

20. plumber
el plomero

21. exterminator
el fumigador/el exterminador

22. termites
las termitas/los comejenes

23. ants
las hormigas

24. bedbugs
los chinches

25. fleas
las pulgas

26. cockroaches / roaches
las cucarachas

27. rats
las ratas

28. mice*
los ratones

*****Note:** one mouse, two mice

Ways to ask about repairs

How much will it cost?
When can you begin?
How long will it take?

Role play. Talk to a repairperson.

A: *Can you <u>fix the roof</u>?*
B: *Yes, but it will take <u>two weeks</u>.*
A: *How much will it cost?*

The Tenant Meeting La reunión de los inquilinos

THE NEXT DAY…

LATER THAT EVENING…

1. roommates
los compañeros/
las compañeras
de habitación

2. party
la fiesta

3. music
la música

4. DJ
el *disc-jockey*

5. noise
el ruido

6. irritated
irritado

7. rules
las normas

8. mess
el desorden

9. invitation
la invitación

A. **dance**
bailar

What do you see in the pictures?

1. What happened in apartment 2B? How many people were there?

2. How did the neighbor feel? Why?

3. What rules did they write at the tenant meeting?

4. What did the roommates do after the tenant meeting?

Read the story.

The Tenant Meeting

Sally Lopez and Tina Green are roommates. They live in apartment 2B. One night they had a big party with music and a DJ. There was a mess in the hallway. Their neighbors were very unhappy. Mr. Clark in 2A was very irritated. He hates noise!

The next day there was a tenant meeting. Everyone wanted rules about parties and loud music. The girls were very embarrassed.

After the meeting, the girls cleaned the mess in the hallway. Then they gave each neighbor an invitation to a new party. Everyone had a good time at the rec room party. Now the tenants have two new rules and a new place to dance.

Reread the story.

1. Find the word "irritated" in paragraph 1. What does it mean in this story?

2. Retell the story in your own words.

What do you think?

3. Imagine you are the neighbor in 2A. What do you say to Tina and Sally?

4. What are the most important rules in an apartment building? Why?

Back from the Market De vuelta del mercado

1. fish
   el pescado
2. meat
   la carne
3. chicken
   el pollo
4. cheese
   el queso
5. milk
   la leche
6. butter
   la mantequilla
7. eggs
   los huevos
8. vegetables
   las verduras y hortalizas

Listen and point. Take turns.

A: *Point to the <u>vegetables</u>.*
B: *Point to the <u>bread</u>.*
A: *Point to the <u>fruit</u>.*

Dictate to your partner. Take turns.

A: *Write <u>vegetables</u>.*
B: *Please spell <u>vegetables</u> for me.*
A: *<u>V-e-g-e-t-a-b-l-e-s</u>.*

9. fruit
   las frutas

10. rice
    el arroz

11. bread
    el pan

12. pasta
    la pasta

13. grocery bag /
    shopping bag
    la bolsa de
    comestibles/
    la bolsa de compras

14. shopping list
    la lista de compra

15. coupons
    los cupones/los vales

Ways to talk about food.

Do we need eggs?
Do we have any pasta?
We have some vegetables, but we need fruit.

Role play. Talk about your shopping list.

A: *Do we need eggs?*
B: *No, we have some.*
A: *Do we have any…?*

67

1. apples
   las manzanas
2. bananas
   los plátanos
3. grapes
   las uvas
4. pears
   las peras
5. oranges
   las naranjas
6. grapefruit
   las toronjas
7. lemons
   los limones
8. limes
   las limas/los limones verdes

9. tangerines
   las mandarinas
10. peaches
    los duraznos/los melocotones
11. cherries
    las cerezas
12. apricots
    los albaricoques
13. plums
    las ciruelas
14. strawberries
    las fresas
15. raspberries
    las frambuesas
16. blueberries
    los arándanos

17. blackberries
    las zarzamoras/las moras
18. watermelons
    las sandías
19. melons
    los melones
20. papayas
    las papayas
21. mangoes
    los mangos
22. kiwi
    los kiwis
23. pineapples
    las piñas
24. coconuts
    los cocos

25. raisins
    las pasas
26. prunes
    las ciruelas pasas
27. figs
    los higos
28. dates
    los dátiles
29. a bunch of bananas
    un racimo de plátanos
30. **ripe** banana
    el plátano **maduro**
31. **unripe** banana
    el plátano **verde**
32. **rotten** banana
    el plátano **podrido/pasado**

Pair practice. Make new conversations.

A: *What's your favorite fruit?*
B: *I like apples. Do you?*
A: *I prefer bananas.*

Survey your class. Record the responses.

1. What kinds of fruit are common in your native country?
2. What kinds of fruit are uncommon?
Report: *According to Luis, papayas are common in Peru.*

1. lettuce
   la lechuga

2. cabbage
   la col

3. carrots
   las zanahorias

4. radishes
   los rábanos

5. beets
   las remolachas/los betabeles

6. tomatoes
   los tomates

7. bell peppers
   los pimientos/
   los pimentones

8. string beans
   las judías verdes/los ejotes

9. celery
   el apio

10. cucumbers
    los pepinos

11. spinach
    la espinaca

12. corn
    el maíz

13. broccoli
    el brócoli

14. cauliflower
    la coliflor

15. bok choy
    el repollo chino

16. turnips
    los nabos

17. potatoes
    las papas

18. sweet potatoes
    las batatas/los camotes

19. onions
    las cebollas

20. green onions / scallions
    las cebollas verdes/
    las cebollitas

21. peas
    los guisantes/los chícharos

22. artichokes
    las alcachofas

23. eggplants
    las berenjenas

24. squash
    la calabaza

25. zucchini
    el calabacín/la calabacita

26. asparagus
    los espárragos

27. mushrooms
    los hongos/las setas

28. parsley
    el perejil

29. chili peppers
    los chiles/los ajíes

30. garlic
    el ajo

31. a **bag of** lettuce
    una **bolsa de** lechuga

32. a **head of** lettuce
    una **cabeza de** lechuga

Pair practice. Make new conversations.

A: *Do you eat <u>broccoli</u>?*
B: *Yes. I like most vegetables, but not <u>peppers</u>.*
A: *Really? Well, I don't like <u>cauliflower</u>.*

Survey your class. Record the responses.

1. Which vegetables do you prefer to eat raw?
2. Which vegetables do you prefer to eat cooked?
Report: ____ *of us prefer <u>raw carrots</u>.* ____ *of us prefer <u>cooked carrots</u>.*

69

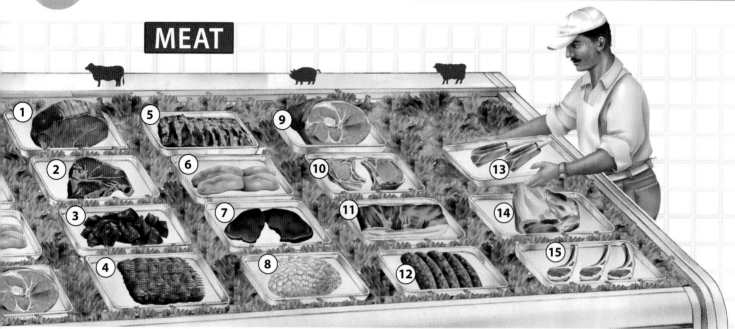

MEAT

Beef Carne de res

1. roast
   el asado
2. steak
   el filete/el bistec
3. stewing beef
   la carne para guisar
4. ground beef
   la carne molida

5. beef ribs
   las costillas de res
6. veal cutlets
   las chuletas de ternera
7. liver
   el hígado
8. tripe
   la tripa/el mondongo

Pork Carne de cerdo

9. ham
   el jamón
10. pork chops
    las chuletas de cerdo
11. bacon
    el tocino
12. sausage
    la salchicha

Lamb Carne de cordero

13. lamb shanks
    los jarretes de cordero
14. leg of lamb
    la pata de cordero
15. lamb chops
    las chuletas de cordero

POULTRY

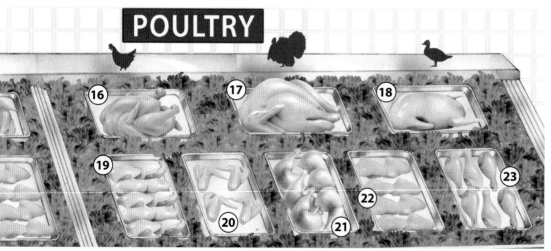

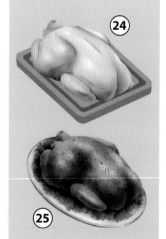

Poultry Carne de aves de corral

16. chicken
    el pollo
17. turkey
    el pavo

18. duck
    el pato
19. breasts
    las pechugas

20. wings
    las alas
21. legs
    las patas

22. thighs
    los contramuslos
23. drumsticks
    los muslos

24. **raw** turkey
    la carne de pavo **cruda**
25. **cooked** turkey
    la carne de pavo **cocida**

More vocabulary

boneless: meat and poultry without bones
skinless: poultry without skin
vegetarian: a person who doesn't eat meat

Ways to ask about meat prices

*How much **is** that <u>roast</u>?*
*How much **are** those <u>cutlets</u>?*
*How much **is** the <u>ground beef</u>?*

SEAFOOD

Fish Pescado

1. trout
la trucha

2. catfish
el bagre

3. whole salmon
el salmón entero

4. salmon steak
el filete de salmón

5. swordfish
el pez espada

6. halibut steak
el filete de halibut

7. tuna
el atún

8. cod
el bacalao

Shellfish Moluscos y crustáceos

9. crab
el cangrejo

10. lobster
la langosta

11. shrimp
el camarón

12. scallops
las vieiras

13. mussels
los mejillones

14. oysters
las ostras

15. clams
las almejas

16. fresh fish
el pescado **fresco**

17. frozen fish
el pescado **congelado**

DELI

18. white bread
el pan blanco

19. wheat bread
el pan de trigo

20. rye bread
el pan de centeno

21. roast beef
el rosbif

22. corned beef
la cecina/la carne en conserva

23. pastrami
el pastrami

24. salami
el salami

25. smoked turkey
el pavo ahumado

26. American cheese
el queso americano

27. Swiss cheese
el queso suizo

28. cheddar cheese
el queso cheddar

29. mozzarella cheese
el queso mozzarella

Ways to order at the counter

I'd like some _roast beef_.
I'll have _a halibut steak_ and some _shrimp_.
Could I get some _Swiss cheese_?

Pair practice. Make new conversations.

A: _What can I get for you?_
B: _I'd like some roast beef_. _How about a pound?_
A: _A pound of roast beef coming up!_

SEAFOOD

DAIRY

2A | 2B

FROZEN FOODS

POULTRY

MEAT

1. customer
el cliente

2. produce section
la sección de verduras,
hortalizas y frutas

3. scale
la balanza

4. grocery clerk
el ayudante de la tienda

5. stocker
el reponedor

6. pet food
la comida para mascotas

7. aisle
el pasillo

8. manager
el gerente

Canned Foods
Alimentos envasados

17. beans
los frijoles/las habichuelas

18. soup
la sopa

19. tuna
el atún

Dairy
Productos lácteos

20. margarine
la margarina

21. sour cream
la crema agria

22. yogurt
el yogur

Grocery Products
Otros productos

23. aluminum foil
el papel de aluminio

24. plastic wrap
el plástico para envolver

25. plastic storage bags
las bolsas de plástico
para almacenar

Frozen Foods
Alimentos congelados

26. ice cream
el helado

27. frozen vegetables
las verduras congeladas

28. frozen dinner
las comidas congeladas

Ways to ask for information in a grocery store

Excuse me, where are <u>the carrots</u>?
Can you please tell me where to find <u>the dog food</u>?
Do you have any <u>lamb chops</u> today?

Pair practice. Make new conversations.

A: *<u>Can you please tell me where to find the dog food</u>?*
B: *Sure. It's in <u>aisle 1B</u>. Do you need anything else?*
A: *Yes, where are <u>the carrots</u>?*

9. **shopping basket**
   la canasta

10. **self-checkout**
    el autopago

11. **line**
    la cola/la fila

12. **cart**
    el carrito

13. **checkstand**
    la caja

14. **cashier / checker**
    la cajera

15. **bagger**
    la persona que empaca
    la compra

16. **cash register**
    la caja registradora

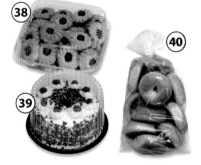

Baking Products
Productos para pastelerías

29. **flour**
    la harina

30. **sugar**
    el azúcar

31. **oil**
    el aceite

Beverages
Bebidas

32. **apple juice**
    el jugo de manzana

33. **coffee**
    el café

34. **soda / pop**
    las bebidas gaseosas

Snack Foods
Botanas/meriendas

35. **potato chips**
    las papas fritas de bolsa

36. **nuts**
    los frutos secos

37. **candy bar**
    las barras de chocolate

Baked Goods
Productos de pastelería

38. **cookies**
    las galletas dulces

39. **cake**
    la torta

40. **bagels**
    los bollos con forma
    de rosquilla

Survey your class. Record the responses.

1. What is your favorite grocery store?
2. Do you prefer to shop alone or with someone?
Report: *Most of us… Some of us…*

Think about it. Discuss.

1. Compare small grocery stores and large supermarkets.
2. Categorize the foods on this page as healthy or unhealthy. Explain your answers.

Containers and Packaging   Contenedores y envases

1. bottles
las botellas

2. jars
los frascos

3. cans
las latas

4. cartons
las cajas de cartón

5. containers
los contenedores

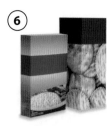

6. boxes
las cajas

7. bags
las bolsas

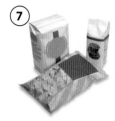

8. packages
los paquetes

9. six-packs
los paquetes
de seis

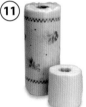

10. loaves
las hogazas

11. rolls
los rollos

12. tubes
los tubos

13. a bottle of water
una botella de agua

14. a jar of jam
un frasco de mermelada

15. a can of beans
una lata de frijoles

16. a carton of eggs
un cartón de huevos

17. a container of cottage cheese
un contenedor de queso fresco

18. a box of cereal
una caja de cereal

19. a bag of flour
una bolsa de harina

20. a package of cookies
un paquete de galletas dulces

21. a six-pack of soda (pop)
un paquete de seis bebidas gaseosas

22. a loaf of bread
una hogaza de pan

23. a roll of paper towels
un rollo de toallas de papel

24. a tube of toothpaste
un tubo de pasta de dientes

Grammar Point: count and noncount

Some foods can be counted: *an apple, two apples*.
Some foods can't be counted: *some rice, some water*.
For noncount foods, count containers: *two bags of rice*.

Pair practice. Make new conversations.

A: *How many <u>boxes of cereal</u> do we need?*
B: *We need <u>two boxes</u>.*

Weights and Measurements

A. **Measure** the ingredients.
Mida los ingredientes.

B. **Weigh** the food.
Pese la comida.

C. **Convert** the measurements.
Convierta las medidas.

1 cup =
237 milliliters

Liquid Measures Medidas para líquidos

(1)
1 fl. oz.

(2)
1 c.

(3)
1 pt.

(4)
1 qt.

(5)
1 gal.

1. a fluid ounce of milk
   una onza líquida de leche

2. a cup of oil
   una taza de aceite

3. a pint of frozen yogurt
   una pinta de yogur congelado

4. a quart of milk
   un cuarto de galón de leche

5. a gallon of water
   un galón de agua

Dry Measures Medidas secas

(6)
1 tsp.

(7)
1 TBS.

(8)
1/4 c.

(9)
1/2 c.

(10)
1 c.

6. a teaspoon of salt
   una cucharadita de sal

7. a tablespoon of sugar
   una cucharada de azúcar

8. a quarter cup of brown sugar
   un cuarto de taza de azúcar morena

9. a half cup of raisins
   media taza de pasas

10. a cup of flour
    una taza de harina

Weight Peso

(11)
11. an ounce of cheese
    una onza de queso

(12)
12. a pound of roast beef
    una libra de rosbif

Equivalencies	
3 tsp. = 1 TBS.	2 c. = 1 pt.
2 TBS. = 1 fl. oz.	2 pt. = 1 qt.
8 fl. oz. = 1 c.	4 qt. = 1 gal.

Volume
1 fl. oz. = 30 ml
1 c. = 237 ml
1 pt. = .47 L
1 qt. = .95 L
1 gal. = 3.79 L

Weight
1 oz. = 28.35 grams (g)
1 lb. = 453.6 g
2.205 lbs. = 1 kilogram (kg)
1 lb. = 16 oz.

75

Food Preparation and Safety
Preparación y seguridad de los alimentos

Food Safety · Seguridad de los alimentos

A. **clean**
limpiar

B. **separate**
separar

C. **cook**
cocinar

D. **chill**
refrigerar

A — Clean counters!
20 SECONDS
Wash your hands!

B — Use separate cutting boards for vegetables and meat!

C — 165 / 160 — Cook to the right temperature!

D — Refrigerate leftovers quickly!

Ways to Serve Meat and Poultry · Maneras de servir las carnes de res y de ave

1. fried chicken
pollo frito

2. barbecued / grilled ribs
costillas a la parrilla

3. broiled steak
filete de res asado a la brasa

4. roasted turkey
pavo al horno

5. boiled ham
jamón hervido

6. stir-fried beef
carne de res sofrita

Ways to Serve Eggs · Maneras de servir los huevos

7. scrambled eggs
huevos revueltos

8. hard-boiled eggs
huevos duros

9. poached eggs
huevos escalfados

10. eggs sunny-side up
huevos fritos

11. eggs over easy
huevos fritos, con una vuelta

12. omelet
tortilla de huevos

More vocabulary

bacteria: very small living things that often cause disease
surface: a counter, a table, or the outside part of something
disinfect: to remove bacteria from a surface

Pair practice. Make new conversations.

A: *How do you like your eggs?*
B: *I like them* <u>scrambled</u>. *And you?*
A: *I like them* <u>hard-boiled</u>.

Cheesy Tofu Vegetable Casserole Estofado de verduras, hortalizas y tofu con queso

A. Preheat the oven.
Precaliente el horno.

B. Grease a baking pan.
Engrase una cazuela para hornear.

C. Slice the tofu.
Rebane el tofu.

D. Steam the broccoli.
Cocine el brócoli **al vapor.**

E. Sauté the mushrooms.
Saltee los hongos/ las setas.

F. Spoon sauce on top.
Échele salsa encima **con una cuchara.**

G. Grate the cheese.
Ralle el queso.

H. Bake.
Hornee.

Easy Chicken Soup Sopa de pollo fácil

I. Cut up the chicken.
Corte el pollo.

J. Dice the celery.
Corte el apio en trocitos.

K. Peel the carrots.
Pele las zanahorias.

L. Chop the onions.
Corte las cebollas.

M. Boil the chicken.
Hierva el pollo.

N. Add the vegetables.
Añada las legumbres y hortalizas.

O. Stir.
Revuelva.

P. Simmer.
Cocine a fuego lento.

Quick and Easy Cake Torta fácil y rápida

Q. Break 2 eggs into a microwave-safe bowl.
Rompa 2 huevos en un tazón para horno microonda.

R. Mix the ingredients.
Mezcle los ingredientes.

S. Beat the mixture.
Bata la mezcla.

T. Microwave for 5 minutes.
Hornee la mezcla en **el horno microondas** durante 5 minutos.

1. can opener
   el abrelatas

2. grater
   el rallador

3. steamer
   la olla/la cacerola a vapor

4. storage container
   el envase con tapa

5. frying pan
   la sartén

6. pot
   la olla/la cacerola

7. ladle
   el cucharón/el cazo

8. double boiler
   la cacerola doble

9. wooden spoon
   la cuchara de madera

10. casserole dish
    el molde refractario/
    el recipiente refractario

11. garlic press
    la prensa para ajo

12. carving knife
    el cuchillo de trinchar

13. roasting pan
    la bandeja para asar

14. roasting rack
    la parrilla para asar

15. vegetable peeler
    el pelador de verduras
    y hortalizas

16. paring knife
    el cuchillo de pelar

17. colander
    el escurridor

18. kitchen timer
    el cronómetro de cocina

19. spatula
    la espátula

20. eggbeater
    el batidor de huevos

21. whisk
    el batidor

22. strainer
    la coladera

23. tongs
    las pinzas/las tenazas

24. lid
    la tapa

25. saucepan
    el cacillo/la olla

26. cake pan
    el molde para torta

27. cookie sheet
    la bandeja para
    galletas dulces

28. pie pan
    el molde para pastel

29. potholders
    los agarraollas

30. rolling pin
    el rodillo

31. mixing bowl
    el tazón para mezclar

Pair practice. Make new conversations.

A: *Please hand me* <u>the whisk</u>.
B: *Here's* <u>the whisk</u>. *Do you need anything else?*
A: *Yes, pass me* <u>the casserole dish</u>.

Use the new words.

Look at page 77. Name the kitchen utensils you see.

A: *This is* <u>a grater</u>.
B: *This is* <u>a mixing bowl</u>.

1. hamburger
   la hamburguesa

2. French fries
   las papas fritas

3. cheeseburger
   la hamburguesa con queso

4. onion rings
   los anillos de cebolla

5. chicken sandwich
   el sándwich de pollo

6. hot dog
   el perro caliente/la salchicha

7. nachos
   los nachos

8. taco
   el taco

9. burrito
   el burrito

10. pizza
    la *pizza*

11. soda
    el refresco

12. iced tea
    el té helado

13. ice-cream cone
    el barquillo de helado

14. milkshake
    la malteada

15. donut
    la rosquilla

16. muffin
    el mollete/el bollo dulce

17. counterperson
    el atendiente en el mostrador

18. straw
    la caña/el sorbeto

19. plastic utensils
    los utensilios de plástico

20. sugar substitute
    el endulzante artificial

21. ketchup
    el kétchup

22. mustard
    la mostaza

23. mayonnaise
    la mayonesa

24. salad bar
    la barra de ensaladas

Grammar Point: yes/no questions (do)

Do you like hamburgers? Yes, I do.
Do you like nachos? No, I don't.
Practice asking about the food on the page.

Think about it. Discuss.

1. Which fast foods are healthier than others? How do you know?
2. Compare the benefits of a fast food lunch and a lunch from home.

79

1. **bacon**
   el tocino

2. **sausage**
   la salchicha

3. **hash browns**
   las papitas doradas

4. **toast**
   la tostada

5. **English muffin**
   el bollo dulce inglés

6. **biscuits**
   los panecillos

7. **pancakes**
   los panqueques

8. **waffles**
   los *waffles*

9. **hot cereal**
   el cereal caliente

10. **grilled cheese sandwich**
    el sándwich de queso
    a la plancha

11. **pickle**
    el pepinillo en vinagre

12. **club sandwich**
    el club sándwich

13. **spinach salad**
    la ensalada de espinaca

14. **chef's salad**
    la ensalada del chef

15. **house salad /
    garden salad**
    la ensalada de la casa/
    la ensalada verde

16. **soup**
    la sopa

17. **rolls**
    los panecillos

18. **coleslaw**
    la ensalada de col

19. **potato salad**
    la ensalada de papas

20. **pasta salad**
    la ensalada de pasta

21. **fruit salad**
    la ensalada de frutas

Menu

Breakfast Special

Served 6 a.m. to 11 a.m.

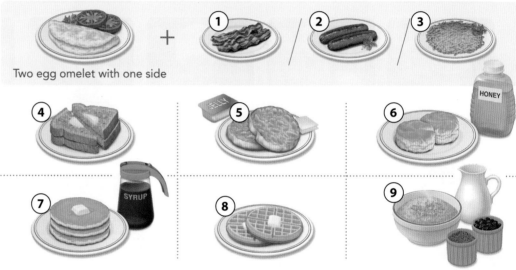

Two egg omelet with one side

Lunch

Served 11 a.m. to 2 p.m • All sandwiches come with soup or salad.

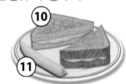

Side salads

Dressings

Thousand Island   Ranch   Italian   Blue Cheese

Survey your class. Record the responses.

1. Do you prefer soup or salad?
2. Which do you prefer, tea or coffee?

Report: *Five* of us prefer *tea*. *Most* of us prefer *soup*.

Pair practice. Make new conversations.

A: *What's your favorite side salad?*
B: *I like coleslaw. How about you?*
A: *I like potato salad.*

Dinner

Desserts

Beverages

22. roast chicken
el pollo asado

23. mashed potatoes
el puré de papas

24. steak
el filete/el bistec

25. baked potato
la papa asada/
la papa al horno

26. spaghetti
el espagueti

27. meatballs
las bolas de carne

28. garlic bread
el pan con ajo

29. grilled fish
el pescado a la parrilla

30. rice
el arroz

31. meatloaf
el rollo de carne

32. steamed vegetables
las verduras y hortalizas
al vapor

33. layer cake
la torta de capas

34. cheesecake
la torta de queso

35. pie
el pastel

36. mixed berries
las bayas mixtas

37. coffee
el café

38. decaf coffee
el café descafeinado

39. tea
el té

40. herbal tea
el té de hierbas

41. cream
la crema

42. low-fat milk
la leche baja en grasa

Ways to order from a menu

I'd like <u>a grilled cheese sandwich</u>.
I'll have <u>a bowl of tomato soup</u>.
Could I get <u>the chef's salad</u> with <u>ranch dressing</u>?

Role play. Order a dinner from the menu.

A: *Are you ready to order?*
B: *I think so. I'll have <u>the roast chicken</u>.*
A: *Would you also like…?*

81

1. **dining room**
   el comedor

2. **hostess**
   la anfitriona/la jefa
   de comedor

3. **high chair**
   la silla alta

4. **booth**
   el compartimiento

5. **to-go box**
   la caja para llevar

6. **patron / diner**
   el cliente

7. **menu**
   el menú

8. **server / waiter**
   el mesero/el camarero

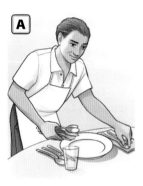

A. **set** the table
   poner la mesa

B. **seat** the customer
   sentar al cliente

C. **pour** the water
   servir el agua

D. **order** from the menu
   pedir del menú

E. **take** the order
   tomar la orden

F. **serve** the meal
   servir la comida

G. **clear / bus** the dishes
   recoger los platos

H. **carry** the tray
   llevar la bandeja

I. **pay** the check
   pagar la cuenta

J. **leave** a tip
   dejar una propina

More vocabulary

eat out: to go to a restaurant to eat
get takeout: to buy food at a restaurant and take it
home to eat

Look at the pictures.
Describe what is happening.

A: *She's <u>seating the customer</u>.*
B: *He's <u>taking the order</u>.*

9. server / waitress
la mesera/la camarera

10. dessert tray
la bandeja de los postres

11. breadbasket
la cesta para el pan

12. busser
el ayudante del camarero

13. dish room
el cuarto de lavado

14. dishwasher
el lavaplatos

15. kitchen
la cocina

16. chef
el chef

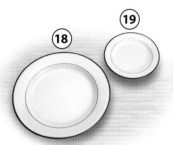

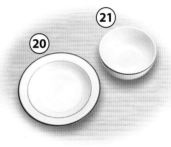

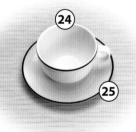

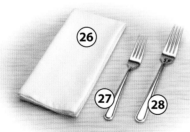

17. place setting
el cubierto

18. dinner plate
el plato

19. bread-and-butter plate
el plato para el pan
y la mantequilla

20. salad plate
el plato para ensalada

21. soup bowl
el tazón de sopa

22. water glass
el vaso de agua

23. wine glass
la copa de vino

24. cup
la taza

25. saucer
el platito/el platillo

26. napkin
la servilleta

27. salad fork
el tenedor para ensalada

28. dinner fork
el tenedor

29. steak knife
el cuchillo para carne

30. knife
el cuchillo

31. teaspoon
la cucharita

32. soup spoon
la cuchara para sopa

Pair practice. Make new conversations.

A: *Excuse me, this spoon is dirty.*
B: *I'm so sorry. I'll get you a clean spoon right away.*
A: *Thanks.*

Role play. A new busser needs help.

A: *Do the salad forks go on the left?*
B: *Yes. They go next to the dinner forks.*
A: *What about the…?*

The Farmers' Market El mercado de agricultores

Take One

GREEN FARMS

USDA ORGANIC

$1.00 each

1, 2, 3, 4 …

4 for $3.00 USDA ORGANIC

BASIL

1. **live music**
   la música en vivo

2. **organic**
   los productos orgánicos

3. **lemonade**
   la limonada

4. **sour**
   agria

5. **samples**
   las muestras

6. **avocados**
   los aguacates/ las paltas

7. **vendors**
   los vendedores

8. **sweets**
   los dulces

9. **herbs**
   las hierbas

A. **count**
   contar

84

What do you see in the picture?

1. How many vendors are at the market today?
2. Which vegetables are organic?
3. What are the children eating?
4. What is the woman counting? Why?

 Read the story.

The Farmers' Market

On Saturdays, the Novaks go to the farmers' market. They like to visit the <u>vendors</u>. Alex Novak always goes to the hot food stand for lunch. His children love to eat the fruit <u>samples</u>. Alex's father usually buys some <u>sweets</u> and <u>lemonade</u>. The lemonade is very <u>sour</u>.

Nina Novak likes to buy <u>organic</u> <u>herbs</u> and vegetables. Today, she is buying <u>avocados</u>. The market worker <u>counts</u> eight avocados. She gives Nina one more for free.

There are other things to do at the market. The Novaks like to listen to the <u>live music</u>. Sometimes they meet friends there. The farmers' market is a great place for families on a Saturday afternoon.

Reread the story.

1. Read the first sentence of the story. How often do the Novaks go to the farmers' market? How do you know?
2. The story says, "The farmers' market is a great place for families." Find examples in the story that support this statement.

What do you think?

3. What's good, bad, or interesting about shopping at a farmers' market?
4. Imagine you are at the farmers' market. What will you buy?

Everyday Clothes La ropa diaria

1. shirt
   la camisa

2. jeans
   los pantalones *jeans*/
   los vaqueros

3. dress
   el vestido

4. T-shirt
   la camiseta

5. baseball cap
   la gorra de béisbol

6. socks
   los calcetines/las medias

7. sneakers
   los tenis

A. **tie**
   amarrar

BEST OF JAZZ CONCERT

TICKETS

BEST OF JAZZ

Listen and point. Take turns.

A: *Point to the dress.*
B: *Point to the T-shirt.*
A: *Point to the baseball cap.*

Dictate to your partner. Take turns.

A: *Write dress.*
B: *Is that spelled d-r-e-s-s?*
A: *Yes, that's right.*

ONE NIGHT ONLY

DOORS OPEN AT 8:00

8. blouse
   la blusa
9. handbag
   el bolso
10. skirt
    la falda
11. suit
    el terno/el traje
12. slacks / pants
    los pantalones
13. shoes
    los zapatos
14. sweater
    el abrigo/el suéter
B. **put on**
   ponérselo

Ways to compliment clothes

That's a pretty <u>dress</u>!
Those are great <u>shoes</u>!
I really like your <u>baseball cap</u>!

Role play. Compliment a friend.

A: *<u>That's a pretty dress</u>! <u>Green</u> is a great color on you.*
B: *Thanks! I really like your…*

87

Casual, Work, and Formal Clothes
Ropa casual, de trabajo y formal

Casual Clothes Ropa casual

1. cap
el gorrito

2. cardigan sweater
el abrigo de lana tejida/el cárdigan

3. pullover sweater
el abrigo cerrado/el pulóver

4. sport shirt
la camisa deportiva

5. maternity dress
el vestido de maternidad

6. overalls
el overol

7. knit top
la blusa bordada

8. capris
el pantalón capri

9. sandals
las sandalias

Work Clothes Ropa de trabajo

10. uniform
el uniforme

11. business suit
el traje formal/el traje de calle

12. tie
la corbata

13. briefcase
el maletín

More vocabulary

in fashion / in style: clothes that are popular now
outfit: clothes that look nice together
three-piece suit: matching jacket, vest, and slacks

Describe the people. Take turns.

A: *She's wearing a maternity dress.*
B: *He's wearing a uniform.*

Casual, Work, and Formal Clothes

Tran Wedding

Formal Clothes Ropa formal

14. sport jacket / sport coat
    la chaqueta deportiva
15. vest
    el chaleco
16. bow tie
    la corbata de moño/lazo
17. tuxedo
    el esmoquin

18. evening gown
    el vestido de noche
19. clutch bag
    el bolso de mano
20. cocktail dress
    el vestido de cóctel
21. high heels
    los tacones altos

Exercise Wear
Ropa para hacer ejercicio

22. sweatshirt / hoodie
    la sudadera
23. sweatpants
    los pantalones de ejercicio
24. tank top
    la camiseta
25. shorts
    los pantalones cortos

Survey your class. Record the responses.

1. Do you prefer to wear formal or casual clothes?
2. Do you prefer to exercise in shorts or sweatpants?
Report: _25% of the class prefers to…_

Think about it. Discuss.

1. Look at pages 170–173. Which jobs require uniforms?
2. What's good and what's bad about wearing a uniform?
3. Describe a popular style. Do you like it? Why or why not?

1. hat	**5. winter scarf**
el gorro	la bufanda para el invierno
2. (over)coat	**6. gloves**
el abrigo/el sobretodo	los guantes
3. headband	**7. headwrap**
la banda de cabeza	el pañuelo de cabeza
4. leather jacket	**8. jacket**
la chaqueta de cuero	la chaqueta

9. parka	**13. earmuffs**
la parka	las orejeras
10. mittens	**14. down vest**
los mitones	el chaleco relleno con plumas
11. ski hat	**15. ski mask**
el gorro para esquiar	la máscara de esquí
12. leggings	**16. down jacket**
los *leggings*/las mallas	la chaqueta rellena con plumas

17. umbrella	**20. rain boots**
el paraguas	las botas para la lluvia
18. raincoat	**21. trench coat**
la gabardina/el impermeable	la trinchera
19. poncho	
el poncho	

22. swimming trunks	**25. cover-up**
el traje de baño	el albornoz/la bata de playa
23. straw hat	**26. swimsuit / bathing suit**
el sombrero de paja	el traje de baño
24. windbreaker	**27. sunglasses**
el cortaviento	las gafas de sol

Grammar Point: *should*

*It's raining. You **should** take an umbrella.*
*It's snowing. You **should** put on a scarf.*
*It's sunny. You **should** wear a straw hat.*

Pair practice. Make new conversations.

A: *It's <u>snowing</u>. You should put on <u>a scarf</u>.*
B: *Don't worry. I'm wearing my <u>parka</u>.*
A: *Good, and don't forget your <u>mittens</u>!*

Underwear and Sleepwear

Unisex Underwear
Ropa interior unisex

1. undershirt
   la camiseta
2. thermal undershirt
   la camiseta térmica
3. long underwear
   la ropa interior de invierno

Men's Underwear
Ropa interior de hombre

4. boxer shorts
   los calzoncillos tipo bóxer
5. briefs
   los calzoncillos
6. athletic supporter / jockstrap
   el suspensor/el soporte atlético

Unisex Socks
Calcetines unisex

7. ankle socks
   los calcetines al tobillo
8. crew socks
   los calcetines de trabajo
9. dress socks
   los calcetines de vestir

Women's Socks
Calcetines de mujer

10. low-cut socks
    los calcetines de tobillo
11. anklets
    los calcetines cortos
12. knee highs
    los calcetines hasta la rodilla

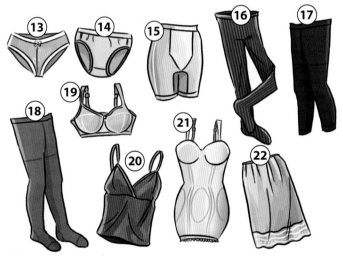

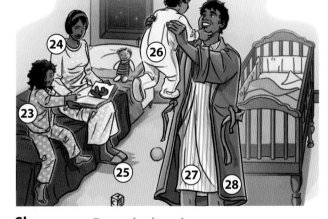

Women's Underwear   Ropa interior de mujer

13. (bikini) panties
    los calzones (bikinis)
14. briefs / underpants
    las pantaletas/
    los calzones
15. body shaper / girdle
    la faja
16. tights
    las medias de malla
17. footless tights
    las medias de malla hasta los talones
18. pantyhose
    las medias panti/las pantimedias
19. bra
    el sostén
20. camisole
    la camisola
21. shapewear slip / slimming slip
    la enagua reductora/el fondo reductor
22. half slip
    la media enagua

Sleepwear   Ropa de dormir

23. pajamas
    la piyama/el pijama
24. nightgown
    el camisón
25. slippers
    las pantuflas
26. blanket sleeper
    la cobija
27. nightshirt
    la camisa de dormir
28. robe
    la bata

More vocabulary

lingerie: underwear or sleepwear for women
loungewear: very casual clothing for relaxing around the home

Survey your class. Record the responses.

1. What color socks do you prefer?
2. What type of socks do you prefer?
Report: _Joe prefers white crew socks._

91

Construction Worker

Road Worker

Automotive Painter

Food Processor

1. hard hat
el casco de protección
para la cabeza

2. work shirt
la camisa de trabajo

3. tool belt
la correa de herramientas

4. high visibility safety vest
el chaleco de seguridad
de alta visibilidad

5. work pants
los pantalones de trabajo

6. steel toe boots
las botas con punta de acero

7. ventilation mask
la máscara de ventilación

8. coveralls
el overol/el mono de trabajo

9. bump cap
el casco de protección

10. safety glasses
las gafas/los anteojos
de seguridad

11. apron
el mandil

Manager

Salesperson

Farmworker

Ranch Hand

12. blazer
el *blazer*

13. tie
la corbata

14. polo shirt
la camisa tipo polo

15. name tag
la etiqueta de identificación

16. bandana
el pañuelo de cabeza

17. work gloves
los guantes de trabajo

18. cowboy hat
el gorro de vaquero

19. jeans
los pantalones *jeans*/
los vaqueros

Use the new words.
Look at pages 170–173. Name the workplace clothing you see.

A: *Look at #37. She's wearing a hard hat.*
B: *Look at #47. He's wearing a lab coat.*

Pair practice. Make sentences.
Dictate them to your classmates.

A. *Farmworkers wear jeans to work.*
B. *A manager often wears a tie to work.*

Security Guard

Emergency Worker

Counterperson

Chef

Line Cook

20. security shirt
la camisa de seguridad

21. badge
la insignia

22. security pants
los pantalones de seguridad

23. helmet
el casco

24. jumpsuit
el mono/el enterito

25. hairnet
la malla para el cabello

26. smock
el blusón

27. disposable gloves
los guantes desechables

28. chef's hat
el gorro de chef

29. chef's jacket
la chaqueta de chef

30. waist apron
el mandil de cintura

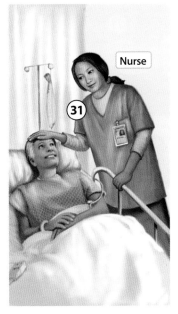

Nurse

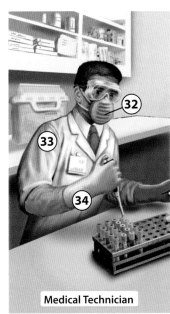

Medical Technician

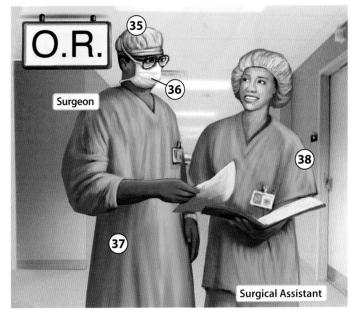

O.R.

Surgeon

Surgical Assistant

31. scrubs
la ropa de la enfermera

32. face mask
máscara facial

33. lab coat
el delantal de laboratorio

34. medical gloves
los guantes médicos

35. surgical scrub cap
el gorro/la gorra de cirugía

36. surgical mask
la máscara de cirugía

37. surgical gown
el camisón de cirugía

38. surgical scrubs
el delantal/el camisón

Identify Anya's problem. Brainstorm solutions.

Anya works at a sandwich counter. Her bus ride to work is an hour. She has to wear a hairnet at work, but today she forgot it at home. What can she do?

Think about it. Discuss.

1. What other jobs require helmets? disposable gloves?
2. Is it better to have a uniform or wear your own clothes at work? Why?

Shoes and Accessories   Zapatos y accesorios

A. purchase
comprar

B. wait in line
esperar en cola/fila

1. suspenders
los tirantes

2. purses / handbags
las carteras

3. salesclerk
la vendedora

4. customer
la clienta

5. display case
la vitrina

6. belts
las correas

13. wallet
la billetera

14. change purse / coin purse
el monedero

15. cell phone case
el estuche para teléfono celular

16. (wrist)watch
el reloj (de pulsera)

17. shoulder bag
la bolsa bandolera

18. backpack
la mochila

19. tote bag
la bolsa

20. belt buckle
la hebilla del cinturón

21. sole
la suela

22. heel
el tacón

23. toe
la punta

24. shoelaces
el cordón del zapato

More vocabulary

athletic shoes: tennis shoes, running shoes, etc.
gift / present: something you give to or receive
from friends or family for a special occasion

Grammar Point: object pronouns

*My **sister** loves jewelry. I'll buy **her** a necklace.*
*My **dad** likes belts. I'll buy **him** a belt buckle.*
*My **friends** love scarves. I'll buy **them** scarves.*

7. shoe department el departamento de calzado	**9.** bracelets los brazaletes	**11.** hats los gorros	**C. try on** shoes **probarse** zapatos
8. jewelry department el departamento de joyería	**10.** necklaces los collares	**12.** scarves las bufandas	**D. assist** a customer **asistir** a un cliente

25. high heels los tacones altos	**29.** oxfords los zapatos Oxford	**33.** chain la cadena	**37.** clip-on earrings los aretes de presilla
26. pumps los zapatos de salón	**30.** loafers los mocasines	**34.** beads las cuentas/los abalorios	**38.** pin el prendedor
27. flats los zapatos de tacón bajo	**31.** hiking boots las botas para excursión	**35.** locket el relicario	**39.** string of pearls el collar de perlas
28. boots las botas	**32.** tennis shoes las zapatillas de tenis	**36.** pierced earrings los aretes de colgar	**40.** ring el anillo

---

Ways to talk about accessories

I need <u>a hat</u> to wear with <u>this scarf</u>.
I'd like a pair of <u>earrings</u> to match <u>this necklace</u>.
Do you have <u>a belt</u> that would go with my <u>shoes</u>?

Role play. Talk to a salesperson.

A: Do you have <u>boots</u> that would go with <u>this skirt</u>?
B: Let me see. How about <u>these brown ones</u>?
A: Perfect. I also need…

95

Describing Clothes   Descripción de la ropa

Sizes Tallas

1. **extra small**
   extrapequeño
2. **small**
   pequeño
3. **medium**
   mediano
4. **large**
   grande
5. **extra large**
   extragrande
6. **one-size-fits-all**
   talla universal

Styles Estilos

7. **crewneck** sweater
   el suéter con **cuello de cisne**

8. **V-neck** sweater
   el suéter con **cuello en V**

9. **turtleneck** sweater
   el suéter con **cuello de tortuga**

10. **scoop neck** sweater
    el suéter con **cuello redondo**

11. **sleeveless** shirt
    la camisa **sin mangas**

12. **short-sleeved** shirt
    la camisa **con mangas cortas**

13. **3/4-sleeved** shirt
    la camisa de **manga de 3/4**

14. **long-sleeved** shirt
    la camisa de **manga larga**

15. **miniskirt**
    la **minifalda**

16. **short** skirt
    la falda **corta**

17. **mid-length / calf-length** skirt
    la falda a **media pierna**

18. **long** skirt
    la falda **larga**

Patterns Patrones

19. solid
    sólido

20. striped
    con rayas

21. polka-dotted
    con lunares

22. plaid
    escocesa

23. print
    estampado

24. checked
    a cuadros

25. floral
    con flores

26. paisley
    estampado de cachemir/
    estampado búlgaro

Survey your class. Record the responses.

1. What type of sweater do you prefer?
2. What patterns do you prefer?
Report: _Three_ out of _ten_ prefer ____.

Role play. Talk to a salesperson.

A: *Excuse me. I'm looking for this V-neck sweater in large.*
B: *Here's a large. It's on sale for $19.99.*
A: *Wonderful! I'll take it. I'm also looking for…*

Comparing Clothing Comparación de la ropa

27. **heavy** jacket
la chaqueta **gruesa**

28. **light** jacket
la chaqueta **liviana**

29. **tight** pants
los pantalones
apretados/ceñidos

30. **loose / baggy** pants
los pantalones
flojos/holgados

31. **low** heels
los tacones **bajos**

32. **high** heels
los tacones **altos**

33. **plain** blouse
la blusa **lisa**

34. **fancy** blouse
la blusa **vistosa**

35. **narrow** tie
la corbata **estrecha**

36. **wide** tie
la corbata **ancha**

Clothing Problems Problemas con la ropa

37. It's **too small**.
Es **demasiado pequeña**.

38. It's **too big**.
Es **demasiado grande**.

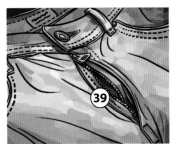

39. The zipper is **broken**.
El cierre está **estropeado**.

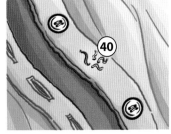

40. A button is **missing**.
Falta un botón.

41. It's **ripped / torn**.
Está **rasgado/descosido**.

42. It's **stained**.
Está **manchado**.

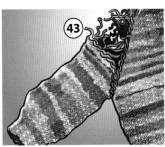

43. It's **unraveling**.
Se está **descosiendo**.

44. It's **too expensive**.
Es **demasiado caro**.

More vocabulary

complaint: a statement that something is not right
customer service: the place customers go with their complaints
refund: money you get back when you return an item to the store

Role play. Return an item to a salesperson.

A: *Welcome to Shopmart. How may I help you?*
B: *This sweater is new, but it's unraveling.*
A: *I'm sorry. Would you like a refund?*

97

Making Clothes   Confección de ropa

Types of Material   Tipos de material

1. cotton
algodón

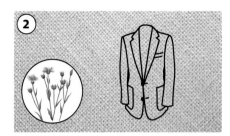

2. linen
hilo

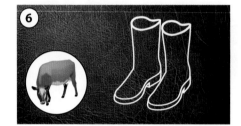

3. wool
lana

4. cashmere
cachemir

5. silk
seda

6. leather
cuero

A Garment Factory   Una fábrica de ropa

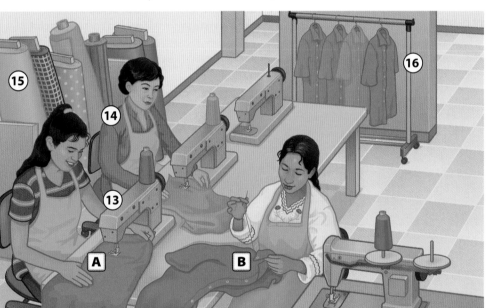

Parts of a Sewing Machine
Partes de una máquina de coser

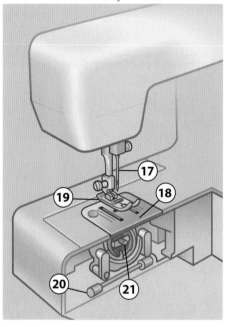

A. sew by machine
coser a máquina

B. sew by hand
coser a mano

13. sewing machine
la máquina de coser

14. sewing machine operator
la operadora de la máquina de coser

15. bolt of fabric
el rollo de tela

16. rack
el bastidor

17. needle
la aguja

18. needle plate
la placa de la aguja

19. presser foot
el pie prensatelas

20. feed dog / feed bar
el alimentador

21. bobbin
la bobina

More vocabulary

fashion designer: a person who draws original clothes
natural materials: cloth made from things that grow in nature
synthetic materials: cloth made by people, such as nylon

Use the new words.

Look at pages 86–87. Name the materials you see.

A: *Look at her pants. They're denim.*
B: *Look at his shoes. They're leather.*

Types of Material Tipos de material

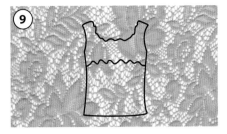

7. denim
tela de *jeans*/tela vaquera

8. suede
gamuza

9. lace
encaje

10. velvet
terciopelo

11. corduroy
pana

12. nylon
nilón

A Fabric Store Una tienda de telas

Closures Cierres

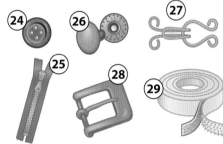

Trim Adornos

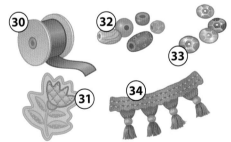

22. pattern
el modelo/el patrón

23. thread
los hilos

24. button
el botón

25. zipper
el cierre

26. snap
la presilla

27. hook and eye
el gancho y ojal

28. buckle
la hebilla

29. hook and loop fastener
la cinta de enganche

30. ribbon
la cinta

31. appliqué
las decoraciones/
los apliques

32. beads
las cuentas

33. sequins
las lentejuelas

34. fringe
el fleco

Survey your class. Record the responses.

1. Can you sew?
2. What's your favorite type of material to wear?
Report: *Five* of us can't sew. *Most* of us like to wear *denim*.

Think about it. Discuss.

1. Which jobs require sewing skills?
2. You're going to make a shirt. What do you do first?
3. Which is better, hand sewn or machine sewn? Why?

99

An Alterations Shop Una tienda de alteraciones

1. **dressmaker**
   la costurera
2. **dressmaker's dummy**
   el maniquí de la costurera
3. **tailor**
   el sastre

4. **collar**
   el cuello
5. **waistband**
   la pretina
6. **sleeve**
   la manga

7. **pocket**
   el bolsillo
8. **hem**
   el dobladillo/el ruedo
9. **cuff**
   el bajo del ruedo

Sewing Supplies Artículos de costura

10. **needle**
    la aguja
11. **thread**
    el hilo

12. **(straight) pin**
    el alfiler
13. **pincushion**
    el alfiletero

14. **safety pin**
    el alfiler de seguridad/
    el imperdible
15. **thimble**
    el dedal

16. **pair of scissors**
    el par de tijeras
17. **tape measure**
    la cinta de medir

18. **seam ripper**
    el abrecostura

Alterations Alteraciones

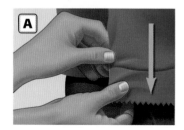

A. **Lengthen** the pants.
   Alargar los pantalones.

B. **Shorten** the pants.
   Acortar los pantalones.

C. **Let out** the pants.
   Extender los pantalones.

D. **Take in** the pants.
   Recoger los pantalones.

Pair practice. Make new conversations.

A: *Would you hand me <u>the thread</u>?*
B: *OK. What are you going to do?*
A: *I'm going to <u>take in</u> <u>these pants</u>.*

Survey your class. Record the responses.

1. How many pockets do you have?
2. How many pairs of scissors do you have at home?
Report: *<u>Most</u> of us have <u>two</u> ____ .*

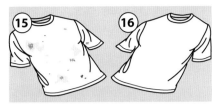

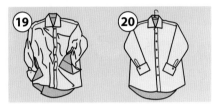

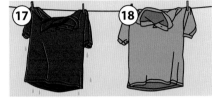

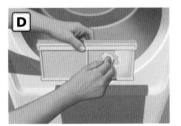

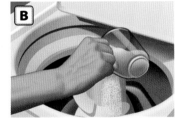

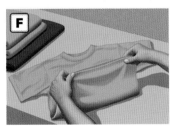

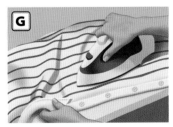

1. **laundry**
   la ropa sucia

2. **laundry basket**
   el cesto para la ropa sucia

3. **washer**
   la lavadora

4. **dryer**
   la secadora

5. **dryer sheets**
   las toallitas para la secadora

6. **fabric softener**
   el suavizante/el suavizador

7. **bleach**
   el cloro/la lejía/
   el blanqueador

8. **laundry detergent**
   el detergente para ropa

9. **clothesline**
   el tendedero/la cuerda

10. **clothespin**
    la pinza para colgar la ropa

11. **hanger**
    el gancho/la percha

12. **spray starch**
    el almidón para rociar

13. **iron**
    la plancha

14. **ironing board**
    la tabla para planchar

15. **dirty** T-shirt
    la camiseta **sucia**

16. **clean** T-shirt
    la camiseta **limpia**

17. **wet** shirt
    la camisa **húmeda**

18. **dry** shirt
    la camisa **seca**

19. **wrinkled** shirt
    la camisa **arrugada**

20. **ironed** shirt
    la camisa **planchada**

A. **Sort** the laundry.
   Separar la ropa.

B. **Add** the detergent.
   Añadir el detergente.

C. **Load** the washer.
   Llenar/cargar la lavadora.

D. **Clean** the lint trap.
   Limpiar el filtro de pelusas.

E. **Unload** the dryer.
   Vaciar/descargar la secadora.

F. **Fold** the laundry.
   Doblar la ropa.

G. **Iron** the clothes.
   Planchar la ropa.

H. **Hang up** the clothes.
   Colgar la ropa.

wash in cold water

no bleach

line dry

dry clean only, do not wash

Pair practice. Make new conversations.

A: *I have to sort the laundry. Can you help?*
B: *Sure. Here's the laundry basket.*
A: *Thanks a lot!*

A Garage Sale   Una venta de garaje

GARAGE SALE
TODAY 7-7
- CLOTHING
- SHOES
- ACCESSORIES
- ELECTRONICS

A Two dollars.

It's stained. I can give you seventy-five cents.

$.50   **$5.00**
$1.00   **$10.00**
$2.00 ASK ME

ALL PURSES $.75

1. **flyer**
   el aviso/el volante

2. **used clothing**
   la ropa usada

3. **sticker**
   la etiqueta/la pegatina

4. **folding card table**
   la mesa plegable

5. **folding chair**
   la silla plegable

6. **clock radio**
   la radio-reloj

7. **VCR**
   la grabadora de videocasete

8. **CD / cassette player**
   el reproductor de casete y CD

A. **bargain**
   regatear

B. **browse**
   mirar

What do you see in the pictures?

1. What kinds of used clothing do you see?
2. What information is on the flyer?
3. Why are the stickers different colors?
4. How much is the clock radio? the VCR?

📄 **Read the story.**

A Garage Sale

Last Sunday, I had a garage sale. At 5:00 a.m., I put up <u>flyers</u> in my neighborhood. Next, I put price <u>stickers</u> on my <u>used clothing</u>, my <u>VCR</u>, my <u>CD / cassette player</u>, and some other old things. At 7:00 a.m., I opened my <u>folding card table</u> and <u>folding chair</u>. Then I waited.

At 7:05 a.m., my first customer arrived. She asked, "How much is the sweatshirt?"

"Two dollars," I said.

She said, "It's stained. I can give you seventy-five cents." We <u>bargained</u> for a minute and she paid $1.00.

All day people came to <u>browse</u>, bargain, and buy. At 7:00 p.m., I had $85.00.

Now I know two things: garage sales are hard work, and nobody wants to buy an old <u>clock radio</u>!

Reread the story.

1. Look at the conversation. Circle the punctuation you see. What do you notice?

What do you think?

2. Do you like to buy things at garage sales? Why or why not?
3. Imagine you want the VCR. How will you bargain for it?

1. **head**
   la cabeza

2. **hair**
   el cabello/el pelo

3. **neck**
   el cuello

4. **chest**
   el pecho

5. **back**
   la espalda

6. **nose**
   la nariz

7. **mouth**
   la boca

8. **foot**
   el pie

Listen and point. Take turns.

A: *Point to the chest.*
B: *Point to the neck.*
A: *Point to the mouth.*

Dictate to your partner. Take turns.

A: *Write hair.*
B: *Did you say hair?*
A: *That's right, h-a-i-r.*

9. leg
   la pierna
10. toe
   el dedo del pie
11. eye
   el ojo
12. ear
   la oreja
13. shoulder
   el hombro
14. arm
   el brazo
15. hand
   la mano
16. finger
   el dedo

Grammar Point: imperatives

*Please **touch** your right foot.*
***Put** your hands on your knees.*
***Don't put** your hands on your shoulders.*

Pair practice. Take turns giving commands.

A: <u>Raise</u> your <u>arms</u>.
B: <u>Touch</u> your <u>feet</u>.
A: <u>Put</u> your <u>hand</u> on your <u>shoulder</u>.

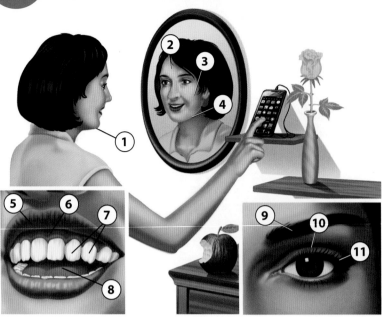

The Face
La cara

1. chin
   la barbilla
2. forehead
   la frente
3. cheek
   la mejilla/el cachete
4. jaw
   la quijada

The Mouth
La boca

5. lip
   el labio
6. gums
   las encías
7. teeth
   los dientes
8. tongue
   la lengua

The Eye
El ojo

9. eyebrow
   la ceja
10. eyelid
    el párpado
11. eyelashes
    las pestañas

The Senses
Los sentidos

A. **see**
   ver
B. **hear**
   oír
C. **smell**
   oler
D. **taste**
   saborear
E. **touch**
   tocar

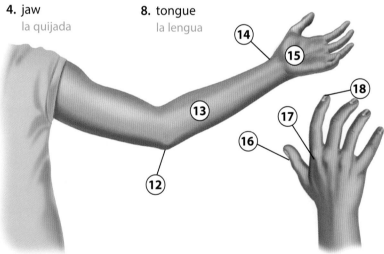

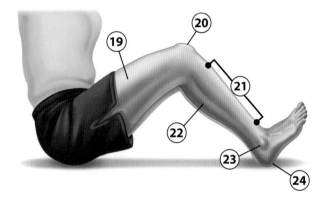

The Arm, Hand, and Fingers   El brazo, la mano y los dedos

12. elbow
    el codo
13. forearm
    el antebrazo
14. wrist
    la muñeca
15. palm
    la palma
16. thumb
    el pulgar
17. knuckle
    el nudillo
18. fingernail
    la uña

The Leg and Foot   La pierna y el pie

19. thigh
    el muslo
20. knee
    la rodilla
21. shin
    la espinilla/la canilla
22. calf
    la pantorrilla
23. ankle
    el tobillo
24. heel
    el talón

More vocabulary

torso: the part of the body from the shoulders to the pelvis
limbs: arms and legs
toenail: the nail on your toe

Pair practice. Make new conversations.

A: *Is your <u>wrist</u> OK?*
B: *Yes, but now my <u>elbow</u> hurts.*
A: *I'm sorry to hear that.*

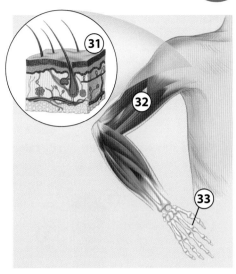

25. breast
el seno/el pecho

26. abdomen
el abdomen

27. hip
la cadera

28. shoulder blade
el omóplato

29. lower back
la parte inferior de la espalda

30. buttocks
las nalgas

31. skin
la piel

32. muscle
el músculo

33. bone
el hueso

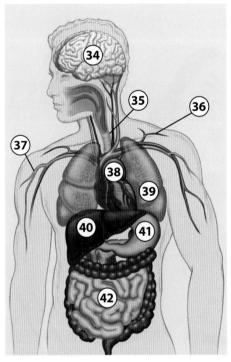

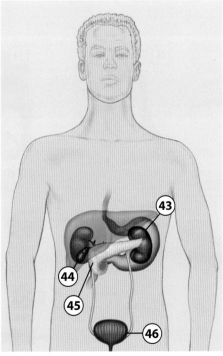

THE SKELETON

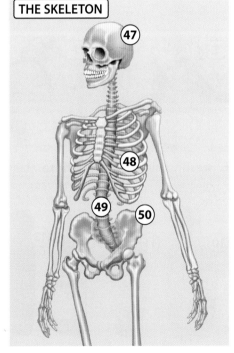

34. brain
el cerebro

35. throat
la garganta

36. artery
la arteria

37. vein
la vena

38. heart
el corazón

39. lung
el pulmón

40. liver
el hígado

41. stomach
el estómago

42. intestines
los intestinos

43. kidney
el riñón

44. gallbladder
la vesícula biliar

45. pancreas
el páncreas

46. bladder
la vejiga

47. skull
el cráneo

48. rib cage
la caja toráxica

49. spinal column
la columna vertebral

50. pelvis
la pelvis

A. **take** a shower / **shower**
tomar una ducha/**ducharse**

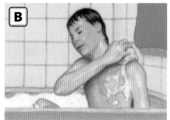

B. **take** a bath / **bathe**
tomar un baño/**bañarse**

C. **use** deodorant
usar desodorante

D. **put on** sunscreen
ponerse protector solar

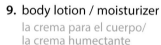

1. shower cap
la gorra de baño

2. shower gel
el gel de ducha

3. soap
el jabón

4. bath powder
el talco

5. deodorant / antiperspirant
el desodorante/el antitranspirante

6. perfume / cologne
el perfume/la colonia

7. sunscreen
el protector solar

8. sunblock
el bloqueador solar

9. body lotion / moisturizer
la crema para el cuerpo/
la crema humectante

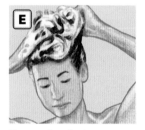

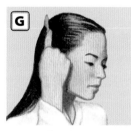

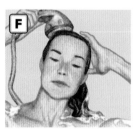

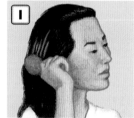

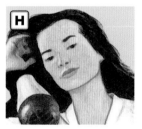

E. **wash**…hair
lavarse…el cabello

F. **rinse**…hair
enjuagarse…
el cabello

G. **comb**…hair
peinarse…el cabello

H. **dry**…hair
secarse…el cabello

I. **brush**…hair
cepillarse…el cabello

10. shampoo
el champú

11. conditioner
el acondicionador

12. hairspray
la laca

13. comb
el peine/la peinilla

14. brush
el cepillo

15. pick
la peineta

16. hair gel
el gel de cabello

17. curling iron
el rizador

18. blow dryer
el secador de cabello

19. hair clip
la pinza/el gancho
para el cabello

20. barrette
el broche

21. bobby pins
los pasadores/las horquillas

More vocabulary

hypoallergenic: a product that is better for people with allergies

unscented: a product without perfume or scent

Think about it. Discuss.

1. Which personal hygiene products are most important to use before a job interview? Why?

2. What is the right age to start wearing makeup? Why?

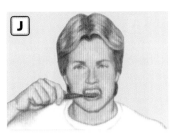
J. brush…teeth
  cepillarse…los dientes

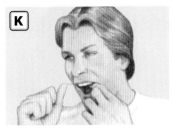
K. floss…teeth
  usar hilo dental

L. gargle
  hacer gárgaras

M. shave
  afeitarse

22. toothbrush
  el cepillo de dientes

23. toothpaste
  la pasta de dientes

24. dental floss
  el hilo dental

25. mouthwash
  el enjuague bucal

26. electric shaver
  la rasuradora eléctrica

27. razor
  la rasuradora

28. razor blade
  la hoja/la cuchilla de afeitar/la navaja

29. shaving cream
  la crema de afeitar

30. aftershave
  la loción para después de afeitarse

N. cut…nails
  cortarse…las uñas

O. polish…nails
  pintarse…las uñas

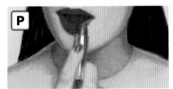
P. put on / apply
  ponerse/aplicarse

Q. take off / remove
  quitarse/limpiarse

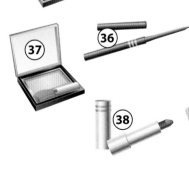

Makeup Maquillaje

31. nail clippers
  el cortauñas

32. emery board
  la lima

33. nail polish
  la pintura/el esmalte
  de uñas

34. eyebrow pencil
  el lápiz de cejas

35. eye shadow
  la sombra

36. eyeliner
  el delineador (de ojos)

37. blush
  el rubor

38. lipstick
  el lápiz de labios

39. mascara
  el rímel

40. foundation
  la base

41. face powder
  el polvo facial

42. makeup remover
  el desmaquillador

  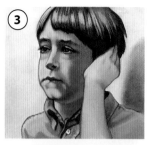 

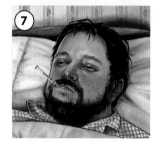   

1. headache
el dolor de cabeza

4. stomachache
el dolor de estómago

7. fever / temperature
la fiebre

A. feel dizzy
sentirse mareado

2. toothache
el dolor de muelas

5. backache
el dolor de espalda

8. chills
los escalofríos

B. feel nauseous
sentir/tener náuseas

3. earache
el dolor de oído

6. sore throat
el dolor de garganta

9. cough
la tos

C. throw up / vomit
vomitar

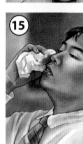  

10. insect bite
la picadura de insecto

11. bruise
el moretón/
el morado/el cardenal

12. cut
el corte

13. sunburn
la quemadura de sol

14. sprained ankle
el tobillo torcido

15. bloody nose
la hemorragia nasal

16. swollen finger
el dedo hinchado

17. blister
la ampolla

18

WORKPLACE ACCIDENT NOTES

Name: Thiu An
Job Title: Packer
Date of accident: Monday, 9/18/17
Location of accident:
warehouse, aisle 3
Description of accident:
3 boxes fell on me
Was safety equipment used?
☑ yes   ☐ no
Were you injured? yes, sprained wrist
and some bruises

PLEASE FILL OUT A COMPLETE ACCIDENT
FORM AS SOON AS POSSIBLE.

18. accident report
el informe de accidente

Look at the pictures.
Describe the symptoms and injuries.

A: *He has a backache.*
B: *She has a toothache.*

Think about it. Discuss.

1. What do you recommend for a stomachache?
2. What is the best way to stop a bloody nose?
3. Who should stay home from work with a cold? Why?

In the Waiting Room En la sala de espera

Health Form

Name: *Andre Zolmar*
Date of birth: *July 8, 1983*
Current symptoms: *stomachache*

Health History:

Childhood Diseases:
- ☑ chicken pox
- ☑ diphtheria
- ☑ rubella
- ☑ measles
- ☐ mumps
- ☐ other

Description of symptoms:

HEALTH FIRST
Name: Andre Zolmar
Group Number: 98765
Membership Number: 60756789

1. appointment
   la cita

2. receptionist
   el/la recepcionista

3. health insurance card
   la tarjeta de seguro médico

4. health history form
   el formulario de
   historial médico

In the Examining Room En la sala de examen

5. doctor
   el médico/el doctor/la doctora

6. patient
   el paciente

7. examination table
   la mesa de examen

8. nurse
   la enfermera/el enfermero

9. blood pressure gauge
   el medidor de presión
   sanguínea

10. stethoscope
    el estetoscopio

11. thermometer
    el termómetro

12. syringe
    la jeringa

Medical Procedures Los procedimientos médicos

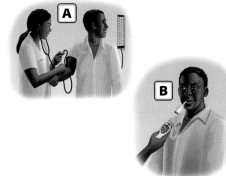

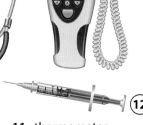

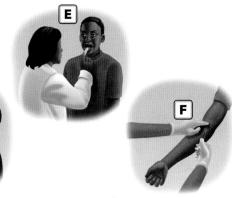

A. **check**…blood pressure
   revisarle…la presión sanguínea

B. **take**…temperature
   tomarle…la temperatura

C. **listen** to…heart
   escucharle el corazón

D. **examine**…eyes
   examinarle…los ojos

E. **examine**…throat
   examinarle…la garganta

F. **draw**…blood
   sacarle…sangre

Patient

First name   Last name   Reason for visit

_____   _____   _____

Common Illnesses Las enfermedades comunes

1. cold
el resfrío

2. flu
la gripe

3. ear infection
la infección de oído

4. strep throat
la infección de la garganta

Medical History
Childhood and Infectious Diseases La niñez y las enfermedades infecciosas

Vaccination date
La fecha de vacunación

5. measles   _____
el sarampión

6. chicken pox   _____
la varicela

7. mumps   _____
las paperas

8. shingles   _____
la culebrilla

9. hepatitis   _____
la hepatitis

10. pneumonia   _____
la pulmonía

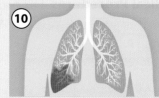

11. allergies
las alergias

I am allergic to:

_____

_____

_____

animals
los animales

shellfish
los moluscos
y crustáceos

peanuts
el maní/
el cacahuate

drugs
los fármacos

Survey your class. Record the responses.

1. Are you allergic to cats?
2. Are you allergic to shellfish?

Report: _Five of us are allergic to ____._

Identify Omar's problem. Brainstorm solutions.

Omar filled out only half of the medical history form at the clinic. Many words on the form were new to him, and two questions were very personal. The nurse was upset.

Allergic Reactions Las reacciones alérgicas

 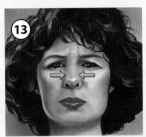  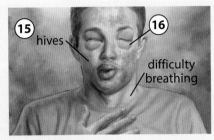

12. sneezing
el estornudo

13. nasal congestion
la congestión nasal

14. rash
la erupción/
el sarpullido

15. anaphylaxis
la anafilaxis

16. swelling
la inflamación

Medical Conditions Los padecimientos

	Patient Yes	No	Family History		Patient Yes	No	Family History
17. cancer / el cáncer	☐	☐	_____	**23.** TB / tuberculosis / la tuberculosis	☐	☐	_____
18. asthma / el asma	☐	☐	_____	**24.** high blood pressure / hypertension / la presión arterial alta/ la hipertensión	☐	☐	_____
19. dementia / la demencia	☐	☐	_____	**25.** intestinal parasites / los parásitos intestinales	☐	☐	_____
20. arthritis / la artritis	☐	☐	_____	**26.** diabetes / la diabetes	☐	☐	_____
21. HIV / AIDS / el VIH/el SIDA	☐	☐	_____	**27.** kidney disease / la insuficiencia renal	☐	☐	_____
22. malaria / el paludismo	☐	☐	_____	**28.** heart disease / las enfermedades cardíacas			

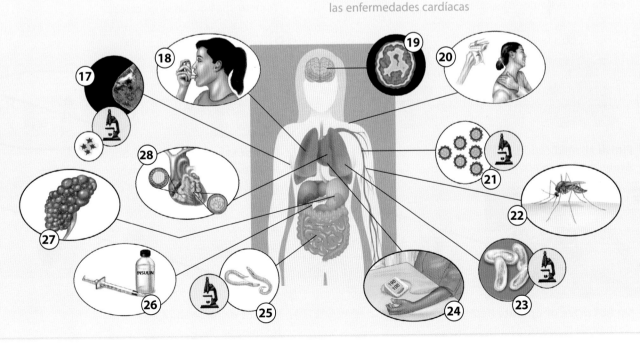

More vocabulary

AIDS (acquired immune deficiency syndrome): a medical condition that results from contracting the HIV virus

Alzheimer's disease: a disease that causes dementia

coronary disease: heart disease

infectious disease: a disease that is spread through air or water

influenza: flu

A Pharmacy   Una farmacia

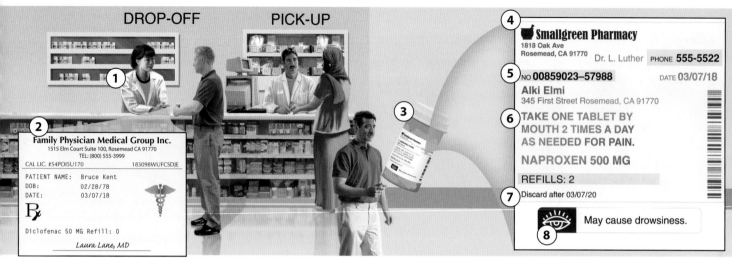

DROP-OFF   PICK-UP

Smallgreen Pharmacy
1818 Oak Ave
Rosemead, CA 91770

Dr. L. Luther   PHONE **555-5522**

NO **00859023–57988**   DATE **03/07/18**

Alki Elmi
345 First Street Rosemead, CA 91770

TAKE ONE TABLET BY MOUTH 2 TIMES A DAY AS NEEDED FOR PAIN.

NAPROXEN 500 MG

REFILLS: 2

Discard after 03/07/20

May cause drowsiness.

Family Physician Medical Group Inc.
1515 Elm Court Suite 100, Rosemead CA 91770
TEL: (800) 555-3999
CAL LIC. #54POI5U170   183098WUFCSDJE

PATIENT NAME: Bruce Kent
DOB: 02/28/78
DATE: 03/07/18

℞

Diclofenac 50 MG Refill: 0

Laura Lane, MD

1. **pharmacist**
   el farmaceuta/el farmacéutico

2. **prescription**
   la prescripción/la receta

3. **prescription medication**
   el medicamento prescrito

4. **prescription label**
   la etiqueta de la receta

5. **prescription number**
   el número de la receta

6. **dosage**
   la dosis

7. **expiration date**
   la fecha de vencimiento

8. **warning label**
   la etiqueta de advertencia

Medical Warnings   Las advertencias medicas

A. **Take** with food or milk.
Tómelo con alimentos o leche.

B. **Take** one hour before eating.
Tómelo una hora antes de comer.

C. **Finish** all medication.
Acabe todo el medicamento.

D. **Do not take** with dairy products.
No lo tome con productos lácteos.

E. **Do not drive or operate** heavy machinery.
No maneje ni opere maquinaria pesada.

F. **Do not drink** alcohol.
No beba alcohol.

More vocabulary

prescribe medication: to write a prescription
fill prescriptions: to prepare medications for patients
pick up a prescription: to get prescription medication

Role play. Talk to the pharmacist.

A: *Hi. I need to pick up a prescription for <u>Jones</u>.*
B: *Here's your medication, <u>Mr. Jones</u>. Take these <u>once a day with milk or food</u>.*

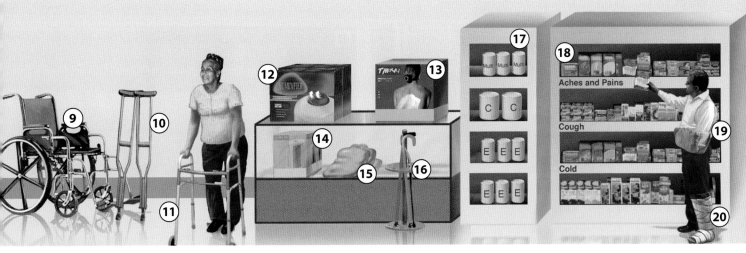

9. wheelchair
la silla de ruedas

10. crutches
las muletas

11. walker
el andador

12. humidifier
el humidificador

13. heating pad
la almohadilla/la bolsa/
el paño de calentamiento

14. air purifier
el purificador de aire

15. hot water bottle
la botella de agua caliente

16. cane
el bastón

17. vitamins
las vitaminas

18. over-the-counter medication
el medicamento sin receta

19. sling
el cabestrillo

20. cast
el yeso

Types of Medication Tipos de medicamento

21. pill
la píldora

22. tablet
la tableta

23. capsule
la cápsula

24. ointment
la pomada/
el ungüento

25. cream
la crema

Over-the-Counter Medication Medicamentos sin receta

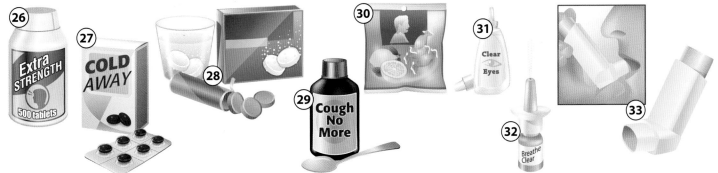

26. pain reliever
el aliviador de dolor/
el analgésico

27. cold tablets
las pastillas para el resfriado

28. antacid
el antiácido

29. cough syrup
el jarabe para la tos

30. throat lozenges
las pastillas para la garganta

31. eye drops
las gotas para los ojos

32. nasal spray
el aerosol nasal

33. inhaler
el inhalador

Ways to talk about medication

Use **take** for pills, tablets, capsules, and cough syrup.
Use **apply** for ointments and creams.
Use **use** for drops, nasal sprays, and inhalers.

Identify Dara's problem. Brainstorm solutions.

Dara's father is 85 and lives alone. She lives nearby.
Her dad has many prescriptions. He often forgets to
take his medication or takes the wrong pills.

Ways to Get Well   Maneras de recuperarse

A. Seek medical attention.
Obtenga atención médica.

B. Get bed rest.
Descanse en la cama.

C. Drink fluids.
Beba líquidos.

D. Take medicine.
Tome un medicamento.

Ways to Stay Well   Maneras para mantenerse sano

E. Stay fit.
Manténgase en buena condición física.

F. Eat a healthy diet.
Coma una dieta saludable.

G. Don't smoke.
No fume.

Ms. Jones, you must stop smoking!

H. Have regular checkups.
Hágase exámenes médicos regularmente.

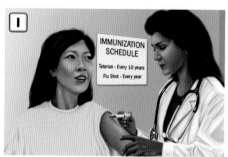

I. Get immunized.
Hágase inmunizar.

J. Follow medical advice.
Cumpla con las indicaciones médicas.

More vocabulary

injection: medicine in a syringe that is put into the body
immunization / vaccination: an injection that stops serious diseases

Survey your class. Record the responses.

1. How do you stay fit?
2. Which two foods are a part of your healthy diet?
Report: *I surveyed ten people who said they ____.*

Types of Health Problems Tipos de problemas de salud

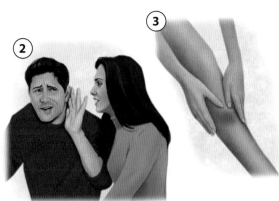

1. vision problems
los problemas de visión

2. hearing loss
la pérdida de la audición

3. pain
el dolor

4. stress
el estrés

5. depression
la depresión

Help with Health Problems Ayuda para los problemas de salud

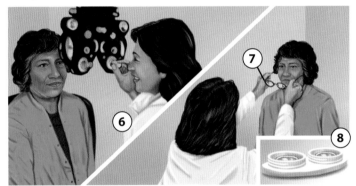

6. optometrist
el optometrista/
el optómetra

8. contact lenses
los lentes de contacto

9. audiologist
el audiólogo

10. hearing aid
el audífono

7. glasses
los anteojos

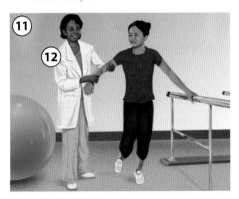

11. physical therapy
la terapia física

13. talk therapy
la terapia del habla

15. support group
el grupo de apoyo

12. physical therapist
el fisioterapeuta

14. therapist
el terapeuta

Ways to ask about health problems

Are you in pain?
Are you having vision problems?
Are you experiencing depression?

Pair practice. Make new conversations.

A: *Do you know a good optometrist?*
B: *Why? Are you having vision problems?*
A: *Yes, I might need glasses.*

117

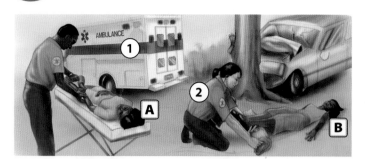

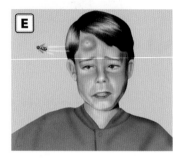
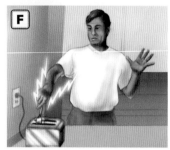

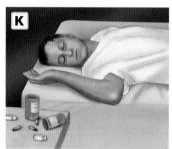
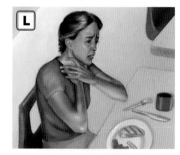

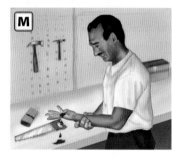

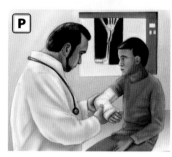

1. ambulance
   la ambulancia

2. paramedic
   el paramédico/el enfermero de urgencias

A. **be** unconscious
   estar inconsciente

B. **be** in shock
   estar en *shock*/choque

C. **be** injured / **be** hurt
   estar lesionado/**estar** herido

D. **have** a heart attack
   tener un ataque al corazón

E. **have** an allergic reaction
   tener una reacción alérgica

F. **get** an electric shock
   recibir una descarga eléctrica

G. **get** frostbite
   quemarse por el frío

H. **burn** (your)self
   quemar(se)

I. **drown**
   ahogarse

J. **swallow** poison
   envenenarse

K. **overdose** on drugs
   tomar una sobredosis de drogas

L. **choke**
   atragantarse/asfixiarse

M. **bleed**
   sangrar

N. **can't breathe**
   asfixiarse/no poder respirar

O. **fall**
   caerse

P. **break** a bone
   fracturarse un hueso

Grammar Point: past tense

For past tense, add *-d* or *-ed*.
burn**ed**, drown**ed**, swallow**ed**,
overdose**d**, choke**d**

These verbs are different (irregular):

be – was, were	bleed – bled	break – broke
have – had	can't – couldn't	
get – got	fall – fell	

First Aid Los primeros auxilios

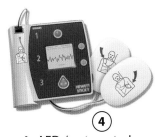

1. first aid kit
el botiquín de primeros auxilios

2. first aid manual
el manual de primeros auxilios

3. medical emergency bracelet
la pulsera/el brazalete de emergencia médica

4. AED / automated external defibrillator
el DEA/el desfibrilador externo automático

Inside the Kit Dentro del botiquín

5. tweezers
las pinzas

6. adhesive bandage
la venda adhesiva

7. sterile pad
el apósito estéril

8. sterile tape
la cinta estéril

9. gauze
la gasa

10. hydrogen peroxide
el peróxido de hidrógeno/ el agua oxigenada

11. antihistamine cream
la crema antihistamínica

12. antibacterial ointment
el ungüento antibacteriano

13. elastic bandage
el vendaje elástico

14. ice pack
la bolsa de hielo

15. splint
la tablilla

First Aid Procedures Los procedimientos de primeros auxilios

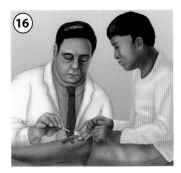

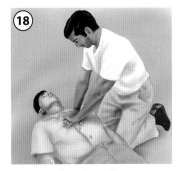
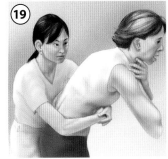

16. stitches
los puntos

17. rescue breathing
la respiración de boca a boca

18. CPR (cardiopulmonary resuscitation)
CPR (la resucitación cardiopulmonar)

19. Heimlich maneuver
la maniobra de Heimlich

Pair practice. Make new conversations.

A: *What do we need in the first aid kit?*
B: *We need tweezers and gauze.*
A: *I think we need sterile tape, too.*

Internet Research: first aid class

Type "first aid," "class," and your ZIP code in the search bar. Look for a class near you.
Report: *I found a first aid class at ____.*

119

Dentistry La odontología

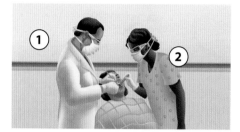

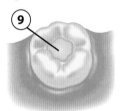

Orthodontics La ortodoncia

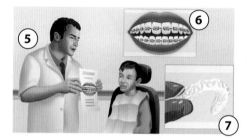
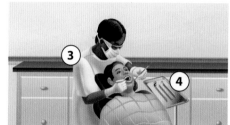

1. dentist
el dentista

2. dental assistant
el asistente dental/
el ayudante del dentista

3. dental hygienist
el higienista dental

4. dental instruments
los instrumentos dentales

5. orthodontist
el ortodoncista

6. braces
los frenos/los frenillos

7. clear aligner
el alineador
transparente

Dental Problems Los problemas dentales

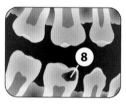

8. cavity / decay
las caries/las picaduras

9. filling
el empaste

10. crown
la corona

11. dentures
la dentadura postiza

12. gum disease
la enfermedad de las encías

13. plaque
el sarro

An Office Visit Una visita a la oficina del dentista

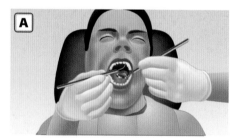

A. clean the teeth
hacer una limpieza dental

B. take X-rays
tomar una radiografía

C. numb the mouth
anestesiar la boca

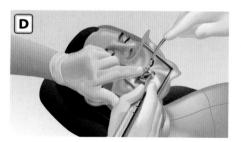
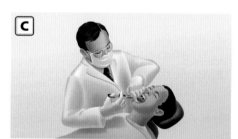

D. drill a tooth
taladrar un diente/una muela

E. fill a cavity
arreglar una caries

F. pull a tooth
sacar/extraer un diente/una muela

Role play. Talk to a dentist.

A: *I think I have a cavity.*
B: *Let me see. Yes. I will need to drill that tooth.*
A: *Oh! How much will that cost?*

Identify Leo's problem. Brainstorm solutions.

Leo has a bad toothache. His wife says, "Call the dentist."
Leo doesn't want to call. He takes pain medication.
The toothache doesn't stop.

	BRONZE	SILVER	GOLD
Monthly Premium	$	$$	$$$
Deductible	$5,000	$3,000	$1,500
Co-pay	$35	$30	none
Out-of-pocket Maximum	$10,000	$6,000	$3,000

BE WELL ONLINE PAYMENTS

JUNE 2018 PAID
JULY 2018 PAID
AUGUST 2018 DUE

BRONZE PLAN
PREMIUM: $834.00

PAY NOW

That's $35. We'll bill your insurance for the other $115.

ABC RADIOLOGY

BEWELL

BEWELL HEALTH EXPLANATION OF BENEFITS

Claim submitted: **5/9/18**   Provider: **ABC Radiology**

Claim processed: **6/1/18**   Patient #**5792321**

Service Date	Type of Service	Total Billed	Allowable Amount	Co-pay	Amount Paid
5/9/18	X-ray	150.00	150.00	35.00	115.00

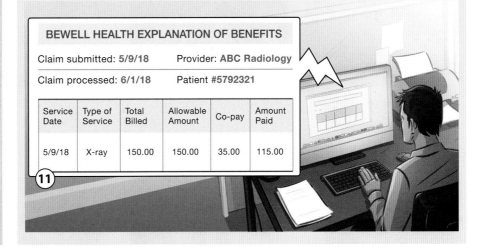

1. carrier
   la empresa aseguradora

2. insurance plans
   los planes de seguro

3. benefits
   las prestaciones

4. insurance policy
   la póliza de seguro

5. insured / policyholder
   el asegurado/el titular de la póliza

6. dependents
   los dependientes

7. premium
   la prima

8. co-pay
   el copago

9. in-network doctor
   un médico de la red

10. out-of-network doctor
    una médica externa a la red

11. explanation of benefits / EOB
    la descripción de prestaciones

A. **compare** plans
   comparar planes

B. **pay** a claim
   pagar una reclamación

Medical Specialists Los especialistas médicos

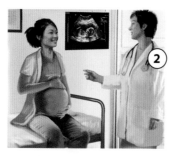

1. internist
el internista

2. obstetrician
la obstetra

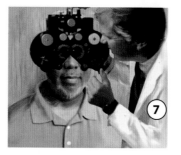

3. cardiologist
el cardiólogo

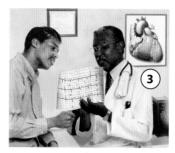

4. pediatrician
el pediatra

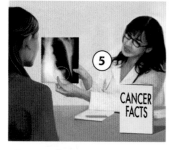

5. oncologist
la oncóloga

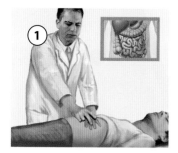

6. radiologist
el radiólogo

7. ophthalmologist
el oftalmólogo

8. psychiatrist
la siquiatra

Nursing Staff El personal de enfermería

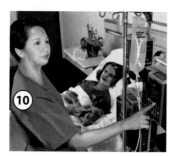

9. surgical nurse
la enfermera quirúrgica

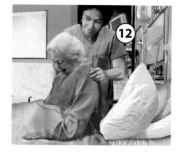

10. registered nurse (RN)
la enfermera registrada

11. licensed practical nurse (LPN)
el enfermero con
licencia práctica

12. certified nursing assistant (CNA)
la asistente certificada
de enfermería

Hospital Staff El personal del hospital

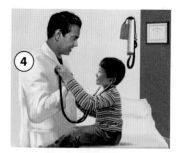

13. administrator
la administradora

14. admissions clerk
el encargado de admisiones

15. dietician
el/la dietista

16. orderly
el camillero/el asistente

More vocabulary

Gynecologists examine and treat women.
Nurse practitioners can give medical exams.
Nurse midwives deliver babies.

Chiropractors move the spine to improve health.
Orthopedists treat bone and joint problems.
Dermatologists treat skin conditions.
Urologists treat bladder and kidney problems.

A Hospital Room Una habitación en el hospital

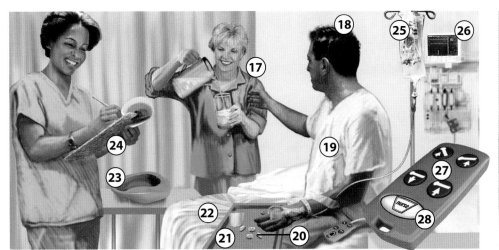

Lab El laboratorio

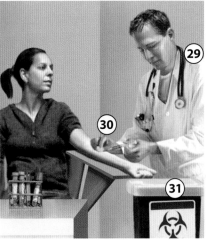

17. volunteer
la voluntaria/
el voluntario

18. patient
el paciente

19. hospital gown
la bata de hospital

20. medication
el medicamento

21. bed table
la mesa de cama

22. hospital bed
la cama de hospital

23. bedpan
la bacinilla

24. medical chart
el expediente médico

25. IV (intravenous drip)
el goteo intravenoso

26. vital signs monitor
el monitor de signos vitales

27. bed control
el control de la cama

28. call button
el botón para llamar

29. phlebotomist
el flebotomista

30. blood work / blood test
el examen de sangre/sanguíneo

31. medical waste disposal
el recipiente para desechos
médicos

Emergency Room Entrance
La entrada de la sala de emergencias

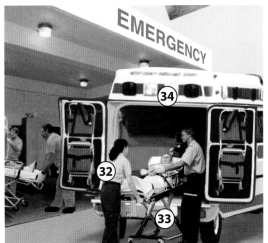

Operating Room La sala de operaciones/el quirófano

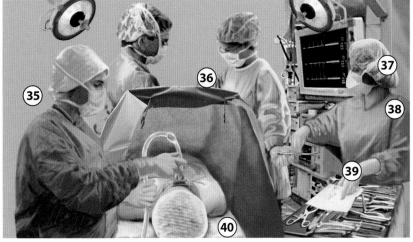

32. emergency medical technician (EMT)
el técnico médico de emergencias

33. stretcher / gurney
la camilla

34. ambulance
la ambulancia

35. anesthesiologist
el anestesiólogo

36. surgeon
el cirujano

37. surgical cap
el gorro quirúrgico

38. surgical gown
la bata quirúrgica

39. surgical gloves
los guantes
quirúrgicos

40. operating table
la mesa quirúrgica

Dictate to your partner. Take turns.

A: *Write this sentence: She's a volunteer.*
B: *She's a what?*
A: *Volunteer. That's v-o-l-u-n-t-e-e-r.*

Role play. Ask about a doctor.

A: *I need to find a good surgeon.*
B: *Dr. Jones is a great surgeon. You should call him.*
A: *I will! Please give me his number.*

A Health Fair Una feria de salud

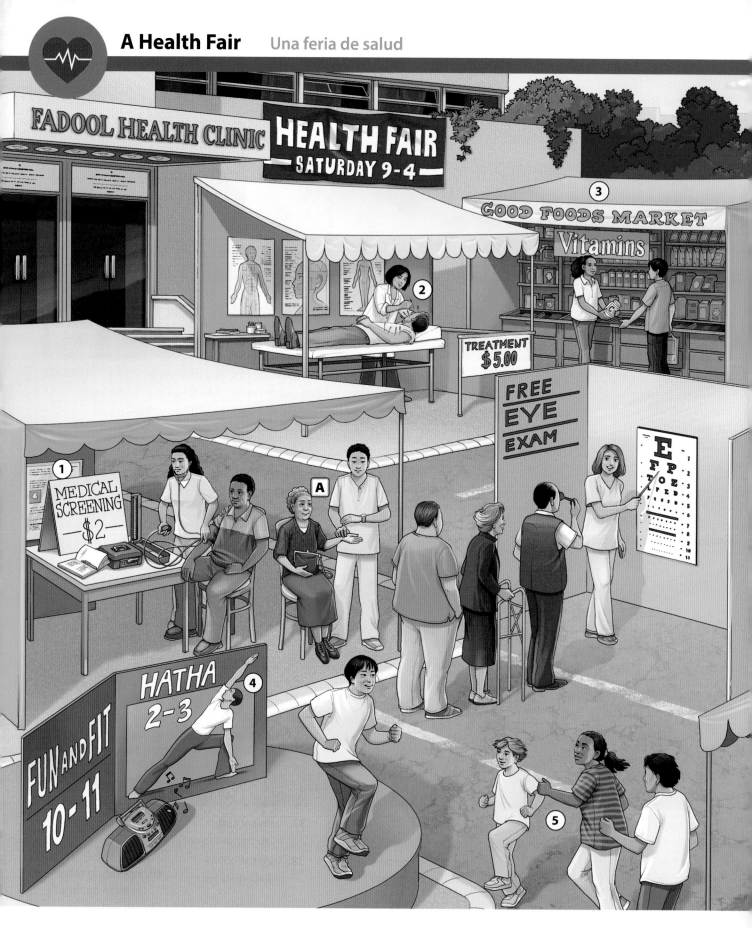

FADOOL HEALTH CLINIC

HEALTH FAIR
SATURDAY 9-4

GOOD FOODS MARKET
Vitamins

TREATMENT
$5.00

FREE
EYE
EXAM

MEDICAL
SCREENING
$2

HATHA
2-3

FUN AND FIT
10-11

1. **low-cost exam**
un examen de bajo costo

2. **acupuncture**
la acupuntura

3. **booth**
el quiosco

4. **yoga**
el yoga

5. **aerobic exercise**
el ejercicio aeróbico

6. **demonstration**
una demostración

7. **sugar-free**
sin azúcar

8. **nutrition label**
la etiqueta de
nutrición

A. **check**…pulse
verificar…el pulso

B. **give** a lecture
dar una clase

124

EAT WELL -BE WELL

"Daily value" means...

What do you see in the picture?

1. Where is this health fair?

2. What kinds of exams and treatments can you get at this fair?

3. What kinds of lectures and demonstrations can you attend here?

4. How much money should you bring? Why?

Read the article.

A Health Fair

Once a month the Fadool Health Clinic has a health fair. You can get a low-cost medical exam at one booth. The nurses check your blood pressure and check your pulse. At another booth, you can get a free eye exam. And an acupuncture treatment is only $5.00.

You can learn a lot at the fair. This month a doctor is giving a lecture on nutrition labels. There is also a demonstration on sugar-free cooking. You can learn to do aerobic exercise and yoga, too.

Do you want to get healthy and stay healthy? Then come to the Fadool Health Clinic Fair! We want to see you there!

Reread the article.

1. Who wrote this article? How do you know?

2. What information in the picture is *not* in the article?

What do you think?

3. Which booths at this fair look interesting to you? Why?

4. Do you read nutrition labels? Why or why not?

125

Downtown El centro de la ciudad

1. **parking garage**
   el estacionamiento/
   el aparcamiento

2. **office building**
   el edificio de oficinas

3. **hotel**
   el hotel

4. **Department of Motor Vehicles**
   el Departamento de
   Vehículos Motorizados

5. **bank**
   el banco

6. **police station**
   la comisaría/la estación
   de policía

7. **bus station**
   la estación de autobuses

THE SHELTON

DMV

Grand Avenue

Elm Street

RED LINE BUS CO.

$ FIRST U.S. $

DOWNTOWN DIVISION

Grand Avenue

Listen and point. Take turns.

A: *Point to the bank.*
B: *Point to the hotel.*
A: *Point to the restaurant.*

Dictate to your partner. Take turns.

A: *Write bank.*
B: *Is that spelled b-a-n-k?*
A: *Yes, that's right.*

126

8. city hall
el palacio municipal/
la alcaldía

9. hospital
el hospital

10. gas station
la gasolinera

11. post office
la oficina de correos

12. fire station
la estación de bomberos

13. courthouse
el tribunal

14. restaurant
el restaurante

15. library
la biblioteca

Grammar Point: *in* and *at* with locations

Use *in* when you are inside the building. *I am in (inside) the bank.* Use *at* to describe your general location. *I am at the bank.*

Pair practice. Make new conversations.

A: *I'm in the <u>bank</u>. Where are you?*

B: *I'm at the <u>bank</u>, too, but I'm outside.*

A: *OK. I'll meet you there.*

127

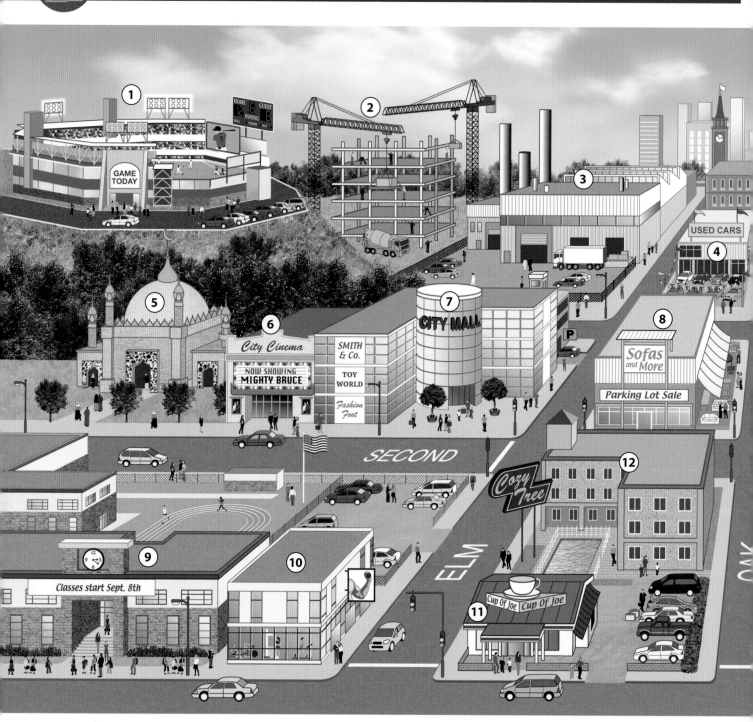

1. **stadium**
   el estadio

2. **construction site**
   la obra

3. **factory**
   la fábrica

4. **car dealership**
   el concesionario de autos

5. **mosque**
   la mezquita

6. **movie theater**
   el cine

7. **shopping mall**
   el centro comercial

8. **furniture store**
   la mueblería

9. **school**
   la escuela

10. **gym**
    el gimnasio

11. **coffee shop**
    la cafetería

12. **motel**
    el motel

Ways to state your destination using *to* and *to the*

Use *to* for schools, churches, and synagogues.
I'm going to school.

Use *to the* for all other locations. *I have to go to the bakery.*

Pair practice. Make new conversations.

A: *Where are you going today?*
B: *I'm going to school. How about you?*
A: *I have to go to the bakery.*

13. skyscraper / high-rise
el rascacielos

14. church
la iglesia

15. cemetery
el cementerio

16. synagogue
la sinagoga

17. community college
el instituto de enseñanza superior

18. supermarket
el supermercado

19. bakery
la panadería

20. home improvement store
la tienda de mejoras para el hogar

21. office supply store
la tienda de artículos de oficina

22. garbage truck
el camión de la basura

23. theater
el teatro

24. convention center
el centro de convenciones

Ways to give locations

The mall is on Second Street.
The mall is on the corner of Second and Elm.
The mall is next to the movie theater.

Survey your class. Record the responses.

1. Do you have a favorite coffee shop? Which one?
2. Which supermarkets do you go to?
Report: *Nine* out of *ten* students go to ____.

129

1. **laundromat**
   la lavandería

2. **dry cleaners**
   la tintorería

3. **convenience store**
   la tienda de conveniencia

4. **pharmacy**
   la farmacia

5. **parking space**
   el lugar para estacionar

6. **handicapped parking**
   el estacionamiento para minusválidos

7. **corner**
   la esquina

8. **traffic light**
   el semáforo

9. **bus**
   el autobús/el camión

10. **fast food restaurant**
    el restaurante de comida rápida

11. **drive-thru window**
    el servicio para automovilistas

12. **newsstand**
    el puesto de periódicos

13. **mailbox**
    el buzón

14. **pedestrian**
    la peatona

15. **crosswalk**
    el cruce peatonal

A. **cross** the street
   cruzar la calle

B. **wait for** the light
   esperar a que cambie el semáforo

C. **jaywalk**
   cruzar imprudentemente una calle

More vocabulary

do errands: to make a short trip from your home to buy or pick up things

neighborhood: the area close to your home

Pair practice. Make new conversations.

A: *I have a lot of errands to do today.*

B: *Me too. First, I'm going to the laundromat.*

A: *I'll see you there after I stop at the copy center.*

16. bus stop la parada de autobús	**22.** bike la bicicleta	**28.** cart el carrito
17. donut shop la tienda de rosquillas	**23.** pay phone el teléfono público	**29.** street vendor el vendedor ambulante
18. copy center el centro de fotocopiado	**24.** sidewalk la acera	**30.** childcare center la guardería infantil
19. barbershop la barbería	**25.** parking meter el parquímetro	**D. ride** a bike **andar** en bicicleta
20. used book store la librería de libros usados	**26.** street sign el letrero	**E. park** the car **estacionar** el auto/el coche
21. curb el borde de la acera/el encintado	**27.** fire hydrant la boca de incendio	**F. walk** a dog **pasear** el perro

---

Internet Research: finding business listings

Type "pharmacy" and your city in the search bar.
Count the pharmacy listings you see.
Report: *I found 25 pharmacies in Chicago.*

Think about it. Discuss.

1. How many different jobs are there at this intersection?
2. Which of these businesses would you like to own? Why?

131

A Mall Un centro comercial

1. music store
   la tienda de música

2. jewelry store
   la joyería

3. nail salon
   el salón de uñas

4. bookstore
   la librería

5. toy store
   la juguetería

6. pet store
   la tienda de mascotas

7. card store
   la tienda de tarjetas

8. florist
   la florería/la floristería

9. optician
   la óptica

10. shoe store
    la zapatería

11. play area
    el área de juegos

12. guest services
    el módulo de información

More vocabulary

beauty shop: hair salon

gift shop: a store that sells T-shirts, mugs, and other small gifts

men's store: men's clothing store

Pair practice. Make new conversations.

A: *Where is the florist?*

B: *It's on the first floor, next to the optician.*

13. department store
la tienda por departamentos

14. travel agency
la agencia de viajes

15. food court
la feria de comida rápida

16. ice cream shop
la heladería

17. candy store
la dulcería

18. hair salon
la peluquería

19. maternity store
la tienda de ropa de maternidad

20. electronics store
la tienda de aparatos electrónicos

21. elevator
el elevador/el ascensor

22. kiosk
el quiosco

23. escalator
la escalera automática

24. directory
el directorio

Ways to talk about plans

Let's go to the <u>card store</u>.
I have to go to the <u>card store</u>.
I want to go to the <u>card store</u>.

Role play. Talk to a friend at the mall.

A: *Let's go to the <u>card store</u>. I need to buy <u>a card</u> for <u>Maggie's birthday</u>.*
B: *OK, but can we go to the <u>shoe store</u> next?*

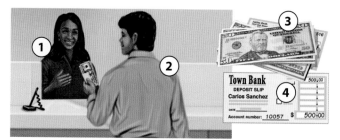
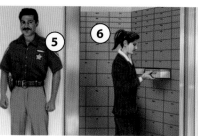

1. teller
el cajero

2. customer
el cliente

3. deposit
el depósito

4. deposit slip
el comprobante de depósito/
la hoja de ingreso

5. security guard
el guardia de seguridad

6. vault
la bóveda

7. safety deposit box
la caja de seguridad

8. valuables
los objetos valiosos

Bank Accounts　Las cuentas bancarias

9. account manager
el gerente de cuentas

10. joint account
la cuenta conjunta

11. opening deposit
el depósito inicial

12. ATM card
la tarjeta de cajero
automático

13. checkbook
la chequera

14. check
el cheque

15. checking account number
el número de cuenta corriente

16. savings account number
el número de cuenta de ahorro

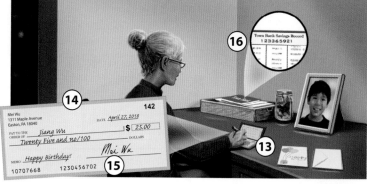

A. Cash a check.
Cobre un cheque.

B. Make a deposit.
Haga un depósito.

17. bank statement
el estado de cuenta

18. balance
el saldo

The ATM (Automated Teller Machine)　El cajero automático

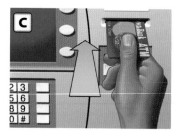
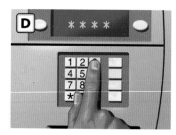

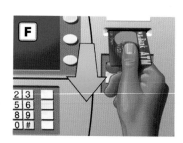

C. Insert your ATM card.
Inserte la tarjeta de
cajero automático.

D. Enter your PIN.*
Introduzca su clave
en el teclado.

E. Withdraw cash.
Retire el efectivo.

F. Remove your card.
Retire la tarjeta.

*PIN = personal identification number

A. get a library card
obtener una tarjeta para uso de la biblioteca

B. look for a book
buscar un libro

C. check out a book
sacar un libro en **préstamo**

D. return a book
devolver un libro

E. pay a late fine
pagar una multa

1. library clerk
el bibliotecario

2. circulation desk
el escritorio de distribución

3. library patron
el usuario de la biblioteca

4. periodicals
las publicaciones periódicas

5. magazine
la revista

6. newspaper
el periódico

7. headline
el titular

8. atlas
el atlas

9. reference librarian
la bibliotecaria de referencias

10. self-checkout
el autoservicio

11. online catalog
el catálogo en línea

12. picture book
el libro de dibujos

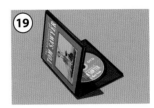

13. biography
la biografía

14. title
el título

15. author
el autor

16. novel
la novela

17. audiobook
el audiolibro/el libro hablado

18. e-book
el libro digital

19. DVD
el DVD

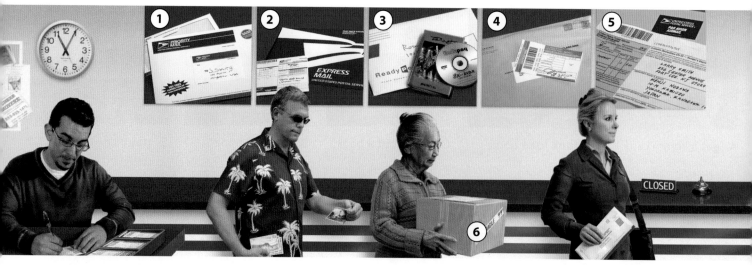

1. Priority Mail®
   Priority Mail® (el correo prioritario)

2. Express Mail®
   Express Mail® (el correo expreso)

3. Media Mail®
   Media Mail® (el correo de otros medios de información)

4. Certified Mail™
   Certified Mail™ (el correo certificado)

5. airmail
   el correo aéreo

6. ground post / parcel post
   el envío por vía terrestre

13. letter
   la carta

14. envelope
   el sobre

15. greeting card
   la tarjeta de felicitación

16. postcard
   la postal

17. package
   el paquete

18. book of stamps
   el libro de estampillas

19. postal forms
   los formularios de correo

20. letter carrier
   el cartero

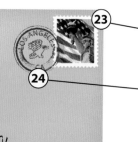

21. return address
   el remitente

22. mailing address
   la dirección del destinatario

21 Sonya Enriquez
   258 Quentin Avenue
   Los Angeles, CA 90068-1416

22 Cindy Lin
   807 Glenn Drive
   Charlotte, NC 28201

23. stamp
   la estampilla

24. postmark
   el matasellos

Ways to talk about sending mail

This letter has to <u>get there tomorrow</u>. (**Express Mail**®)
This letter has to <u>arrive in two days</u>. (**Priority Mail**®)
This letter can go in <u>regular mail</u>. (**First Class**)

Pair practice. Make new conversations.

A: *Hi. <u>This letter has to get there tomorrow</u>.*
B: *You can send it by <u>Express Mail</u>®.*
A: *OK. I need <u>a book of stamps</u>, too.*

7. **postal clerk**
   el empleado de correos

8. **scale**
   la máquina franqueadora

9. **post office box (PO box)**
   el apartado postal (PO box)

10. **automated postal center (APC)**
    el centro postal automático (CPA)

11. **post office lobby drop**
    el buzón del vestíbulo de la oficina de correos

12. **mailbox**
    el buzón

Sending a Card Enviar una tarjeta

A. **Write** a note in a card.
Escriba un mensaje en la tarjeta.

B. **Address** the envelope.
Escriba la dirección en el sobre.

C. **Put on** a stamp.
Póngale la estampilla.

D. **Mail** the card.
Envíe la tarjeta.

E. **Deliver** the card.
Entregue la tarjeta.

F. **Receive** the card.
Reciba la tarjeta.

G. **Read** the card.
Lea la tarjeta.

H. **Write** back.
Responda.

More vocabulary

junk mail: mail you don't want
overnight / next-day mail: Express Mail®
postage: the cost to send mail

Survey your class. Record the responses.

1. Do you send greeting cards by mail or online?
2. Do you pay bills by mail or online?
Report: _25%_ of us _send cards_ _by mail_.

137

1. DMV handbook
   el manual del DMV

2. testing area
   el área de examen

3. DMV clerk
   el empleado del DMV

4. photo
   la fotografía

5. fingerprint
   la huella digital

6. vision exam
   el examen de visión

7. window
   la ventanilla

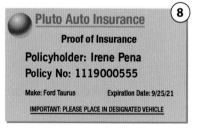

8. proof of insurance
   la prueba de seguro

9. driver's license
   la licencia de manejar

10. expiration date
    la fecha de vencimiento

11. driver's license number
    el número de licencia de conductor

12. license plate
    la placa/la tablilla

13. registration sticker / tag
    el marbete/la etiqueta de registro

More vocabulary

expire: A license is no good, or **expires**, after the expiration date.
renew a license: to apply to keep a license before it expires
vanity plate: a more expensive, personal license plate

Internet Research: DMV locations

Type "DMV" and your ZIP code in the search bar. How many DMVs are there?
Report: *I found _____ DMV office(s) near me.*

138

Getting Your First License Obteniendo su primera licencia

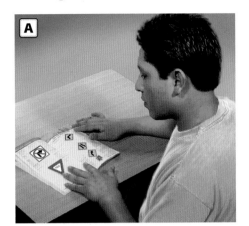

A. Study the handbook.
Estudie el manual.

B. Take a driver education course.*
Tome un curso de manejo.

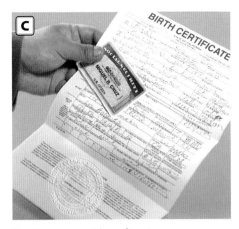

C. Show your identification.
Muestre su identificación.

D. Pay the application fee.
Pague los costos de solicitud.

E. Take a written test.
Tome una prueba escrita.

F. Get a learner's permit.
Obtenga un permiso de aprendiz.

G. Take a driver's training course.*
Tome un curso de capacitación
para conductores.

H. Pass a driving test.
Pase una prueba de manejo.

I. Get your license.
Obtenga su licencia.

*Note: This is not required for drivers 18 and older.

Ways to request more information

What do I do next?
What's the next step?
Where do I go from here?

Role play. Talk to a DMV clerk.

A: *I want to apply for <u>a driver's license</u>.*
B: *Did you <u>study the handbook</u>?*
A: *Yes, I did. <u>What do I do next</u>?*

Federal Government　El Gobierno federal

Legislative Branch
La rama legislativa

1. U.S. Capitol
   El capitolio de EE. UU.

2. Congress
   el Congreso

3. House of Representatives
   la Cámara de Representantes

4. congressperson
   el/la congresista

5. Senate
   el Senado

6. senator
   el senador

435　100

Executive Branch
La rama ejecutiva

7. White House
   la Casa Blanca

8. president
   el presidente

9. vice president
   el vicepresidente

10. Cabinet
    el Gabinete

STATE　DEFENSE　LABOR

Judicial Branch
La rama judicial

11. Supreme Court
    la Corte Suprema

12. justices
    los jueces

13. chief justice
    el presidente de la Corte Suprema

State Government　El Gobierno estatal

Tallahassee

FLORIDA

ASSEMBLY　STATE SENATE

14. governor
    el gobernador

15. lieutenant governor
    el vicegobernador

16. state capital
    la capital del estado

17. Legislature
    la Asamblea Legislativa

18. assemblyperson
    el asambleísta

19. state senator
    el senador del estado

City Government　El Gobierno municipal

MARYLAND

Baltimore

CITY OF BALTIMORE

20. mayor
    el alcalde

21. city council
    el Consejo Municipal

22. councilperson
    el concejal

The U.S. Military Las Fuerzas Armadas de EE. UU.

23. **Pentagon**
    el Pentágono

24. **Secretary of Defense**
    el ministro de Defensa

25. **general**
    el general

26. **admiral**
    el almirante

27. **officer**
    el oficial

Military Service El servicio militar

A. be a recruit
ser recluta

B. be on active duty
estar de servicio activo

C. be on reserve
estar en la reserva

D. be a veteran
ser veterano

Branches of the Military Las ramas de las Fuerzas Armadas

28. **Army**
    el Ejército

29. **soldier**
    el soldado

30. **Navy**
    la Marina

31. **seaman / sailor**
    la marina/la marinera

32. **Air Force**
    la Fuerza Aérea

33. **airman**
    el aviador

34. **Marines**
    los Infantes de Marina

35. **marine**
    el infante de marina

36. **Coast Guard**
    la Guardia Costera

37. **coast guardsman**
    la guardacostas

38. **National Guard***
    la Guardia Nacional

39. **national guardsman**
    el guardia nacional

*Each state has an Army National Guard. The national guardsmen are reservists.

Civic Engagement La participación ciudadana

Responsibilities Responsabilidades

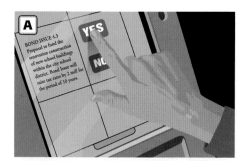

A. vote
votar

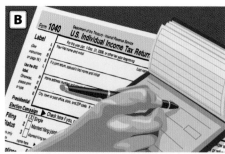

B. pay taxes
pagar impuestos

C. obey the law
obedecer/acatar las leyes

D. register with Selective Service*
inscribirse en el servicio selectivo del ejército

E. serve on a jury
servir en un jurado

F. be informed
estar informado

Citizenship Requirements Requisitos de ciudadanía

G. be 18 or older
tener 18 o más años de edad

H. live in the U.S. for five years
vivir en EE. UU. por cinco años

I. take a citizenship test
tomar un examen de ciudadanía

Rights Los derechos

1. peaceful assembly
la reunión pacífica

2. free speech
la libertad de expresión

3. freedom of religion
la libertad de religión

4. freedom of the press
la libertad de prensa

5. a fair trial
un juicio justo

*Note: All males 18 to 26 who live in the U.S. are required to register with Selective Service.

142

An Election Una elección

J. run for office
postularse para un cargo

6. candidate
el candidato

K. campaign
hacer campaña

7. rally
reunirse en apoyo
a un candidato

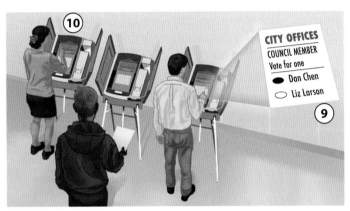

L. debate
debatir

8. opponent
el oponente

9. ballot
la papeleta

10. voting booth /
polling booth
la cabina electoral/
la cabina de votación

M. get elected
ser electo

11. election results
los resultados de
las elecciones

N. serve
servir

12. elected official
el funcionario electo

More vocabulary

political party: a group of people with the same
political goals
term: the period of time an elected official serves

Think about it. Discuss.

1. Should everyone have to vote? Why or why not?
2. Are candidate debates important? Why or why not?
3. Would you prefer to run for city council or mayor? Why?

143

A. **arrest** a suspect
arrestar a un sospechoso

1. police officer
el oficial de policía/el policía

2. handcuffs
las esposas

B. **hire** a lawyer / **hire** an attorney
contratar a un abogado

3. guard
el guardia

4. defense attorney
el abogado defensor

C. **appear** in court
comparecer ante el tribunal

5. defendant
el acusado

6. judge
el juez

D. **stand** trial
ser juzgado

7. courtroom
la sala del tribunal

8. jury
el jurado

9. evidence
la evidencia/las pruebas

10. prosecuting attorney
el fiscal

11. witness
el testigo

12. court reporter
el escribiente/el secretario

13. bailiff
el alguacil

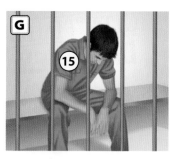

E. **convict** the defendant
condenar al acusado

14. verdict*
el veredicto

F. **sentence** the defendant
sentenciar al acusado

G. **go** to jail / **go** to prison
ir a la cárcel/ir a prisión

15. convict / prisoner
el condenado/el preso

H. **be** released
salir en libertad

*Note: There are two possible verdicts, "guilty" and "not guilty."

Look at the pictures.
Describe what happened.

A: *The police officer arrested a suspect.*
B: *He put handcuffs on him.*

Think about it. Discuss.

1. Would you want to serve on a jury? Why or why not?
2. Look at the crimes on page 145. What sentence would you give for each crime? Why?

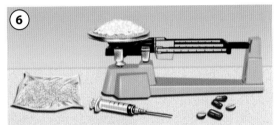

1. **vandalism**
   el vandalismo

2. **burglary**
   el robo

3. **assault**
   la agresión

4. **gang violence**
   el pandillismo

5. **drunk driving**
   manejar en estado
   de embriaguez

6. **illegal drugs**
   las sustancias/
   las drogas ilegales

7. **arson**
   el incendio provocado

8. **shoplifting**
   los hurtos en
   comercios

9. **identity theft**
   la usurpación
   de identidad

10. **victim**
    la víctima

11. **mugging**
    el ataque

12. **murder**
    el asesinato

13. **gun**
    la pistola

More vocabulary

commit a crime: to do something illegal
criminal: someone who does something illegal
steal: to take money or things from someone illegally

Identify the tenants' problem. Brainstorm solutions.

The apartment tenants at 65 Elm Street are upset.
There were three burglaries on their block last month.
This month there were five burglaries and a mugging!

145

A. Walk with a friend.
Camine con un amigo.

B. Stay on well-lit streets.
Permanezca en calles bien iluminadas.

C. Conceal your PIN number.
Resguarde su clave.

D. Protect your purse or wallet.
Proteja el bolso o la cartera/billetera.

E. Lock your doors.
Cierre las puertas con llave.

F. Don't **open** your door to strangers.
No abra la puerta a extraños.

G. Don't **drink** and **drive**.
No maneje en estado de embriaguez.

H. Shop on secure websites.
Haga compras en sitios Web seguros.

I. Be aware of your surroundings.
Esté pendiente de sus alrededores.

J. Report suspicious packages.
Denuncie los paquetes sospechosos.

K. Report crimes to the police.
Denuncie los delitos a la policía.

L. Join a Neighborhood Watch.
Únase al grupo de vigilancia del vecindario.

More vocabulary

sober: not drunk

designated drivers: sober drivers who drive drunk people home safely

Survey your class. Record the responses.

1. Do you always lock your doors?
2. Do you belong to a Neighborhood Watch?
Report: _75%_ of us _always lock our doors_.

Online Dangers for Children
Los riesgos de Internet para los niños

1. cyberbullying
   el ciberacoso

2. online predators
   los depredadores cibernéticos

3. inappropriate material
   el material inapropiado

Ways to Protect Children **Las formas de proteger a los niños**

A. **Turn on** parental controls.
   Active los controles de padres.

B. **Monitor** children's Internet use.
   Supervise el uso que hacen los niños de Internet.

C. **Block** inappropriate sites.
   Bloquee los sitios inapropiados.

Internet Crime **Los delitos a través de Internet**

4. phishing
   el fraude electrónico

5. hacking
   la piratería informática

Safety Solutions **Las medidas de seguridad**

D. **Create** secure passwords.
   Cree contraseñas seguras.

E. **Update** security software.
   Actualice el *software* de seguridad.

F. **Use** encrypted / secure sites.
   Use sitios cifrados/ sitios seguros.

G. **Delete** suspicious emails.
   Elimine los correos electrónicos sospechosos.

1. lost child
el niño perdido

2. car accident
el accidente automovilístico

3. airplane crash
el accidente aéreo

4. explosion
la explosión

5. earthquake
el terremoto

6. mudslide
el derrumbe

7. forest fire
el incendio forestal

8. fire
el incendio

9. firefighter
el bombero

10. fire truck
el camión de bomberos

Ways to report an emergency

First, give your name. *My name is <u>Tim Johnson</u>.*
Then, state the emergency and give the address.
There was <u>a car accident</u> at <u>219 Elm Street</u>.

Role play. Call 911.

A: *911 emergency operator.*
B: *My name is <u>Lisa Diaz</u>. There is <u>a fire</u> at <u>323 Oak Street</u>.*
Please hurry!

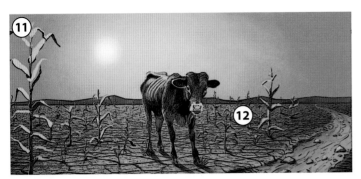

11. drought
la sequía

12. famine
el hambre epidémica

13. blizzard
la ventisca

14. hurricane
el huracán

15. tornado
el tornado

16. volcanic eruption
la erupción volcánica

17. tidal wave / tsunami
el maremoto

18. avalanche
la avalancha

19. flood
la inundación

20. search and rescue team
las brigadas de búsqueda y rescate

Survey your class. Record the responses.

1. Which natural disaster worries you the most?

2. Which natural disaster worries you the least?

Report: _Five_ of us are _most_ worried about _earthquakes_.

Think about it. Discuss.

1. What organizations can help you in an emergency?

2. What are some ways to prepare for natural disasters?

3. Where would you go in an emergency?

Before an Emergency   Antes de una emergencia

A. **Plan** for an emergency.
   Planifique para una emergencia.

1. meeting place
   el lugar de encuentro

2. out-of-state contact
   los contactos fuera del estado

3. escape route
   la ruta de escape

4. gas shut-off valve
   la válvula de cierre del gas

5. evacuation route
   la ruta de evacuación

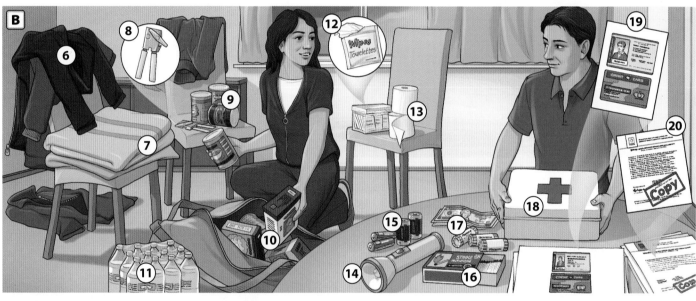

B. **Make** a disaster kit.
   Prepare un equipo de suministros en caso de desastres.

6. warm clothes
   las vestimentas calientes

7. blankets
   las cobijas/las mantas

8. can opener
   el abrelatas

9. canned food
   la comida enlatada

10. packaged food
   la comida envasada

11. bottled water
   el agua en botella

12. moist towelettes
   las toallitas húmedas

13. toilet paper
   el papel higiénico

14. flashlight
   la linterna/la lámpara de mano

15. batteries
   las pilas

16. matches
   las cerillas/los fósforos

17. cash and coins
   el efectivo y las monedas

18. first aid kit
   el botiquín de primeros auxilios

19. copies of ID and credit cards
   las copias de las tarjetas de identificación y de crédito

20. copies of important papers
   las copias de documentos importantes

Pair practice. Make new conversations.

A: *What do we need for our disaster kit?*
B: *We need blankets and matches.*
A: *I think we also need batteries.*

Survey your class. Record the responses.

1. Do you have a disaster kit?
2. Do you have an out-of-state contact?
Report: *Ten of us have a disaster kit.*

During an Emergency Durante una emergencia

C. **Watch** the weather.
  Esté pendiente de los informes del tiempo.

D. **Pay attention** to warnings.
  Preste atención a las advertencias.

E. **Remain** calm.
  Permanezca tranquilo.

F. **Follow** directions.
  Siga las instrucciones.

G. **Help** people with disabilities.
  Ayude a las personas discapacitadas.

H. **Seek** shelter.
  Busque refugio.

I. **Stay away** from windows.
  Manténgase alejado de las ventanas.

J. **Take** cover.
  Busque resguardo.

K. **Evacuate** the area.
  Evacue el área.

After an Emergency Luego de una emergencia

L. **Call** out-of-state contacts.
  Llame a sus contactos fuera del estado.

M. **Clean up** debris.
  Limpie los escombros.

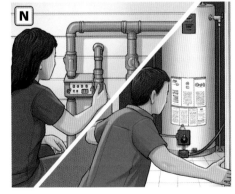

N. **Inspect** utilities.
  Revise los servicios básicos.

Ways to say you're OK
I'm fine.
We're OK here.
Everything's under control.

Ways to say you need help
We need help.
Someone is hurt.
I'm injured. Please get help.

Role play. Prepare for an emergency.
A: *They just issued a hurricane warning.*
B: *OK. We need to stay calm and follow directions.*
A: *What do we need to do first?*

Community Cleanup   Limpieza comunitaria

1. **graffiti**
   el grafiti

2. **litter**
   la basura

3. **streetlight**
   la luz de la calle

4. **hardware store**
   la ferretería

5. **petition**
   la petición

A. **give** a speech
   dar un discurso

B. **applaud**
   aplaudir

C. **change**
   cambiar

What do you see in the pictures?

1. What were the problems on Main Street?

2. What was the petition for?

3. Why did the city council applaud?

4. How did the volunteers change the street?

Read the story.

Community Cleanup

Marta Lopez has a donut shop on Main Street. One day she looked at her street and was very upset. She saw <u>graffiti</u> on her donut shop and the other stores. <u>Litter</u> was everywhere. All the <u>streetlights</u> were broken. Marta wanted to fix the lights and clean up the street.

Marta started a <u>petition</u> about the streetlights. Five hundred people signed it. Then she <u>gave a speech</u> to the city council. The council members voted to repair the streetlights. Everyone <u>applauded</u>. Marta was happy, but her work wasn't finished.

Next, Marta asked for volunteers to clean up Main Street. The <u>hardware store</u> manager gave the volunteers free paint. Marta gave them free donuts and coffee. The volunteers painted and cleaned. They <u>changed</u> Main Street. Now Main Street is beautiful and Marta is proud.

Reread the story.

1. Find "repair" in paragraph 2. Find another word for "repair" in the story.

What do you think?

2. What are the benefits of being a volunteer?

3. What do you think Marta said in her speech? How do you know?

Basic Transportation   El transporte básico

1. car
   el automóvil
2. passenger
   el pasajero
3. taxi
   el taxi
4. motorcycle
   la motocicleta
5. street
   la calle
6. truck
   la camioneta
7. train
   el tren
8. (air)plane
   el avión

Listen and point. Take turns.

A: Point to _the motorcycle_.
B: Point to _the truck_.
A: Point to _the train_.

Dictate to your partner. Take turns.

A: Write _motorcycle_.
B: Could you repeat that for me?
A: I said _motorcycle_.

9. helicopter
   el helicóptero
10. airport
    el aeropuerto
11. subway station
    la estación del metro
12. subway
    el metro/el tren
    subterráneo
13. bus stop
    la parada de autobús
14. bus
    el autobús
15. bicycle
    la bicicleta

Ways to talk about using transportation

Use *take* for buses, trains, subways, taxis, planes, and helicopters. Use *drive* for cars and trucks. Use *ride* for bicycles and motorcycles.

Pair practice. Make new conversations.

A: *How do you get to school?*
B: *I take the bus. How about you?*
A: *I ride a bicycle to school.*

155

A Bus Stop   Una parada de autobús

BUS 10 Northbound

Main	Elm	Oak
6:00	6:10	6:13
6:30	6:40	6:43
7:00	7:10	7:13
7:30	7:40	7:43

TRANSFER →

Valid for $2\frac{1}{2}$ hours

A Subway Station   Una estación de metro/de tren subterráneo

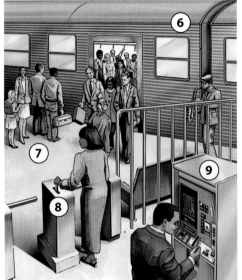

1. bus route
la ruta de autobús

3. rider
el pasajero

5. transfer
el billete de
transbordo

6. subway car
el vagón del tren
subterráneo

7. platform
la plataforma

8. turnstile
el molinete

9. vending machine
la máquina
expendedora

10. token
la ficha/el vale

11. fare card
el boleto/
el billete

2. fare
el pasaje

4. schedule
el horario

A Train Station   Una estación de tren

AMTRAK

LIZ   LK98S
KOENIG   3/12/2017

TRIP
CHICAGO, IL   5:15 PM
ST. LOUIS, MO 10:45 PM

RAIL FARE 70.00
PAYMENT STATUS PAID
RAIL PLANS G0517B
ISSUE CHICAGO UNION STATION
TICKET 1 OF 1

Fresno

Los Angeles

Fresno

Los Angeles

Airport Transportation   Transporte para ir y volver del aeropuerto

TAXIS

J&J Hotel

TAXI

1036081

22.00

12. ticket window
la ventanilla de
boletos/billetes

13. conductor
el conductor

14. track
la vía férrea

15. ticket
el boleto/el billete

16. one-way trip
el viaje de ida

17. round trip
el viaje de ida y vuelta

18. taxi stand
la parada de taxis

19. shuttle
el autobús de servicio
regular/el autobús puente

20. town car
el automóvil urbano

21. taxi driver
el chofer de taxi

22. taxi license
la licencia del taxi

23. meter
el taxímetro

More vocabulary

hail a taxi: to raise your hand to get a taxi
miss the bus: to get to the bus stop after the bus leaves

Internet Research: taxi fares

Type "taxi fare finder" and your city in the search bar.
Enter a starting address and an ending address.
Report: *The fare from my house to school is $10.00.*

Prepositions of Motion

A. go under the bridge
ir debajo del puente

B. go over the bridge
ir sobre el puente

C. walk up the steps
ascender los peldaños

D. walk down the steps
descender los peldaños

E. get into the taxi
subirse al taxi

F. get out of the taxi
bajarse del taxi

G. run across the street
cruzar corriendo la calle

H. run around the corner
correr alrededor de la esquina

I. get on the highway
entrar en la autopista

J. get off the highway
salir de la autopista

K. drive through the tunnel
conducir a través del túnel

Grammar Point: *into, out of, on, off*

Use *get into* for taxis and cars.
Use *get on* for buses, trains, planes, and highways.

Use *get out of* for taxis and cars.
Use *get off* for buses, trains, planes, and highways.

1. stop
detenerse/pararse

2. do not enter / wrong way
no entrar/sentido contrario

3. one way
un solo sentido

4. speed limit
el límite de velocidad

5. U-turn OK
la vuelta en U permitida

6. no outlet / dead end
el callejón sin salida/
la calle sin salida

7. right turn only
solo giro a la derecha

8. no left turn
no se permite girar
a la izquierda

9. yield
ceda el paso

10. merge
convergir

11. no parking
no estacionarse

12. handicapped parking
el estacionamiento
para minusválidos

13. pedestrian crossing
el cruce peatonal

14. railroad crossing
el cruce del ferrocarril

15. school crossing
el cruce escolar

16. roadwork
trabajos en carretera

17. U.S. route / highway marker
la ruta de EE. UU./el marcador
de autopista

18. hospital
el hospital

Pair practice. Make new conversations.

A: *Watch out! The sign says <u>no left turn</u>.*
B: *Sorry, I was looking at the <u>stop</u> sign.*
A: *That's OK. Just be careful!*

Survey your class. Record the responses.

1. Which traffic signs are different in your native country?
2. Which traffic signs are similar in your native country?
Report: *The U.S. and <u>Mexico</u> have similar <u>stop</u> signs.*

Directions *Direcciones*

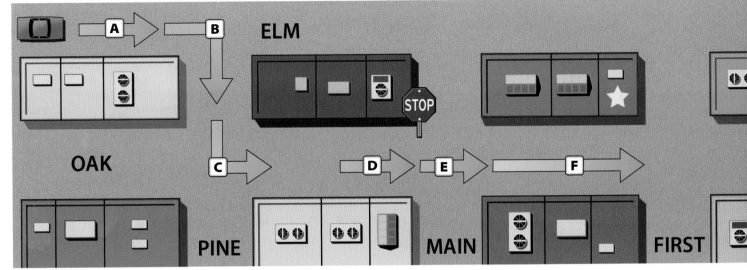

ELM

OAK

STOP

PINE   MAIN   FIRST

A. Go straight on Elm Street.
Vaya directo en Elm Street.

B. Turn right on Pine Street.
Gire a la derecha en Pine Street.

C. Turn left on Oak Street.
Gire a la izquierda en Oak Street.

D. Stop at the corner.
Deténgase en la esquina.

E. Go past Main Street.
Pase Main Street.

F. Go one block to First Street.
Vaya una cuadra a First Street.

Maps *Mapas*

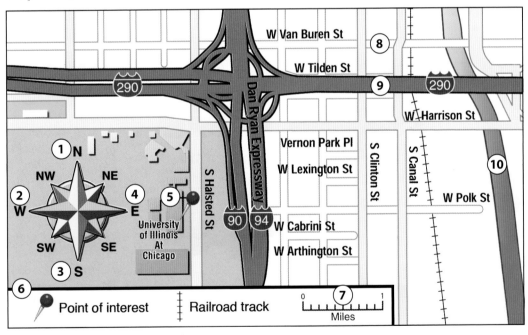

1. north
   el norte

2. west
   el oeste

3. south
   el sur

4. east
   el este

5. symbol
   el símbolo

6. key
   la clave

7. scale
   la escala

8. street
   la calle

9. highway
   la autopista

10. river
    el río

11. GPS (global positioning system)
    el GPS (sistema de posicionamiento global)

12. Internet map
    el mapa Internet

Role play. Ask for directions.

A: *I'm lost. I need to get to Elm and Pine.*
B: *Go straight on Oak and make a right on Pine.*
A: *Thanks so much.*

Think about it. Discuss.

1. What are the pros and cons of using a GPS?
2. Which types of jobs require map-reading skills?

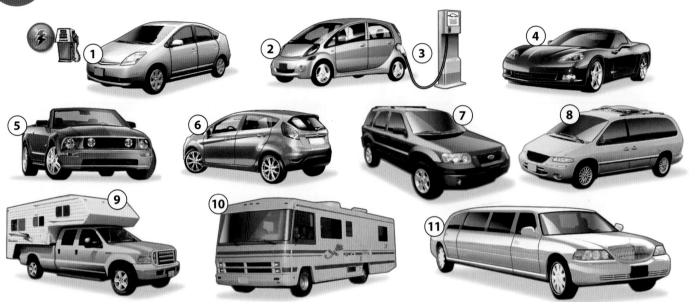

1. **hybrid**
   el híbrido

2. **electric vehicle / EV**
   el vehículo eléctrico

3. **EV charging station**
   la estación de recarga de
   vehículos eléctricos

4. **sports car**
   el automóvil deportivo

5. **convertible**
   el convertible

6. **hatchback**
   el automóvil con puerta trasera

7. **SUV (sport utility vehicle)**
   el SUV (vehículo deportivo utilitario)/
   el vehículo de doble tracción

8. **minivan**
   la miniván/la furgoneta

9. **camper**
   el *camper*

10. **RV (recreational vehicle)**
    el RV (vehículo recreacional)

11. **limousine / limo**
    la limusina

12. **pickup truck**
    el *pickup*/
    la camioneta

13. **cargo van**
    el furgón de carga

14. **tow truck**
    la grúa

15. **tractor-trailer / semi**
    el camión
    semirremolque/
    el tráiler

16. **cab**
    la cabina

17. **trailer**
    el remolque

18. **moving van**
    el camión de
    mudanza

19. **dump truck**
    el camión volquete

20. **tank truck**
    el camión tanque

21. **school bus**
    el ómnibus escolar

More vocabulary

sedan: a 4-door car

coupe: a 2-door car

make and model: the car manufacturer and style: *Ford Fiesta*

Pair practice. Make new conversations.

A: *I have a new car!*

B: *Did you get a hybrid?*

A: *Yes, but I really wanted a sports car.*

Buying a Used Car Compra de un automóvil usado

'09 compact. Only $8,500.

A

'13 sedan. Must sell. Great deal!

A. Look at car ads.
Mire los anuncios de automóviles.

How many miles does it have?

B

FOR SALE

B. Ask the seller about the car.
Pregúntele al vendedor sobre el automóvil.

It's in good condition.

C

C. Take the car to a mechanic.
Lleve el automóvil a un mecánico.

D

It's $8,500.

I can give you $8,000.

D. Negotiate a price.
Negocie un precio.

E

E. Get the title from the seller.
Obtenga el título del vendedor.

F

F. Register the car.
Registre el automóvil.

Taking Care of Your Car El cuidado de su automóvil

G

G. Fill the tank with gas.
Llene el tanque con gasolina.

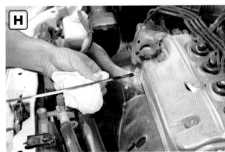

H

H. Check the oil.
Revise el aceite.

I

I. Put in coolant.
Póngale refrigerante.

J

J. Go for a smog and safety check.*
Vaya para que le hagan a su automóvil una inspección de seguridad y control de emisiones.

K

K. Replace the windshield wipers.
Reemplace los limpiaparabrisas.

L

L. Fill the tires with air.
Infle los neumáticos.

*smog check = emissions test

Ways to request service

Please check the oil.
Could you fill the tank?
Put in coolant, please.

Think about it. Discuss.

1. What's good and bad about a used car?
2. Do you like to negotiate car prices? Why or why not?
3. Do you know any good mechanics? Why are they good?

At the Dealer En el concesionario

1. windshield el parabrisas	**5. tire** el neumático/la llanta
2. windshield wipers los limpiaparabrisas	**6. turn signal** la luz direccional
3. side-view mirror el espejo lateral	**7. headlight** la luz delantera
4. hood el capó/la capota	**8. bumper** el parachoques/la defensa

At the Mechanic En el taller del mecánico

9. hubcap / wheel cover el tapacubos/la tapa de rueda	**13. taillight** la luz trasera
10. gas tank el tanque de gasolina	**14. brake light** la luz de freno
11. trunk la maletera/el baúl	**15. tailpipe** el escape
12. license plate la placa/la tablilla	**16. muffler** el silenciador

Under the Hood Debajo del capó

17. fuel injection system el sistema inyector de combustible	**19. radiator** el radiador
18. engine el motor	**20. battery** la batería

Inside the Trunk Dentro de la maletera

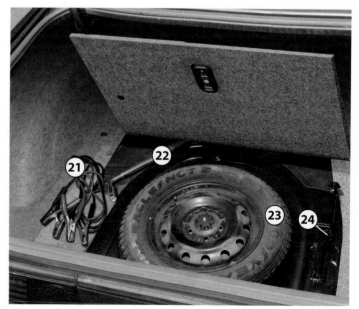

21. jumper cables los cables puente/los cables para pasar corriente	**23. spare tire** el neumático de repuesto/la llanta de repuesto
22. lug wrench la llave de tuerca	**24. jack** el gato hidráulico

The Dashboard and Instrument Panel El tablero y el panel de instrumentos

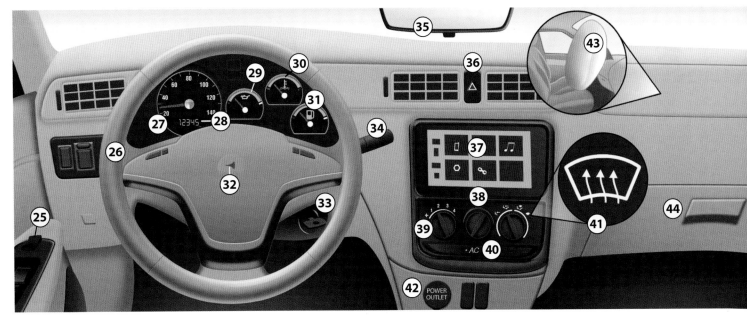

25. door lock
el seguro de puerta

26. steering wheel
el volante/el timón

27. speedometer
el velocímetro

28. odometer
el odómetro

29. oil gauge
el indicador/medidor
de aceite

30. temperature gauge
el indicador/medidor
de temperatura

31. gas gauge
el indicador/medidor
de gasolina

32. horn
el claxon/la bocina

33. ignition
el arranque/la ignición

34. turn signal
la palanca de luz direccional

35. rearview mirror
el espejo retrovisor

36. hazard lights
las luces de peligro

37. touch screen / audio
display
la pantalla táctil/la audiopantalla

38. temperature control dial
el selector de control
de temperatura

39. fan speed
la velocidad del ventilador

40. air conditioning /
AC button
el botón de encendido
del aire acondicionado

41. defroster
el descongelador

42. power outlet
el tomacorriente

43. airbag
la bolsa de aire

44. glove compartment
el compartimiento de
guantes/la guantera

An Automatic Transmission
Una transmisión automática

A Manual Transmission
Una transmisión manual

Inside the Car
Dentro del automóvil

45. brake pedal
el pedal de freno

46. gas pedal /
accelerator
el pedal de gasolina/el
acelerador

47. gearshift
la palanca de cambio
de velocidad

48. handbrake
el freno de mano

49. clutch
el embrague

50. stick shift
la palanca de
velocidades

51. front seat
el asiento delantero

52. seat belt
el cinturón de
seguridad

53. child safety seat
el asiento para niños

54. back seat
el asiento trasero

An Airport *Un aeropuerto*

In the Airline Terminal *En la terminal de la línea aérea*

1. skycap
el maletero

2. check-in kiosk
el quiosco para registrarse

3. ticket agent
el agente de pasajes

4. screening area
el área de control de seguridad

At the Security Checkpoint *En el punto de inspección de seguridad*

5. TSA* agent / security screener
el agente de la TSA/el inspector de
seguridad/el revisor de seguridad

6. bin
la caja

Taking a Flight *Para tomar un vuelo*

A. Check in electronically.
Regístrese
electrónicamente.

B. Check your bags.
Registre su equipaje.

C. Show your boarding pass
and ID.
Muestre su tarjeta
de embarque y su
identificación.

D. Go through security.
Pase por el área de
seguridad.

E. Board the plane.
Aborde el avión.

F. Find your seat.
Encuentre su asiento.

G. Stow your carry-on bag.
Guarde su equipaje
de mano.

H. Fasten your seat belt.
Abróchese el cinturón
de seguridad.

I. Put your cell phone in
airplane mode.
Ponga su teléfono celular
en modo avión.

J. Take off. / Leave.
Despega/se va.

K. Land. / Arrive.
Aterriza/llega.

L. Claim your baggage.
Reclame su equipaje.

* Transportation Security Administration

At the Gate En la puerta

7. arrival and departure monitors
los monitores de salidas y llegadas

8. gate
la puerta

9. boarding area
la zona de embarque

On the Airplane En el avión

10. cockpit
la cabina del piloto

11. pilot
el piloto

12. flight attendant
la aeromoza/la azafata

13. overhead compartment
el compartimiento para el equipaje de mano

14. emergency exit
la salida de emergencia

15. passenger
el pasajero

At Customs En la aduana

16. declaration form
la declaración de aduana

17. customs officer
el agente de aduana

18. luggage / bag
el equipaje

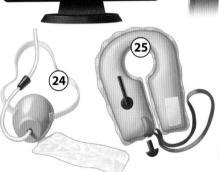

19. e-ticket
el pasaje electrónico

20. mobile boarding pass
la tarjeta de embarque móvil

21. tray table
la mesita

22. turbulence
la turbulencia

23. baggage carousel
el carrusel de equipajes

24. oxygen mask
la máscara de oxígeno

25. life vest
el chaleco salvavidas

26. emergency card
la tarjeta de emergencia

27. reclined seat
el asiento reclinado

28. upright seat
el asiento en posición vertical

29. on time
a tiempo

30. delayed
retrasado

More vocabulary

departure time: the time the plane takes off
arrival time: the time the plane lands
nonstop flight: a trip with no stops

Pair practice. Make new conversations.

A: *Excuse me. Where do I <u>check in</u>?*
B: *At the <u>check-in kiosk</u>.*
A: *Thanks.*

A Road Trip   Un viaje por carretera

Seattle, WA

YELLOWSTONE NATIONAL PARK

1. **ranger**
   el guardaparques/
   el guardabosque

2. **wildlife**
   la fauna silvestre

3. **stars**
   las estrellas

4. **scenery**
   el paisaje

5. **automobile club card**
   la tarjeta del club
   de conductores

6. **destination**
   el destino

A. **pack**
   empacar

B. **be** lost
   estar perdidos

C. **have** a flat tire
   tener un neumático reventado

D. **get** a ticket
   recibir una boleta
   de infracción

E. **run out** of gas
   quedarse sin gasolina

F. **break down**
   averiarse

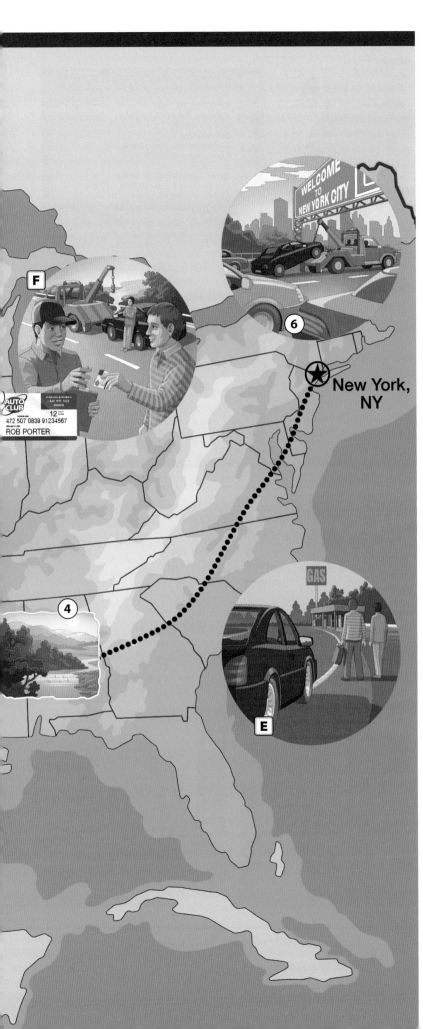

What do you see in the pictures?

1. Where are the young men from? What's their destination?

2. Do they have a good trip? How do you know?

Read the story.

A Road Trip

On July 7, Joe and Rob <u>pack</u> their bags and start their road trip to New York City.

Their first stop is Yellowstone National Park. They listen to a <u>ranger</u> talk about the <u>wildlife</u> in the park. That night they go to bed under a sky full of <u>stars</u>, but Rob can't sleep. He's nervous about the wildlife.

The next day, their GPS breaks. "We're not going in the right direction!" Rob says. "<u>We're lost!</u>"

"No problem," says Joe. "We can take the southern route. We'll see some beautiful <u>scenery</u>."

But there are *a lot* of problems. They <u>have a flat tire</u> in west Texas and <u>get a</u> speeding <u>ticket</u> in east Texas. In South Carolina, they <u>run out of gas</u>. Then, five miles from New York City, their car <u>breaks down</u>. "Now, *this* is a problem," Joe says.

"No, it isn't," says Rob. He calls the number on his <u>automobile club card</u>. Help arrives in 20 minutes.

After 5,000 miles of problems, Joe and Rob finally reach their <u>destination</u>—by tow truck!

Reread the story.

1. Find the phrase "Help arrives." What does that phrase mean?

What do you think?

2. What is good, bad, or interesting about taking a road trip?

3. Imagine you are planning a road trip. Where will you go?

167

Job Search *En busca de trabajo*

A. **set** a goal
   fijarse una meta

B. **write** a resume
   escribir un currículum

C. **contact** references
   comunicarse con los contactos para referencias

D. **research** local companies
   investigar las empresas locales

E. **talk** to friends / **network**
   hablar con los amigos/ **relacionarse** con otros

F. **go** to an employment agency
   ir a una agencia de empleos

G. **look** for help wanted signs
   buscar avisos de "se solicita ayuda"

H. **check** employment websites
   revisar los sitios web de empleo

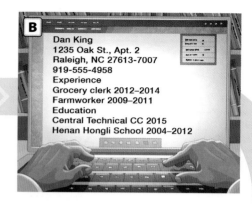

Listen and point. Take turns.

A: *Point to a resume.*
B: *Point to a help wanted sign.*
A: *Point to an application.*

Dictate to your partner. Take turns.

A: *Write contact.*
B: *Is it spelled c-o-n-t-a-c-t?*
A: *Yes, that's right, contact.*

Can you come in for an interview at 9:00?

Tell me about your experience.

I worked in a market for two years.

Take these to aisle 9.

OK!

Mr. King, the job is yours.

I. **apply** for a job
   solicitar un trabajo

J. **complete** an application
   llenar una solicitud

K. **write** a cover letter
   escribir una carta de presentación

L. **submit** an application
   presentar una solicitud

M. **set up** an interview
   concertar una entrevista

N. **go on** an interview
   ir a una entrevista

O. **get** a job /
   be hired
   conseguir un trabajo/
   ser contratado

P. **start** a new job
   empezar a trabajar

Ways to talk about the job search

It's important to <u>set a goal</u>.
You have to <u>write a resume</u>.
It's a good idea to <u>network</u>.

Role play. Talk about a job search.

A: *I'm looking for a job. What should I do?*
B: *Well, it's important to <u>set a goal</u>.*
A: *Yes, and I have to <u>write a resume</u>.*

1. accountant
el contador/la contadora

2. actor
el actor/la actriz

3. administrative assistant
el asistente administrativo/
la asistente administrativa

4. appliance repairperson
el técnico de reparación de
aparatos electrodomésticos

5. architect
el arquitecto/la arquitecta

6. artist
el artista/la artista

7. assembler
el ensamblador/
la ensambladora

8. auto mechanic
el mecánico de
automóviles

9. babysitter
la niñera

10. baker
el panadero/la panadera

11. business owner
el dueño/la dueña
de negocios

12. businessperson
la persona de negocios

13. butcher
el carnicero

14. carpenter
el carpintero

15. cashier
el cajero/la cajera

16. childcare worker
la trabajadora de
cuidado de niños

Ways to ask about someone's job

What's her job?

What does he do?

170 *What does he do for a living?*

Pair practice. Make new conversations.

A: *What does she do for a living?*

B: *She's an accountant. What do they do?*

A: *They're actors.*

17. commercial fisher
el pescador comercial

18. computer software engineer
el ingeniero de *software* de computadoras

19. computer technician
el técnico de computadoras

We have that shirt in red.

20. customer service representative
el representante de servicio al cliente

21. delivery person
el repartidor

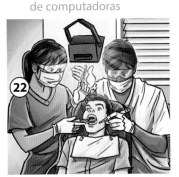

22. dental assistant
el/la asistente dental

23. dock worker
el trabajador portuario/ el estibador

24. electronics repairperson
el técnico de reparación electrónica

25. engineer
el ingeniero

26. firefighter
el bombero

27. florist
la florista

28. gardener
el jardinero

29. garment worker
el empleado/la empleada de una fábrica de ropa

30. graphic designer
el diseñador gráfico

31. hairdresser / hairstylist
la peluquera

32. home healthcare aide
la asistenta de atención de la salud a domicilio

Ways to talk about jobs and occupations

Sue's <u>a garment worker</u>. She works **in** a factory.
Tom's <u>an engineer</u>. He works **for** a large company.
Luis is <u>a gardener</u>. He's self-employed.

Role play. Talk about a friend's new job.

A: *Does your friend like <u>his</u> new job?*
B: *Yes, <u>he</u> does. <u>He's a graphic designer</u>.*
A: *Who does <u>he</u> work for?*

33. homemaker
el ama de casa

34. housekeeper
la limpiadora/la recamarera

你好   He says, "Hi."

35. interpreter / translator
el intérprete/el traductor

36. lawyer
el abogado

37. machine operator
el operador/la operadora
de maquinaria

38. manicurist
la manicurista

**39. medical records
technician**
la técnica de registros
médicos

40. messenger / courier
el mensajero

41. model
la modelo

42. mover
el empleado de una
casa de mudanzas

43. musician
el músico

44. nurse
la enfermera

45. occupational therapist
el/la terapista ocupacional

46. (house) painter
el pintor (de casas)

47. physician assistant
el/la asistente del médico

48. police officer
el/la oficial de policía

Grammar Point: past tense of be

I **was** a machine operator for five years.
She **was** a model from 2010 to 2012.
Before they **were** movers, they **were** painters.

Pair practice. Make new conversations.

A: What was your first job?
B: I was _a musician_. How about you?
A: I was _a messenger for a small company_.

49. postal worker
el empleado/la empleada
de correos

50. printer
el impresor

51. receptionist
la recepcionista

52. reporter
el reportero/la reportera

53. retail clerk
el dependiente de la
tienda minorista

54. sanitation worker
el empleado de servicios
de la higiene pública

55. security guard
el/la guardia de seguridad

56. server
la camarera

Here are some programs
that will help you.

HELPING
HEART
AGENCY

57. social worker
la trabajadora social

58. soldier
el soldado

59. stock clerk
el empleado de almacén

Hello. I'm
calling with a
very special
offer.

60. telemarketer
la persona que realiza
ventas por teléfono

61. truck driver
el camionero

62. veterinarian
el doctor/la doctora
en veterinaria

63. welder
el soldador

Norma's
Story

64. writer / author
el escritor/la escritora/
el autor/la autora

Survey your class. Record the responses.

1. What is one job you don't want to have?
2. Which jobs do you want to have?
Report: *Tom wants to be a(n) ____, but not a(n) ____.*

Think about it. Discuss.

Q: What kind of person makes a good <u>interpreter</u>? Why?
A: To be a(n) ____, you need to be able to ____ and
have ____, because…

173

Planning and Goal Setting La planificación y el establecimiento de objetivos

A. **visit** a career planning center
   visite un centro de planificación profesional

B. **explore** career options
   explore opciones profesionales

C. **take** an interest inventory
   responda un cuestionario de intereses

D. **identify** your technical skills
   identifique sus destrezas técnicas

E. **list** your soft skills
   enumere sus destrezas no técnicas

F. **consult** with a career counselor
   consulte con un orientador de carrera

G. **set** a long-term goal
   fíjese un objetivo de largo plazo

H. **set** a short-term goal
   fíjese un objetivo de corto plazo

I. **attend** a job fair
   asista a una feria de empleos

J. **speak** with a recruiter
   converse con un reclutador

Career Path Trayectoria de carrera

1. basic education
   la educación básica
2. entry-level job
   el trabajo de nivel de entrada
3. training
   la capacitación
4. new job
   el trabajo nuevo

5. college degree
   el diploma universitario
6. career advancement
   la superación profesional
7. continuing education / professional development
   la educación permanente/ el desarrollo profesional
8. promotion
   el ascenso

Types of Training Tipos de capacitación

9. career and technical training / vocational training
   la capacitación profesional y técnica/ la capacitación vocacional
10. apprenticeship
    el aprendizaje
11. internship
    las prácticas/la pasantía
12. on-the-job training
    la capacitación en el trabajo
13. online course
    el curso en línea
14. workshop
    el taller

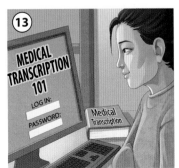

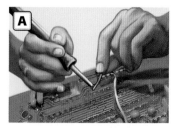

A. assemble components
ensamblar componentes

B. assist medical patients
ayudar a los pacientes

C. cook
cocinar

D. do manual labor
hacer labores manuales

E. drive a truck
conducir un camión

F. fly a plane
volar un avión

G. make furniture
hacer muebles

H. operate heavy machinery
operar maquinaria pesada

I. program computers
programar computadoras

J. repair appliances
reparar electrodomésticos

K. sell cars
vender automóviles

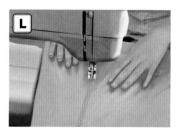

L. sew clothes
coser ropa

4% interest of 5K = x

M. solve math problems
resolver problemas matemáticos

ПРИВЕТ

N. speak another language
hablar otro idioma

O. supervise people
supervisar a las personas

P. take care of children
cuidar niños

Q. teach
enseñar

R. type
mecanografiar

S. use a cash register
usar una caja registradora

T. wait on customers
atender a los clientes

Grammar Point: can, can't

*I am a chef. I **can** cook.*
*I'm not a pilot. I **can't** fly a plane.*
*I **can't** speak French, but I **can** speak Spanish.*

Role play. Talk to a job counselor.

A: *Let's talk about your skills. Can you <u>type</u>?*
B: *<u>No, I can't, but</u> I can <u>use a cash register</u>.*
A: *That's good. What else can you do?*

Customers need better service…

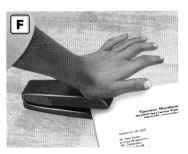

Scan Complete

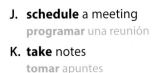

Let's meet at 2:00.
Sure.

Hello. ABC Company. How may I help you?
Please hold.
Mr. Perez, I'm transferring you.

Hello. This is Sue Jones. Please call me.

Message Pad
Call From: Ana Puerta
Tel: 555-1234
Message:
Please Call!

This is Lee Tran. Please call me back.

Office Skills
Las destrezas de oficina

A. **type** a letter
   mecanografiar una carta

B. **enter** data
   introducir datos

C. **transcribe** notes
   transcribir notas

D. **make** copies
   hacer copias

E. **collate** papers
   compaginar papeles

F. **staple**
   engrapar

G. **fax** a document
   enviar un documento por fax

H. **scan** a document
   escanear un documento

I. **print** a document
   imprimir un documento

J. **schedule** a meeting
   programar una reunión

K. **take** notes
   tomar apuntes

L. **organize** materials
   organizar materiales

Telephone Skills
Las destrezas telefónicas

M. **greet** the caller
   saludar al que llama

N. **put** the caller on hold
   poner en espera al que llama

O. **transfer** the call
   transferir la llamada

P. **leave** a message
   dejar un mensaje

Q. **take** a message
   tomar un mensaje

R. **check** messages
   revisar los mensajes

177

Soft Skills   Destrezas no técnicas

Leadership Skills   Las destrezas de liderazgo

A. **solve** problems
resolver problemas

Which is better for us?

B. **think** critically
pensar de manera crítica

Let's do this!

C. **make** decisions
tomar decisiones

Let's take five minutes to review our timeline.

D. **manage** time
administrar el tiempo

Interpersonal Skills   Las destrezas interpersonales

I have three suggestions.

E. **communicate** clearly
comunicarse claramente

Let's start with line 15.

I'll get the data.

I can type.

F. **cooperate** with teammates
cooperar con los compañeros de equipo

On line 15 or 50?

G. **clarify** instructions
aclarar las instrucciones

Good, but fix page 5.

Thank you. I will.

H. **respond** well to feedback
responder bien a los comentarios

Personal Qualities   Las cualidades personales

Your wait time is approximately ten minutes.

1. patient
paciente

We can do this!

2. positive
positiva

You need to sort by date.

Please show me how.

3. willing to learn
dispuesta a aprender

I think this is yours!

Thanks!

4. honest
honrado

Ways to talk about your skills
I **can** solve problems. I communicate clearly.
Ways to talk about your qualities
I **am** patient and honest.

Talk about your skills and abilities.
A: Tell me about your leadership skills.
B: I can solve problems. How about you?
A: I can think critically.

A. **Prepare** for the interview.
   Prepárese para la entrevista.

B. **Dress** appropriately.
   Vístase con ropa adecuada.

C. **Be** neat.
   Esté bien arreglado.

D. **Bring** your resume and ID.
   Lleve su currículum y su identificación.

E. **Don't be** late.
   No llegue tarde.

F. **Be** on time.
   Sea puntual.

Hello, I'm Elias Ortiz.

Hello, Mr. Ortiz. I'm Mrs. Perez.

G. **Turn off** your cell phone.
   Apague su teléfono celular.

H. **Greet** the interviewer.
   Salude al entrevistador.

I. **Shake** hands.
   Estréchense las manos.

Computer skills are important.

I have those skills.

I worked with computers on my last job.

J. **Make** eye contact.
   Haga contacto visual.

K. **Listen** carefully.
   Escuche cuidadosamente.

L. **Talk** about your experience.
   Hable sobre su experiencia.

Do you offer training?

Thank you for your time.

Dear Mrs. Perez, Thank you for the opportunity to meet with you.

M. **Ask** questions.
   Haga preguntas.

N. **Thank** the interviewer.
   Agradézcale al entrevistador.

O. **Write** a thank-you note.
   Escríbale una nota de agradecimiento.

More vocabulary

benefits: health insurance, vacation pay, or other things the employer can offer an employee

inquire about benefits: to ask about benefits

Identify Dan's problem. Brainstorm solutions.

Dan has an interview tomorrow. Making eye contact with strangers is hard for him. He doesn't like to ask questions. What can he do?

179

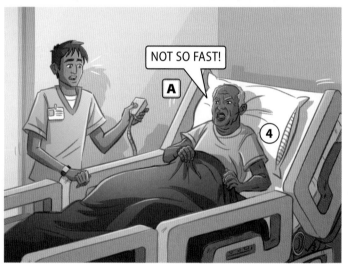

1. facility
   las instalaciones

2. staff
   el personal

3. team player
   el trabajador en equipo

4. resident
   el interno

5. co-worker
   la compañera

6. shift
   el turno

A. **yell**
   gritar

B. **complain**
   quejarse

C. **direct**
   dar instrucciones

D. **distribute**
   repartir

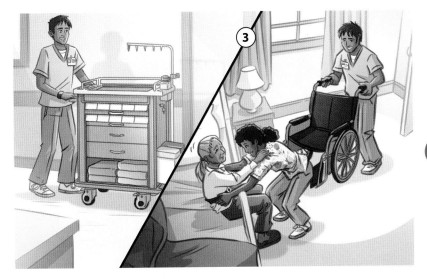

Not 10B, Leo! 10D – down the hall.

How did it go, Leo?

I learned a lot!

	FROM	TO	CNA STAFF
1ST	7:00AM	3:30PM	MARY, LIZ, LEO
2ND	3:00PM	11:30PM	BEN, SARA, TOM
3RD	11:00PM	7:30AM	MEI, KARA, JOSH

What do you see in the pictures?

1. What time does Leo arrive at the nursing home?

2. What other types of workers are on the staff?

3. Is Leo a team player? How do you know?

4. How long was Leo's shift on his first day?

 Read the story.

First Day on the Job

Leo Reyes arrives at the Lakeview nursing home <u>facility</u> at 7 a.m. It's his first day as a CNA. The nurse, Ms. Castro, introduces him to the <u>staff</u>. He meets Lakeview's receptionist, cook, social worker, physical therapists, and the other CNAs. Then it's time for work.

Leo has a positive attitude. He is a <u>team player</u>. He also makes mistakes.

One elderly <u>resident</u> <u>yells</u> at Leo. Another <u>complains</u> about him. Leo goes to the wrong room, but a <u>co-worker</u> <u>directs</u> him to the right one.

The afternoon is better. Leo listens to the residents talk about their careers. He drives the van to the mall. He helps another CNA <u>distribute</u> the afternoon snacks.

At the end of his <u>shift</u>, Ms. Castro asks Leo about his day. He tells her, "I worked hard, made mistakes, and learned a lot!" Ms. Castro smiles and says, "Sounds like a good first day!"

Reread the story.

1. Highlight the word "distribute" in paragraph 4. What other words can you use here?

2. Underline two examples of negative feedback in the story.

What do you think?

3. Should Leo respond to the residents' feedback? Why or why not?

181

1. entrance
   la entrada

2. customer
   el cliente

3. office
   la oficina

4. employer / boss
   la empleadora/la jefa

5. receptionist
   la recepcionista

6. safety regulations
   los reglamentos
   de seguridad

7. time clock
   el reloj registrador/
   el marcador de tiempo

Listen and point. Take turns.

A: *Point to the <u>front entrance</u>.*
B: *Point to the <u>receptionist</u>.*
A: *Point to the <u>time clock</u>.*

Dictate to your partner. Take turns.

A: *Can you spell <u>employer</u>?*
B: *I'm not sure. Is it <u>e-m-p-l-o-y-e-r</u>?*
A: *Yes, that's right.*

8. supervisor
   el supervisor
9. employee
   el empleado
10. payroll clerk
    el encargado
    de nómina
11. pay stub
    el talón de pago
12. wages
    los sueldos
13. deductions
    las deducciones
14. paycheck
    el cheque de pago

Ways to talk about wages

I **earn** $800 a week.
He **makes** $10 an hour.
I'm **paid** $2,000 a month.

Role play. Talk to an employer.

A: *Is everything correct on your paycheck?*
B: *No, it isn't. I make $619 a week, not $519.*
A: *Let's talk to the payroll clerk. Where is she?*

183

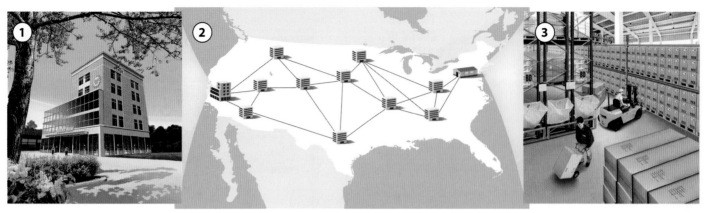

1. corporate offices / headquarters
las oficinas corporativas/la sede central

2. branch locations
las sucursales

3. warehouse
el almacén

4. human resources
recursos humanos

5. research and development
investigación y desarrollo

6. marketing
mercadeo

Sales are up!

7. sales
ventas

8. logistics
logística

9. accounting
contabilidad

10. IT / information technology
TI/tecnología de la información

11. customer service
servicio al cliente

12. building maintenance
mantenimiento de instalaciones

13. security
seguridad

Use the new words.

Look at pages 170–173. Find jobs for each department.
A: *Accountants* work in *accounting*.
B: *Security guards* work in *security*.

Survey your class. Record the responses.

Which department(s) would you like to work in?
Report: *Ten of us would like to work in logistics.*
Nobody wants to work in security.

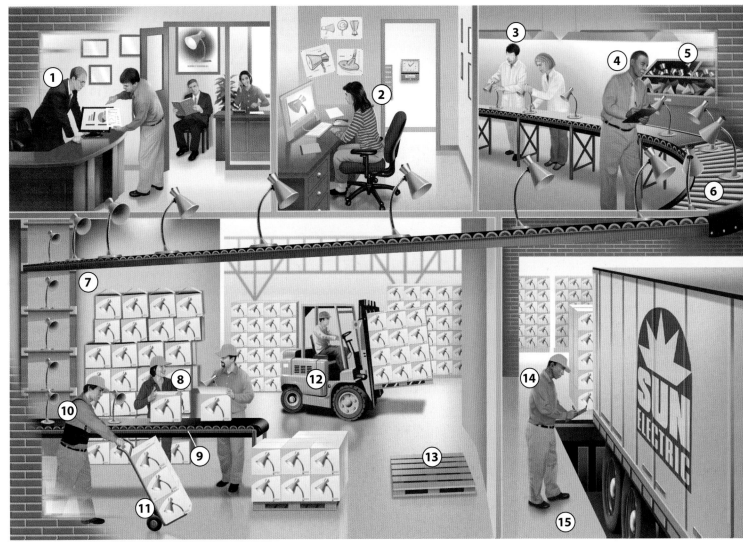

1. factory owner
   el dueño de la fábrica
2. designer
   el diseñador/la diseñadora
3. factory worker
   el obrero
4. line supervisor
   el supervisor de línea/
   de la cadena

5. parts
   las piezas
6. assembly line
   la línea de montaje/
   la línea de ensamblaje
7. warehouse
   la bodega/el almacén
8. packer
   el empacador/
   la empacadora

9. conveyer belt
   la cinta transportadora
10. order puller
    el encargado de pedidos
11. hand truck
    la carretilla de mano
12. forklift
    el elevador de carga

13. pallet
    la paleta
14. shipping clerk
    el dependiente encargado
    del despacho de
    mercadería
15. loading dock
    el muelle de carga

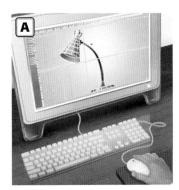

A. **design**
diseñar

B. **manufacture**
fabricar

C. **assemble**
ensamblar/montar/armar

D. **ship**
despachar

185

1. **gardening crew**
   el personal de jardinería

2. **leaf blower**
   el soplador de hojas

3. **wheelbarrow**
   la carretilla

4. **gardening crew leader**
   el jefe del personal de jardinería

5. **landscape designer**
   la diseñadora paisajista

6. **lawn mower**
   la cortadora de césped

7. **shovel**
   la pala

8. **rake**
   el rastrillo

9. **pruning shears**
   las tijeras de podar

10. **trowel**
    el desplantador

11. **hedge clippers**
    las tijeras para setos

12. **weed whacker / weed eater**
    el recortador/el cortador

A. **mow** the lawn
   cortar el césped

B. **trim** the hedges
   podar los setos

C. **rake** the leaves
   rastrillar las hojas

D. **fertilize / feed** the plants
   fertilizar/abonar las plantas

E. **plant** a tree
   plantar un árbol

F. **water** the plants
   regar las plantas

G. **weed** the flower beds
   quitar la maleza de las flores

H. **install** a sprinkler system
   instalar un sistema
   de rociador

Use the new words.
Look at page 53. Name what you can do in the yard.

A: I can _mow the lawn_.
B: I can _weed the flower bed_.

Identify Inez's problem. Brainstorm solutions.

Inez works on a gardening crew. She wants to learn to install sprinklers. The crew leader has no time to teach her. What can she do?

Crops Las siembras

1. rice
   el arroz

2. wheat
   el trigo

3. soybeans
   los frijoles de soya

4. corn
   el maíz

5. alfalfa
   la alfalfa

6. cotton
   el algodón

7. field
   el campo

8. farmworker
   el trabajador agrícola

9. tractor
   el tractor

10. orchard
    la huerta

11. barn
    la granja

12. farm equipment
    el equipo para trabajar
    en el campo

13. farmer / grower
    el agricultor/el cultivador

14. vegetable garden
    el huerto/la huerta de
    verduras y hortalizas

15. livestock
    el ganado

16. vineyard
    la viña

17. corral
    el corral

18. hay
    el heno

19. fence
    la cerca

20. hired hand
    el mozo de campo/
    el peón de labranza

21. cattle
    el ganado

22. rancher
    el ganadero

A. **plant**
   sembrar

B. **harvest**
   cosechar

C. **milk**
   ordeñar

D. **feed**
   alimentar

1. **supply cabinet**
   el gabinete de artículos de oficina

2. **clerk**
   el empleado

3. **janitor**
   el limpiador

4. **conference room**
   la sala de conferencias

5. **executive**
   el ejecutivo/la ejecutiva

6. **presentation**
   la presentación

7. **cubicle**
   el cubículo

8. **office manager**
   el gerente de oficina

9. **desk**
   el escritorio

10. **file clerk**
    el archivista

11. **file cabinet**
    el archivero/el fichero

12. **computer technician**
    el técnico de computadoras

13. **PBX**
    la centralita telefónica

14. **receptionist**
    la recepcionista

15. **reception area**
    el área de recepción

16. **waiting area**
    el área de espera

Ways to greet a receptionist

Good <u>morning</u>. I'm here for a <u>job interview</u>.
Hello. I have a <u>9 a.m.</u> appointment with <u>Mr. Lee</u>.
Hi. I'm here to see <u>Mr. Lee</u>. <u>He's</u> expecting me.

Role play. Talk to a receptionist.

A: Hello. How can I help you?
B: <u>I'm here for a job interview with Mr. Lee</u>.
A: OK. What is your name?

Office Equipment Los equipos de oficina

17. computer
la computadora

18. inkjet printer
la impresora de chorro
de tinta

19. laser printer
la impresora láser

20. scanner
el escáner

21. fax machine
la máquina de fax/el fax

22. paper cutter
la cortadora de papel/
la guillotina

23. photocopier
la fotocopiadora

24. paper shredder
la trituradora de papel

25. calculator
la calculadora

26. electric pencil sharpener
el sacapuntas eléctrico

27. postal scale
la máquina franqueadora

Office Supplies Los artículos de oficina

28. stapler
la engrapadora/la grapadora

29. staples
las grapas

30. clear tape
la cinta adhesiva transparente

31. paper clip
el clip/el sujetapapeles

32. packing tape
la cinta adhesiva para
empacar

33. glue
la goma/la pega

34. rubber band
la liga elástica

35. pushpin
la tachuela

36. correction fluid
el líquido corrector

37. correction tape
la cinta correctora

38. legal pad
el cuaderno de papel de
tamaño oficio

39. sticky notes
el papel de notas adhesivo

40. mailer
el envase especial para
remitir objetos por correo

41. mailing label
la etiqueta engomada
de dirección postal

42. letterhead / stationery
el papel membreteado/
el papel de escribir

43. envelope
el sobre

44. rotary card file
el archivo de tarjetas giratorio

45. ink cartridge
el cartucho de tinta

46. ink pad
la almohadilla de tinta

47. stamp
el sello

48. appointment book
la libreta de citas

49. organizer
el organizador

50. file folder
la carpeta de archivo

189

1. mainframe computer
la computadora central

2. computer operations specialist
la especialista en operaciones informáticas

3. data
los datos

4. cybersecurity
la ciberseguridad

5. virus alert
la alerta antivirus

6. tablet
la tableta

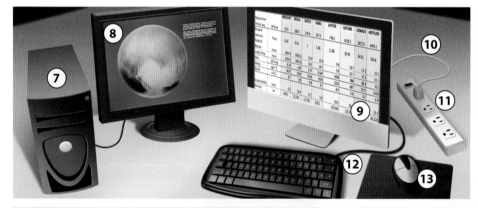

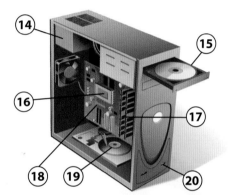

7. tower
la torre/la caja

8. monitor
el monitor

9. desktop computer
la computadora
de escritorio

10. power cord
el cable de alimentación

11. surge protector
el protector de sobretensión

12. cable
el cable

13. mouse
el ratón

14. power supply unit
la fuente de alimentación

15. DVD and CD-ROM drive
la unidad de DVD y CD-ROM

16. microprocessor / CPU
el microprocesador/la CPU

17. RAM (random access memory)
la memoria RAM (memoria de acceso aleatorio)

18. motherboard
la tarjeta madre

19. hard drive
el disco duro

20. USB port
el puerto USB

21. printer
la impresora

22. laptop computer
la computadora portátil

23. keyboard
el teclado

24. track pad
el panel táctil

25. flash drive / thumb drive
la memoria *flash*/
la llave USB

26. hub
el concentrador USB

27. external hard drive
el disco duro externo

28. speaker
el altavoz

Information Technology (IT)

Software / Applications El *software*/las aplicaciones

29. word processing program
el procesador de textos

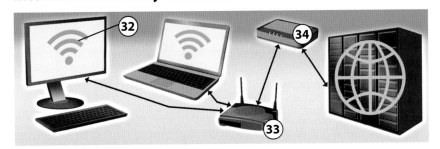

30. spreadsheet program
el programa de hojas de cálculo

31. presentation program
el programa de presentaciones

Internet Connectivity La conexión a Internet

Web Conferencing
La conferencia web

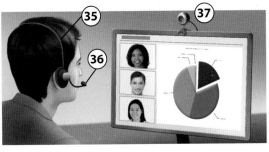

32. Wi-Fi connection
la conexión wifi

33. router
el enrutador

34. modem
el módem

35. headset
el audífono

36. mic / microphone
el micrófono

37. webcam
la cámara web

A. The computer **won't start**.
La computadora **no enciende**.

B. The screen **froze**.
La pantalla **se congeló**.

C. I **can't install** the update.
Yo **no puedo instalar** la actualización.

D. I **can't log on**.
Yo **no puedo iniciar sesión**.

E. It **won't print**.
No imprime.

F. I **can't stream** video.
Yo **no puedo ver la transmisión** del video.

VALET PARKING

1. **doorman**
   el portero

2. **revolving door**
   la puerta giratoria

3. **parking attendant**
   el auxiliar de estacionamiento

4. **concierge**
   el conserje

5. **gift shop**
   la tienda de regalos

6. **bell captain**
   el capitán de botones

7. **bellhop**
   el botones

8. **luggage cart**
   el carrito de maletas

9. **elevator**
   el elevador/el ascensor

10. **guest**
    el huésped

11. **desk clerk**
    el recepcionista

12. **front desk**
    la recepción

13. **guest room**
    la habitación para huésped

14. **double bed**
    la cama matrimonial

15. **king-size bed**
    la cama *king-size*

16. **suite**
    la *suite*

17. **room service**
    el servicio en la habitación

18. **hallway**
    el pasillo

19. **housekeeping cart**
    el carrito de la limpieza

20. **housekeeper**
    la limpiadora/la recamarera

21. **pool service**
    el servicio en la alberca/piscina

22. **pool**
    la alberca/la piscina

23. **maintenance**
    el mantenimiento

24. **gym**
    el gimnasio

25. **meeting room**
    la sala de conferencias

26. **ballroom**
    el salón de bailes

A Restaurant Kitchen Una cocina de restaurante

1. short-order cook
   el cocinero de platos rápidos

2. dishwasher
   el lavaplatos

3. walk-in freezer
   la cámara congeladora/
   el almacén-congelador

4. food preparation worker
   el preparador de comidas

5. storeroom
   el almacén/la bodega

6. sous-chef
   el chef de partida/
   el subchef

7. head chef / executive chef
   el chef principal/
   el chef ejecutivo

Restaurant Dining Comer en un restaurante

8. server
   la mesera/la camarera

9. diner
   el cliente

10. buffet
    el bufé

11. maitre d'
    el jefe de comedor

12. headwaiter
    el capitán de meseros

13. bus person
    el ayudante de meseros

14. banquet room
    la sala de banquetes

15. runner
    el servidor de comida

16. caterer
    la encargada del servicio de
    comida y bebidas

More vocabulary

line cook: short-order cook

wait staff: servers, headwaiters, and runners

Think about it. Discuss.

1. What is the hardest job in a hotel or restaurant? Explain.
   (*Being a _____ is hard because these workers have to _____.*)

2. Pick two jobs on these pages. Compare them.

193

Tools and Building Supplies   Herramientas y materiales de construcción

HAND TOOLS

HARDWARE

POWER TOOLS

1. hammer
   el martillo
2. mallet
   el mazo
3. ax
   el hacha

4. handsaw
   el serrucho
5. hacksaw
   la sierra de arco
6. C-clamp
   la abrazadera en forma de C

7. pliers
   los alicates
8. electric drill
   el taladro eléctrico
9. circular saw
   la sierra circular

10. jigsaw
    la sierra alternativa vertical
11. power sander
    la lijadora eléctrica
12. router
    la buriladora/
    el contorneador

26. vise
    el tornillo de banco/
    la prensa de tornillo
27. blade
    la cuchilla
28. drill bit
    la broca/la barrena
29. level
    el nivel

30. screwdriver
    el destornillador
31. Phillips screwdriver
    el destornillador de estrella/el
    destornillador Phillips
32. machine screw
    el tornillo para máquina
33. wood screw
    el tornillo para madera

34. nail
    el clavo
35. bolt
    el perno
36. nut
    la tuerca
37. washer
    la arandela

38. toggle bolt
    el tornillo articulado
39. hook
    el gancho
40. eye hook
    el gancho de ojo
41. chain
    la cadena

Use the new words.
Look at pages 62–63. Name the tools you see.

A: *There's a hammer.*
B: *There's a pipe wrench.*

Survey your class. Record the responses.

1. Are you good with tools?
2. Which tools do you have at home?
Report: *75% of us are… Most of us have…*

194

ELECTRICAL PLUMBING LUMBER PAINT

13. wire
el alambre

14. extension cord
el cordón prolongador/
la extensión

15. bungee cord
el cable elástico

16. yardstick
la regla

17. pipe
el tubo

18. fittings
los accesorios

19. 2 x 4 (two by four)
la madera de 2 x 4
(dos por cuatro)

20. particle board
la tabla de partículas

21. spray gun
la pistola rociadora

22. paintbrush
la brocha

23. paint roller
el rodillo de pintar

24. wood stain
la tintura para madera

25. paint
la pintura

42. wire stripper
los alicates pelacables

43. electrical tape
la cinta de aislar/
la cinta aislante

44. work light
la luz de trabajo

45. tape measure
la cinta de medir

46. outlet cover
la tapa del tomacorriente

47. pipe wrench
la llave corrediza/la llave
inglesa para tubos

48. adjustable wrench
la llave ajustable

49. duct tape
la cinta adhesiva para conductos

50. plunger
el desatascador/el chupón

51. paint pan
la bandeja de pintura

52. scraper
el raspador/la espátula

53. masking tape
la cinta adhesiva protectora

54. drop cloth
el trapo para cubrir

55. chisel
el cincel

56. sandpaper
el papel de lija

57. plane
el cepillo

Role play. Find an item in a building supply store.

A: *Where can I find particle board?*
B: *It's on the back wall, in the lumber section.*
A: *Great. And where are the nails?*

Identify Jean's problem. Brainstorm solutions.

Jean borrowed Jody's drill last month. Now she can't find it. She doesn't know what to do!

Construction   La construcción

1. construction worker
el obrero de construcción

2. ladder
la escalera

3. I beam / girder
la viga I/la viga maestra

4. scaffolding
el andamiaje

5. cherry picker
la grúa alzacarro

6. bulldozer
el tractor nivelador/el buldózer

7. crane
la grúa

8. backhoe
la retroexcavadora

9. jackhammer / pneumatic drill
el martillo perforador/
el taladro neumático

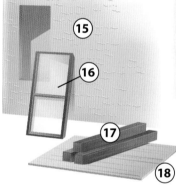
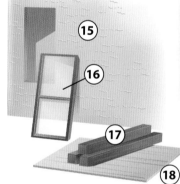

10. concrete
el cemento

11. tile
las losas/
las baldosas

12. bricks
los ladrillos

13. trowel
la llana de albañil

14. insulation
el aislamiento

15. stucco
el estuco

16. windowpane
la hoja de vidrio

17. wood / lumber
la madera/el madero

18. plywood
la madera terciada/
contrachapada

19. drywall
la pared de yeso

20. shingles
las tejas de madera

21. pickax
el azadón de pico

22. shovel
la pala

23. sledgehammer
el mazo

A. paint
pintar

B. lay bricks
colocar ladrillos

C. install tile
instalar losas

D. hammer
martillar

Safety Hazards and Hazardous Materials Peligros de seguridad y materiales peligrosos

1. careless worker
el trabajador descuidado

2. careful worker
el trabajador cuidadoso

3. poisonous fumes
los gases venenosos

4. broken equipment
el equipo averiado o roto

5. frayed cord
el cable desgastado

6. slippery floor
el piso resbaloso

7. radioactive materials
los materiales radioactivos

8. flammable liquids
los líquidos inflamables

Safety Equipment Equipo de seguridad

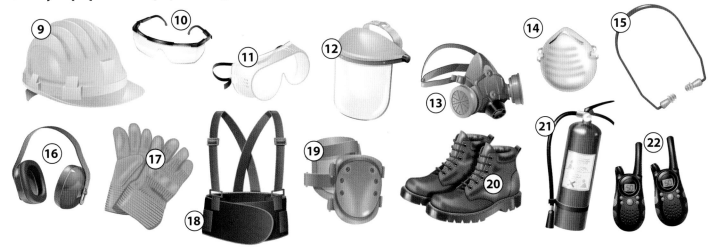

9. hard hat
el casco protector

10. safety glasses
las gafas de seguridad

11. safety goggles
las gafas protectoras

12. safety visor
la visera de seguridad

13. respirator
la careta antigás

14. particle mask
la mascarilla

15. earplugs
los tapones para el oído

16. earmuffs
las orejeras

17. work gloves
los guantes de trabajo

18. back support belt
la correa de soporte
para la espalda

19. knee pads
las rodilleras

20. safety boots
las botas de seguridad

21. fire extinguisher
el extintor/extinguidor
de incendios

22. two-way radio
el/la radio bidireccional

197

A Bad Day at Work
Un mal día en el trabajo

1. **dangerous**
   peligroso
2. **clinic**
   la clínica
3. **budget**
   el presupuesto
4. **floor plan**
   la planta
5. **contractor**
   el contratista
6. **electrical hazard**
   el peligro eléctrico
7. **wiring**
   el cableado
8. **bricklayer**
   el albañil
A. **call in** sick
   llamar para avisar que uno está enfermo

198

What do you see in the pictures?

1. How many workers are there? How many are working?

2. Why did two workers call in sick?

3. What is dangerous at the construction site?

Read the story.

A Bad Day at Work

Sam Lopez is the <u>contractor</u> for a new building. He makes the schedule and supervises the <u>budget</u>. He also solves problems. Today there are a lot of problems.

Two <u>bricklayers</u> <u>called in sick</u> this morning. So Sam has only one bricklayer at work. One hour later, a construction worker fell. He had to go to the <u>clinic</u>.

Construction work is <u>dangerous</u>. Sam always tells his workers to be careful. Yesterday he told them about the new <u>wiring</u> on the site. It's an <u>electrical hazard</u>.

Right now, the building owner is in Sam's office. Her new <u>floor plan</u> has 25 more offices. Sam has a headache. Maybe he needs to call in sick tomorrow.

Reread the story.

1. Make a timeline of the events in this story. What happened first? next? last?

2. Find the sentence "He had to go to the clinic" in paragraph 2. Is "he" the worker or Sam? How do you know?

What do you think?

3. Give examples of good reasons (or excuses) to give when you can't come in to work. Give an example of a bad excuse. Why is it bad?

4. Imagine you are Sam. What do you tell the building owner? Why?

Schools and Subjects
Las escuelas y materias

1. preschool / nursery school
   la escuela de párvulos/ el centro de enseñanza preescolar

2. elementary school
   la escuela primaria

3. middle school / junior high school
   la escuela intermedia

4. high school
   la escuela secundaria

5. career and technical school / vocational school
   la escuela profesional y técnica/el instituto de capacitación vocacional

6. community college
   el instituto de enseñanza superior

7. college / university
   la universidad

8. adult school
   la escuela para adultos

Listen and point. Take turns.

A: Point to the <u>preschool</u>.
B: Point to the <u>high school</u>.
A: Point to the <u>adult school</u>.

Dictate to your partner. Take turns.

A: Write <u>preschool</u>.
B: Is that <u>p-r-e-s-c-h-o-o-l</u>?
A: Yes, that's right.

9. How does Ishmael see the whale?

It's evil.

But here it says …

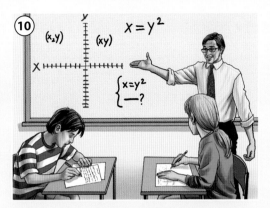

$x = y^2$

(x_2y) (xy)

X

$\begin{cases} x = y^2 \\ —? \end{cases}$

11. H_2O →

12. US Civil War
1861–1865
Reasons for the war:

A –
B –
C –

9. **language arts**
   las artes del lenguaje

10. **math**
    las matemáticas

11. **science**
    las ciencias

12. **history**
    la historia

13. **world languages**
    los idiomas
    del mundo

14. **English language instruction**
    la enseñanza de inglés

15. **arts**
    las artes

16. **music**
    la música

17. **physical education**
    la educación física

13.

Muy bien!

GENTE | COSAS
estudiante | lápiz

很好

人 | 物
学生 | 铅笔

14. Good work!

PEOPLE | THINGS
student | pencil

15.

16.

17.

More vocabulary

core course: a subject students have to take.
Math is a core course.
elective: a subject students choose to take. Art is an elective.

Pair practice. Make new conversations.

A: *I go to a community college.*
B: *What subjects are you taking?*
A: *I'm taking history and science.*

1
factory

1. word
la palabra

2
I worked in a factory.

2. sentence
la oración

3
Little by little, work and success came to me. My first job wasn't good. I worked in a small factory. Now, I help manage two factories.

3. paragraph
el párrafo

4

4. essay
el ensayo/la composición

Parts of an Essay
Las partes de un ensayo

5. title
el título

6. introduction
la introducción

7. evidence
la prueba

8. body
el cuerpo

9. conclusion
la conclusión

10. quotation
la cita

11. citation
la fuente de la cita

12. footnote
la nota al pie de la página

13. source
la fuente

Carlos Lopez
Eng. Comp.
10/03/16

5 Success in the U.S.

6 I came to Los Angeles from Mexico in 2006. I had no job, no friends, and no family here. I was homesick and scared, but I did not go home. I took English classes (always at night) and I studied hard. I believed in my future success!

7 According to the U.S. Census, more than 400,000 new immigrants come to the U.S. every year.[1] Most of us need to find work. During my first year here, my routine was the same: get up; look for work; go to class; go to bed. I had to take jobs with long hours and low pay. Often I had two or three jobs.

8 Little by little, work and success came to me. My first job wasn't good. I worked in a small factory. Now, I help manage two factories.

9 Hard work makes success possible, and **10** "men were born to succeed, not to fail" (Thoreau, 1853). My story **11** demonstrates the truth of that statement.

12 [1] U.S. Census, 2015 **13**

Punctuation
La puntuación

14. period
el punto

15. question mark
el signo de interrogación

16. exclamation mark / exclamation point
el signo de admiración

17. comma
la coma

18. quotation marks
las comillas

19. apostrophe
el apóstrofe

20. colon
los dos puntos

21. semicolon
el punto y coma

22. parentheses
los paréntesis

23. hyphen
el guion

Writing Rules Las reglas de escritura

A
Carlos
Mexico
Los Angeles

A. Capitalize names.
Escribir en mayúsculas la inicial de los nombres.

B
Hard work makes success possible.

B. Capitalize the first letter in a sentence.
Escribir en mayúsculas la primera letra de una oración.

C
I was homesick and scared, but I did not go home.

C. Use punctuation.
Usar la puntuación.

D
I came to Los Angeles from Mexico in 2006. I had no job, no friends, and no family here. I was homesick and scared, but I did not go home. I took English classes (always at night) and I studied hard. I believed in my future success!

D. Indent the first sentence in a paragraph.
Sangrar la primera oración de un párrafo.

Ways to ask for suggestions on your compositions

What do you think of this title?
Is this paragraph OK? Is the punctuation correct?
Do you have any suggestions for the conclusion?

Pair practice. Make new conversations.

A: What do you think of this *title*?
B: *I think you need to revise it.*
A: *Thanks. How would you revise it?*

The Writing Process El proceso de escritura

PREWRITING

E. **Think about** the assignment.
Piense sobre la tarea.

F. **Brainstorm** ideas.
Fórmese ideas.

G. **Organize** your ideas.
Organice las ideas.

WRITING AND REVISING

H. **Write** a first draft.
Escriba un primer borrador.

I. **Edit**. / **Proofread**.
Edítelo/corríjalo.

J. **Revise**. / **Rewrite**.
Revíselo/reescríbalo.

SHARING AND RESPONDING

K. **Get** feedback.
Reciba comentarios.

L. **Write** a final draft.
Escriba el borrador final.

M. **Turn in / Hand in** your paper.
Entregue/presente su composición.

Survey your class. Record the responses.

1. Do you prefer to write essays or read them?
2. Which is more difficult: writing a first draft or revising?
Report: *Five people I surveyed said ___.*

Think about it. Discuss.

1. What are interesting topics for essays?
2. Do you like to read quotations? Why or why not?
3. In which jobs are writing skills important?

Integers Los números enteros

$$\ldots -4\ -3\ -2\ -1\ 0\ 1\ 2\ 3\ 4\ \ldots$$

① ②

1. negative integers
los números enteros negativos

2. positive integers
los números enteros positivos

Fractions Las fracciones

③ 1, 3, 5, 7, 9, 11 …

④ 2, 4, 6, 8, 10 …

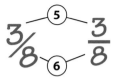

3. odd numbers
los números impares

4. even numbers
los números pares

5. numerator
el numerador

6. denominator
el denominador

Math Operations Las operaciones matemáticas

A. add
sumar

B. subtract
restar

C. multiply
multiplicar

D. divide
dividir

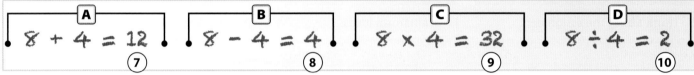

$$8 + 4 = 12 \quad 8 - 4 = 4 \quad 8 \times 4 = 32 \quad 8 \div 4 = 2$$

⑦ ⑧ ⑨ ⑩

7. sum
la suma

8. difference
la diferencia

9. product
el producto

10. quotient
el cociente

A Math Problem Un problema matemático

⑪ Tom is 10 years older than Kim. Next year he will be twice as old as Kim. How old is Tom this year?

⑫ x = Kim's age now
$x + 10$ = Tom's age now
$x + 1$ = Kim's age next year
$2(x + 1)$ = Tom's age next year

$x + 10 + 1 = 2(x + 1)$
$x + 11 = 2x + 2$ ⑬
$11 - 2 = 2x - x$

$x = 9$, Kim is 9, Tom is 19 ⑭

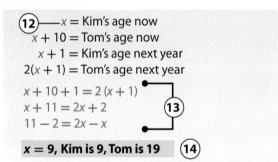

⑮

horizontal axis

vertical axis

11. word problem
un problema expresado con palabras

12. variable
la variable

13. equation
la ecuación

14. solution
la solución

15. graph
la gráfica

Types of Math Las ramas de las matemáticas

⑯ How much are they?

x = the sale price
$x = 79.00 - .40(79.00)$
$x = \$47.40$

16. algebra
el álgebra

⑰ How many do I need?

area of path = 24 square ft.
area of brick = 2 square ft.
$24 / 2$ = 12 bricks

17. geometry
la geometría

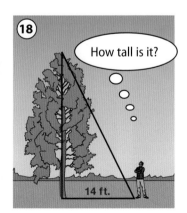

⑱ How tall is it?

14 ft.

$\tan 63° = \text{height} / 14 \text{ feet}$
height = 14 feet $(\tan 63°)$
height $\approx$ 27.48 feet

18. trigonometry
la trigonometría

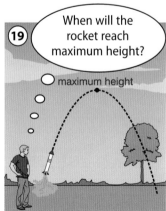

⑲ When will the rocket reach maximum height?

maximum height

$s(t) = -\frac{1}{2} gt^2 + V_0 t + h$
$s^{l}(t) = -gt + V_0 = 0$
$t = V_0 / g$

19. calculus
el cálculo

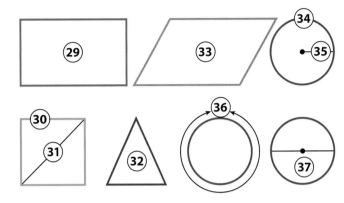

Lines Las líneas

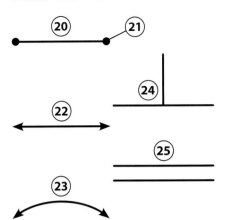

Angles Los ángulos

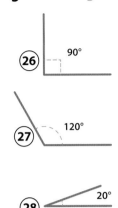

90°

120°

20°

Shapes Las formas

20. line segment
el segmento de línea

21. endpoint
el punto extremo

22. straight line
la línea recta

23. curved line
la línea curva

24. perpendicular lines
las líneas perpendiculares

25. parallel lines
las líneas paralelas

26. right angle / 90° angle
el ángulo recto/
el ángulo de 90°

27. obtuse angle
el ángulo obtuso

28. acute angle
el ángulo agudo

29. rectangle
el rectángulo

30. square
el cuadrado

31. diagonal
la diagonal

32. triangle
el triángulo

33. parallelogram
el paralelogramo

34. circle
el círculo

35. radius
el radio

36. circumference
la circunferencia

37. diameter
el diámetro

Geometric Solids Los sólidos geométricos

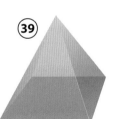
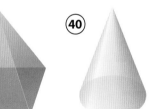

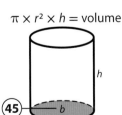

Measuring Area and Volume
La medición del área y el volumen

$\ell \times w = $ area

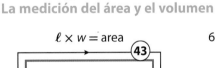

w

ℓ

$6 \times f = $ surface area

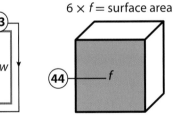

f

38. cube
el cubo

39. pyramid
la pirámide

40. cone
el cono

43. perimeter
el perímetro

44. face
el lado

$\pi \times r^2 \times h = $ volume

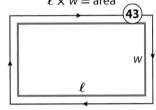

h

b

$\frac{4}{3} \times \pi \times r^3 = $ volume

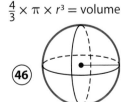

$\pi \approx 3.14$

41. cylinder
el cilindro

42. sphere
la esfera

45. base
la base

46. pi
pi

Survey your class. Record the responses.

1. Is division easy or difficult?

2. Is algebra easy or difficult?

Report: _50% of the class thinks ____ is difficult._

Think about it. Discuss.

1. What's the best way to learn mathematics?

2. How can you find the area of your classroom?

3. Which jobs use math? Which don't?

Biology   La biología

1. organisms
   los organismos

2. biologist
   el biólogo

3. slide
   el portaobjetos

4. cell
   la célula

5. cell wall
   la pared celular

6. cell membrane
   la membrana de
   la célula

7. nucleus
   el núcleo

8. chromosome
   el cromosoma

9. cytoplasm
   el citoplasma

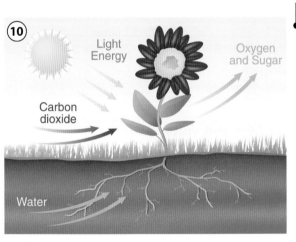

10. photosynthesis
    la fotosíntesis

11. habitat
    el hábitat

12. vertebrates
    los vertebrados

13. invertebrates
    los invertebrados

A Microscope   Un microscopio

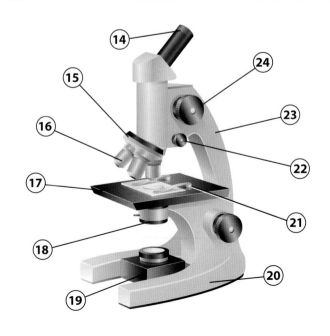

14. eyepiece
    el ocular

15. revolving nosepiece
    el revólver

16. objective
    el objetivo

17. stage
    la platina

18. diaphragm
    el condensador

19. light source
    el foco

20. base
    la base

21. stage clips
    las pinzas

22. fine adjustment knob
    el tornillo micrométrico

23. arm
    el brazo

24. coarse adjustment knob
    el tornillo macrométrico

Chemistry La química

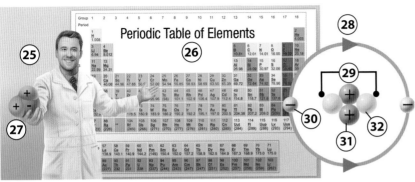

25. chemist
el químico

26. periodic table
la tabla periódica

27. molecule
la molécula

28. atom
el átomo

29. nucleus
el núcleo

30. electron
el electrón

Physics La física

31. proton
el protón

32. neutron
el neutrón

33. physicist
el físico

34. formula
la fórmula

35. prism
el prisma

36. magnet
el imán

A Science Lab Un laboratorio de ciencias

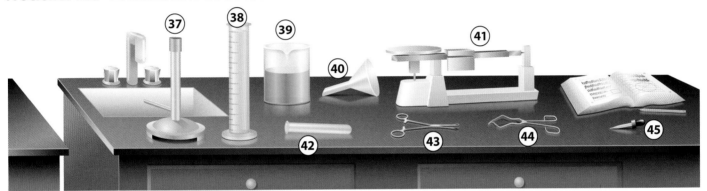

37. Bunsen burner
el quemador Bunsen

38. graduated cylinder
el cilindro graduado

39. beaker
el vaso de laboratorio

40. funnel
el embudo

41. balance / scale
la balanza/la báscula

42. test tube
el tubo de pruebas

43. forceps
las tenazas

44. crucible tongs
las tenazas de crisol

45. dropper
el gotero

An Experiment Un experimento

Salt and sugar crystals will grow the same way.

Salt crystals grow faster than sugar crystals.

A. State a hypothesis.
Establezca una hipótesis.

B. Do an experiment.
Haga un experimento.

C. Observe.
Observe.

D. Record the results.
Anote los resultados.

E. Draw a conclusion.
Saque una conclusión.

207

U.S. History   La historia de EE. UU.

Colonial Period El período colonial

1. thirteen colonies
   las trece colonias

2. colonists
   los colonos

3. Native American
   los indígenas
   norteamericanos

4. slaves
   los esclavos

5. Declaration of Independence
   la Declaración de Independencia

6. First Continental Congress
   el primer congreso continental

7. founders
   los fundadores

8. Revolutionary War
   la guerra de la
   Independencia de EE. UU.

9. redcoat
   los casacas rojas

10. minuteman
    los milicianos

11. first president
    el primer
    presidente

12. Constitution
    la Constitución

13. Bill of Rights
    la Declaración
    de Derechos

Western Expansion
803–1893

Civil War
1861–1865

World War I
1914–1918

Jazz Age
1920–1929

World War II
1941–1945

Civil Rights Movement
1954–1972

Information Age
1959–now

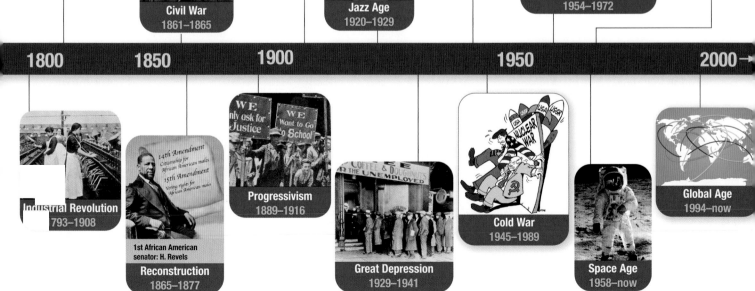

1800　　**1850**　　**1900**　　**1950**　　**2000 →**

Industrial Revolution
793–1908

1st African American senator: H. Revels
Reconstruction
1865–1877

Progressivism
1889–1916

Great Depression
1929–1941

Cold War
1945–1989

Space Age
1958–now

Global Age
1994–now

Civilizations Las civilizaciones

Pyramids Parthenon

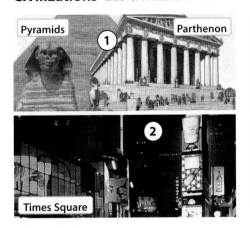

Times Square

Julius Caesar

King Sobhuza II

Benito Juárez

3

4

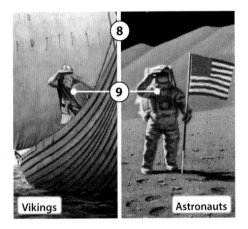

Qin Shi Huang

Queen Elizabeth I

Benito Mussolini

Shinzo Abe

1. ancient
antiguas

2. modern
modernas

3. emperor
el emperador

4. monarch
el monarca

5. president
el presidente

6. dictator
el dictador

7. prime minister
el primer ministro

Historical Terms Los términos históricos

Vikings Astronauts

8. exploration
la exploración

9. explorer
el explorador

10. war
la guerra

11. army
el ejército

12. immigration
la inmigración

13. immigrant
el inmigrante

Wolfgang Mozart Duke Ellington

Susan B. Anthony César Chávez

Thomas Edison Guillermo Camarena

14. composer
el compositor

15. composition
la composición

16. political movement
el movimiento político

17. activist
el activista

18. inventor
el inventor

19. invention
la invención

Creating a Document   La creación de un documento

A. **open** the program
   abra el programa

B. **create** a new document
   cree un documento nuevo

C. **type**
   teclee/mecanografíe

D. **save** the document
   guarde el documento

E. **close** the document
   cierre el documento

F. **quit** the program
   salga del programa

Selecting and Changing Text   Seleccionar y modificar texto

G. **click** on the screen
   haga clic en la pantalla

H. **double-click** to select a word
   haga doble clic para seleccionar una palabra

I. **delete** a word
   elimine una palabra

J. **drag** to select text
   arrastre el cursor para seleccionar el texto

K. **copy** text
   copie el texto

L. **paste** text
   pegue el texto

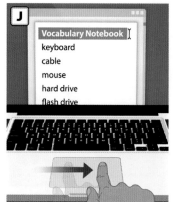

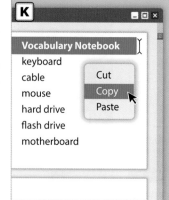

More vocabulary

keyboard shortcut: use of the keys on the keyboard to cut, copy, paste, etc. For example, press "control" on a PC ("command" on a Mac) and "C" to copy text.

Identify Diego's problem. Brainstorm solutions.

Diego is nervous around computers. He needs to complete an online job application. His brother, Luis, offers to apply for him. What could Diego do?

Moving around the Screen Moverse por la pantalla

M. scroll
desplace la imagen

N. use the arrow keys
use las teclas de flecha

O. create a username
cree un nombre de usuario

P. create a password
cree una contraseña

Q. reenter the password /
type the password again
vuelva a ingresar la contraseña/
teclee la contraseña de nuevo

Registering an Account Abrir una cuenta

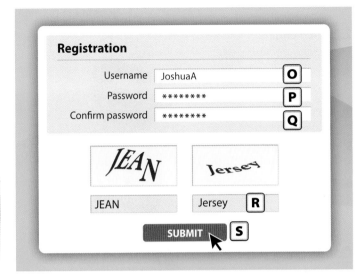

R. type the verification code
teclee el código de verificación

S. click submit
haga clic en enviar

Sending Email Enviar correo electrónico

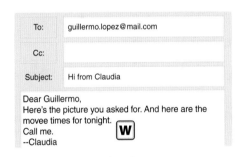

T. log in to your account
inicie sesión en su cuenta

U. address the email
escriba la dirección del destinatario
del correo electrónico

V. type the subject
teclee el asunto

W. compose / write the message
redacte/escriba el mensaje

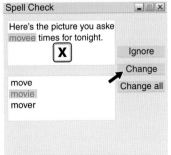

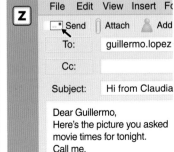

X. check your spelling
revise la ortografía

Y. attach a file
adjunte un archivo

Z. send the email
envíe el correo electrónico

Internet Research   Búsqueda en Internet

1. research question
el interrogante de la investigación

2. search engine
el motor de búsqueda

3. search box
el campo de búsqueda

4. keywords
las palabras clave

5. search results
los resultados de la búsqueda

6. links
los enlaces

Conducting Research   Llevar a cabo una investigación

A. **select** a search engine
seleccione un motor de búsqueda

B. **type** in a phrase
teclee una frase

C. **type** in a question
teclee una pregunta

D. **click** the search icon / **search**
haga clic en el icono de búsqueda/**buscar**

E. **look** at the results
revise los resultados

F. **click** on a link
haga clic en un enlace

G. **bookmark** a site
marque como favorito un sitio

H. **keep** a record of sources
lleve un registro de las fuentes

I. **cite** sources
cite las fuentes

More vocabulary

research: to search for and record information that answers a question

investigate: to research a problem or situation

Ways to talk about your research

My research shows ____.

According to my research, ____.

These are the results of my research: ____.

7. menu bar
la barra de menús

8. browser window
la ventana del navegador

9. back button
el botón de retorno

10. URL / website address
el URL/la dirección
de un sitio web

11. refresh button
el botón actualizar

12. web page
la página web

13. source
la fuente

14. tab
la pestaña

15. drop-down menu
el menú desplegable

16. content
el contenido

17. pop-up ad
el aviso emergente

18. video player
el reproductor de video

19. social media links
los enlaces a redes
sociales

20. date
la fecha

Internet Research: online practice

Type "practice" in the search bar. Add more keywords. ("ESL vocabulary," etc.)

Report: *I found <u>vocabulary</u> practice on a site called ____.*

Think about it. Discuss.

1. Which is better for Internet research: searching with a question, a phrase, or keywords? Explain.
2. Do you enjoy research? Why or why not?

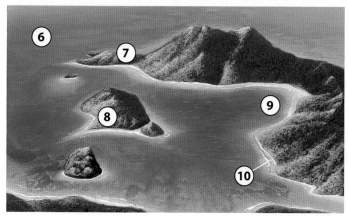

1. **rain forest**
   el bosque húmedo/
   la selva tropical
   húmeda

2. **waterfall**
   la cascada/el salto
   de agua/la catarata

3. **river**
   el río

4. **desert**
   el desierto

5. **sand dune**
   la duna

6. **ocean**
   el océano

7. **peninsula**
   la península

8. **island**
   la isla

9. **bay**
   la bahía

10. **beach**
    la playa

11. **forest**
    el bosque

12. **shore**
    la orilla

13. **lake**
    el lago

14. **mountain peak**
    el pico/la cima
    de la montaña

15. **mountain range**
    la cordillera/
    la sierra

16. **hills**
    las colinas

17. **canyon**
    el cañón

18. **valley**
    el valle

19. **plains**
    el llano/la llanura

20. **meadow**
    la pradera/el prado

21. **pond**
    el estanque/
    la charca/la laguna

More vocabulary

body of water: a river, a lake, or an ocean
stream / creek: a very small river
inhabitants: the people and animals living in a habitat

Survey your class. Record the responses.

1. Would you rather live by the ocean or a lake?
2. Would you rather live in a desert or a rainforest?
Report: *Fifteen of us would rather ____ than ____.*

The Solar System and the Planets El sistema solar y los planetas

Sun

asteroid belt

orbit

1. Mercury Mercurio	**3.** Earth Tierra	**5.** Jupiter Júpiter	**7.** Uranus Urano
2. Venus Venus	**4.** Mars Marte	**6.** Saturn Saturno	**8.** Neptune Neptuno

PHASES OF THE MOON

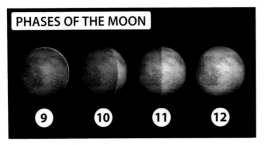

SPACE

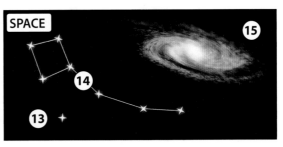

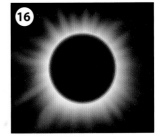

9. new moon la luna nueva	**11.** quarter moon el cuarto menguante	**13.** star la estrella	**15.** galaxy la galaxia
10. crescent moon la media luna	**12.** full moon la luna llena	**14.** constellation la constelación	**16.** solar eclipse el eclipse solar

SPACE EXPLORATION

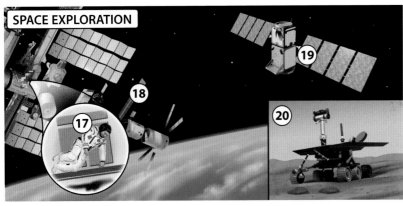

ASTRONOMY

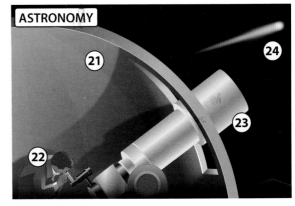

17. astronaut el astronauta	**19.** satellite el satélite	**21.** observatory el observatorio	**23.** telescope el telescopio
18. space station la estación espacial	**20.** probe / rover el astromóvil/el vehículo de exploración espacial	**22.** astronomer el astrónomo	**24.** comet el cometa

More vocabulary

lunar eclipse: when the moon is in the earth's shadow
Big Dipper: a famous part of the constellation Ursa Major
Sirius: the brightest star in the night sky

Think about it. Discuss.

1. Do you want to travel in space? Why or why not?
2. Who should pay for space exploration? Why?
3. What do you like best about the night sky?

Trees and Plants Árboles y plantas

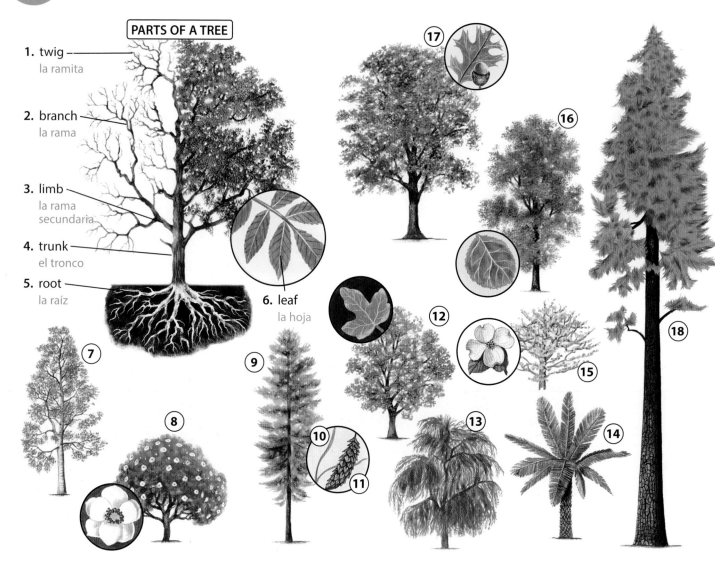

PARTS OF A TREE

1. twig
   la ramita
2. branch
   la rama
3. limb
   la rama secundaria
4. trunk
   el tronco
5. root
   la raíz
6. leaf
   la hoja

7. birch
   el abedul
8. magnolia
   la magnolia
9. pine
   el pino

10. needle
    la aguja
11. pine cone
    la piña/el cono
12. maple
    el arce

13. willow
    el sauce
14. palm
    la palma
15. dogwood
    el cornejo/el cerezo silvestre

16. elm
    el olmo
17. oak
    el roble
18. redwood
    la secoya

Plants Las plantas

19. holly
    el acebo
20. berries
    las bayas

21. cactus
    el cactus
22. vine
    la enredadera

23. poison sumac
    el zumaque venenoso
24. poison oak
    el árbol de las pulgas

25. poison ivy
    la hiedra venenosa

Parts of a Flower Partes de una flor

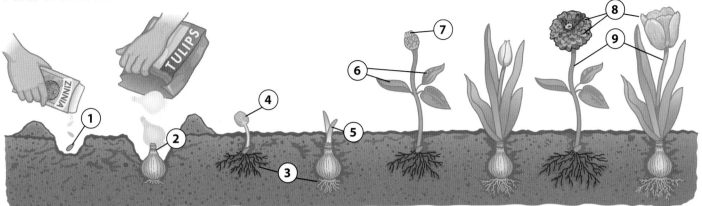

1. **seed**
   la semilla

2. **bulb**
   el bulbo

3. **roots**
   las raíces

4. **seedling**
   la plántula/el pimpollo

5. **shoot**
   el brote

6. **leaves**
   las hojas

7. **bud**
   el capullo

8. **petals**
   los pétalos

9. **stems**
   los tallos

10. **sunflower**
    el girasol

11. **tulip**
    el tulipán

12. **hibiscus**
    el hibisco

13. **marigold**
    la maravilla/el clavelón

14. **daisy**
    la margarita

15. **rose**
    la rosa

16. **iris**
    el lirio

17. **crocus**
    el azafrán

18. **gardenia**
    la gardenia

19. **orchid**
    la orquídea

20. **carnation**
    el clavel

21. **chrysanthemum**
    el crisantemo

22. **jasmine**
    el jazmín

23. **violet**
    la violeta

24. **poinsettia**
    la flor de Nochebuena/
    la flor de Pascua

25. **daffodil**
    el narciso atrompetado/
    el trompón

26. **lily**
    la azucena/el lirio

27. **houseplant**
    la planta de interiores

28. **bouquet**
    el ramo/el ramillete

29. **thorn**
    la espina

217

Sea Animals   Fauna marina

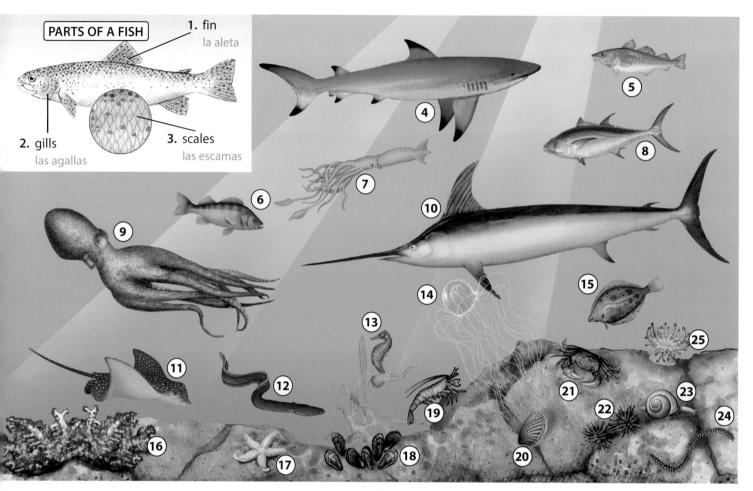

PARTS OF A FISH

1. fin
   la aleta

2. gills
   las agallas

3. scales
   las escamas

4. shark el tiburón	**9.** octopus el pulpo	**14.** jellyfish la medusa	**19.** shrimp el camarón	**24.** worm la lombriz/ el gusano
5. cod el bacalao/el abadejo	**10.** swordfish el pez espada	**15.** flounder el lenguado	**20.** scallop la vieira	**25.** sea anemone la anémona de mar
6. bass el róbalo/la percha	**11.** ray la raya	**16.** coral el coral	**21.** crab el cangrejo	
7. squid el calamar	**12.** eel la anguila	**17.** starfish la estrella de mar	**22.** sea urchin el erizo de mar	
8. tuna el atún	**13.** seahorse el caballo de mar	**18.** mussel el mejillón	**23.** snail el caracol	

Amphibians   Los anfibios

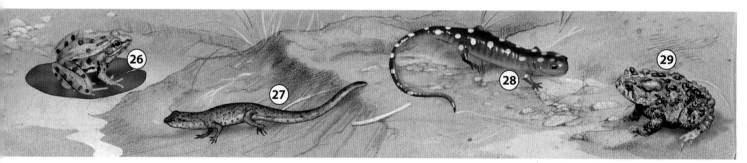

26. frog
la rana

27. newt
la salamandra acuática/
el tritón

28. salamander
la salamandra

29. toad
el sapo

Marine Life, Amphibians, and Reptiles

Sea Mammals Mamíferos marinos

30. water
el agua

31. dolphin
el delfín

32. porpoise
la marsopa

33. whale
la ballena

34. walrus
la morsa

35. sea lion
el león marino

36. seal
la foca

37. sea otter
la nutria marina

38. rock
la roca

Reptiles Los reptiles

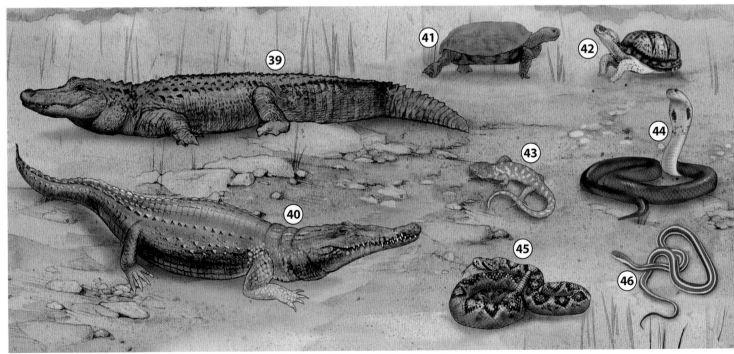

39. alligator
el caimán

40. crocodile
el cocodrilo

41. tortoise
la tortuga de tierra

42. turtle
la tortuga

43. lizard
la lagartija

44. cobra
la cobra

45. rattlesnake
la serpiente de cascabel

46. garter snake
la culebra americana
no venenosa

219

PARTS OF A BIRD

1. wing
el ala

2. claw
la garra

3. beak / bill
el pico

4. feather
la pluma

5. nest
el nido

6. owl
el búho/la lechuza

7. blue jay
el arrendajo azul/
el grajo azul

8. sparrow
el gorrión

9. woodpecker
el pájaro carpintero

10. eagle
el águila

11. hummingbird
el colibrí/el picaflor

12. penguin
el pingüino

13. duck
el pato

14. goose
el ganso

15. peacock
el pavo real

16. pigeon
la paloma

17. robin
el petirrojo

Insects and Arachnids Los insectos y los arácnidos

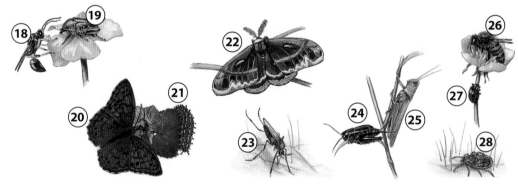

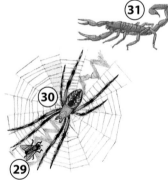

18. wasp
la avispa

19. beetle
el escarabajo

20. butterfly
la mariposa

21. caterpillar
la oruga

22. moth
la mariposa nocturna/
la polilla

23. mosquito
el mosquito

24. cricket
el grillo

25. grasshopper
el saltamontes

26. honeybee
la abeja melífera

27. ladybug
la mariquita/la catarinita

28. tick
la garrapata

29. fly
la mosca

30. spider
la araña

31. scorpion
el escorpión

Domestic Animals and Rodents

Farm Animals / Livestock Los animales de granja/el ganado

1. cow la vaca	**3.** donkey el burro	**5.** goat la cabra	**7.** rooster el gallo
2. pig el cerdo/el puerco/ el cochino	**4.** horse el caballo	**6.** sheep la oveja	**8.** hen la gallina

Pets Las mascotas

9. cat el gato	**11.** dog el perro	**13.** rabbit el conejo	**15.** parakeet el periquito
10. kitten el gatito	**12.** puppy el perrito	**14.** guinea pig el conejillo de indias/ el cuy	**16.** goldfish la carpa dorada

Rodents Los roedores

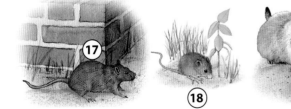

17. rat la rata	**19.** gopher la tuza	**21.** squirrel la ardilla
18. mouse el ratón	**20.** chipmunk la ardilla listada	**22.** prairie dog la marmota de las praderas

More vocabulary

Farm animals and pets are **domesticated**. They work for and/or live with people. Animals that are not domesticated are **wild**. Most rodents are wild.

Survey your class. Record the responses.

1. Have you worked with farm animals? Which ones?
2. Are you afraid of rodents? Which ones?

Report: *Lee has worked with cows. He's afraid of rats.*

221

1. moose
   el alce

2. mountain lion
   el puma

3. coyote
   el coyote

4. opossum
   la zarigüeya/la comadreja

5. wolf
   el lobo

6. buffalo / bison
   el búfalo/el bisonte

7. bat
   el murciélago

8. armadillo
   el armadillo

9. beaver
   el castor

10. porcupine
    el puerco espín

11. bear
    el oso

12. skunk
    el zorrillo/la mofeta

13. raccoon
    el mapache

14. deer
    el venado

15. fox
    el zorro

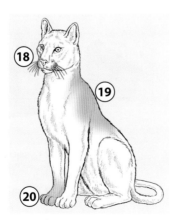

16. antlers
    las astas

17. hooves
    las pezuñas

18. whiskers
    los bigotes

19. coat / fur
    el pelaje/la piel

20. paw
    la garra/la zarpa

21. horn
    el cuerno

22. tail
    la cola

23. quill
    la púa

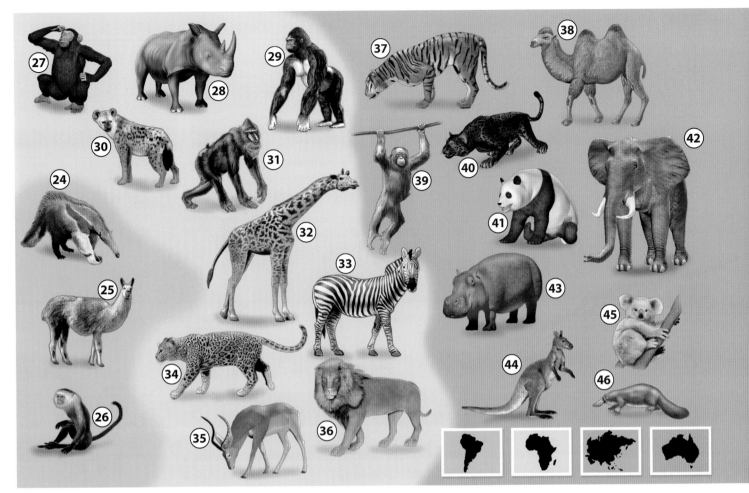

24. anteater el oso hormiguero	**29.** gorilla el gorila	**34.** leopard el leopardo	**39.** orangutan el orangután	**44.** kangaroo el canguro
25. llama la llama	**30.** hyena la hiena	**35.** antelope el antílope	**40.** panther la pantera	**45.** koala el koala
26. monkey el mono	**31.** baboon el mandril	**36.** lion el león	**41.** panda el panda	**46.** platypus el ornitorrinco
27. chimpanzee el chimpancé	**32.** giraffe la jirafa	**37.** tiger el tigre	**42.** elephant el elefante	
28. rhinoceros el rinoceronte	**33.** zebra la cebra	**38.** camel el camello	**43.** hippopotamus el hipopótamo	

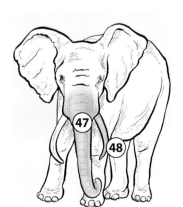

47. trunk
la trompa

48. tusk
el colmillo

49. mane
la melena/la crin

50. pouch
la bolsa

51. hump
la joroba

Energy and the Environment　La energía y el medio ambiente

Energy Sources　Fuentes de energía

1. solar energy
la energía solar

2. wind power
la energía eólica

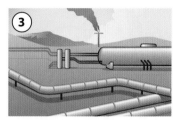

3. natural gas
el gas natural

4. coal
el carbón

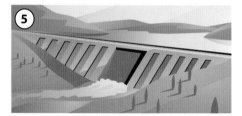

5. hydroelectric power
la energía hidroeléctrica

6. oil / petroleum
el petróleo

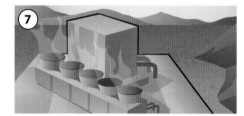

7. geothermal energy
la energía geotérmica

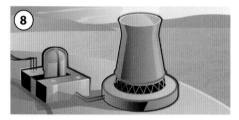

8. nuclear energy
la energía nuclear

9. biomass / bioenergy
la energía de biomasas/la bioenergía

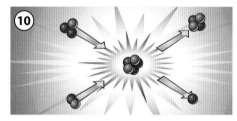

10. fusion
la energía de fusión

Pollution　La contaminación/polución

11. air pollution / smog
la contaminación del aire/el esmog

12. hazardous waste
los desechos peligrosos

13. acid rain
la lluvia ácida

14. water pollution
la contaminación del agua

15. radiation
la radiación

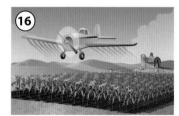

16. pesticide poisoning
el envenenamiento
con insecticidas

17. oil spill
el derrame de petróleo

More vocabulary

Environmental Protection Agency (EPA): the federal group that responds to pollution and environmental disasters

Internet Research: recycling

Type "recycle" and your city in the search bar. Look for information on local recycling centers.
Report: *You can recycle cans at ____.*

Ways to Conserve Energy and Resources · Formas de conservar la energía y los recursos

A. reduce trash
reducir la basura

B. reuse shopping bags
volver a usar las bolsas de compra

C. recycle
reciclar

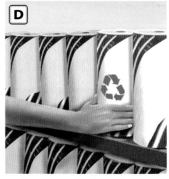

D. buy recycled products
comprar productos reciclados

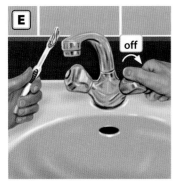

E. save water
ahorrar agua

F. fix leaky faucets
reparar los grifos con goteras

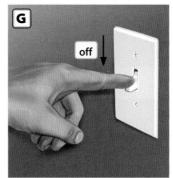

G. turn off lights
apagar las luces

H. use energy-efficient bulbs
usar bulbos de bajo consumo energético

I. carpool
compartir el vehículo

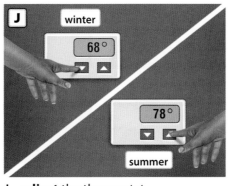

J. adjust the thermostat
ajustar el termostato

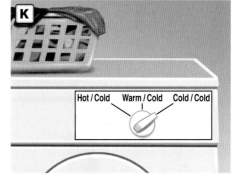

K. wash clothes in cold water
lavar la ropa en agua fría

L. don't litter
no tirar basura

M. compost food scraps
convertir en abono las sobras de alimentos

N. plant a tree
plantar un árbol

A Graduation   Una graduación

All Adelia's photos

I loved Art History.

My last economics lesson

Marching Band is great!

The photographer was upset.

We look good!

I get my diploma.

Dad and his digital camera

1. **photographer**
   el fotógrafo

2. **funny photo**
   la foto chistosa

3. **serious photo**
   la foto seria

4. **guest speaker**
   el orador invitado

5. **podium**
   el podio

6. **ceremony**
   la ceremonia

7. **cap**
   el birrete

8. **gown**
   la toga

A. **take** a picture
   tomar una foto

B. **cry**
   llorar

C. **celebrate**
   celebrar

226

People	Comments	
Sara	June 29th 8:19 p.m. Great pictures! What a day!	Delete
Zannie baby	June 30th 10 a.m. Love the funny photo.	Delete

Videos | Music | Classifieds |

I'm behind the mayor.

We're all very happy.

What do you see in the pictures?

1. Which classes are Adelia's favorites?
2. Do you prefer the funny or the serious graduation photo? Why?
3. Who is standing at the podium?
4. What are the graduates throwing in the air? Why?

Read the story.

A Graduation

Look at these great photos on my web page! The first three are from my favorite classes, but the other pictures are from graduation day.

There are two pictures of my classmates in <u>caps</u> and <u>gowns</u>. In the first picture, we're laughing and the <u>photographer</u> is upset. In the second photo, we're serious. I like the <u>serious photo</u>, but I love the <u>funny photo</u>!

There's also a picture of our <u>guest speaker</u>, the mayor. She is standing at the <u>podium</u>. Next, you can see me at the graduation <u>ceremony</u>. My dad wanted to <u>take a picture</u> of me with my diploma. That's my mom next to him. She <u>cries</u> when she's happy.

After the ceremony, everyone was happy, but no one cried. We wanted to <u>celebrate</u> and we did!

Reread the story.

1. Which events happened before the graduation? After?
2. Why does the author say, "but no one cried" in paragraph 4?

What do you think?

3. What kinds of ceremonies are important for children? for teens? for adults?

Places to Go
Lugares a donde ir

1. zoo
   el zoológico
2. movies
   el cine
3. botanical garden
   el jardín botánico
4. bowling alley
   la pista de boliche
5. rock concert
   el concierto de
   música rock
6. swap meet /
   flea market
   el bazar/el mercado
   de pulgas
7. aquarium
   el acuario

File   Edit   View   History   Bookmarks   Tools

Places to Go in Our City

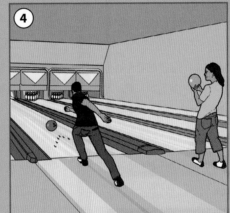

T-SHIRTS $3 2 FOR $5

SUNGLASSES $10

ANTIQU

Listen and point. Take turns.

A: *Point to the <u>zoo</u>.*

B: *Point to the <u>flea market</u>.*

A: *Point to the <u>rock concert</u>.*

Dictate to your partner. Take turns.

A: *Write these words: <u>zoo, movies, aquarium</u>.*

B: *<u>Zoo, movies</u>, and what?*

A: *And <u>aquarium</u>.*

8. play
   la obra teatral

9. art museum
   el museo de arte

10. amusement park
    el parque de
    atracciones

11. opera
    la ópera

12. nightclub
    el club nocturno

13. county fair
    la feria del condado

14. classical concert
    el concierto de
    música clásica

Ways to make plans using *Let's go*

Let's go to <u>the amusement park</u> tomorrow.

Let's go to <u>the opera</u> on Saturday.

Let's go to <u>the movies</u> tonight.

Pair practice. Make new conversations.

A: <u>*Let's go to the zoo this afternoon*</u>.

B: *OK. And let's go to* <u>*the movies tonight*</u>.

A: *That sounds like a good plan.*

The Park and Playground El parque y el patio de recreo

1. **ball field**
   el campo de béisbol

2. **cyclist**
   el ciclista

3. **bike path**
   el camino para bicicletas

4. **jump rope**
   la cuerda para saltar

5. **fountain**
   la fuente

6. **tennis court**
   la cancha de tenis

7. **skateboard**
   el monopatín

8. **picnic table**
   la mesa para comidas
   campestres

9. **water fountain**
   la fuente de agua para
   beber/el bebedero

10. **bench**
    la banca

11. **swings**
    los columpios

12. **tricycle**
    el triciclo

13. **slide**
    el tobogán

14. **climbing apparatus**
    el aparato para trepar

15. **sandbox**
    la caja de arena

16. **outdoor grill**
    la parrilla al aire libre

A. pull the wagon
arrastrar el cochecito

B. push the swing
empujar el columpio

C. climb the bars
trepar las barras

D. picnic / have a picnic
hacer una comida
campestre

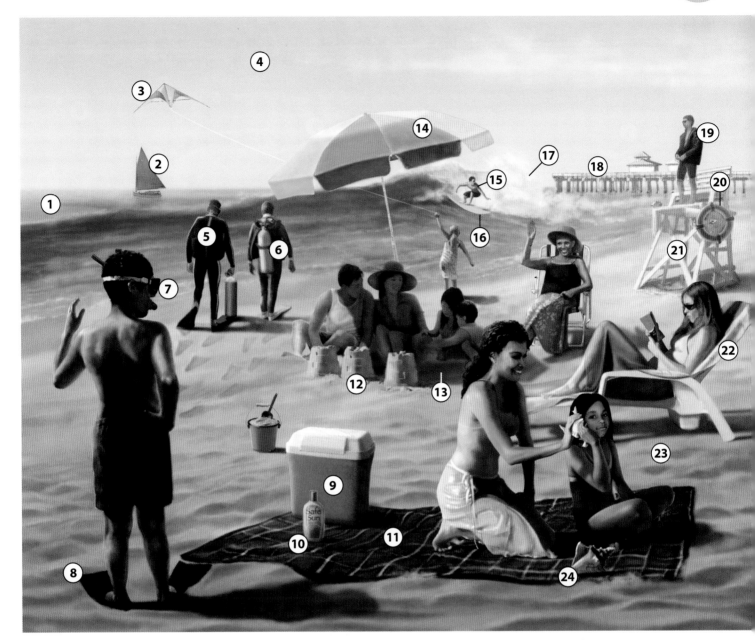

1. ocean / water el océano/el agua	**7.** diving mask la careta de buzo	**13.** shade la sombra	**19.** lifeguard el salvavidas
2. sailboat el velero	**8.** fins las aletas	**14.** beach umbrella la sombrilla de playa	**20.** lifesaving device el dispositivo salvavidas
3. kite la cometa	**9.** cooler la hielera/la nevera de playa	**15.** surfer el surfista	**21.** lifeguard station la estación del salvavidas
4. sky el cielo	**10.** sunscreen / sunblock el protector solar	**16.** surfboard la tabla hawaiana	**22.** beach chair la silla de playa
5. wetsuit el traje de buzo	**11.** blanket la manta/la toalla de playa	**17.** wave la ola	**23.** sand la arena
6. scuba tank el tanque de buceo	**12.** sandcastle el castillo de arena	**18.** pier el muelle	**24.** seashell la concha de mar

More vocabulary

seaweed: a plant that grows in the ocean
tide: the level of the ocean. The tide goes in and out every 12 hours.

Grammar Point: prepositions *in, on, under*

*Where are the little kids? They're **under** the umbrella.*
*Where's the cooler? It's **on** the blanket.*
*Where's the kite? It's **in** the sky.*

231

1. boating
   el paseo en bote

2. rafting
   el paseo en balsa

3. canoeing
   el piragüismo

4. fishing
   la pesca

5. camping
   el campamento

6. backpacking
   ir de campamento

7. hiking
   la caminata/la excursión

8. mountain biking
   el ciclismo de montañas

9. horseback riding
   la equitación/el paseo a caballo

10. tent
    la carpa/la tienda de campaña

11. campfire
    la fogata/la hoguera

12. sleeping bag
    el saco para dormir

13. foam pad
    la colchoneta de gomaespuma

14. life vest
    el chaleco salvavidas

15. backpack
    la mochila

16. camping stove
    la cocina de campamento

17. fishing net
    la red de pescar

18. fishing pole
    la caña de pescar

19. rope
    la cuerda

20. multi-use knife
    el cuchillo multiusos

21. matches
    las cerillas/los fósforos

22. lantern
    la linterna

23. insect repellent
    el repelente de insectos

24. canteen
    la cantimplora

1. downhill skiing
el esquí de descenso

2. snowboarding
el *snowboard*

3. cross-country skiing
el esquí de fondo

4. ice skating
el patinaje sobre hielo

5. figure skating
el patinaje artístico de figuras

6. sledding
montar en trineo

7. waterskiing
el esquí acuático

8. sailing
el velerismo

9. surfing
el surf

10. windsurfing
el *windsurf*

11. snorkeling
el buceo de superficie

12. scuba diving
el buceo con escafandra

More vocabulary

speed skating: racing while ice skating
kitesurfing: surfing with a small surfboard and a kite

Internet Research: popular winter sports

Type "popular winter sports" in the search bar.
Compare the information on two sites.
Report: *Two sites said _____ is a popular winter sport.*

233

1. archery
el tiro con arco

2. billiards / pool
el billar

3. bowling
el boliche

4. boxing
el boxeo

5. cycling / biking
el ciclismo

6. badminton
el bádminton

7. fencing
la esgrima

8. golf
el golf

9. gymnastics
la gimnasia

10. inline skating
el patinaje sobre ruedas

11. martial arts
las artes marciales

12. racquetball
el ráquetbol

13. skateboarding
el monopatinaje

14. table tennis
el tenis de mesa

15. tennis
el tenis

16. weightlifting
el levantamiento de pesas

17. wrestling
la lucha

18. track and field
el atletismo

19. horse racing
la carrera de caballos

Pair practice. Make new conversations.

A: *What sports do you like?*
B: *I like <u>bowling</u>. What do you like?*
A: *I like <u>gymnastics</u>.*

Internet Research: dangerous sports

Type "most dangerous sports" in the search bar.
Look for information on two or more sites.
Report: *According to my research, ____ is dangerous.*

1. **score**
   el tanteo/el marcador

2. **coach**
   el entrenador

3. **team**
   el equipo

4. **fan**
   el admirador/el entusiasta

5. **player**
   el jugador

6. **official / referee**
   el oficial/el árbitro

7. **basketball court**
   la cancha de baloncesto

8. **basketball hoop**
   el aro de baloncesto

9. **basketball**
   el baloncesto

10. **baseball**
    el béisbol

11. **softball**
    el sófbol

12. **football**
    el fútbol americano

13. **soccer**
    el fútbol/el balompié

14. **ice hockey**
    el *hockey* sobre hielo

15. **volleyball**
    el voleibol

16. **water polo**
    el polo acuático

More vocabulary

win: to have the best score
lose: the opposite of win
tie: to have the same score

captain: the team leader
goalie: the team member who protects the goal in soccer, ice hockey, and water polo
umpire: the referee in baseball
Little League: a baseball and softball program for children

235

A. **pitch**
lanzar

B. **hit**
pegar

C. **throw**
arrojar/aventar

D. **catch**
atrapar/agarrar

E. **kick**
patear

F. **tackle**
atajar/tumbar

G. **pass**
pasar

H. **shoot**
disparar/tirar

I. **jump**
saltar

J. **dribble**
driblar/regatear/rebotar

K. **dive**
tirarse/aventarse

L. **swim**
nadar

M. **stretch**
estirarse

N. **exercise / work out**
hacer ejercicios/entrenar

O. **bend**
doblarse

P. **serve**
servir

Q. **swing**
girar

R. **start**
comenzar

S. **race**
competir en una carrera

T. **finish**
terminar

U. **skate**
patinar

V. **ski**
esquiar

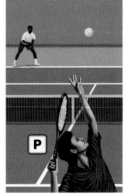

Use the new words.
Look at page 235. Name the actions you see.

A: *He's throwing.*
B: *She's jumping.*

Ways to talk about your sports skills

I can throw, but I can't catch.
I swim well, but I don't dive well.
I'm good at skating, but I'm terrible at skiing.

1. golf club
el palo de golf

2. tennis racket
la raqueta de tenis

3. volleyball
la bola de voleibol

4. basketball
la bola de baloncesto

5. bowling ball
la bola de boliche

6. bow
el arco

7. target
el blanco

8. arrows
las flechas

9. ice skates
los patines de hielo

10. inline skates
los patines de rueda

11. hockey stick
el palo de *hockey*

12. soccer ball
la bola de fútbol

13. shin guards
las espinilleras

14. baseball bat
el bate de béisbol

15. catcher's mask
la careta del receptor

16. uniform
el uniforme

17. glove
el guante

18. baseball
la pelota de béisbol

19. football helmet
el casco de fútbol americano

20. shoulder pads
las hombreras

21. football
el balón de fútbol americano

22. weights
las pesas

23. snowboard
la tabla de *snowboard*

24. skis
los esquíes

25. ski poles
los bastones de esquí

26. ski boots
las botas de esquí

27. flying disc*
el disco volador

*** Note:** one brand is
Frisbee®, of Wham-O, Inc.

Use the new words.
Look at pages 234–235. Name the sports equipment you see.

A: *Those are ice skates.*
B: *That's a football.*

Survey your class. Record the responses.

1. What sports equipment do you own?
2. What sports stores do you recommend?
Report: *Sam owns a ____. He recommends ____.*

237

Hobbies and Games Pasatiempos y juegos

A. collect things
coleccionar objetos

B. play games
participar en juegos

C. quilt
acolchar

D. do crafts
hacer artesanías

Collectibles

1. figurine
   la figurilla
2. baseball cards
   las tarjetas de béisbol
3. video game console
   la consola de videojuegos
4. video game controller
   el control del juego
   de video

5. board game
   el juego de mesa
6. dice
   los dados
7. checkers
   las damas
8. chess
   el ajedrez

9. model kit
   el juego para construir
   modelos a escala
10. acrylic paint
    la pintura de acrílico
11. glue stick
    el pegamento
12. glue gun
    la pistola de pegamento

13. construction paper
    el papel de construcción
14. woodworking kit
    el juego de artesanía
    en madera
15. quilt block
    el bloque de colcha
16. rotary cutter
    el cortador rotatorio

Grammar Point: used to

When I was a kid, I **used to** play cards every day.
Now, I don't play very often.

Pair practice. Make new conversations.

A: *What were your hobbies when you were a kid?*
B: *I used to <u>collect baseball cards</u>. And you?*
A: *I used to <u>play video games</u>.*

E. paint
pintar

F. knit
tejer

G. pretend
hacer creer/actuar

H. play cards
jugar a los naipes

17. canvas
   el lienzo

18. easel
   el caballete

19. oil paint
   la pintura de óleo

20. paintbrush
   el pincel

21. watercolors
   las acuarelas

22. yarn
   el hilo

23. knitting needles
   las agujas de tejer

24. embroidery
   el bordado

25. crochet
   el ganchillo/el croché

26. action figure
   el muñeco de acción

27. model train
   el tren a escala

28. dolls
   las muñecas

29. diamonds
   diamantes

30. spades
   espadas

31. hearts
   corazones

32. clubs
   tréboles

Ways to talk about hobbies and games

*This <u>board game</u> is **interesting**. It makes me think.*
*That <u>video game</u> is **boring**. Nothing happens.*
*I love to <u>play cards</u>. It's **fun** to play with my friends.*

Internet Research: popular hobbies

Type "most popular hobbies" in the search bar.
Look for information on one or more sites.
Report: *I read that _____ is a popular hobby.*

239

Electronics and Photography Electrónica y fotografía

1. **boom box**
   el estéreo portátil

2. **video MP3 player**
   el reproductor de video y MP3

3. **dock / charging station**
   el cargador/la estación de recarga

4. **lightweight headphones**
   los auriculares livianos

5. **earbuds / in-ear headphones**
   los audífonos intraurales/
   los intrauriculares

6. **noise-canceling headphones**
   los auriculares con cancelación de ruido

7. **personal CD player**
   el reproductor personal de CD

8. **flat-screen TV / flat-panel TV**
   el televisor de pantalla plana

9. **Blu-ray player**
   el reproductor de Blu-ray

10. **universal remote**
    el control remoto universal

11. **DVD player**
    el reproductor de DVD

12. **turntable**
    el tocadiscos

13. **tuner**
    el sintonizador

14. **speakers**
    los parlantes

15. **portable charger**
    el cargador portátil

16. **microphone**
    el micrófono

17. digital camera
la cámara digital

18. memory card
la tarjeta de memoria

19. zoom lens
el *zoom*/el teleobjetivo

20. tripod
el trípode

21. camcorder
la cámara de video y audio

22. camera case / bag
el estuche/el bolso para la cámara

23. battery pack
el bloque de pilas secas

24. battery charger
el cargador de pilas

25. plug
el enchufe

26. international power adapter
el adaptador de corriente internacional

27. LCD projector
el proyector LCD

28. screen
la pantalla

29. photo album
el álbum de fotos

30. digital photo album
el álbum de fotos digital

31. out of focus
desenfocada/fuera de foco

32. overexposed
sobreexpuesta

33. underexposed
subexpuesta

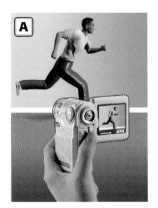

A. record
grabar

B. play
reproducir

C. rewind
rebobinar

D. fast forward
avanzar rápido

E. pause
pausar

241

Types of TV Programs Tipos de programas de televisión

1. news program
los programas de noticias

2. sitcom (situation comedy)
la comedia de situación

3. cartoon
los dibujos animados

4. talk show
los programas de entrevistas

5. soap opera
las telenovelas

6. reality show
los programas de telerrealidad

7. nature program
los documentales sobre la naturaleza

8. game show
los programas de juegos/de preguntas

9. children's program
los programas para niños

10. shopping program
los programas de ventas por televisión

11. sports program
los programas deportivos

12. drama
los programas dramáticos

Types of Movies Tipos de películas

13. comedy
de comedia

14. tragedy
de tragedia

15. western
del oeste

16. romance
románticas

17. horror story
de horror

18. science fiction story
de ciencia-ficción

19. action story / adventure story
de acción/de aventuras

20. mystery / suspense
de misterio/de suspenso

Types of Music Tipos de música

21. classical
clásica

22. blues
blues

23. rock
rock

24. jazz
jazz

25. pop
pop

26. hip-hop
hip hop

27. country
country

28. R&B / soul
R&B/soul

29. folk
folclórica/tradicional

30. gospel
góspel

31. reggae
reggae

32. world music
música internacional

Music   Música

A. play an instrument
tocar un instrumento

B. sing a song
cantar una canción

C. conduct an orchestra
dirigir una orquesta

D. be in a rock band
ser miembro de una
banda de *rock*

Woodwinds
Instrumentos de viento de madera

1. flute
   la flauta
2. clarinet
   el clarinete
3. oboe
   el oboe
4. bassoon
   el fagot
5. saxophone
   el saxofón

Strings
Instrumentos de cuerda

6. violin
   el violín
7. cello
   el violoncelo
8. bass
   el bajo
9. guitar
   la guitarra

Brass
Instrumentos de bronce o metales

10. trombone
    el trombón
11. trumpet /
    horn
    la trompeta/
    el corno
12. tuba
    la tuba
13. French horn
    el corno
    francés

Percussion   Instrumentos de percusión

14. piano
    el piano
15. xylophone
    el xilófono
16. drums
    los tambores
17. tambourine
    la pandereta/el pandero

Other Instruments   Otros instrumentos

18. electric keyboard
    el teclado electrónico
19. accordion
    el acordeón
20. organ
    el órgano
21. harmonica
    la armónica

1. parade
   el desfile

2. float
   la carroza

3. confetti
   el confeti

4. couple
   la pareja

5. card
   la tarjeta

6. heart
   el corazón

7. fireworks
   los fuegos artificiales

8. flag
   la bandera

9. mask
   la máscara/la careta/
   el antifaz

10. jack-o'-lantern
    la linterna hecha de
    calabaza

11. costume
    el disfraz

12. candy
    los dulces

13. feast
    el festín

14. turkey
    el pavo

15. ornament
    el adorno

16. Christmas tree
    el árbol de Navidad

17. candy cane
    los bastones dulces

18. string lights
    las luces navideñas

*Thanksgiving is on the fourth Thursday in November.

A Birthday Party
Una fiesta de cumpleaños

1. decorations
   las decoraciones

2. deck
   el entarimado

3. present / gift
   el presente/el regalo

A. **videotape**
   grabar en video

B. **make** a wish
   pedir un deseo

C. **blow out**
   soplar las velas

D. **hide**
   esconderse

E. **bring**
   traer

F. **wrap**
   envolver

Happy Birthday!

What do you see in the picture?

1. What kinds of decorations do you see?
2. What are people doing at this birthday party?
3. What wish did the teenager make?
4. How many presents did people bring?

Read the story.

A Birthday Party

Today is Lou and Gani Bombata's birthday barbecue. There are <u>decorations</u> around the backyard, and food and drinks on the <u>deck</u>. There are also <u>presents</u>. Everyone in the Bombata family likes to <u>bring</u> presents.

Right now, it's time for cake. Gani <u>is blowing out</u> the candles, and Lou <u>is making a wish</u>. Lou's mom wants to <u>videotape</u> everyone, but she can't find Lou's brother, Todd. Todd hates to sing, so he always <u>hides</u> for the birthday song.

Lou's sister, Amaka, has to <u>wrap</u> some <u>gifts</u>. She doesn't want Lou to see. Amaka isn't worried. She knows her family loves to sing. She can put her gifts on the present table before they finish the first song.

Reread the story.

1. Which paragraph gives you the most information about the Bombata family? Explain why.
2. Tell the story in your own words.

What do you think?

3. What wish do you think Gani made? Give your reasons.
4. Imagine you are invited to this party. You want to get one special gift for Gani **and** Lou to share. What's one gift they could both enjoy?

Verb Guide

Verbs in English are either regular or irregular in the past tense and past participle forms.

Regular Verbs

The regular verbs below are marked 1, 2, 3, or 4 according to four different spelling patterns.
(See page 250 for the irregular verbs, which do not follow any of these patterns.)

Spelling Patterns for the Past and the Past Participle	Example	
1. Add -ed to the end of the verb.	ASK	ASKED
2. Add -d to the end of the verb.	LIVE	LIVED
3. Double the final consonant and add -ed to the end of the verb.	DROP	DROPPED
4. Drop the final y and add -ied to the end of the verb.	CRY	CRIED

The Oxford Picture Dictionary List of Regular Verbs

accept (1)
add (1)
address (1)
adjust (1)
agree (2)
answer (1)
apologize (2)
appear (1)
applaud (1)
apply (4)
arrange (2)
arrest (1)
arrive (2)
ask (1)
assemble (2)
assist (1)
attach (1)
attend (1)
bake (2)
bargain (1)
bathe (2)
block (1)
board (1)
boil (1)
bookmark (1)
borrow (1)
bow (1)
brainstorm (1)
breathe (2)
browse (2)
brush (1)
bubble (2)
buckle (2)
burn (1)
bus (1)
calculate (2)
call (1)

capitalize (2)
carpool (1)
carry (4)
cash (1)
celebrate (2)
change (2)
check (1)
chill (1)
choke (2)
chop (3)
circle (2)
cite (2)
claim (1)
clarify (4)
clean (1)
clear (1)
click (1)
climb (1)
close (2)
collate (2)
collect (1)
color (1)
comb (1)
comfort (1)
commit (3)
compare (2)
complain (1)
complete (2)
compliment (1)
compose (2)
compost (1)
conceal (1)
conduct (1)
consult (1)
contact (1)
convert (1)
convict (1)

cook (1)
cooperate (2)
copy (4)
correct (1)
cough (1)
count (1)
create (2)
cross (1)
cry (4)
dance (2)
debate (2)
decline (2)
delete (2)
deliver (1)
design (1)
dial (1)
dice (2)
dictate (2)
die (2)
direct (1)
disagree (2)
discipline (2)
discuss (1)
disinfect (1)
distribute (2)
dive (2)
divide (2)
double-click (1)
drag (3)
dress (1)
dribble (2)
drill (1)
drop (3)
drown (1)
dry (4)
dust (1)
dye (2)

earn (1)
edit (1)
empty (4)
end (1)
enter (1)
erase (2)
evacuate (2)
examine (2)
exchange (2)
exercise (2)
expire (2)
explain (1)
explore (2)
exterminate (2)
fast forward (1)
fasten (1)
fax (1)
fertilize (2)
fill (1)
finish (1)
fix (1)
floss (1)
fold (1)
follow (1)
garden (1)
gargle (2)
graduate (2)
grate (2)
grease (2)
greet (1)
hail (1)
hammer (1)
hand (1)
harvest (1)
help (1)
hire (2)
hug (3)

identify (4)
immigrate (2)
indent (1)
inquire (2)
insert (1)
inspect (1)
install (1)
introduce (2)
investigate (2)
invite (2)
iron (1)
jaywalk (1)
join (1)
jump (1)
kick (1)
kiss (1)
knit (3)
label (1)
land (1)
laugh (1)
learn (1)
lengthen (1)
lift (1)
list (1)
listen (1)
litter (1)
live (2)
load (1)
lock (1)
log (3)
look (1)
mail (1)
manufacture (2)
match (1)
measure (2)
microwave (2)
milk (1)
misbehave (2)
miss (1)
mix (1)
monitor (1)
mop (3)
move (2)
mow (1)
multiply (4)
negotiate (2)
network (1)
numb (1)
nurse (2)

obey (1)
observe (2)
offer (1)
open (1)
operate (2)
order (1)
organize (2)
overdose (2)
pack (1)
paint (1)
park (1)
participate (2)
pass (1)
paste (2)
pause (2)
peel (1)
perm (1)
pick (1)
pitch (1)
plan (3)
plant (1)
play (1)
polish (1)
pour (1)
praise (2)
preheat (1)
prepare (2)
prescribe (2)
press (1)
pretend (1)
print (1)
program (3)
protect (1)
pull (1)
purchase (2)
push (1)
quilt (1)
race (2)
raise (2)
rake (2)
receive (2)
record (1)
recycle (2)
redecorate (2)
reduce (2)
reenter (1)
refuse (2)
register (1)
relax (1)

remain (1)
remove (2)
renew (1)
repair (1)
replace (2)
report (1)
request (1)
research (1)
respond (1)
retire (2)
return (1)
reuse (2)
revise (2)
rinse (2)
rock (1)
sauté (1)
save (2)
scan (3)
schedule (2)
scroll (1)
scrub (3)
search (1)
seat (1)
select (1)
sentence (2)
separate (2)
serve (2)
share (2)
shave (2)
ship (3)
shop (3)
shorten (1)
shower (1)
sign (1)
simmer (1)
skate (2)
ski (1)
slice (2)
smell (1)
smile (2)
smoke (2)
solve (2)
sort (1)
spell (1)
spoon (1)
staple (2)
start (1)
state (2)
stay (1)

steam (1)
stir (3)
stop (3)
stow (1)
stretch (1)
study (4)
submit (3)
subtract (1)
supervise (2)
swallow (1)
tackle (2)
talk (1)
taste (2)
thank (1)
tie (2)
touch (1)
transcribe (2)
transfer (3)
translate (2)
travel (1)
trim (3)
try (4)
turn (1)
type (2)
underline (2)
undress (1)
unload (1)
unpack (1)
unscramble (2)
update (2)
use (2)
vacuum (1)
videotape (2)
visit (1)
volunteer (1)
vomit (1)
vote (2)
wait (1)
walk (1)
wash (1)
watch (1)
water (1)
wave (2)
weed (1)
weigh (1)
wipe (2)
work (1)
wrap (3)
yell (1)

Verb Guide

Irregular Verbs

These verbs have irregular endings in the past and/or the past participle.

The Oxford Picture Dictionary List of Irregular Verbs

simple	past	past participle	simple	past	past participle
be	was	been	make	made	made
beat	beat	beaten	meet	met	met
become	became	become	pay	paid	paid
bend	bent	bent	picnic	picnicked	picnicked
bleed	bled	bled	proofread	proofread	proofread
blow	blew	blown	put	put	put
break	broke	broken	quit	quit	quit
bring	brought	brought	read	read	read
buy	bought	bought	rewind	rewound	rewound
catch	caught	caught	rewrite	rewrote	rewritten
choose	chose	chosen	ride	rode	ridden
come	came	come	run	ran	run
cut	cut	cut	say	said	said
do	did	done	see	saw	seen
draw	drew	drawn	seek	sought	sought
drink	drank	drunk	sell	sold	sold
drive	drove	driven	send	sent	sent
eat	ate	eaten	set	set	set
fall	fell	fallen	sew	sewed	sewn
feed	fed	fed	shake	shook	shaken
feel	felt	felt	shoot	shot	shot
find	found	found	show	showed	shown
fly	flew	flown	sing	sang	sung
freeze	froze	frozen	sit	sat	sat
get	got	gotten	speak	spoke	spoken
give	gave	given	stand	stood	stood
go	went	gone	steal	stole	stolen
hang	hung	hung	sweep	swept	swept
have	had	had	swim	swam	swum
hear	heard	heard	swing	swung	swung
hide	hid	hidden	take	took	taken
hit	hit	hit	teach	taught	taught
hold	held	held	think	thought	thought
keep	kept	kept	throw	threw	thrown
lay	laid	laid	wake	woke	woken
leave	left	left	win	won	won
lend	lent	lent	withdraw	withdrew	withdrawn
let	let	let	write	wrote	written
lose	lost	lost			

Index

Index Key

Font

bold type = verbs or verb phrases (example: **catch**)
ordinary type = all other parts of speech (example: baseball)
ALL CAPS = unit titles (example: MATHEMATICS)
Initial caps = subunit titles (example: Equivalencies)

Numbers/Letters

first number in **bold** type = page on which word appears

second number, or letter, following number in **bold** type = item number on page

(examples: cool **13**–5 means that the word *cool* is item number 5 on page 13; across **157**–G means that the word *across* is item G on page 157).

Symbols

✦ = word found in exercise band at bottom of page

🔑 = The keywords of the **Oxford 3000™** have been carefully selected by a group of language experts and experienced teachers as the words which should receive priority in vocabulary study because of their importance and usefulness.

AWL = **The Academic Word List** is the most principled and widely accepted list of academic words. Averil Coxhead gathered information from academic materials across the academic disciplines to create this word list.

Abbreviations **48**
abdomen **107**–26
about **48**–B, **179**–L, **203**–E 🔑
above **25**–4 🔑
accelerator **163**–46
accept **12** ✦, **12**–H, **12**–J 🔑 AWL
access number **15**–24 🔑 AWL
Accessories **59**, **94**–95
ACCESSORIES **94**–95
accident **148**–2 🔑
    accident report **110**–18 🔑
accordion **244**–19
account **211**–T 🔑
    account manager **134**–9 🔑
    checking account number **134**–15 🔑
    joint account **134**–10 🔑
    log in to your account **211**–T
    savings account number **134**–16 🔑
Account **134**, **211** 🔑
accountant **170**–1
accounting **184**–9
ache
    backache **110**–5
    earache **110**–3
    headache **110**–1 🔑
    stomachache **110**–4
    toothache **110**–2
acid rain **224**–13 🔑
across **157**–G 🔑
acrylic paint **238**–10 🔑
action 🔑
    action figure **239**–26 🔑
    action story **243**–19 🔑
activist **209**–17
actor **170**–2 🔑
acupuncture **124**–2
acute angle **205**–28 🔑
ad 🔑
    classified ad **48**–2
    pop-up ad **213**–17
adapter **241**–26
add **33**–C, **77**–N, **101**–B, **204**–A 🔑
additional charges **15**–32 🔑
address 🔑
    mailing address **136**–22

return address **136**–21 🔑
street address **4**–5 🔑
website address **213**–10 🔑
address **137**–B, **211**–U
adhesive bandage **119**–6 🔑
adjust **225**–J 🔑 AWL
    adjustable wrench **195**–48
    adjustment **206**–22, **206**–24 AWL
administrative assistant **170**–3 🔑 AWL
administrator **122**–13 AWL
Administrators **5** AWL
admiral **141**–26
admissions clerk **122**–14 🔑
adult school **200**–8 🔑 AWL
ADULTS AND CHILDREN **30**–31 🔑 AWL
adventure story **243**–19 🔑
AED / automated external defibrillator **119**–4
aerobic exercise **124**–5 🔑
afraid **43**–23 🔑
after 🔑
    afternoon **18**–17 🔑
    aftershave **109**–30
    five after one **18**–7 🔑
    quarter after one **18**–9 🔑
    ten after one **18**–8 🔑
    twenty after one **18**–10 🔑
After an Emergency **151** 🔑
Age **32** 🔑
agency **133**–14, **168**–F 🔑
agent **164**–3, **164**–5 🔑
agree **12**–L 🔑
agreement **51**–28 🔑
aid 🔑 AWL
    first aid kit **119**–1, **150**–18
    first aid manual **119**–2 🔑 AWL
    hearing aid **117**–10 🔑
AID **119** 🔑
Aid **119** 🔑
aide **5**–16, **171**–32
AIDS (acquired immune deficiency syndrome) **113**–21, **113** ✦
air 🔑
    air conditioning **163**–40
    Air Force **141**–32

air pollution **224**–11 🔑
air purifier **115**–14
airbag **163**–43 🔑
airmail **136**–5
airplane **154**–8
airplane crash **148**–3 🔑
airport **155**–10 🔑
Airline Terminal **164** AWL
airman **141**–33
Airplane **165**
AIRPORT **164**–165 🔑
Airport Transportation **156** 🔑 AWL
aisle **72**–7
alarm clock **58**–24 🔑
Alaska time **19**–28
album **241**–29, **241**–30
alfalfa **187**–5
algebra **204**–16
allergic reaction **118**–E 🔑 AWL
Allergic Reactions **113** 🔑 AWL
allergies **112**–11
alley **51**–24, **228**–4
alligator **219**–39
alphabet **7**–13 🔑
Alteration Shop **100** 🔑 AWL
ALTERATIONS **100** AWL
Alterations **100** AWL
aluminum foil **72**–23
Alzheimer's disease **113** ✦
a.m. **18**–4 🔑
ambulance **118**–1, **123**–34 🔑
American **208**–3
American cheese **71**–26
AMPHIBIANS **218**–219
Amphibians **218**
amusement park **229**–10 🔑
anaphylaxis **113**–15
ancient **209**–1 🔑
anemone **218**–25
anesthesiologist **123**–35
angle 🔑
    acute angle **205**–28 🔑
    90° angle **205**–26 🔑
    obtuse angle **205**–27 🔑
    right angle **205**–26 🔑

Angles **205** 🔑

angry **43**–29 🔑

animals **59**–15 🔑

ANIMALS **221** 🔑

Animals **218, 221** 🔑

ankle **106**–23, **110**–14 🔑

   ankle socks **91**–7 🔑

anklets **91**–11

anniversary **22**–3 🔑

answer **8**–L

answer sheet **10**–2 🔑

antacid **115**–28

anteater **223**–24

antelope **223**–35

antibacterial ointment **119**–12

antihistamine cream **119**–11

antiperspirant **108**–5

antlers **222**–16

ants **63**–23

apartment **48**–3, **48**–4 🔑

   apartment building **50**–1 🔑

   apartment number **4**–6 🔑

Apartment **48** 🔑

Apartment Complex **51** 🔑 AWL

Apartment Entryway **51**

apartment search tool **48**–1 🔑

APARTMENTS **50–51** 🔑

APC (automated postal center) **137**–10

apologize **12**–G 🔑

apostrophe **202**–19

apparatus **230**–14

appear **144**–C 🔑

Appearance **32** 🔑

applaud **152**–B

apples **68**–1 🔑

   apple juice **73**–32 🔑

appliance repairperson **170**–4

application **48**–C, **139**–D, **169**–J, **169**–L 🔑

Applications **191** 🔑

appliqué **99**–31

apply **109**–P, **169**–I 🔑

appointment **22**–4, **111**–1 🔑

   appointment book **189**–48 🔑

apprenticeship **175**–10

apricots **68**–12

April **21**–28 🔑

apron **92**–11, **93**–30

aquarium **228**–7

ARACHNIDS **220**

Arachnids **220**

archery **234**–1

architect **170**–5

area 🔑 AWL

   area code **4**–10, **15**–28 🔑 AWL

   boarding area **165**–9 🔑

   dining area **46**–8

   play area **132**–11 🔑 AWL

   reception area **188**–15 🔑 AWL

   rural area **52**–4 🔑 AWL

   screening area **164**–4

   testing area **138**–2 🔑 AWL

   waiting area **188**–16

   urban area **52**–1 🔑 AWL

AREA **55** 🔑

Area and Volume **205** 🔑 AWL

arm **105**–14, **206**–23 🔑

   armchair **56**–22

Arm, Hand, and Fingers **106** 🔑

armadillo **222**–8

Army **141**–28, **209**–11 🔑

around **157**–H 🔑

Around Campus **5**

arrange **49**–Q 🔑

arrest **144**–A 🔑

arrival and departure monitors **165**–7 🔑

arrival time **165** ✦ 🔑

arrive **164**–K 🔑

arrows **237**–8 🔑

arson **145**–7

artery **107**–36

arthritis **113**–20

artichokes **69**–22

artist **170**–6 🔑

arts **201**–15 🔑

   art museum **229**–9 🔑

   language arts **201**–9 🔑

   martial arts **234**–11

ask **2**–B 🔑

   ask about **48**–B, **161**–B 🔑

   ask for help **10**–F 🔑

   ask questions **8**–K, **179**–M 🔑

asparagus **69**–26

assault **145**–3

assemble **176**–A, **185**–C AWL

assembler **170**–7

assembly AWL

   assembly line **185**–6 🔑 AWL

   peaceful assembly **142**–1 🔑 AWL

   assemblyperson **140**–18

assist **95**–D, **176**–B 🔑 AWL

assistance **14**–21 🔑 AWL

assistant 🔑 AWL

   administrative assistant **170**–3 AWL

   assistant principal **5**–5 🔑 AWL

   certified nursing assistant (CNA) **122**–12 🔑

   dental assistant **120**–2, **171**–22

   physician assistant **172**–47

Assistant **93** 🔑 AWL

asthma **113**–18

astronaut **215**–17

astronomer **215**–22

Astronomy **215**

At Customs **165** 🔑

At the Dealer **162**

At the Gate **165** 🔑

At the Mechanic **162**

At the Security Checkpoint **164** 🔑 AWL

athletic

   athletic shoes **94** ✦

   athletic supporter **91**–6

Atlantic time **19**–33

atlas **135**–8

ATM (Automated Teller Machine) **134**

ATM card **134**–12

atom **207**–28 🔑

attach **211**–Y 🔑 AWL

attachments **61**–11 AWL

attack **118**–D

attendant

   flight attendant **165**–12

   parking attendant **192**–3

attic **47**–9

attorney 🔑

   defense attorney **144**–4

   hire an attorney **144**–B

   prosecuting attorney **144**–10

attractive **32**–13 🔑

audio display / touch screen **163**–37 🔑

audiobook **135**–17

audiologist **117**–9

auditorium **5**–18

August **21**–32 🔑

aunt **34**–7 🔑

author **135**–15, **173**–64 🔑 AWL

auto

   auto mechanic **170**–8

   automobile club card **166**–5 🔑

automated AWL

   automated external defibrillator / AED **119**–4

   automated phone system **14**–22 🔑 AWL

   automated postal center (APC) **137**–10 AWL

Automated Teller Machine **134**

Automatic Transmission **163** 🔑 AWL

Automotive Painter **92**

autumn **21**–39 🔑

avalanche **149**–18

average 🔑

   average height **32**–5 🔑

   average weight **32**–8 🔑

avocados **84**–6

ax **194**–3

baboon **223**–31

baby **31**–7 🔑

   baby carrier **37**–17

   baby food **37**–4 🔑

   baby lotion **37**–13

   baby monitor **59**–7 🔑 AWL

   baby powder **37**–14 🔑

   baby's room **47**–11 🔑

   babysitter **170**–9

back **104**–5 🔑

   back button **213**–9 🔑

   back seat **163**–54 🔑

   back support belt **197**–18 🔑

   backache **110**–5

   backhoe **196**–8

   backpack **94**–18, **232**–15

   backpacking **232**–6

   go back **11**–M 🔑

   hatchback **160**–6

   horseback riding **232**–9 🔑

   lower back **107**–29 🔑

   write back **137**–H 🔑

   pay back **26**–D 🔑

BACK FROM THE MARKET **66–67** 🔑

Backyard **53**

bacon **70**–11, **80**–1

bacteria **76** ✦ 🔑

bad **23**–17 🔑
BAD DAY AT WORK **198**–**199** 🔑
badge **93**–21
badminton **234**–6
bag **69**–31, **74**–7, **74**–19, **165**–18 🔑
   airbag **163**–43 🔑
   camera case / bag **241**–22 🔑
   clutch bag **89**–19
   diaper bag **37**–11
   grocery bag **67**–13 🔑
   handbag **87**–9, **94**–2
   plastic storage bags **72**–25 🔑
   shopping bag **67**–13 🔑
   shoulder bag **94**–17 🔑
   sleeping bag **232**–12 🔑
   tote bag **94**–19
   trash bags **61**–24 🔑
   vacuum cleaner bag **61**–12
bagels **73**–40
baggage 🔑
   baggage carousel **165**–23 🔑
bagger **73**–15
baggy **97**–30
bailiff **144**–13
bake **77**–H 🔑
Baked Goods **73** 🔑
baked potato **81**–25 🔑
baker **170**–10
bakery **129**–19
balance **134**–18, **207**–41 🔑
balcony **51**–20
bald **33**–24
ball **59**–12, **237**–5, **237**–12 🔑
   ball field **230**–1 🔑
   ballroom **192**–26
   baseball **235**–10, **237**–18 🔑
   basketball **235**–9, **237**–4 🔑
   basketball court **235**–7 🔑
   basketball hoop **235**–8
   football **235**–12, **237**–21 🔑
   meatballs **81**–27
   racquetball **234**–12
   softball **235**–11
   volleyball **235**–15, **237**–3
balloons **44**–4
ballot **143**–9
bananas **68**–2
   a bunch of bananas **68**–29
   ripe banana **68**–30
   rotten banana **68**–32
   unripe banana **68**–31
band **189**–34 🔑
   headband **90**–3
   waistband **100**–5
bandage **119**–6, **119**–13 🔑
bandana **92**–16
bangs **33**–8
bank **126**–5 🔑
   bank statement **134**–17 🔑
BANK **134** 🔑
Bank Accounts **134**
banner **44**–1
banquet room **193**–14

bar 🔑
   bar code **27**–4 🔑
   candy bar **73**–37 🔑
   feed bar **98**–20
   grab bar **57**–11 🔑
   menu bar **213**–7 🔑
   salad bar **79**–24 🔑
barbecued ribs **76**–2
barbershop **131**–19
bargain **102**–A
barn **187**–11
barrette **108**–20
base **14**–3, **205**–45, **206**–20 🔑
baseball **235**–10, **237**–18 🔑
   baseball bat **237**–14
   baseball cap **86**–5
   baseball cards **238**–2 🔑
   baseball game **44**–2 🔑
basement **47**–14
Basement **50**
Basic Colors **24** 🔑
basic education **175**–1 🔑
BASIC TRANSPORTATION **154**–**155** 🔑 AWL
basket **56**–3
   basketball **235**–9, **237**–4 🔑
   basketball court **235**–7 🔑
   basketball hoop **235**–8
   breadbasket **83**–11
   laundry basket **101**–2
   shopping basket **73**–9
   wastebasket **57**–26
bass **218**–6, **244**–8
bassoon **244**–4
bat **222**–7, **237**–14
bath 🔑
   bath mat **57**–28
   bath powder **108**–4 🔑
   bath towel **57**–16 🔑
   bathroom **46**–5 🔑
   bathtub **57**–2
   take a bath **108**–B
   half bath **57** ✦
bathe **36**–F, **108**–B
bathing suit **90**–26 🔑
BATHROOM **57** 🔑
battery / batteries **150**–15, **162**–20 🔑
   battery charger **241**–24 🔑
   battery pack **241**–23 🔑
bay **214**–9 🔑
be 🔑
   be a recruit **141**–A
   be a veteran **141**–D
   be aware **146**–I 🔑 AWL
   be born **40**–A 🔑
   be 18 or older **142**–G 🔑
   be hired **169**–O 🔑
   be hurt **118**–C 🔑
   be in a rock band **244**–D 🔑
   be in class **38**–J 🔑
   be in shock **118**–B 🔑
   be informed **142**–F 🔑
   be injured **118**–C 🔑 AWL
   be lost **166**–B 🔑

be neat **179**–C 🔑
be on active duty **141**–B 🔑
be on reserve **141**–C
be on time **179**–F 🔑
be released **144**–H 🔑 AWL
be unconscious **118**–A 🔑
don't be late **179**–E 🔑
beach **214**–10 🔑
   beach chair **231**–22 🔑
   beach umbrella **231**–14 🔑
BEACH **231** 🔑
beads **95**–34, **99**–32
beak **220**–3 🔑
beaker **207**–39
beam **196**–3
beans **72**–17
   string beans **69**–8
   soybeans **187**–3
bear **37**–24, **222**–11 🔑
beard **33**–6 🔑
beat **77**–S 🔑
beater
   eggbeater **78**–20
beautiful **23**–21 🔑
beauty shop **132** ✦ 🔑
beaver **222**–9
become **40**–G, **41**–N 🔑
bed **58**–9 🔑
   bed control **123**–27 🔑
   bed frame **58**–18 🔑
   bed table **123**–21 🔑
   bedbugs **63**–24
   bedpan **123**–23 🔑
   bedroom **46**–3 🔑
   bedspread **59**–11
   bunk beds **59**–9 🔑
   double bed **192**–14 🔑
   flower bed **53**–20 🔑
   hospital bed **123**–22 🔑
   kids' bedroom **47**–10 🔑
   king-size bed **192**–15 🔑
BEDROOM **58, 59** 🔑
bee
   honeybee **220**–26
beef 🔑
   beef ribs **70**–5
   corned beef **71**–22
   ground beef **70**–4
   roast beef **71**–21
   stewing beef **70**–3
   stir-fried beef **76**–6 🔑
Beef **70** 🔑
beetle **220**–19
beets **69**–5
Before an Emergency **150** 🔑
behind **25**–8 🔑
beige / tan **24**–18
bell 🔑
   bell captain **192**–6 🔑
   bell peppers **69**–7 🔑
   bellhop **192**–7
   doorbell **53**–14
below **25**–5 🔑

belts **94**–6 🔑
  back support belt **197**–18 🔑
  belt buckle **94**–20
  conveyer belt **185**–9
  seat belt **163**–52 🔑
  tool belt **92**–3 🔑
bench **230**–10
bend 236–O 🔑
benefits **121**–3, **179** ✦🔑 AWL
  explanation of benefits **121**–11
berries **216**–20
  blackberries **68**–17
  blueberries **68**–16
  mixed berries **81**–36
  raspberries **68**–15
  strawberries **68**–14
between **25**–12 🔑
Beverages **73, 81**
bib **37**–5
bicycle / bike **131**–22, **155**–15 🔑
  bike path **230**–3 🔑
big **23**–2, **97**–38 🔑
  Big Dipper **215** ✦
  big-screen TV **50**–14 🔑
bike / bicycle **131**–22 🔑
  bike path **230**–3 🔑
biking **232**–8, **234**–5
bikini panties **91**–13
bill **220**–3 🔑
Bill **15** 🔑
Bill of Rights **208**–13
billiards **234**–2
billing period **15**–30
Bills **26** 🔑
bin **164**–6 🔑
  recycling bin **61**–2
  trash bin **51**–23
bioenergy **224**–9
biography **135**–13
biologist **206**–2
Biology **206** 🔑
biomass **224**–9
birch **216**–7
Bird **220** 🔑
BIRDS, INSECTS, AND ARACHNIDS **220** 🔑
birth 🔑
  birth certificate **40**–1 🔑
  birthday **22**–1 🔑
  date of birth **4**–14 🔑
  place of birth **4**–15 🔑
BIRTHDAY PARTY **246**–**247** 🔑
biscuits **80**–6 🔑
bison **222**–6
bit **194**–28 🔑
bite **110**–10 🔑
black **24**–13 🔑
  black hair **33**–12 🔑
  blackberries **68**–17
bladder **107**–46
blade **194**–27
  razor blade **109**–28
  shoulder blade **107**–28 🔑

blankets **58**–15, **150**–7, **231**–11
  blanket sleeper **91**–26
blazer **92**–12
bleach **101**–7
bleachers **5**–3
bleed 118–M
blender **54**–12
blind **32**–11 🔑
blister **110**–17
blizzard **13**–24, **149**–13
block 147–C
blocks **59**–19 🔑
  go one block **159**–F 🔑
  quilt block **238**–15
  sunblock **108**–8, **231**–10
blond hair **33**–14 🔑
blood 🔑
  blood pressure gauge **111**–9 🔑
  blood test **123**–30 🔑
  blood work **123**–30 🔑
  bloody nose **110**–15 🔑
  check blood pressure **111**–A 🔑
  draw blood **111**–F 🔑
  high blood pressure **113**–24 🔑
blouse **87**–8
blow dryer **33**–21, **108**–18
blow out 246–C 🔑
blower **186**–2
blue **24**–3 🔑
  blue jay **220**–7
  blueberries **68**–16
  bright blue **24**–12 🔑
  dark blue **24**–10 🔑
  light blue **24**–11 🔑
  navy blue **28**–5 🔑
blues **243**–22
Bluetooth headset **14**–14
Blu-ray player **240**–9
blush **109**–37
board 🔑
  board game **238**–5 🔑
  bulletin board **7**–14
  chalkboard **6**–3
  cutting board **54**–27
  electric keyboard **244**–18 🔑
  emery board **109**–32
  headboard **58**–10
  ironing board **101**–14 🔑
  keyboard **190**–23 🔑
  keyboard shortcut **210** ✦
  motherboard **190**–18
  particle board **195**–20
  skateboard **230**–7
  snowboard **237**–23
  surfboard **231**–16
  whiteboard **6**–1
board 164–E
boarding 🔑
  boarding area **165**–9 🔑 AWL
  boarding pass **165**–20 🔑
  skateboarding **234**–13
  snowboarding **233**–2

boat 🔑
  sailboat **231**–2
boating **232**–1 🔑
bobbin **98**–21
bobby pins **108**–21
body **202**–8 🔑
  body lotion **108**–9
  body of water **214** ✦🔑
  body shaper **91**–15
BODY **104**–**105**, **106**–**107** 🔑
boil 77–M 🔑
boiled ham **76**–5
boiler **78**–8
bok choy **69**–15
bolt **51**–35, **194**–35
  bolt of fabric **98**–15
  toggle bolt **194**–38
bone **107**–33, **118**–P 🔑
  boneless **70** ✦
book 🔑
  appointment book **189**–48 🔑
  audiobook **135**–17
  book of stamps **136**–18 🔑
  bookcase **7**–10
  bookstore **132**–4
  checkbook **134**–13
  coloring book **59**–13
  DMV handbook **138**–1
  e-book **135**–18
  notebook **7**–28
  picture book **135**–12 🔑
  spiral notebook **7**–30
  test booklet **10**–1
  textbook **7**–26
  used book store **131**–20 🔑
  workbook **7**–27
bookmark a site **212**–G
boom box **240**–1
booster car seat **37**–21 🔑
booth **82**–4, **124**–3
boots **95**–28 🔑
  hiking boots **95**–31
  rain boots **90**–20 🔑
  safety boots **197**–20 🔑
  ski boots **237**–26
  steel toe boots **92**–6 🔑
bored **43**–25 🔑
borrow 26–B 🔑
boss **182**–4 🔑
botanical garden **228**–3
bottle **37**–1, **74**–1, **74**–13 🔑
  hot water bottle **115**–15 🔑
bottled water **150**–11 🔑
bouquet **217**–28
bow **237**–6
  bow tie **89**–16
bow 3–I
bowl **55**–2 🔑
  mixing bowl **54**–28, **78**–31 🔑
  serving bowl **55**–21 🔑
  soup bowl **83**–21 🔑
  sugar bowl **55**–14 🔑

bowling **234**–3 ✎
   bowling alley **228**–4 ✎
   bowling ball **237**–5 ✎
box / boxes **74**–6, **74**–18 ✎
   boom box **240**–1
   box spring **58**–19 ✎
   fuse box **62**–13
   mailbox **53**–1, **130**–13, **137**–12
   mailboxes **50**–11
   post office box (PO box) **137**–9
   safety deposit box **134**–7 ✎
   sandbox **230**–15
   search box **212**–3 ✎
   to-go box **82**–5 ✎
boxer shorts **91**–4 ✎
boxing **234**–4 ✎
boy **31**–9 ✎
bra **91**–19
bracelets **95**–9, **119**–3
braces **120**–6
brain **107**–34 ✎
brainstorm 8–H, **203**–F
brake
   brake light **162**–14
   brake pedal **163**–45
   handbrake **163**–48
branch **216**–2 ✎
   branch locations **184**–2 ✎ AWL
   Branches of the Military **141** ✎ AWL
Branch **140** ✎
Brass **244**
bread **67**–11 ✎
   bread-and-butter plate **83**–19 ✎
   breadbasket **83**–11
   garlic bread **81**–28
   loaf of bread **74**–22
   rye bread **71**–20
   wheat bread **71**–19
   white bread **71**–18 ✎
break 77–Q, **118**–P ✎
   break down 166–F ✎
Breakfast Special **80** ✎
breast **70**–19, **107**–25 ✎
breathe 118–N ✎
breathing **119**–17 ✎
bricklayer **198**–8
bricks **196**–12, **196**–B ✎
briefcase **88**–13
briefs **91**–5, **91**–14
bright blue **24**–12 ✎
bring 179–D, **246**–E ✎
broccoli **69**–13
broiled steak **76**–3
broiler **54**–21
broken **62**–5, **62**–6, **62**–7, **63**–15,
   97–39 ✎
   broken equipment **197**–4 ✎
broom **61**–16
brother **34**–6 ✎
   brother-in-law **34**–17
   half brother **35**–28 ✎
   stepbrother **35**–30

brown **24**–17 ✎
   brown hair **33**–15 ✎
   hash browns **80**–3
browse 102–B
   browser window **213**–8
bruise **110**–11
brush **33**–20, **108**–14 ✎
   paintbrush **195**–22, **239**–20
   scrub brush **61**–20
   toilet brush **57**–20 ✎
   toothbrush **57**–23, **109**–22
brush 108–I, **109**–J
bubble in 10–K ✎
bucket **61**–7
buckle **94**–20, **99**–28
buckle up 36–L
bud **217**–7
budget **198**–3 ✎
buffalo **222**–6
buffet **55**–24, **193**–10
bugs
   bedbugs **63**–24
building **50**–1, **126**–2 ✎
building maintenance **184**–12 ✎ AWL
BUILDING SUPPLIES **194**–**195** ✎
bulb **217**–2
bulldozer **196**–6
bulletin board **7**–14
bump cap **92**–9
bumper **162**–8
   bumper pad **59**–4
bunch ✎
   bunch of bananas **68**–29
bungee cord **195**–15
bunk beds **59**–9 ✎
Bunsen burner **207**–37
bureau **58**–1
burger
   cheeseburger **79**–3
   hamburger **79**–1
burglary **145**–2
burn
   sunburn **110**–13
burn 118–H ✎
burner **54**–19, **207**–37
burrito **79**–9
bus **130**–9, **155**–14 ✎
   bus person **193**–13 ✎
   bus route **156**–1 ✎ AWL
   bus station **126**–7 ✎
   bus stop **131**–16, **155**–13 ✎
   miss the bus **156** ✦✎
   school bus **160**–21 ✎
bus 82–G
Bus Stop **156** ✎
business ✎
   business owner **170**–11 ✎
   business suit **88**–11 ✎
   businessperson **170**–12 ✎
busser **83**–12
butcher **170**–13
butter **66**–6, **83**–19 ✎

butterfly **220**–20
buttocks **107**–30
button **99**–24 ✎
   AC button **163**–40
   back button **213**–9 ✎
   call button **123**–28 ✎
   refresh button **213**–11
buy 27–G ✎
   buy a home **41**–M ✎
   buy a snack **11**–K
   buy recycled products **225**–D ✎
Buying a House **49** ✎
Buying a Used Car **161** ✎
BUYING AND MAINTAINING A CAR
   161 ✎ AWL
buzzer **51**–32

cab **160**–16
cabbage **69**–2
cabinet **54**–1 ✎
   file cabinet **188**–11 ✎ AWL
   medicine cabinet **57**–22 ✎
   supply cabinet **188**–1 ✎
Cabinet **140**–10 ✎
cables **162**–21, **190**–12 ✎
cactus **216**–21
cafeteria **5**–14
cage **107**–48
cake **73**–39 ✎
   cake pan **78**–26 ✎
   cheesecake **81**–34
   layer cake **81**–33 ✎
   pancakes **80**–7
Cake **77**
calculate 17–B ✎
calculator **17**–6, **189**–25
calculus **204**–19
CALENDAR **20**–**21**
CALENDAR EVENTS **22**
calf **106**–22
   calf-length **96**–17
call
   call button **123**–28 ✎
   international call **15**–35 ✎
   Internet phone call **14**–19 ✎
   local call **15**–33 ✎
   missed call **14**–16 ✎
   long-distance call **15**–34
call 48–A, **151**–L ✎
   call in 198–A ✎
Call **15**
calm **42**–8 ✎
camcorder **241**–21
camel **223**–38
camera ✎
   camera case / bag **241**–22 ✎
   digital camera **241**–17 ✎
   document camera **7**–16 ✎ AWL
   security camera **50**–19 ✎ AWL
camisole **91**–20
campaign 143–K
camper **160**–9 ✎

campfire **232**–11
camping **232**–5 🔑
   camping stove **232**–16 🔑
Campus **5**
can **74**–3, **74**–15
   can opener **78**–1, **150**–8
   electric can opener **54**–14
   garbage can **53**–24 🔑
cancer **113**–17 🔑
candidate **143**–6 🔑
candle **56**–20
   candle holder **56**–21
candy **245**–12 🔑
   candy bar **73**–37 🔑
   candy cane **245**–17
   candy store **133**–17 🔑
cane **115**–16
canned food **150**–9 🔑
Canned Foods **72** 🔑
canoeing **232**–3
can't breathe 118–N 🔑
can't install 191–C 🔑
can't log on 191–D
can't stream 191–F
canteen **232**–24
canvas **239**–17
canyon **214**–17
cap **88**–1, **226**–7 🔑
   baseball cap **86**–5 🔑
   bump cap **92**–9
   shower cap **108**–1 🔑
   surgical cap **123**–37
   surgical scrub cap **93**–35
capital **140**–16 🔑
capitalize 202–A, **202**–B
Capitol **140**–1
capris **88**–8
capsule **115**–23
captain **235 ✦** 🔑
car **154**–1 🔑
   car accident **148**–2 🔑
   car dealership **128**–4
   car safety seat **37**–20 🔑
   sports car **160**–4
   subway car **156**–6
   town car **156**–20 🔑
   2-door car **160 ✦**
CAR **160, 161, 162** 🔑
Car **161, 163** 🔑
card **245**–5 🔑
   ATM card **134**–12
   automobile club card **166**–5 🔑
   baseball cards **238**–2 🔑
   card store **132**–7 🔑
   copies of ID and credit cards **150**–19 🔑
   emergency card **165**–26 🔑
   fare card **156**–11
   folding card table **102**–4 🔑
   green card **40**–2 🔑
   greeting card **136**–15
   health insurance card **111**–3 🔑
   memory card **241**–18 🔑
   phone card **15**–23 🔑

postcard **136**–16
Resident Alien card **40**–2
rotary card file **189**–44 🔑
Social Security card **40**–5
Card **137** 🔑
cardigan sweater **88**–2 🔑
Cardinal Numbers **16**
cardiologist **122**–3
cardiopulmonary resuscitation (CPR)
   119–18
care **171**–32 🔑
   careful worker **197**–2 🔑
   careless worker **197**–1 🔑
   childcare worker **170**–16
CARE **111, 116–117, 120** 🔑
Care of Your Car **161** 🔑
career 🔑
   career advancement **175**–6
   career and technical school **200**–5 🔑
   career and technical training
      175–9 🔑
Career Path **175** 🔑
CAREER PLANNING **174–175** 🔑
cargo van **160**–13 🔑
carnation **217**–20
carousel
   baggage carousel **165**–23
carpenter **62**–12, **170**–14
carpet **56**–24 🔑
carpool 225–I
carriage **37**–19
carrier **15**–27, **121**–1
   baby carrier **37**–17
   letter carrier **136**–20
carrots **69**–3 🔑
carry 11–F, **82**–H 🔑
CARS AND TRUCKS **160** 🔑
cart **73**–12, **131**–28
   housekeeping cart **192**–19
   luggage cart **192**–8
cartons **74**–4, **74**–16
cartoon **242**–3
cartridge **189**–45
carving knife **78**–12
case 🔑
   camera case / bag **241**–22 🔑
   cell phone case **94**–15 🔑
   display case **94**–5 🔑
cash 🔑
   cash and coins **150**–17 🔑
   cash register **27**–10, **73**–16 🔑 AWL
cash 27–F, **134**–A
cashier **73**–14, **170**–15
cashmere **98**–4
Casserole **77**
casserole dish **78**–10
cassette
   CD / cassette player **102**–8 🔑
cast **115**–20 🔑
castle **231**–12 🔑
CASUAL, WORK, AND FORMAL
   CLOTHES **88–89** 🔑
Casual Clothes **88**

cat **221**–9 🔑
   catfish **71**–2
catalog **135**–11
catch 236–D 🔑
catcher's mask **237**–15
caterer **193**–16
caterpillar **220**–21
cattle **187**–21
cauliflower **69**–14
cavity **120**–8
C-clamp **194**–6
CD 🔑
   CD / cassette player **102**–8 🔑
   CD-ROM drive **190**–15 🔑
   personal CD player **240**–7 🔑
celebrate 226–C 🔑
celery **69**–9
cell **206**–4 🔑
   cell membrane **206**–6
   cell phone **4**–13, **14**–8 🔑
   cell phone case **94**–15 🔑
   cell wall **206**–5 🔑
cello **244**–7
Celsius **13**–2
cemetery **129**–15
cent **26**–1, **26**–2, **26**–3, **26**–4 🔑
center 🔑
   automated postal center (APC) **137**–10
   childcare center **131**–30
   convention center **129**–24 🔑 AWL
   copy center **131**–18 🔑
   entertainment center **56**–5 🔑
   visit a career planning center **174**–A 🔑
centimeter [cm] **17**–14 🔑
Central time **19**–31
cereal **80**–9
   box of cereal **74**–18
ceremony **226**–6 🔑
certificate 🔑
   birth certificate **40**–1 🔑
   Certificate of Naturalization **40**–6
   death certificate **41**–11 🔑
certified
   Certified Mail® **136**–4
   certified nursing assistant (CNA)
      122–12 🔑
chain **51**–34, **95**–33, **194**–41 🔑
chair **7**–11 🔑
   armchair **56**–22
   beach chair **231**–22 🔑
   dining room chair **55**–8
   easy chair **56**–22 🔑
   folding chair **102**–5 🔑
   hard chair **23**–5 🔑
   high chair **37**–6, **82**–3 🔑
   rocking chair **37**–22
   soft chair **23**–6 🔑
   wheelchair **115**–9
chalk **7**–18
   chalkboard **6**–3
challenged **32**–10 🔑
change 36–G, **60**–P, **152**–C 🔑
change purse **94**–14

changing 🔑
  changing pad **59**–2
  changing table **59**–1 🔑
Changing Text **210** 🔑 AWL
charger **240**–15, **241**–24
  charger cord **14**–9
  charger plug **14**–10
  portable charger **240**–15
charging station / dock **240**–3 🔑
chart **123**–24 🔑 AWL
cheap **23**–20 🔑
check **134**–14
  checkbook **134**–13
  check-in kiosk **164**–2
  checkstand **73**–13
  paycheck **183**–14
check 🔑
  check blood pressure **111**–A 🔑
  check email **39**–W 🔑
  check employment websites
    168–H 🔑
  check in **164**–A 🔑
  check messages **177**–R 🔑
  check out **135**–C 🔑
  check pulse **124**–A
  check the correct boxes **9**–U 🔑
  check the oil **161**–H 🔑
  check the pronunciation **8**–D 🔑
  check your bags **164**–B 🔑
  check your spelling **211**–X 🔑
  check your understanding **12**–O 🔑
  check your work **10**–L 🔑
checked **96**–24
checker / cashier **73**–14
checkers **238**–7
checking account number **134**–15 🔑
checkout
  self-checkout **73**–10, **135**–10
Checkpoint **164**
cheddar cheese **71**–28
cheek **106**–3 🔑
cheese **66**–4 🔑
  American cheese **71**–26
  cheddar cheese **71**–28
  cheeseburger **79**–3
  cheesecake **81**–34
  grilled cheese sandwich **80**–10
  mozzarella cheese **71**–29
  Swiss cheese **71**–27
Cheesy Tofu Vegetable Casserole **77**
chef **83**–16
  chef's hat **93**–28
  chef's jacket **93**–29
  chef's salad **80**–14
  executive chef **193**–7
  head chef **193**–7
  sous-chef **193**–6
Chef **93**
chemist **207**–25 🔑
Chemistry **207** 🔑
cherries **68**–11
cherry picker **196**–5
chess **238**–8

chest **104**–4 🔑
  chest of drawers **59**–6 🔑
  toy chest **59**–16 🔑
chicken **66**–3, **70**–16 🔑
  chicken pox **112**–6
  chicken sandwich **79**–5
  fried chicken **76**–1
  roast chicken **81**–22
Chicken **77** 🔑
chief justice **140**–13 🔑
child / children 🔑
  child safety seat **163**–53 🔑
  childcare center **131**–30
  childcare worker **170**–16
  children's program **242**–9
  grandchild **34** ✦🔑
  lost child **148**–1 🔑
CHILDCARE AND PARENTING **36**–**37** 🔑
Childhood and Infectious Diseases **112** 🔑
CHILDREN **30**–**31** 🔑
Children **147** 🔑
chili peppers **69**–29 🔑
chill **76**–D
chills **110**–8
chimney **53**–4
chimpanzee **223**–27
chin **106**–1 🔑
chipmunk **221**–20
chips **73**–35 🔑
chiropractors **122** ✦
chisel **195**–55
choke **118**–L
choose **9**–P 🔑
chop **77**–L 🔑
chops **70**–10, **70**–15
Christmas **22**–18
  Christmas tree **245**–16
chromosome **206**–8
chrysanthemum **217**–21
church **129**–14 🔑
chute **51**–26
circle **205**–34 🔑
circle **9**–Q
circular saw **194**–9
circulation desk **135**–2
circumference **205**–36
citation **202**–11 AWL
cite sources **212**–I 🔑 AWL
citizen 🔑
  senior citizen **30**–5 🔑
Citizenship Requirements **142** 🔑
city **4**–7, **52**–1 🔑
  city council **140**–21 🔑
  city hall **127**–8 🔑
City Government **140** 🔑
CITY STREETS **128**–**129** 🔑
CIVIC ENGAGEMENT **142**–**143**
Civilizations **209**
claim **164**–L 🔑
clamp **194**–6
clams **71**–15
clarify instructions **178**–G 🔑 AWL
clarinet **244**–2

classical **243**–21 AWL
  classical concert **229**–14 🔑 AWL
classified ad **48**–2
Classmates **8**
classroom **5**–7 🔑
CLASSROOM **6**–**7** 🔑
claw **220**–2
clean **101**–16 🔑
clean **76**–A
  clean the house **39**–O 🔑
  clean the lint trap **101**–D 🔑
  clean the oven **60**–C 🔑
  clean the teeth **120**–A 🔑
  clean up **151**–M 🔑
cleaner
  dry cleaners **130**–2
  glass cleaner **61**–14
  multipurpose cleaner **61**–18
  oven cleaner **61**–3
  vacuum cleaner **61**–10
  vacuum cleaner attachments **61**–11
  vacuum cleaner bag **61**–12
cleaning cloths **61**–9 🔑
CLEANING SUPPLIES **61** 🔑
CLEANUP **152**–**153**
clear **13**–9 🔑
  clear aligner **120**–7
  clear tape **189**–30 🔑 AWL
clear **82**–G 🔑
  clear off **10**–I 🔑
clerk **5**–13, **188**–2 🔑
  admissions clerk **122**–14
  desk clerk **192**–11 🔑
  DMV clerk **138**–3 🔑
  file clerk **188**–10 🔑 AWL
  grocery clerk **72**–4 🔑
  library clerk **135**–1 🔑
  payroll clerk **183**–10
  postal clerk **137**–7
  retail clerk **173**–53
  salesclerk **94**–3 🔑
  shipping clerk **185**–14
  stock clerk **173**–59 🔑
click **210**–G 🔑
  click on a link **212**–F 🔑
  click submit **211**–S 🔑 AWL
  click the search icon **212**–D 🔑
  double-click **210**–H 🔑
climb **230**–C 🔑
climbing apparatus **230**–14
clinic **198**–2
clippers **109**–31, **186**–11
clip
  clip-on earrings **95**–37
  hair clip **108**–19
  paper clip **189**–31
  stage clips **206**–21
clock **7**–9 🔑
  alarm clock **58**–24 🔑
  clock radio **102**–6 🔑
  time clock **183**–7 🔑
close **6**–H, **210**–E 🔑
closet **57** ✦, **58**–5 🔑

Closures **99**
cloth **195**–54 🔑
  cleaning cloth **61**–9
  cloth diaper **37**–8
  tablecloth **55**–12
  washcloth **57**–6
clothes **150**–6 🔑
  clothesline **101**–9
  clothespin **101**–10
CLOTHES **86**–**87**, **88**–**89**, **96**–**97**, **98**–**99** 🔑
clothing **102**–2 🔑
CLOTHING **90, 92**–**93** 🔑
Clothing **97** 🔑
cloudy **13**–10
club 🔑
  automobile club card **166**–5
  club sandwich **80**–12
  golf club **237**–1
  nightclub **229**–12
clubs **239**–32 🔑
clutch **163**–49
  clutch bag **89**–19
CNA (certified nursing assistant) **122**–12 🔑
coach **5**–20, **235**–2 🔑
coal **224**–4 🔑
coarse adjustment knob **206**–24
Coast Guard **141**–36
coast guardsman **141**–37 🔑
coat **90**–2, **222**–19 🔑
  lab coat **93**–33 🔑
  raincoat **90**–18 🔑
  redcoat **208**–9
  sport coat **89**–14 🔑
  trench coat **90**–21
cobra **219**–44
cockpit **165**–10
cockroaches **63**–26
cocktail dress **89**–20
coconuts **68**–24
cod **71**–8, **218**–5
code 🔑 AWL
  area code **4**–10, **15**–28 🔑 AWL
  bar code **27**–4 🔑
  ZIP code **4**–9
coffee **73**–33, **81**–37, **81**–38 🔑
  coffee maker **54**–6
  coffee mug **55**–7
  coffee shop **128**–11 🔑
  coffee table **56**–19 🔑
COFFEE SHOP MENU **80**–**81** 🔑
coins **150**–17 🔑
  coin purse **94**–14
Coins **26** 🔑
colander **78**–17
cold **13**–6, **42**–4, **112**–1 🔑
  cold tablets **115**–27 🔑
  cold water **57**–10 🔑
coleslaw **80**–18
collar **100**–4
collate 177–E
collect 238–A 🔑
college **200**–7 🔑
  college degree **41**–7, **175**–5 🔑

college dormitory **52**–8
  community college **129**–17, **200**–6 🔑 AWL
cologne **108**–6
colon **202**–20
Colonial Period **208**
colonies **208**–1
colonists **208**–2
color 🔑
  watercolors **239**–21
color 33–D
coloring book **59**–13 🔑
COLORS **24** 🔑
Colors **24** 🔑
Columbus Day **22**–15
column **107**–49 🔑
comb **33**–19, **108**–13
comb 108–G
come 39–R 🔑
comedy **242**–2, **243**–13 🔑
comet **215**–24
comfort 36–I 🔑
comma **202**–17
commercial fisher **171**–17
commit a crime **145** ✦ 🔑 AWL
Common Illnesses **112** 🔑
communicate clearly **178**–E 🔑 AWL
COMMUNITY CLEANUP **152**–**153**
community college **129**–17, **200**–6 🔑 AWL
compare plans **121**–A 🔑
Comparing Clothing **97** 🔑
compartment **163**–44, **165**–13
complain 180–B 🔑
complaint **97** ✦
complete an application **169**–J 🔑
Complex **51** 🔑 AWL
compliment **12** ✦
compliment 12–C
compose / write the message **211**–W 🔑
composer **209**–14
composition **209**–15
Composition **202**
compost 225–M
compost pile **53**–25
computer **7**–15, **189**–17 🔑 AWL
  computer lab **5**–15 🔑
  computer operations specialist **190**–2 🔑
  computer software engineer **171**–18 🔑
  computer technician **171**–19, **188**–12
  computer **won't start 191**–A 🔑
  desktop computer **190**–9 AWL
  laptop computer **190**–22 AWL
  mainframe computer **190**–1
  program computers **176**–I
conceal 146–C
concert **228**–5, **229**–14 🔑
concierge **192**–4
conclusion **202**–9 🔑 AWL
concrete **196**–10 🔑
conditioner **108**–11
CONDITIONS **112**–**113** 🔑
Conditions **13, 112**–**113** 🔑
condominium / condo **52**–5
conduct 244–C 🔑 AWL

Conducting Research **212** 🔑 AWL
conductor **156**–13
cone **205**–40
  ice-cream cone **79**–13
  pine cone **216**–11
conference room **188**–4 🔑 AWL
confetti **245**–3
confused **43**–26 🔑
congestion **113**–13
Congress **140**–2, **208**–6 🔑
congressperson **140**–4
Conserve Energy and Resources **225** 🔑 AWL
console **238**–3
constellation **215**–14
Constitution **208**–12 AWL
construction 🔑 AWL
  construction paper **238**–13 🔑
  construction site **128**–2 🔑 AWL
  construction worker **196**–1 🔑 AWL
CONSTRUCTION **196** 🔑 AWL
Construction Worker **92** 🔑 AWL
consult 174–F 🔑 AWL
contact 150–2 🔑 AWL
  contact lenses **117**–8 🔑
  contact list **14**–15 🔑 AWL
  contact references **168**–C 🔑
container **74**–5, **74**–17, **78**–4 🔑
CONTAINERS AND PACKAGING **74** 🔑
content **213**–16 🔑
continental
  First Continental Congress **208**–6
continuing education **175**–7 🔑
contractor **198**–5 AWL
control **123**–27 🔑
controller **238**–4
convenience store **130**–3
convention center **129**–24 🔑 AWL
CONVERSATION **12** 🔑
convert 17–D, **75**–C 🔑 AWL
convertible **160**–5 AWL
conveyer belt **185**–9
convict 144–E
convict / prisoner **144**–15
cook **193**–1 🔑
  line cook **93, 193** ✦ 🔑
  short-order cook **193**–1
cook 39–Q, **76**–C, **176**–C 🔑
Cook **93** 🔑
cooked **70**–25 🔑
cookies **73**–38 🔑
  cookie sheet **78**–27 🔑
cool **13**–5 🔑
cooler **231**–9
co-op **52** ✦
cooperate with teammates **178**–F AWL
co-pay **121**–8
copier
  photocopier **189**–23
copies / copy 🔑
  copies of ID and credit cards **150**–19 🔑
  copies of important papers **150**–20 🔑
  copy center **131**–18 🔑
  make copies **177**–D 🔑

copy 8–E, 210–K
coral 218–16
cord
  bungee cord 195–15
  extension cord 195–14
  frayed cord 197–5
  power cord 190–10
corduroy 99–11
corn 69–12, 187–4
  cornrows 33–22
corned beef 71–22
corner 130–7
coronary disease 113 ♦
corporate offices / headquarters 184–1 AWL
corral 187–17
correct 10–N
correction
  correction fluid 189–36
  correction tape 189–37
cost 27–7
  low-cost exam 124–1
costume 245–11
cotton 98–1, 187–6
couch 56–18
cough 110–9
cough syrup 115–29
council 140–21
  councilperson 140–22
counselor 5–6, 174–F
count 84–A
counter 54–22
  counterperson 79–17
Counterperson 93
country 52–4, 243–27
county fair 229–13
coupe 160 ♦
couple 35–20, 35–21, 245–4 AWL
coupons 67–15
courier 172–40
course 175–13
court
  basketball court 235–7
  court reporter 144–12
  courthouse 127–13
  courtroom 144–7
  courtyard 51–21
  food court 133–15
  Supreme Court 140–11
  tennis court 230–6
cousin 34–9
cover 162–9, 195–46
  coveralls 92–8
  cover-up 90–25
cow 221–1
cowboy hat 92–18
co-worker 180–5
coyote 222–3
CPR (cardiopulmonary resuscitation) 119–18
CPU 190–16
crab 71–9, 218–21
cracked 62–4
cradle 59–20

crane 196–7
crash 148–3
crayons 59–14
cream 81–41, 115–25
  antihistamine cream 119–11
  ice cream 72–26
  ice-cream cone 79–13
  ice cream shop 133–16
  shaving cream 109–29
  sour cream 72–21
cream / ivory 24–16
creamer 55–15
create AWL
  create a new document 210–B AWL
  create a password 211–P
  create a username 211–O
  create secure passwords 147–D
Creating a Document 210 AWL
credit 150–19 AWL
creek / stream 214 ♦
crescent moon 215–10
crew 186–1, 186–4
  crew socks 91–8
  crewneck sweater 96–7
crib 59–3
cricket 220–24
CRIME 145
Crime 147
criminal 145 ♦
crochet 239–25
crocodile 219–40
crocus 217–17
cross
  cross-country skiing 233–3
  crosswalk 130–15
cross 130–A
  cross out 9–R
crossing 158–13, 158–14, 158–15
crown 120–10
crucible tongs 207–44
crutches 115–10
cry 226–B
cube 205–38
cubicle 188–7
cucumbers 69–10
cuff 100–9
cup 75–2, 75–10, 83–24
  1/2 cup 75–9
  1/4 cup 75–8
  teacup 55–6
curb 131–21
curling iron 108–17
curly hair 33–11
curtains 56–16, 57–14, 58–7
curved line 205–23
cushion 56 ♦, 100–13
customer 72–1, 94–4, 134–2, 182–2
  customer service 97 ♦, 184–11
  customer service representative 171–20
Customs 165
customs officer 165–17
cut 91–10, 110–12

cut 33–A, 109–N
  cut up 77–I
cute 32–14
cutlets 70–6
cutter 189–22, 238–16
cutting board 54–27
CYBER SAFETY 147
cyberbullying 147–1
cybersecurity 190–4 AWL
cycling 234–5 AWL
cyclist 230–2
cylinder 205–41, 207–38
cytoplasm 206–9

daffodil 217–25
daily 20–21
DAILY ROUTINES 38–39
Dairy 72
daisy 217–14
dance 64–A
Danger 147
dangerous 198–1
dark blue 24–10
Dashboard and Instrument Panel 163 AWL
data 15–36, 190–3 AWL
date 20–1, 68–28, 213–20
  date of birth 4–14
  expiration date 114–7, 138–10
daughter 34–14
  daughter-in-law 34 ♦
  granddaughters 34 ♦
  stepdaughter 35 ♦
day 20–2
  birthday 22–1
  Columbus Day 22–15
  daylight saving time 19–25
  every day 20–21
  Independence Day 22–13
  Labor Day 22–14
  Martin Luther King Jr. Day 22–10
  Memorial Day 22–12
  New Year's Day 22–9
  Presidents' Day 22–11
  Veterans Day 22–16
Day 18
DAY AT SCHOOL 11
DAY AT WORK 198–199
Days of the Week 20
dead 41 ♦
  dead end 158–6
  dead-bolt lock 51–35
deaf 32–12
Dealer 162
dealership 128–4
death certificate 41–11
debate 143–L AWL
decaf coffee 81–38
decay 120–8
deceased 41 ♦
December 21–36
decimal point 17–7
Decimals 17
deck 246–2

declaration
declaration form **165**–16
Declaration of Independence **208**–5
decline **12**–K AWL
decorations **246**–1 🔑
deductions **183**–13 AWL
deed **41**–9
deer **222**–14
defendant **144**–5
defense attorney **144**–4 🔑
defroster **163**–41
degrees **13**–8, **205**–26 🔑
delayed **165**–30 🔑
delete **147**–G, **210**–I
DELI **71**
deliver **11**–G, **137**–E 🔑
delivery person **171**–21 🔑
dementia **113**–19
demonstration **124**–6 AWL
denim **99**–7
denominator **204**–6
dental
dental assistant **120**–2, **171**–22
dental floss **109**–24
dental hygienist **120**–3
dental instruments **120**–4
DENTAL CARE **120**
Dental Problems **120**
dentist **120**–1 🔑
Dentistry **120**
dentures **120**–11
deodorant **108**–5
department **95**–7, **95**–8 🔑
Department of Motor Vehicles **126**–4
department store **133**–13 🔑
DEPARTMENT OF MOTOR VEHICLES (DMV)
138–**139**
departure **165**–7 🔑
departure time **165** ✦ 🔑
dependents **121**–6
deposit **134**–3 🔑
deposit slip **134**–4 🔑
opening deposit **134**–11
safety deposit box **134**–7 🔑
depression **117**–5 AWL
depth **17**–18 🔑
dermatologists **122** ✦
DESCRIBING CLOTHES **96**–**97** 🔑
DESCRIBING HAIR **33** 🔑
DESCRIBING PEOPLE **32** 🔑
DESCRIBING THINGS **23** 🔑
desert **214**–4 🔑
design **185**–A AWL
designated drivers **146** ✦
designer **98** ✦, **171**–30, **185**–2,
186–5 AWL
desk **6**–7, **188**–9 🔑
circulation desk **135**–2
desk clerk **192**–11 🔑
front desk **192**–12 🔑
desktop computer **190**–9 AWL
dessert tray **83**–10
Desserts **81**

destination **166**–6
detector **51**–30 AWL
detergent **101**–8
device **231**–20 🔑 AWL
diabetes **113**–26
diagonal **205**–31
dial **15**–A, **15**–E
diameter **205**–37
diamonds **239**–29 🔑
diaper **37**–8, **37**–10
diaper bag **37**–11
diaper pail **37**–7
diaphragm **206**–18
dice **238**–6
dice **77**–J
dictate **8**–N
dictator **209**–6
dictionary **7**–31, **7**–32 🔑
die **41**–R 🔑
dietician **122**–15
difference **204**–8 🔑
different **23**–16 🔑
DIFFERENT **28**–**29** 🔑
DIFFERENT PLACES TO LIVE **52** 🔑
difficult **23**–24 🔑
digital 🔑
digital camera **241**–17 🔑
digital photo album **241**–30 🔑
digital video recorder (DVR) **56**–7
DIGITAL LITERACY **210**–**211**
dime / 10 cents **26**–3
Dimensions **17** AWL
diner **82**–6, **193**–9
dining
dining area **46**–8
dining room **82**–1
dining room chair **55**–8
dining room table **55**–9
Dining **193**
DINING AREA **55**
dinner **72**–28 🔑
dinner fork **83**–28 🔑
dinner plate **83**–18 🔑
Dinner **81** 🔑
diploma **40**–3
direct **180**–C 🔑
Directions **9**, **159** 🔑
DIRECTIONS AND MAPS **159** 🔑
directory **133**–24
directory assistance **14**–21
dirty **101**–15 🔑
Disabilities **32**
disagree **12**–M 🔑
disappointed **28**–4 🔑
DISASTERS **148**–**149** 🔑
disc **237**–27 🔑
discipline **36**–K
discuss **8**–G 🔑
disease **113**–27, **113**–28, **120**–12 🔑
Diseases **112** 🔑
disgusted **42**–7 🔑
dish **55**–1 🔑
casserole dish **78**–10

dish rack **54**–5
dish room **83**–13 🔑
dish towel **61**–22 🔑
dishwasher **54**–8, **83**–14, **193**–2
dishwashing liquid **61**–21 🔑
satellite dish **53**–5
soap dish **57**–3 🔑
disinfect **76** ✦
disinfectant wipes **61**–23
display case **94**–5 🔑 AWL
disposable AWL
disposable diaper **37**–10
disposable gloves **93**–27 🔑 AWL
disposal **54**–7, **123**–31 AWL
distribute **180**–D 🔑 AWL
dive **236**–K
divide **17**–A, **204**–D 🔑
diving **233**–12
diving mask **231**–7
divorced couple **35**–21 🔑
DJ **64**–4
DMV
DMV clerk **138**–3
DMV handbook **138**–1
do **39**–T 🔑
do an experiment **207**–B 🔑
do crafts **238**–D 🔑
do errands **130** ✦
do manual labor **176**–D 🔑 AWL
do not drink **114**–F 🔑
do not drive or operate **114**–E 🔑
do not enter **158**–2 🔑
do not take **114**–D 🔑
don't be late **179**–E 🔑
don't litter **225**–L
don't smoke **116**–G
dock **185**–15, **240**–3
dock worker **171**–23
doctor **111**–5 🔑
Document **210** 🔑 AWL
document camera **7**–16 🔑 AWL
DOCUMENTS **40**–**41** 🔑 AWL
dog **221**–11
feed dog **98**–20
hot dog **79**–6
prairie dog **221**–22
dogwood **216**–15
DOING THE LAUNDRY **101** 🔑
doll **59**–21, **239**–28
dollhouse **59**–18
dollar **26**–7 🔑
dollar coin **26**–6 🔑
fifty dollars **26**–11
five dollars **26**–8
half dollar **26**–5 🔑
one hundred dollars **26**–12
ten dollars **26**–9
twenty dollars **26**–10
dolphin **219**–31
DOMESTIC ANIMALS AND RODENTS
221 🔑 AWL
domesticated **221** ✦ AWL
donkey **221**–3

donut **79**–15
  donut shop **131**–17
door **46**–4 🔑
  door chain **51**–34 🔑
  door lock **163**–25 🔑
  doorbell **53**–14
  doorknob **53**–12
  doorman **192**–1
  front door **53**–11 🔑
  garage door **53**–7 🔑
  revolving door **192**–2
  screen door **53**–15 🔑
  sliding glass door **53**–18 🔑
  storm door **53**–10 🔑
  2-door car **160** ✦
dorm / dormitory **52**–8
dosage **114**–6
double 🔑
  double bed **192**–14 🔑
  double boiler **78**–8
double-click 210–H
down 🔑
  break down 166–F
  down jacket **90**–16
  down vest **90**–14
  downhill skiing **233**–1
  drop-down menu **213**–15
  put down 6–J
  sit down 6–F 🔑
  walk down **157**–D
downstairs **51** ✦🔑
DOWNTOWN **126**–**127** 🔑
drag 210–J 🔑
drain **57**–7
drama **242**–12 🔑 AWL
drapes **56**–16
draw 8–F, **111**–F, **207**–E 🔑
drawer **54**–23, **58**–2, **59**–6 🔑
dress **86**–3, **88**–5, **89**–20 🔑
  dress socks **91**–9 🔑
  dressmaker **100**–1
  dressmaker's dummy **100**–2
dress 36–H, **179**–B
dressed **38**–D
dresser **58**–1
Dressings **80**
dribble 236–J
drill **194**–8, **196**–9
  drill bit **194**–28
drill 120–D
drink 11–J
  do not drink 114–F 🔑
  don't drink and **drive 146**–G 🔑
  drink fluids **116**–C
drip **123**–25
dripping 63–17
drive **190**–15, **190**–19, **190**–25,
  190–27
  drive-thru window **130**–11
  driveway **53**–8
drive 🔑
  don't **drink** and **drive 146**–G 🔑
  drive a truck **176**–E 🔑

drive through **157**–K 🔑
drive to work **38**–I 🔑
driver **156**–21, **173**–61 🔑
  designated drivers **146** ✦
  driver's license **40**–4, **138**–9 🔑 AWL
  driver's license number **138**–11 🔑
  Phillips screwdriver **194**–31
  screwdriver **194**–30
driving **145**–5 🔑
drop 🔑
  drop cloth **195**–54 🔑
  drop-down menu **213**–15 🔑
  post office lobby drop **137**–11 🔑
drop off 38–G
dropper **207**–45
drops **115**–31 🔑
drought **149**–11
drown 118–I
drugs **118**–K, **145**–6 🔑
drums **244**–16 🔑
drumsticks **70**–23
drunk driving **145**–5 🔑
dry **101**–18 🔑
  dry cleaners **130**–2
  dry erase marker **7**–17
  drywall **196**–19
dry 60–N, **108**–H 🔑
Dry Measures **75** 🔑
dryer **50**–13, **101**–4
  blow dryer **33**–21, **108**–18
  dryer sheets **101**–5
duck **70**–18, **220**–13
duct tape **195**–49 🔑
dummy **100**–2
dump truck **160**–19 🔑
dune **214**–5
duplex **52** ✦
During an Emergency **151** 🔑
dust 🔑
  dust ruffle **58**–17
  dust storm **13**–20 🔑
  dustpan **61**–17
dust 60–A
duster **61**–1
DVD **135**–19 🔑
  DVD and CD-ROM drive **190**–15 🔑
  DVD player **240**–11 🔑
dye 33–D

eagle **220**–10
ear **105**–12 🔑
  ear infection **112**–3 🔑
  earache **110**–3
  earbuds / in-ear headphones **240**–5
  earmuffs **90**–13, **197**–16
  earplugs **197**–15
  pierced ear **32**–17
  pierced earrings **95**–36
early **19**–22 🔑
Earth **215**–3 🔑
earthquake **148**–5
easel **239**–18
east **159**–4 🔑

Eastern time **19**–32
easy **23**–23, **76**–11 🔑
  easy chair **56**–22 🔑
Easy Chicken Soup **77** 🔑
eat 11–I 🔑
  eat a healthy diet **116**–F 🔑
  eat breakfast **38**–E 🔑
  eat dinner **39**–S 🔑
  eat out **82** ✦🔑
eater
  weed eater **186**–12
e-book **135**–18
eclipse **215**–16
edit 203–I AWL
education 🔑
  basic education **175**–1 🔑
  continuing education **175**–7 🔑
  physical education **201**–17 🔑 AWL
eel **218**–12
eggplants **69**–23
eggs **66**–7 🔑
  eggbeater **78**–20
  eggs over easy **76**–11 🔑
  eggs sunny-side up **76**–10 🔑
  hard-boiled eggs **76**–8 🔑
  poached eggs **76**–9
  scrambled eggs **76**–7
Eggs **76** 🔑
eight **16**
eighteen **16**
eighteenth **16**
eighth **16**
eightieth **16**
eighty **16**
elastic bandage **119**–13 🔑
elbow **106**–12 🔑
elderly **32**–3 🔑
elected **143**–M 🔑
  elected official **143**–12 🔑
Election **143** 🔑
election results **143**–11 🔑
elective **201** ✦
electric **118**–F 🔑
  electric can opener **54**–14
  electric drill **194**–8
  electric keyboard **244**–18 🔑
  electric mixer **54**–25
  electric pencil sharpener **189**–26
  electric shaver **109**–26
  electric vehicle / EV **160**–2 🔑
electrical 🔑
  electrical hazard **198**–6
  electrical tape **195**–43 🔑
electrician **62**–9
electron **207**–30
electronics
  electronics repairperson **171**–24
  electronics store **133**–20
ELECTRONICS AND PHOTOGRAPHY
  240–**241** 🔑
elementary school **200**–2 🔑
elephant **223**–42
elevator **50**–9, **133**–21, **192**–9 🔑

eleven **16**
eleventh **16**
elm **216**–16
email 🔑
  address the email **211**–U
  check email **39**–W 🔑
  delete suspicious emails **147**–G 🔑
  send the email **211**–Z 🔑
Email **211** 🔑
embarrassed **43**–24 🔑
embroidery **239**–24
EMERGENCIES **118** 🔑
EMERGENCIES AND NATURAL
  DISASTERS **148**–**149** 🔑
emergency **119**–3 🔑
  emergency card **165**–26 🔑
  emergency exit **51**–25, **165**–14 🔑
  emergency medical technician (EMT)
    123–32
Emergency **150, 151** 🔑
Emergency Call **15** 🔑
EMERGENCY PROCEDURES **150**–**151** 🔑 AWL
Emergency Room Entrance **123** 🔑
Emergency Worker **93** 🔑
emery board **109**–32
emperor **209**–3
employee **183**–9 🔑
employer **182**–4 🔑
empty **23**–10 🔑
empty 60–L
EMT (emergency medical technician)
  123–32
end 🔑
  dead end **158**–6 🔑
  end table **56**–14 🔑
  end the call **15**–D
  endpoint **205**–21
energy **224**–1, **224**–7, **224**–8 🔑 AWL
  bioenergy **224**–9
Energy and Resources **225** 🔑 AWL
ENERGY AND THE ENVIRONMENT
  224–**225** 🔑 AWL
Energy Sources **224** 🔑 AWL
engine **162**–18, **212**–2 🔑
engineer **171**–18, **171**–25 🔑
ENGLISH COMPOSITION **202**–**203**
English language instruction **201**–14 🔑
English muffin **80**–5
enter 🔑
  do not **enter 158**–2 🔑
  enter data **177**–B 🔑 AWL
  enter the room **11**–C 🔑
  enter your PIN **134**–D
ENTERTAINMENT **242**–**243** 🔑
entertainment center **56**–5 🔑
entrance **182**–1 🔑
Entrance **50, 123** 🔑
entry-level job **175**–2 🔑 AWL
Entryway **51**
envelope **136**–14, **189**–43 🔑
ENVIRONMENT **224**–**225** 🔑 AWL
Environmental Protection Agency (EPA) **224** ✦
EPA (Environmental Protection Agency) **224** ✦

equation **204**–13 AWL
equipment **187**–12, **197**–4 🔑 AWL
EQUIPMENT **237** 🔑 AWL
Equipment **189, 197** 🔑 AWL
Equivalencies **17, 75**
erase 10–M
eraser **7**–19, **7**–21
errands **130** ✦
eruption **149**–16
escalator **133**–23
escape **50**–2 🔑
  escape route **150**–3 🔑 AWL
essay **202**–4 🔑
Essay **202** 🔑
e-ticket **165**–19
EV / electric vehicle **160**–2 🔑
evacuate 151–K
evacuation route **150**–5 🔑 AWL
even numbers **204**–4 🔑
evening **18**–19 🔑
  evening gown **89**–18
EVENTS **22, 40**–**41** 🔑
every day **20**–21 🔑
EVERYDAY CLOTHES **86**–**87**
EVERYDAY CONVERSATION **12**
evidence **144**–9, **202**–7 🔑 AWL
exam **124**–1, **138**–6 🔑
examination table **111**–7 🔑
examine 11–E, **111**–D 🔑
Examining Room **111** 🔑
exchange 27–I
excited **43**–22 🔑
exclamation mark / exclamation point
  202–16
executive **188**–5 🔑
  executive chef **193**–7
Executive Branch **140**
exercise **124**–5 🔑
exercise 39–P, **236**–N
Exercise Wear **89** 🔑
exhausted **43** ✦
ex-husband **35** ✦
exit **51**–25, **165**–14 🔑
expensive **23**–19, **97**–44 🔑
Experiment **207** 🔑
expiration date **114**–7, **138**–10
expire 138 ✦
explain 12–N 🔑
explanation of benefits / EOB **121**–11 🔑 AWL
exploration **209**–8
explore 174–B
explorer **209**–9
explosion **148**–4 🔑
exposed 🔑 AWL
  overexposed **241**–32
  underexposed **241**–33
Express Mail® **136**–2
Extended Family **34** 🔑
extension cord **195**–14
exterminate 62 ✦
exterminator **63**–21
external hard drive **190**–27
extinguisher **197**–21

extra 🔑
  extra large **96**–5 🔑
  extra small **96**–1 🔑
ex-wife **35** ✦
eye **105**–11 🔑
  eye drops **115**–31
  eye hook **194**–40 🔑
  eye shadow **109**–35 🔑
  eyebrow **106**–9
  eyebrow pencil **109**–34
  eyeglasses **117**–7 🔑
  eyelashes **106**–11
  eyelid **106**–10
  eyeliner **109**–36
  eyepiece **206**–14
  hook and eye **99**–27
Eye **106** 🔑

fabric **98**–15
  fabric softener **101**–6
Fabric Store **99**
face **205**–44 🔑
  face mask **93**–32
  face powder **109**–41 🔑
Face **106** 🔑
facility **180**–1 🔑 AWL
factory **128**–3 🔑
  factory owner **185**–1 🔑
  factory worker **185**–3 🔑
Factory **98**
Fahrenheit **13**–1
fair
  county fair **229**–13
  fair trial **142**–5 🔑
  job fair **174**–I 🔑 AWL
FAIR **124**–**125**
fall 118–O 🔑
  fall in love **40**–H 🔑
fall / autumn **21**–39 🔑
FAMILIES **34**–**35** 🔑
Family **34** 🔑
FAMILY REUNION **44**–**45**
famine **149**–12
fan **55**–19, **235**–4 🔑
  fan speed **163**–39 🔑
fancy **97**–34 🔑
far from **25** ✦🔑
fare **156**–2
  fare card **156**–11
farm **52**–9 🔑
  farm equipment **187**–12 🔑
  farmworker **187**–8 🔑
Farm Animals **221** 🔑
farmer **187**–13 🔑
FARMERS' MARKET **84**–**85** 🔑
FARMING AND RANCHING **187** 🔑
Farmworker **92** 🔑
fashion designer **98** ✦🔑 AWL
fast **23**–3 🔑
  fast food restaurant **130**–10 🔑
FAST FOOD RESTAURANT **79** 🔑
fast forward 241–D 🔑
fasten 164–H 🔑

fastener **99**–29 🔑
fat / heavy **32**–7 🔑
father **34**–4, **35**–23 🔑
    father-in-law **34**–11
    grandfather **34**–2 🔑
    stepfather **35**–25
faucet **57**–8
fax 177–G
fax machine **189**–21
feast **245**–13
feather **220**–4 🔑
    feather duster **61**–1
February **21**–26 🔑
Federal Government **140** 🔑 AWL
feed 36–C, **186**–D, **187**–D 🔑 AWL
feed dog / feed bar **98**–20
feedback
    respond well to feedback **178**–H
feel 110–A, **110**–B 🔑
FEELINGS **42** 🔑
female **4**–18 🔑
fence **187**–19 🔑
fencing **234**–7
fertilize 186–D
fever **110**–7 🔑
fiction **243**–18
field **5**–2, **187**–7 🔑
    ball field **230**–1
    track and field **234**–18 🔑
fifteen **16**
fifteenth **16**
fifth **16**
fiftieth **16**
fifty **16**
    fifty dollars **26**–11
    50 percent **17**–10 🔑
fighter
    firefighter **148**–9, **171**–26
figs **68**–27
figure **239**–26 🔑
    figure skating **233**–5
figurine **238**–1
file **189**–44 🔑 AWL
    attach a file **211**–Y 🔑 AWL
    file cabinet **188**–11 🔑 AWL
    file clerk **188**–10 🔑 AWL
    file folder **189**–50
fill 🔑
    fill a cavity **120**–E
    fill in 9–O 🔑
    fill prescriptions **114** ✦
    fill the tank **161**–G 🔑
    fill the tires **161**–L 🔑
filling **120**–9 🔑
Filling Out a Form **4** 🔑
fin **218**–1
find 164–F 🔑
FINDING A HOME **48**–**49** 🔑
fine adjustment knob **206**–22
finger **105**–16 🔑
    fingernail **106**–18
    fingerprint **138**–5
    swollen finger **110**–16 🔑

Fingers **106** 🔑
finish 236–T 🔑
    finish all medication **114**–C
fins **231**–8
fire **148**–7, **148**–8 🔑
    campfire **232**–11
    fire escape **50**–2 🔑
    fire exit **51** ✦🔑
    fire extinguisher **197**–21
    fire hydrant **131**–27
    fire screen **56**–12 🔑
    fire station **127**–12 🔑
    fire truck **148**–10 🔑
    firefighter **148**–9, **171**–26
    fireplace **56**–13
    fireworks **245**–7
first **16** 🔑
    first aid kit **119**–1, **150**–18 🔑
    first aid manual **119**–2 🔑 AWL
    First Continental Congress **208**–6
    first name **4**–2 🔑
    first president **208**–11 🔑
FIRST AID **119** 🔑
First Aid **119** 🔑
First Aid Procedures **119** 🔑 AWL
FIRST DAY ON THE JOB **180**–**181** 🔑
First Floor **50** 🔑
First License **139** 🔑 AWL
fish **66**–1, **81**–29 🔑
    catfish **71**–2
    goldfish **221**–16
    jellyfish **218**–14
    starfish **218**–17
    swordfish **71**–5, **218**–10
Fish **71, 218** 🔑
fisher **171**–17
fishing **232**–4 🔑
    fishing net **232**–17 🔑
    fishing pole **232**–18 🔑
fitted sheet **58**–12
fittings **195**–18
five **16**
    five after one **18**–7 🔑
    five dollars **26**–8
fix 62 ✦, **225**–F 🔑
fixture **55**–18
flag **245**–8 🔑
flammable liquids **197**–8
flash drive / thumb drive **190**–25
flashlight **150**–14
flat 🔑
    flat sheet **58**–13 🔑
    flat-panel TV **240**–8 🔑
    flat-screen TV **240**–8 🔑
    have a flat tire **166**–C 🔑
flats **95**–27
fleas **63**–25
    flea market **228**–6
flight 🔑
    flight attendant **165**–12
    nonstop flight **165** ✦
Flight **164** 🔑
float **245**–2 🔑

flood **149**–19 🔑
floor **46**–7, **58**–21, **197**–6 🔑
    floor lamp **56**–15 🔑
    floor plan **198**–4 🔑
Floor **50** 🔑
floral **96**–25
florist **132**–8, **171**–27
floss **109**–24
floss 109–K
flounder **218**–15
flour **73**–29 🔑
Flower **217** 🔑
flowers 🔑
    flower bed **53**–20 🔑
FLOWERS **217** 🔑
flu **112**–2 🔑
fluid
    correction fluid **189**–36
    fluid ounce **75**–1
flute **244**–1
fly **220**–29
fly 176–F 🔑
flyer **102**–1
flying disc **237**–27 🔑
foam pad **232**–13
focus **241**–31 🔑 AWL
foggy **13**–21
foil **72**–23
fold 101–F 🔑
folder **189**–50
folding 🔑
    folding card table **102**–4 🔑
    folding chair **102**–5 🔑
folk **243**–29
follow 116–J, **151**–F 🔑
Following Directions **9** 🔑
food 🔑
    baby food **37**–4 🔑
    canned food **150**–9
    fast food restaurant **130**–10 🔑
    food court **133**–15 🔑
    food preparation worker **193**–4 🔑
    food processor **54**–26
    packaged food **150**–10 🔑
    pet food **72**–6 🔑
FOOD **79** 🔑
FOOD PREPARATION AND SAFETY **76**–**77** 🔑
Food Processor **92**
Food Safety **76** 🔑
FOOD SERVICE **193** 🔑
Foods **72, 73** 🔑
foot **104**–8 🔑
    football **235**–12, **237**–21 🔑
    football helmet **237**–19
    footless tights **91**–17
    footnote **202**–12
    presser foot **98**–19
Foot **106** 🔑
forceps **207**–43
forearm **106**–13
forehead **106**–2
forest **214**–1, **214**–11 🔑
    forest fire **148**–7 🔑

fork **55**–3, **83**–27, **83**–28 🔑
  forklift **185**–12
Form **4** 🔑
Formal Clothes **89** 🔑
former husband **35** ✦🔑
former wife **35** ✦🔑
forms **111**–4, **136**–19, **165**–16 🔑
formula **37**–3, **207**–34 🔑 AWL
fortieth **16**
forty **16**
forward **241**–D 🔑
foundation **109**–40 🔑 AWL
founders **208**–7
fountain **230**–5, **230**–9
four **16**
  4-door car **160** ✦🔑
  2 x 4 (two by four) **195**–19
fourteen **16**
fourteenth **16**
fourth **16**
Fourth Floor **50**
Fourth of July / Independence Day **22**–13
fox **222**–15
Fractions **204**
Fractions and Decimals **17**
frame **58**–4, **58**–18 🔑
frayed cord **197**–5
free 🔑
  free speech **142**–2 🔑
  sugar-free **124**–7
freedom 🔑
  freedom of religion **142**–3 🔑
  freedom of the press **142**–4 🔑
freezer **54**–10, **193**–3
freezing **13**–7
French
  French fries **79**–2
  French horn **244**–13
Frequency **20**
fresh **71**–16 🔑
Friday **20**–13 🔑
fried
  fried chicken **76**–1
  stir-fried beef **76**–6 🔑
fringe **99**–34
Frisbee® **237**–27
frog **218**–26
front **25**–7 🔑
  front desk **192**–12 🔑
  front door **53**–11 🔑
  front seat **163**–51 🔑
  front walk **53**–2
Front Porch **53**
Front Yard and House **53** 🔑
frostbite **118**–G
froze 191–B
frozen 🔑
  frozen dinner **72**–28 🔑
  frozen fish **71**–17
  frozen vegetables **72**–27 🔑
  frozen yogurt **75**–3
  pipes are frozen **63**–16 🔑

Frozen Foods **72** 🔑
fruit **67**–9 🔑
  fruit salad **80**–21 🔑
FRUIT **68** 🔑
frustrated **43**–27
frying pan **78**–5 🔑
fuel injection system **162**–17 🔑
full **23**–9, **42**–6 🔑
  full moon **215**–12 🔑
  full-length mirror **58**–6 🔑
fumes **197**–3
funnel **207**–40
funny photo **226**–2 🔑
fur **222**–19 🔑
furious **43** ✦
furnished apartment **48**–3 🔑
furniture **53**–19 🔑
  furniture polish **61**–8 🔑
  furniture store **128**–8 🔑
Furniture and Accessories **59** 🔑
fuse box **62**–13
fusion **224**–10

galaxy **215**–15
gallbladder **107**–44
gallon **75**–5 🔑
game 🔑
  baseball game **44**–2 🔑
  board game **238**–5 🔑
  game show **242**–8 🔑
  video game console **238**–3
  video game controller **238**–4
GAMES **238**–**239** 🔑
Games **59** 🔑
gang violence **145**–4
garage **47**–15, **126**–1 🔑
  garage door **53**–7 🔑
Garage **50** 🔑
GARAGE SALE **102**–**103** 🔑
garbage 🔑
  garbage can **53**–24 🔑
  garbage disposal **54**–7 🔑 AWL
  garbage truck **129**–22 🔑
garden 🔑
  botanical garden **228**–3
  garden salad **80**–15 🔑
  roof garden **50**–4 🔑
  vegetable garden **53**–27, **187**–14 🔑
garden 53–B
gardener **171**–28
gardenia **217**–18
gardening 🔑
  gardening crew **186**–1
  gardening crew leader **186**–4 🔑
GARDENING **186** 🔑
gargle 109–L
garlic **69**–30
  garlic bread **81**–28
  garlic press **78**–11
Garment Factory **98**
garment worker **171**–29
garter
  garter snake **219**–46

gas **224**–3 🔑
  gas gauge **163**–31
  gas meter **62**–14 🔑
  gas pedal **163**–46
  gas shut-off valve **150**–4
  gas station **127**–10 🔑
  gas tank **162**–10 🔑
gate **50**–16, **53**–9, **165**–8 🔑
Gate **165**
gauge
  blood pressure gauge **111**–9 🔑
  gas gauge **163**–31
  oil gauge **163**–29
  temperature gauge **163**–30
gauze **119**–9
gearshift **163**–47 🔑
gel **108**–2, **108**–16
gender **4**–16 AWL
general **141**–25
GEOGRAPHY AND HABITATS **214** 🔑
Geometric Solids **205** 🔑
geometry **204**–17
geothermal energy **224**–7 🔑 AWL
get 🔑
  get a job **40**–F, **169**–O 🔑 AWL
  get a learner's permit **139**–F 🔑
  get a library card **135**–A 🔑
  get a loan **49**–J 🔑
  get a ticket **166**–D 🔑
  get an electric shock **118**–F 🔑
  get bed rest **116**–B 🔑
  get change **26**–A 🔑
  get dressed **38**–D 🔑
  get elected **143**–M 🔑
  get engaged **41**–J 🔑
  get feedback **203**–K
  get frostbite **118**–G
  get good grades **10**–H 🔑
  get home **39**–R 🔑
  get immunized **116**–I
  get into **157**–E 🔑
  get married **41**–K 🔑
  get off **157**–J 🔑
  get on **157**–I 🔑
  get out of **157**–F 🔑
  get takeout **82** ✦
  get the title **161**–E 🔑
  get up 38–B 🔑
  get your license **139**–I 🔑 AWL
Get Well **116** 🔑
Getting Your First License **139** 🔑 AWL
gift **94** ✦, **246**–3 🔑
gift shop **132** ✦, **192**–5 🔑
gills **218**–2
giraffe **223**–32
girder **196**–3
girdle **91**–15
girl **31**–10 🔑
give 15–F, **152**–A 🔑
  give a lecture **124**–B 🔑 AWL
glad **44**–5 🔑
glass **53**–18, **83**–22, **83**–23 🔑
  glass cleaner **61**–14

glasses **117**–7 🔑
  safety glasses **92**–10, **197**–10 🔑
  sunglasses **90**–27
global positioning system (GPS)
  159–11
gloves **90**–6, **237**–17 🔑
  disposable gloves **93**–27 🔑 AWL
  glove compartment **163**–44
  medical gloves **93**–34 🔑 AWL
  rubber gloves **61**–4 🔑
  surgical gloves **123**–39
  work gloves **92**–17, **197**–17 🔑
glue **189**–33 🔑
  glue gun **238**–12 🔑
  glue stick **238**–11 🔑
GO **228**–**229** 🔑
go 🔑
  go back **11**–M 🔑
  go for **161**–J 🔑
  go on an interview **169**–N 🔑
  go one block **159**–F 🔑
  go over **157**–B 🔑
  go past **159**–E 🔑
  go straight **159**–A 🔑
  go through **164**–D 🔑
  go to an employment agency **168**–F 🔑
  go to bed **39**–Y 🔑
  go to college **41**–I 🔑
  go to jail **144**–G 🔑
  go to prison **144**–G 🔑
  go to sleep **39**–Z 🔑
  go to the grocery store **38**–L 🔑
  go to work **38**–I 🔑
  go under **157**–A 🔑
  to-go box **82**–5 🔑
goalie **235** ✦
goat **221**–5
goggles **197**–11
goldfish **221**–16
golf **234**–8
  golf club **237**–1 🔑
good **23**–18 🔑
Goods **73** 🔑
goose **220**–14
gopher **221**–19
gorilla **223**–29
gospel **243**–30
Government **140** 🔑
GOVERNMENT AND MILITARY SERVICE
  140–**141** 🔑 AWL
governor **140**–14, **140**–15 🔑
gown **226**–8
  evening gown **89**–18
  hospital gown **123**–19
  nightgown **91**–24
  surgical gown **93**–37, **123**–38
GPS (global positioning system)
  159–11
grab bar **57**–11 🔑
grades **10**–4 🔑 AWL
graduate **40**–D 🔑
graduated cylinder **207**–38
GRADUATION **226**–**227**

graffiti **152**–1
grandchild **34** ✦🔑
granddaughters **34** ✦🔑
grandfather **34**–2 🔑
grandmother **34**–1 🔑
Grandparents **34** 🔑
grandson **34** ✦🔑
grapefruit **68**–6
grapes **68**–3
graph **204**–15
graphic designer **171**–30 AWL
grasshopper **220**–25
grate **77**–G
grater **78**–2
gray **24**–15 🔑
  gray hair **33**–23 🔑
grease **77**–B
green **24**–5 🔑
  green card **40**–2 🔑
  green onions **69**–20
greet **3**–H, **177**–M, **179**–H
GREETING **2**–**3**
greeting card **136**–15
grill **53**–17
grilled
  grilled cheese sandwich **80**–10
  grilled fish **81**–29
  grilled ribs **76**–2
grocery 🔑
  grocery bag **67**–13 🔑
  grocery clerk **72**–4 🔑
Grocery Products **72** 🔑
GROCERY STORE **72**–**73** 🔑
ground 🔑
  ground beef **70**–4
  ground post **136**–6
  playground **50**–3
group **117**–15 🔑
grower **187**–13
guard **144**–3 🔑
  Coast Guard **141**–36
  lifeguard **231**–19 🔑
  lifeguard station **231**–21 🔑
  National Guard **141**–38
  security guard **134**–5, **173**–55 🔑 AWL
  shin guards **237**–13
Guard **93** 🔑
guest **192**–10 🔑
  guest room **192**–13 🔑
  guest services **132**–12 🔑
  guest speaker **226**–4 🔑
guinea pig **221**–14
guitar **244**–9
gums **106**–6
  gum disease **120**–12
gun **145**–13 🔑
  glue gun **238**–12 🔑
  spray gun **195**–21 🔑
gurney **123**–33
gutter **53**–6
gym **5**–19, **128**–10, **192**–24
gymnastics **234**–9
gynecologists **122** ✦

habitat **206**–11
HABITATS **214**
hacking **147**–5
hacksaw **194**–5
hail **13**–22
hail a taxi **156** ✦
hair **104**–2 🔑
  black hair **33**–12 🔑
  blond hair **33**–14 🔑
  brown hair **33**–15 🔑
  curly hair **33**–11 🔑
  gray hair **33**–23 🔑
  hair clip **108**–19
  hair gel **108**–16
  hair salon **133**–18
  hairdresser **171**–31
  hairnet **93**–25
  hairspray **108**–12
  hairstylist **171**–31
  long hair **33**–3 🔑
  red hair **33**–13 🔑
  short hair **33**–1 🔑
  shoulder-length hair **33**–2
  straight hair **33**–9 🔑
  wavy hair **33**–10
HAIR **33** 🔑
half 🔑
  half bath **57** ✦🔑
  half brother **35**–28 🔑
  1/2 cup **75**–9 🔑
  half dollar **26**–5 🔑
  half past one **18**–11 🔑
  half sister **35**–27 🔑
  half slip **91**–22
halibut steak **71**–6
hall **126**–8 🔑
  hallway **5**–10, **192**–18
Hallway **51**
ham **70**–9, **76**–5
hamburger **79**–1
hammer **194**–1 🔑
  jackhammer **196**–9
  sledgehammer **196**–23
hammer **196**–D
hammock **53**–23
hamper **57**–1
hand **105**–15 🔑
  DMV handbook **138**–1
  hand towel **57**–17 🔑
  hand truck **185**–11 🔑
  handbag **87**–9
  handbags **94**–2
  handcuffs **144**–2
  handsaw **194**–4
  handset **14**–4
  hired hand **187**–20 🔑
Hand **106**
hand in **10**–O, **203**–M
handbrake **163**–48
handicapped parking **130**–6, **158**–12
hang up **15**–D, **101**–H 🔑
hanger **101**–11
happy **28**–6, **43**–31 🔑

hard **23**–5, **23**–24 🔑
   external hard drive **190**–27 🔑
   hard drive **190**–19 🔑
   hard hat **92**–1, **197**–9 🔑
   hard-boiled eggs **76**–8 🔑
hardware store **152**–4
harmonica **244**–21
harvest 187–B
hash browns **80**–3
hatchback **160**–6
hats **90**–1, **95**–11 🔑
   chef's hat **93**–28
   cowboy hat **92**–18
   hard hat **92**–1, **197**–9 🔑
   ski hat **90**–11
   straw hat **90**–23
have 🔑
   have a baby **41**–L 🔑
   have a conversation **11**–L 🔑
   have a flat tire **166**–C 🔑
   have a heart attack **118**–D 🔑
   have a picnic **230**–D
   have an allergic reaction **118**–E 🔑 AWL
   have dinner **39**–S 🔑
   have regular checkups **116**–H
Hawaii-Aleutian time **19**–27
hay **187**–18
hazard **198**–6
   hazard lights **163**–36
Hazardous Materials **197**
hazardous waste **224**–12
Hazards **197**
head **104**–1 🔑
   Bluetooth headset **14**–14
   head chef **193**–7
   head of lettuce **69**–32
   headache **110**–1 🔑
   headband **90**–3
   headboard **58**–10
   headlight **162**–7
   headline **135**–7
   headphones **6**–8, **240**–4, **240**–5, **240**–6
   headset **14**–13, **191**–35
   headwaiter **193**–12
   headwrap **90**–7
   letterhead **189**–42
   overhead compartment **165**–13
headquarters / corporate offices **184**–1 🔑 AWL
health 🔑
   health history form **111**–4 🔑
   health insurance card **111**–3 🔑
HEALTH **116**–**117** 🔑
HEALTH FAIR **124**–**125** 🔑
HEALTH INSURANCE **121** 🔑
Health Problems **117** 🔑
hear 106–B 🔑
hearing 🔑
   hearing aid **117**–10 🔑 AWL
   hearing impaired **32**–12
   hearing loss **117**–2 🔑
heart **107**–38, **245**–6 🔑
   have a heart attack **118**–D 🔑
   heart disease **113**–28 🔑

hearts **239**–31 🔑
heat wave **13**–15 🔑
heating pad **115**–13
heavy **23**–13, **32**–7, **97**–27 🔑
hedge clippers **186**–11
heel **94**–22, **106**–24 🔑
   high heels **89**–21, **95**–25, **97**–32 🔑
   low heels **97**–31 🔑
height **17**–16, **32**–5 🔑
Height **32** 🔑
Heimlich maneuver **119**–19
helicopter **155**–9
helmet **93**–23, **237**–19
help 8–J, **151**–G 🔑
Help with Health Problems **117** 🔑
hem **100**–8
hen **221**–8
hepatitis **112**–9
herbal tea **81**–40 🔑
herbs **84**–9
hibiscus **217**–12
hide 246–D 🔑
high **97**–32 🔑
   high blood pressure **113**–24 🔑
   high chair **37**–6, **82**–3 🔑
   high heels **89**–21, **95**–25 🔑
   high school **200**–4 🔑
   high-rise **129**–13
   high visibility safety vest **92**–4 🔑 AWL
   junior high school **200**–3 🔑
   knee highs **91**–12 🔑
highlighter **7**–25
highway **159**–9 🔑
   highway marker **158**–17
hiking **232**–7
   hiking boots **95**–31 🔑
hills **214**–16 🔑
   downhill skiing **233**–1
hip **107**–27 🔑
hip-hop **243**–26
hippopotamus **223**–43
hire 144–B 🔑
hired hand **187**–20 🔑
Historical Terms **209** 🔑
history **111**–4, **201**–12 🔑
HISTORY **209** 🔑
hit 236–B 🔑
HIV / AIDS **113**–21
HOBBIES AND GAMES **238**–**239** 🔑
hockey **235**–14
   hockey stick **237**–11
hold 36–A 🔑
holder
   candle holder **56**–21
   policyholder **121**–5
   potholders **78**–29
   toothbrush holder **57**–24
holiday **22**–7, **22**–8 🔑
HOLIDAYS **245** 🔑
Holidays **22** 🔑
holly **216**–19
home **52**–7, **52**–12 🔑
   home healthcare aide **171**–32

home improvement store **129**–20 🔑
home phone **4**–12 🔑
homemaker **172**–33
homesick **43**–20
HOME **46**–**49** 🔑
honest **178**–4 🔑
honeybee **220**–26
hood **162**–4
Hood **162**
hoodie **89**–22
hoof / hooves **222**–17
hook **194**–39 🔑
   eye hook **194**–40 🔑
   hook and eye **99**–27 🔑
   hook and loop fastener **99**–29
horn **163**–32, **222**–21, **244**–11 🔑
   French horn **244**–13
horror story **243**–17 🔑
horse **221**–4 🔑
   horse racing **234**–19 🔑
   horseback riding **232**–9 🔑
   seahorse **218**–13
hose **53**–21
   pantyhose **91**–18
hospital **127**–9, **158**–18 🔑
   hospital bed **123**–22 🔑
   hospital gown **123**–19
HOSPITAL **122**–**123** 🔑
Hospital Room **123** 🔑
Hospital Staff **122** 🔑
hostess **82**–2
hot **13**–3, **42**–1 🔑
   hot cereal **80**–9
   hot dog **79**–6
   hot water **57**–9 🔑
   hot water bottle **115**–15 🔑
hotel **126**–3 🔑
A HOTEL **192** 🔑
hour **18**–1 🔑
house 🔑
   courthouse **127**–13
   dollhouse **59**–18
   House of Representatives **140**–3
   house painter **172**–46 🔑
   house salad **80**–15 🔑
   housekeeper **172**–34, **192**–20
   housekeeping cart **192**–19
   houseplant **56**–4, **217**–27
   townhouse **52**–6
   two-story house **52** ♦🔑
   warehouse **184**–3, **185**–7
   White House **140**–7
House **49** 🔑
HOUSE AND YARD **53** 🔑
HOUSEHOLD PROBLEMS AND REPAIRS
   62–**63** 🔑
HOUSEWORK **60**
housing **52**–11 🔑
hub **190**–26
hubcap **162**–9
hug 2–F
human resources **184**–4 🔑 AWL
humid **13**–17

humidifier **115**–12

humiliated **43** ✦

hummingbird **220**–11

hump **223**–51

hungry **42**–5 🔑

hurricane **13**–18, **149**–14

hurt **42**–16, **118**–C 🔑

husband **34**–13 🔑

   ex-husband **35** ✦

   former husband **35** ✦🔑

hutch **55**–22

hybrid **160**–1

hydrant **131**–27

hydroelectric power **224**–5

hydrogen peroxide **119**–10

hyena **223**–30

HYGIENE **108**–**109**

hygienist **120**–3

hypertension **113**–24

hyphen **202**–23

hypoallergenic **108** ✦

I beam **196**–3

ice 🔑

   ice cream **72**–26 🔑

   ice-cream cone **79**–13

   ice cream shop **133**–16 🔑

   ice hockey **235**–14

   ice pack **119**–14

   ice skates **237**–9

   ice skating **233**–4

iced tea **79**–12 🔑

icy **13**–23

ID **150**–19

identify **174**–D 🔑 AWL

identity theft **145**–9

ignition **163**–33

illegal drugs **145**–6 🔑 AWL

ILLNESSES AND MEDICAL
   CONDITIONS **112**–**113** 🔑 AWL

Immediate Family **34** 🔑

immigrant **209**–13 AWL

immigrate **40**–C AWL

immigration **209**–12 AWL

immunization **116** ✦

impaired **32**–11, **32**–12

important **150**–20 🔑

improvement **129**–20 🔑

in **25**–6 🔑

   be in shock **118**–B 🔑

   bubble in **10**–K 🔑

   call in **198**–A 🔑

   check in **164**–A 🔑

   check-in kiosk **164**–2

   fall in love **40**–H 🔑

   fill in **9**–O 🔑

   hand in **10**–O 🔑

   in fashion / in style **88** ✦🔑 AWL

   in front of **25**–7 🔑

   in-network doctor **121**–9 🔑 AWL

   in pain **42**–11 🔑

   in the middle **25**–2 🔑

log in to your account **211**–T

   move in **48**–F 🔑

   take in **100**–D 🔑

   turn in **203**–M 🔑

   walk-in freezer **193**–3

In the Airline Terminal **164** AWL

In the Examining Room **111** 🔑

In the Waiting Room **111** 🔑

inappropriate material **147**–3 🔑 AWL

inch [in.] **17**–15 🔑

indent **202**–D

independence 🔑

   Declaration of Independence **208**–5

   Independence Day **22**–13

INDIVIDUAL SPORTS **234** 🔑 AWL

infant **31**–6

infection **112**–3 🔑

infectious disease **113** ✦🔑

Infectious Diseases **112** 🔑

influenza **113** ✦

INFORMATION **4** 🔑

information technology / IT **184**–10

INFORMATION TECHNOLOGY (IT)
   190–**191**

inhabitants **214** ✦

inhaler **115**–33

injection **116** ✦, **162**–17

injured **118**–C 🔑 AWL

INJURIES **110** 🔑 AWL

ink 🔑

   ink cartridge **189**–45

   ink pad **189**–46

   inkjet printer **189**–18 🔑

inline

   inline skates **237**–10

   inline skating **234**–10

inquire about benefits **179** ✦🔑 AWL

insects 🔑

   insect bite **110**–10 🔑

   insect repellent **232**–23

INSECTS **220** 🔑

Insects **220** 🔑

insert **134**–C AWL

INSIDE A COMPANY **184** 🔑

INSIDE AND OUTSIDE THE BODY **106**–**107** 🔑

Inside the Car **163** 🔑

Inside the Kit **119**

Inside the Trunk **162**

inspect **151**–N AWL

install **186**–H, **196**–C 🔑

instructor **6**–4 AWL

Instrument Panel **163** 🔑 AWL

instruments **120**–4 🔑

Instruments **244** 🔑

insulation **196**–14

insurance **111**–3, **138**–8 🔑

   insurance plans **121**–2 🔑

   insurance policy **121**–4 🔑 AWL

INSURANCE **121** 🔑

insured / policyholder **121**–5

integers **204**–1, **204**–2

Integers **204**

intercom **50**–5

international call **15**–35 🔑

international power adapter **241**–26 🔑

Internet 🔑

   Internet crime **147** 🔑

   Internet map **159**–12 🔑

   Internet phone call **14**–19 🔑

   monitor children's Internet use
      147–B 🔑 AWL

INTERNET **212**–**213** 🔑

Internet Connectivity **191** 🔑

INTERNET RESEARCH **212**–**213** 🔑 AWL

internist **122**–1

internship **175**–11

Interpersonal Skills **178**

interpreter **172**–35

INTERSECTION **130**–**131**

interview 🔑

   go on an interview **169**–N 🔑

   set up an interview **169**–M 🔑

INTERVIEW SKILLS **179** 🔑

intestinal parasites **113**–25

intestines **107**–42

into **157**–E 🔑

intravenous drip (IV) **123**–25

introduce **2**–D, **3**–J 🔑

introduction **202**–6 🔑

invention **209**–19 🔑

inventor **209**–18

invertebrates **206**–13

investigate **212** ✦🔑 AWL

invitation **64**–9 🔑

   accept an invitation **12**–J 🔑

   decline an invitation **12**–K 🔑 AWL

invite **12**–I 🔑

iris **217**–16

iron **101**–13, **108**–17 🔑

iron **101**–G 🔑

ironed **101**–20 🔑

ironing board **101**–14 🔑

irritated **64**–6 🔑

island **214**–8 🔑

IT / information technology **184**–10

IV (intravenous drip) **123**–25

ivory **24**–16

ivy **216**–25

jack **162**–24

jacket **90**–8 🔑

   chef's jacket **93**–29

   down jacket **90**–16 🔑

   leather jacket **90**–4 🔑

   sport jacket **89**–14 🔑

jackhammer **196**–9

jack-o'-lantern **245**–10

janitor **188**–3

January **21**–25 🔑

jar **74**–2, **74**–14

   sanitizing jar **33**–16

jasmine **217**–22

jaw **106**–4

jay **220**–7

jaywalk **130**–C

jazz **243**–24

jeans **86**–2, **92**–19 🔑
jellyfish **218**–14
jewelry 🔑
   jewelry department **95**–8 🔑
   jewelry store **132**–2 🔑
jigsaw **194**–10
job **175**–2, **175**–4, **175**–12 🔑 AWL
   attend a job fair **174**–I 🔑
JOB SAFETY **197** 🔑
JOB SEARCH **168**–**169** 🔑
JOB SKILLS **176** 🔑
JOBS AND OCCUPATIONS **170**–**173** 🔑 AWL
jockstrap **91**–6
join **146**–L 🔑
joint account **134**–10 🔑
judge **144**–6 🔑
Judicial Branch **140**
juice **73**–32 🔑
July **21**–31 🔑
jump **236**–I 🔑
jump rope **230**–4 🔑
jumper cables **162**–21
jumpsuit **93**–24
June **21**–30 🔑
junior high school **200**–3 🔑
junk mail **137** ✦
Jupiter **215**–5
jury **144**–8 🔑
justices **140**–12, **140**–13 🔑

kangaroo **223**–44
keep **28**–B, **212**–H 🔑
ketchup **79**–21
kettle **54**–17
key **51**–31, **159**–6 🔑
   keypad **14**–5
   pound key **14**–7 🔑
   star key **14**–6 🔑
keyboard **190**–23, **244**–18 🔑
   keyboard shortcut **210** ✦
keywords **212**–4
kick **236**–E 🔑
kidney **107**–43
   kidney disease **113**–27
kids' bedroom **47**–10 🔑
KIDS' BEDROOM **59** 🔑
king-size bed **192**–15 🔑
kiosk **133**–22, **164**–2
kiss **3**–L, **36**–P 🔑
kit
   first aid kit **119**–1, **150**–18
   model kit **238**–9
   woodworking kit **238**–14
Kit **119**
kitchen **46**–6, **83**–15 🔑
   kitchen timer **78**–18
A KITCHEN **54** 🔑
Kitchen **193** 🔑
KITCHEN UTENSILS **78**
kite **231**–3
   kitesurfing **233** ✦
kitten **221**–10
kiwi **68**–22

knee **106**–20 🔑
   knee highs **91**–12 🔑
   knee pads **197**–19
knife **55**–4, **83**–30 🔑
   carving knife **78**–12
   multi-use knife **232**–20
   paring knife **78**–16
   steak knife **83**–29
knit **239**–F
knit top **88**–7
knitting needles **239**–23
knob **206**–22, **206**–24
   doorknob **53**–12
knuckle **106**–17
koala **223**–45

lab **5**–15 🔑
   lab coat **93**–33 🔑
Lab **123**, **207** 🔑
label 🔑 AWL
   mailing label **189**–41
   nutrition label **124**–8
   prescription label **114**–4
   warning label **114**–8 🔑
label **9**–V AWL
Labor Day **22**–14
lace **99**–9
   shoelaces **94**–24
ladder **196**–2
ladle **78**–7
ladybug **220**–27
lake **214**–13 🔑
lamb **70**–14
   lamb chops **70**–15
   lamb shanks **70**–13
Lamb **70**
lamp **56**–15, **58**–25
   lampshade **58**–26
land **164**–K
landlord **51**–27
landscape designer **186**–5 🔑 AWL
LANDSCAPING AND GARDENING **186** 🔑
languages **201**–13 🔑
   language arts **201**–9 🔑
lantern **232**–22, **245**–10
laptop **190**–22
large **96**–4, **96**–5 🔑
laser printer **189**–19 🔑
lashes
   eyelashes **106**–11
last 🔑
   last name **4**–4 🔑
   last week **20**–18 🔑
late **19**–24 🔑
laugh **44**–A 🔑
laundromat **130**–1
laundry **101**–1 🔑
   laundry basket **101**–2
   laundry detergent **101**–8
LAUNDRY **101** 🔑
Laundry Room **50** 🔑
lawn **53**–26
   lawn mower **186**–6

lawyer **172**–36 🔑
lay **196**–B
layer cake **81**–33 🔑
LCD projector **6**–5, **241**–27
leader **186**–4 🔑
Leadership Skills **178** 🔑
leaf / leaves **216**–6, **217**–6 🔑
   leaf blower **186**–2
leaking **62**–3
learn **40**–E, **178**–3 🔑
learner's dictionary **7**–31
Learning New Words **8** 🔑
lease **48** ✦, **51**–28
leather **98**–6 🔑
   leather jacket **90**–4 🔑
leave **11**–O, **38**–N, **82**–J, **164**–J, **177**–P 🔑
leaves / leaf **216**–6, **217**–6 🔑
   leaf blower **186**–2
lecture **124**–B 🔑 AWL
left **25**–1, **158**–8, **159**–C 🔑
Leg and Foot **106** 🔑
legal 🔑 AWL
   legal holiday **22**–8 🔑
   legal pad **189**–38
Legal Holidays **22** 🔑
LEGAL SYSTEM **144** 🔑 AWL
leggings **90**–12
Legislature **140**–17 AWL
legs **70**–21, **105**–9 🔑
   leg of lamb **70**–14
lemonade **84**–3
lemons **68**–7 🔑
lend **26**–C 🔑
length **17**–17 🔑
lengthen **100**–A
lens / lenses **117**–8, **241**–19
leopard **223**–34
let out **100**–C 🔑
letter **136**–13 🔑
   letter carrier **136**–20
   letterhead **189**–42
lettuce **69**–1
level **175**–2, **194**–29 🔑
librarian **135**–9
library **5**–17, **127**–15 🔑
   library clerk **135**–1 🔑
   library patron **135**–3
LIBRARY **135** 🔑
license 🔑 AWL
   driver's license **40**–4, **138**–9 🔑 AWL
   driver's license number **138**–11 🔑
   license plate **138**–12, **162**–12 🔑 AWL
   marriage license **41**–8 🔑 AWL
   renew a license **138** ✦
   taxi license **156**–22 🔑
License **139** 🔑 AWL
licensed practical nurse (LPN) **122**–11
lid **78**–24 🔑
lieutenant governor **140**–15 🔑
life 🔑
   life vest **165**–25, **232**–14
   lifeguard **231**–19 🔑
   lifeguard station **231**–21 🔑

lifesaving device **231**–20 ⚷ AWL
wildlife **166**–2
LIFE **218–219** ⚷
LIFE EVENTS AND DOCUMENTS **40–41** ⚷ AWL
lift **11**–E ⚷
light **23**–14, **97**–28 ⚷
  brake light **162**–14
  daylight saving time **19**–25 ⚷
  flashlight **150**–14
  hazard lights **163**–36
  headlight **162**–7
  light blue **24**–11 ⚷
  light fixture **55**–18
  light source **206**–19 ⚷ AWL
  light switch **58**–27 ⚷
  night light **37**–28 ⚷
  porch light **53**–13
  streetlight **152**–3
  string lights **245**–18 ⚷
  taillight **162**–13
  traffic light **130**–8 ⚷
  work light **195**–44 ⚷
light bulb **56** ✦
lightning **13**–14
lily **217**–26
limbs **106** ✦, **216**–3
limes **68**–8
limit **158**–4 ⚷
limo / limousine **160**–11
line **73**–11 ⚷
  assembly line **185**–6 ⚷ AWL
  clothesline **101**–9
  curved line **205**–23 ⚷
  headline **135**–7
  line cook **93**, **193** ✦⚷
  line segment **205**–20
  line supervisor **185**–4
  parallel lines **205**–25 ⚷ AWL
  perpendicular lines **205**–24
  phone line **14**–1 ⚷
  straight line **205**–22 ⚷
linen **98**–2
  linen closet **57** ✦
liner
  eyeliner **109**–36
Lines **205** ⚷
lingerie **91** ✦
links **212**–6, **213**–19 ⚷ AWL
lion **219**–35, **222**–2, **223**–36
lip **106**–5 ⚷
  lipstick **109**–38
Liquid Measures **75** ⚷
liquids **61**–21, **197**–8 ⚷
list ⚷
  contact list **14**–15 ⚷ AWL
  list your soft skills **174**–E
  shopping list **67**–14 ⚷
listen **6**–C, **111**–C, **179**–K ⚷
listing **48**–2
litter **152**–2
litter **225**–L
little **23**–1 ⚷
Little League **235** ✦

LIVE **52** ⚷
live **142**–H ⚷
live music **84**–1 ⚷
liver **70**–7, **107**–40
livestock **187**–15
Livestock **221**
living room **47**–13 ⚷
LIVING ROOM **56** ⚷
lizard **219**–43
llama **223**–25
load **101**–C
loading dock **185**–15
loaf **74**–22
  meatloaf **81**–31
loafers **95**–30
loaves **74**–10
Lobby **50**
lobster **71**–10
local call **15**–33 ⚷
lock **51**–35, **163**–25
  locksmith **62**–11
lock **146**–E ⚷
locker **5**–11, **50**–17
locket **95**–35
log in to your account **211**–T
logistics **184**–8
lonely **42**–17 ⚷
long **96**–18 ⚷
  long hair **33**–3 ⚷
  long underwear **91**–3 ⚷
  long-distance call **15**–34 ⚷
  long-sleeved **96**–14 ⚷
look ⚷
  look at **49**–H, **161**–A, **212**–E ⚷
  look for **135**–B, **168**–G ⚷
  look up **8**–A ⚷
loop **99**–29
loose **97**–30 ⚷
lose **235** ✦⚷
loss **117**–2 ⚷
lost child **148**–1 ⚷
lotion **37**–13, **108**–9
loud **23**–11 ⚷
loungewear **91** ✦
love **40**–H, **42**–18 ⚷
  love seat **56**–1 ⚷
low **97**–31 ⚷
  low-cost exam **124**–1 ⚷
  low-cut socks **91**–10 ⚷
  low-fat milk **81**–42 ⚷
lower back **107**–29 ⚷
lozenges **115**–30
LPN (licensed practical nurse) **122**–11
lug wrench **162**–22
luggage **165**–18
  luggage cart **192**–8
lumber **196**–17
lunar eclipse **215** ✦
Lunch **80** ⚷
lung **107**–39 ⚷

machine ⚷
  fax machine **189**–21

machine operator **172**–37
machine screw **194**–32 ⚷
sewing machine **98**–13 ⚷
sewing machine operator **98**–14
vending machine **156**–9
Machine **98**, **134** ⚷
magazine **135**–5 ⚷
  magazine rack **56** ✦
magnet **207**–36
magnolia **216**–8
mail ⚷
  airmail **136**–5
  Certified Mail® **136**–4
  Express Mail® **136**–2
  junk mail **137** ✦
  mailbox **50**–11, **53**–1, **130**–13, **137**–12
  Media Mail® **136**–3
  next-day mail / overnight **137** ✦⚷
  Priority Mail® **136**–1
  voice mail **14**–17 ⚷
mail **137**–D
mailer **189**–40
mailing
  mailing address **136**–22
  mailing label **189**–41
main office **5**–12 ⚷
mainframe computer **190**–1
MAINTAINING A CAR **161** ⚷ AWL
maintenance **184**–12, **192**–23 AWL
maitre d' **193**–11
make ⚷
  make a deposit **134**–B ⚷
  make a disaster kit **150**–B ⚷
  make a mortgage payment **49**–L ⚷
  make a request **12** ✦⚷
  make a wish **246**–B ⚷
  make an offer **49**–I ⚷
  make copies **177**–D ⚷
  make decisions **178**–C ⚷
  make dinner **39**–Q ⚷
  make eye contact **179**–J ⚷ AWL
  make furniture **176**–G ⚷
  make lunch **38**–F ⚷
  make progress **10**–G ⚷
  make small talk **12**–B ⚷
  make the bed **60**–F ⚷
make and model **160** ✦⚷
maker
  coffee maker **54**–6
  dressmaker **100**–1
  dressmaker's dummy **100**–2
  homemaker **172**–33
Makeup **109**
makeup remover **109**–42
Making a Phone Call **15** ⚷
MAKING ALTERATIONS **100** ⚷ AWL
Making an Emergency Call **15** ⚷
MAKING CLOTHES **98–99** ⚷
malaria **113**–22
male **4**–17 ⚷
mall **128**–7 ⚷
MALL **132–133** ⚷
mallet **194**–2

MAMMALS **222**–**223**
Mammals **219**
man / men **30**–1, **30**–4 🔑
    doorman **192**–1
    men's store **132** ✦🔑
    minuteman **208**–10
manage time **178**–D
manager **72**–8 🔑
    account manager **134**–9 🔑
    office manager **188**–8 🔑
Manager **92** 🔑
manager / superintendent **50**–8 🔑
mane **223**–49
maneuver **119**–19
mangoes **68**–21
manicurist **172**–38
mantle **56**–11
manual **119**–2 AWL
Manual Transmission **163** AWL
manufacture **185**–B 🔑
MANUFACTURING **185** 🔑
map **7**–12, **159**–12 🔑
Map **13** 🔑
maple **216**–12
MAPS **159** 🔑
Maps **159** 🔑
March **21**–27 🔑
margarine **72**–20
marigold **217**–13
marine **141**–35
MARINE LIFE, AMPHIBIANS, AND
    REPTILES **218**–**219**
Marines **141**–34
mark **202**–15, **202**–16, **202**–18 🔑
    postmark **136**–24
markers **7**–17, **7**–24, **158**–17
market **228**–6 🔑
    supermarket **129**–18 🔑
MARKET **66**–**67** 🔑
marketing **184**–6 🔑
marriage license **41**–8 🔑 AWL
married couple **35**–20 🔑 AWL
Mars **215**–4
martial arts **234**–11
Martin Luther King Jr. Day **22**–10
mascara **109**–39
mashed potatoes **81**–23
mask **245**–9
    catcher's mask **237**–15
    diving mask **231**–7
    face mask **93**–32
    oxygen mask **165**–24
    particle mask **197**–14
    ski mask **90**–15
    surgical mask **93**–36
    ventilation mask **92**–7
masking tape **195**–53
mat **57**–5, **57**–28
    placemat **55**–11
match **9**–T
matches **150**–16, **232**–21 🔑
matching **28**–3 🔑

material 🔑
    inappropriate material **147**–3 🔑 AWL
    natural materials **98** ✦🔑
    radioactive materials **197**–7
    synthetic materials **98** ✦
Material **98**–**99** 🔑
Materials **197** 🔑
maternity
    maternity dress **88**–5
    maternity store **133**–19
math **201**–10 🔑
Math Operations **204** 🔑
Math Problem **204** 🔑
MATHEMATICS **204**–**205** 🔑
mattress **58**–20
May **21**–29 🔑
mayonnaise **79**–23
mayor **140**–20 🔑
meadow **214**–20
measles **112**–5
measure **100**–17, **195**–45
measure **17**–C, **75**–A 🔑
Measurement **17** 🔑
MEASUREMENTS **17, 75** 🔑
Measures **75** 🔑
Measuring Area and Volume **205** 🔑 AWL
meat **66**–2 🔑
    meatballs **81**–27
    meatloaf **81**–31
Meat **76** 🔑
MEAT AND POULTRY **70** 🔑
mechanic **170**–8
Mechanic **162**
Media Mail® **136**–3
medical 🔑 AWL
    emergency medical technician (EMT)
        123–32
    medical chart **123**–24 🔑 AWL
    medical emergency bracelet
        119–3 🔑
    medical records technician **172**–39 🔑
    medical waste disposal **123**–31 🔑 AWL
MEDICAL CARE **111** 🔑
MEDICAL CONDITIONS **112**–**113** 🔑
Medical Conditions **113** 🔑
MEDICAL EMERGENCIES **118** 🔑
medical gloves **93**–34 🔑
Medical Procedures **111** 🔑 AWL
Medical Specialists **122** 🔑
Medical Technician **93**
Medical Warnings **114** 🔑
medication **114**–3, **115**–18, **123**–20
    prescribe medication **114** ✦
Medication **115**
medicine cabinet **57**–22 🔑
medium **96**–3 🔑 AWL
meet **228**–6
meet **49**–G, **49**–R 🔑
meeting 🔑
    meeting place **150**–1 🔑
    meeting room **192**–25 🔑
MEETING AND GREETING **2**–**3** 🔑

melons **68**–19
    watermelons **68**–18
membrane **206**–6
Memorial Day **22**–12
memory card **241**–18 🔑
men / man **30**–1, **30**–4
    doorman **192**–1
    men's store **132** ✦🔑
    minuteman **208**–10
Men's Underwear **91** 🔑
menu **82**–7, **213**–15 🔑
    menu bar **213**–7 🔑
MENU **80**–**81** 🔑
Mercury **215**–1
merge **158**–10
mess **64**–8 🔑
message 🔑
    compose / **write** the message
        211–W 🔑
    text message **14**–18 🔑 AWL
messenger **172**–40
meter **62**–14, **131**–25, **156**–23 🔑
mice / mouse **63**–28, **190**–13, **221**–18 🔑
microphone / mic **191**–36, **240**–16
microprocessor **190**–16
Microscope **206**
microwave **77**–T
microwave oven **54**–13
middle **25**–2 🔑
    middle initial **4**–3 🔑 AWL
    middle school **200**–3 🔑
    middle-aged **32**–2
mid-length **96**–17
midnight **18**–21 🔑
Military **141** 🔑 AWL
MILITARY SERVICE **140**–**141** 🔑 AWL
milk **66**–5, **81**–42 🔑
    milkshake **79**–14
milk **187**–C
mini
    mini-blinds **58**–8
    minivan **160**–8
miniskirt **96**–15
minister **209**–7 🔑
minuteman **208**–10
minutes **18**–2 🔑
mirror **57**–18 🔑
    full-length mirror **58**–6 🔑
    rearview mirror **163**–35 🔑
    side-view mirror **162**–3 🔑
misbehave **44**–B
miss the bus **156** ✦🔑
missed call **14**–16 🔑
missing **97**–40 🔑
mittens **90**–10
mix **77**–R 🔑
mixed berries **81**–36
mixer **54**–25 🔑
mixing bowl **54**–28, **78**–31 🔑
mobile **59**–5 🔑
    mobile boarding pass **165**–20
    mobile home **52**–7 🔑

model **172**–41 🔑
  model kit **238**–9
  model train **239**–27 🔑
modem **191**–34
modern **209**–2 🔑
moist towelettes **150**–12
moisturizer **108**–9
mole **32**–16
molecule **207**–27
monarch **209**–4
Monday **20**–9 🔑
MONEY **26** 🔑
monitor 147–B AWL
monitor **190**–8 🔑 AWL
  arrival and departure monitors **165**–7 🔑 AWL
  baby monitor **59**–7 🔑 AWL
  vital signs monitor **123**–26 🔑 AWL
monkey **223**–26
month **20**–3 🔑
  monthly charges **15**–31 🔑
Months of the Year **21** 🔑
moon 🔑
  crescent moon **215**–10 🔑
  full moon **215**–12 🔑
  new moon **215**–9 🔑
  quarter moon **215**–11 🔑
moose **222**–1
mop **61**–6
mop 60–D
morning **18**–15 🔑
mosque **128**–5
mosquito **220**–23
motel **128**–12
moth **220**–22
mother **34**–3, **35**–22 🔑
  grandmother **34**–1 🔑
  motherboard **190**–18
  mother-in-law **34**–10
  stepmother **35**–26
MOTION **157** 🔑
motorcycle **154**–4 🔑
mountain 🔑
  mountain biking **232**–8
  mountain lion **222**–2
  mountain peak **214**–14 🔑
  mountain range **214**–15 🔑 AWL
  Mountain time **19**–30
mouse / mice **63**–28, **190**–13, **221**–18 🔑
mouth **104**–7 🔑
  mouthwash **109**–25
Mouth **106** 🔑
move in 48–F 🔑
move out 48 ✦🔑
movement **209**–16 🔑
mover **172**–42
movies **228**–2 🔑
  movie theater **128**–6 🔑
Movies **243** 🔑
Moving around the Screen **211** 🔑 AWL
Moving In **49** 🔑
moving van **160**–18 🔑
mow 186–A

mower **186**–6
mozzarella cheese **71**–29
MP3 player **240**–2
mudslide **148**–6
muffin **79**–16, **80**–5
muffler **162**–16
muffs **197**–16
mug **55**–7
mugging **145**–11
multiply 204–C 🔑
multi-use knife **232**–20
mumps **112**–7
murder **145**–12 🔑
muscle **107**–32
mushrooms **69**–27
music **64**–3, **201**–16 🔑
  live music **84**–1 🔑
  music store **132**–1 🔑
  world music **243**–32 🔑
MUSIC **244** 🔑
Music **243** 🔑
musician **172**–43 🔑
mussels **71**–13, **218**–18
mustache **33**–5
mustard **79**–22
mystery **243**–20 🔑

nachos **79**–7 🔑
nail **194**–34 🔑
  fingernail **106**–18
  nail clippers **109**–31
  nail polish **109**–33
  nail salon **132**–3
  toenail **106** ✦
name **4**–1, **4**–2, **4**–4 🔑
  name tag **92**–15
napkin **55**–10, **83**–26
narrow **97**–35 🔑
nasal
  nasal congestion **113**–13
  nasal spray **115**–32
National Guard **141**–38
national guardsman **141**–39 🔑
Native American **208**–3
NATURAL DISASTERS **148**–**149** 🔑
natural gas **224**–3 🔑
natural materials **98** ✦🔑
nature program **242**–7 🔑
Navy **141**–30 🔑
navy blue **28**–5 🔑
near **25** ✦🔑
neck **104**–3 🔑
  crewneck **96**–7
  necklaces **95**–10
  scoop neck **96**–10
  turtleneck **96**–9
  V-neck **96**–8
needle **98**–17, **100**–10, **216**–10 🔑
needle plate **98**–18 🔑
needles **239**–23 🔑
negative integers **204**–1 🔑 AWL
negotiate 161–D

neighborhood **130** ✦🔑
nephew **34**–19 🔑
Neptune **215**–8
nervous **42**–10 🔑
nest **220**–5 🔑
net 🔑
  fishing net **232**–17 🔑
  hairnet **93**–25
network 168–E AWL
Neutral Colors **24** 🔑 AWL
neutron **207**–32
new 🔑
  new job **175**–4 🔑 AWL
  new moon **215**–9 🔑
  New Year's Day **22**–9
New Words **8** 🔑
news 🔑
  news program **242**–1
  newspaper **135**–6 🔑
  newsstand **130**–12
newt **218**–27
next 🔑
  next to **25**–9 🔑
  next week **20**–20 🔑
  next-day mail **137** ✦🔑
nickel / 5 cents **26**–2
niece **34**–18
night **18**–20 🔑
  night light **37**–28 🔑
  night table **58**–23 🔑
  nightclub **229**–12
  nightgown **91**–24
  nightshirt **91**–27
  nightstand **58**–23
  overnight **137** ✦
nine **16**
nineteen **16**
nineteenth **16**
ninetieth **16**
ninety **16**
  90° angle **205**–26 🔑
ninth **16**
nipple **37**–2
no 🔑
  no left turn **158**–8 🔑
  no outlet **158**–6
  no parking **158**–11
noise **64**–5 🔑
  noise-canceling headphones **240**–6
noisy **23**–11 🔑
nonstop flight **165** ✦
noon **18**–16
  afternoon **18**–17
north **159**–1 🔑
nose **104**–6, **110**–15 🔑
  revolving nosepiece **206**–15
not 🔑
  can't breathe 118–N 🔑
  can't install 191–C 🔑
  can't log on 191–D
  can't stream 191–F

do not drink 114–F 🔑
do not drive 114–E 🔑
do not enter 158–2 🔑
do not operate 114–E 🔑
do not take 114–D 🔑
don't be late 179–E 🔑
don't litter 225–L
don't smoke 116–G
not working 62–1 🔑
won't print 191–E 🔑
note 189–39 🔑
footnote 202–12
notebook 7–28
notebook paper 7–29
spiral notebook 7–30
novel 135–16 🔑
November 21–35 🔑
nuclear energy 224–8 🔑 AWL
nucleus 206–7, 207–29
numb 120–C
number 🔑
access number 15–24 🔑 AWL
apartment number 4–6 🔑
checking account number 134–15 🔑
driver's license number 138–11 🔑
even numbers 204–4 🔑
odd numbers 204–3 🔑 AWL
phone number 4–11, 15–29 🔑
prescription number 114–5
savings account number 134–16 🔑
SKU number 27–5
Social Security number 4–19
NUMBERS 16 🔑
Numbers 16 🔑
Numerals 16 🔑
numerator 204–5
nurse 111–8, 172–44 🔑
licensed practical nurse (LPN)
122–11
nurse midwives 122 ✦
nurse practitioners 122 ✦🔑 AWL
registered nurse (RN) 122–10
surgical nurse 122–9
nurse 36–B
Nurse 93 🔑
nursery 47–11
nursery rhymes 37–23
nursery school 200–1
nursing
certified nursing assistant (CNA) 122–12
nursing home 52–12
Nursing Staff 122 🔑
nut 194–36 🔑
nutrition label 124–8
nuts 73–36 🔑
nylon 99–12

oak 216–17, 216–24
obey 142–C 🔑
objective 206–16 🔑 AWL
oboe 244–3
observatory 215–21
observe 207–C 🔑

obstetrician 122–2
obtuse angle 205–27 🔑
occupational therapist 172–45 AWL
OCCUPATIONS 170–173 AWL
ocean 214–6, 231–1 🔑
o'clock 18–6
October 21–34 🔑
octopus 218–9
odd numbers 204–3 🔑 AWL
odometer 163–28
off 🔑
clear off 10–I 🔑
drop off 38–G 🔑
gas shut-off valve 150–4
get off 157–J 🔑
take off 109–Q, 164–J 🔑
turn off 11–P, 179–G, 225–G 🔑
offer 12–E 🔑
office 182–3 🔑
corporate offices 184–1 🔑 AWL
main office 5–12 🔑
office building 126–2 🔑
office manager 188–8 🔑
office supply store 129–21 🔑
post office 127–11 🔑
post office box (PO box) 137–9
run for office 143–J 🔑
OFFICE 136–137, 188–189 🔑
Office 51 🔑
Office Equipment 189 🔑
OFFICE SKILLS 177 🔑
Office Skills 177 🔑
Office Supplies 189 🔑
Office Visit 120 🔑
OFFICE WORK 188–189 🔑
officer 141–27, 144–1, 165–17, 172–48 🔑
official 143–12, 235–6 🔑
oil 73–31, 224–6 🔑
oil gauge 163–29
oil paint 239–19 🔑
oil spill 224–17
ointment 115–24, 119–12
OK 158–5
old 31–9, 31–10 🔑
omelet 76–12
on 25–11 🔑
get on 157–I 🔑
go on 169–N 🔑
on hold 177–P
on the left 25–1 🔑
on the right 25–3 🔑
on time 19–23, 165–29 🔑
on-the-job training 175–12 🔑
overdose on drugs 118–K 🔑
put on 87–B, 108–D, 109–P, 137–C 🔑
try on 95–C 🔑
turn on 11–D, 147–D 🔑
On the Airplane 165
once a week 20–22 🔑
oncologist 122–5
one 16 🔑
five after one 18–7 🔑
one billion 16

one eighth 17–5
one fourth 17–4
one half 17–2 🔑
one hundred 16
one hundred dollars 26–12
one hundred one 16
100 percent 17–8 🔑
one hundred thousand 16
one hundredth 16
one million 16
one o'clock 18–6 🔑
one third 17–3
one thousand 16
one thousandth 16
one way 158–3 🔑
one whole 17–1 🔑
one-fifteen 18–9
one-forty 18–12
one-forty-five 18–13
one-oh-five 18–7
one-size-fits-all 96–6 🔑
one-ten 18–8
one-thirty 18–11
one-twenty 18–10
one-way trip 156–16 🔑
quarter after one 18–9 🔑
ten after one 18–8 🔑
twenty after one 18–10 🔑
onions 69–19, 69–20 🔑
onion rings 79–4 🔑
online 🔑
online catalog 135–11
online course 175–13 🔑
Online Dangers 147 🔑
online predators 147–2
online test 10–5 🔑
only 158–7 🔑
open 6–G, 146–F 🔑
open the program 210–A 🔑
opener 54–14, 78–1, 150–8
opening deposit 134–11
opera 229–11, 242–5
operate 114–E, 176–H 🔑
Operating Room 123 🔑
operating table 123–40 🔑
Operations 204 🔑
operator 14–20, 98–14, 172–37
ophthalmologist 122–7
opinion 44–3 🔑
opossum 222–4
opponent 143–8 🔑
optician 132–9
optometrist 117–6
orange 24–4 🔑
oranges 68–5 🔑
orangutan 223–39
orchard 187–10
orchid 217–19
order 🔑
order puller 185–10
short-order cook 193–1
order 82–D
orderly 122–16

Ordinal Numbers **16**
organ **244**–20
organic **84**–2
organisms **206**–1
organize **177**–L, **203**–G
organizer **189**–49
ornament **245**–15
Orthodontics **120**
orthodontist **120**–5
orthopedists **122** ✦
Other Instruments **244**
otter **219**–37
ottoman **56**–23
ounce **75**–1, **75**–11
out **62**–2
   blow out **246**–C
   check out **135**–C
   cross out **9**–R
   eat out **82** ✦
   get out of **157**–F
   let out **100**–C
   out of focus **241**–31 AWL
   outfit **88** ✦
   out-of-network doctor **121**–10 AWL
   out-of-state contact **150**–2 AWL
   run out of gas **166**–E
   take out **9**–Y, **60**–Q
   work out **236**–N
outdoor grill **230**–16
OUTDOOR RECREATION **232**
outlet **58**–28, **158**–6, **163**–42
   outlet cover **195**–46
OUTSIDE THE BODY **106**–**107**
oven **54**–15, **54**–20
   oven cleaner **61**–3
over **76**–11, **157**–B
   overalls **88**–6
   overcoat **90**–2
   overexposed **241**–32
   overflowing **63**–18
   overhead compartment **165**–13
   overnight / next-day mail **137** ✦
   over-the-counter medication **115**–18
overdose **118**–K
Over-the-Counter Medication **115**
owl **220**–6
owner **170**–11, **185**–1
oxfords **95**–29
oxygen mask **165**–24
oysters **71**–14

Pacific time **19**–29
pacifier **37**–25
pack **74**–9, **119**–14, **241**–23
   backpack **94**–18, **232**–15
pack **49**–M, **166**–A
package **74**–8, **74**–20, **136**–17
packaged food **150**–10
PACKAGING **74**
packer **185**–8
packing tape **189**–32
pad
   bumper pad **59**–4

changing pad **59**–2
foam pad **232**–13
heating pad **115**–13
ink pad **189**–46
keypad **14**–5
knee pads **197**–19
legal pad **189**–38
shoulder pads **237**–20
steel-wool soap pads **61**–5
sterile pad **119**–7
track pad **190**–24
pail **37**–7, **61**–7
pain **42**–11, **117**–3
   pain reliever **115**–26
paint **195**–25, **238**–10, **239**–19
   paint pan **195**–51
   paint roller **195**–23
   paintbrush **195**–22, **239**–20
paint **49**–P, **196**–A, **239**–E
painter **172**–46
Painter **92**
painting **56**–9
pair of scissors **100**–16
paisley **96**–26
pajamas **91**–23
pallet **185**–13
palm **106**–15, **216**–14
pan **54**–24
   bedpan **123**–23
   cake pan **78**–26
   dustpan **61**–17
   frying pan **78**–5
   paint pan **195**–51
   pancakes **80**–7
   pie pan **78**–28
   roasting pan **78**–13
   saucepan **78**–25
pancreas **107**–45
panda **223**–41
pane **196**–16
panel AWL
   flat-panel TV **240**–7
Panel **163** AWL
panther **223**–40
panties **91**–13
pants **87**–12
   security pants **93**–22 AWL
   training pants **37**–16
   work pants **92**–5
pantyhose **91**–18
papayas **68**–20
paper
   construction paper **238**–13
   copies of important papers **150**–20
   newspaper **135**–6
   notebook paper **7**–29
   paper clip **189**–31
   paper cutter **189**–22
   paper shredder **189**–24
   paper towels **54**–3
   sandpaper **195**–56
   toilet paper **57**–19, **150**–13
   wallpaper **59**–8

parade **245**–1
paragraph **202**–3 AWL
parakeet **221**–15
parallel lines **205**–25 AWL
parallelogram **205**–33
paramedic **118**–2
parasites **113**–25
parcel post **136**–6
parentheses **202**–22
PARENTING **36**–**37**
Parents **34**
parent-teacher conference **22**–5
paring knife **78**–16
park **229**–10
park **131**–E
PARK AND PLAYGROUND **230**
parka **90**–9
parking **130**–6, **158**–11, **158**–12
   parking attendant **192**–3
   parking garage **126**–1
   parking meter **131**–25
   parking space **50**–18, **130**–5
parochial school **5** ✦
parsley **69**–28
part **33**–4
participate **10**–B AWL
particle
   particle board **195**–20
   particle mask **197**–14
Partner **8** AWL
parts **185**–5
Parts of a Bird **220**
PARTS OF A CAR **162**–**163**
Parts of a Fish **218**
Parts of a Flower **217**
Parts of a Sewing Machine **98**
Parts of a Tree **216**
Parts of an Essay **202**
party **64**–2
pass **165**–20
   passport **41**–10
pass **10**–E, **139**–H, **236**–G
passenger **154**–2, **165**–15
password
   create a password **211**–P
   create secure passwords **147**–D
   reenter the password **211**–Q
   type the password again **211**–Q
past **159**–E
pasta **67**–12
   pasta salad **80**–20
paste
   paste text **210**–L
   toothpaste **109**–23
pastrami **71**–23
path **230**–3
Path **175**
patient **111**–6, **123**–18, **178**–1
patio **53**–16
   patio furniture **53**–19
patron **82**–6, **135**–3
pattern **99**–22
Patterns **96**

pause **241**–E ♪
paw **222**–20
pay ♪
  pay phone **131**–23 ♪
  pay stub **183**–11
  paycheck **183**–14
  payroll clerk **183**–10
pay ♪
  pay a claim **121**–B
  pay a late fine **135**–E ♪
  pay attention **151**–D ♪
  pay back 26–D ♪
  pay cash **27**–A ♪
  pay for 27–G ♪
  pay taxes **142**–B ♪
  pay the application fee **139**–D ♪
  pay the check **82**–I
  pay the rent **48**–E ♪
Pay **27** ♪
PBX **188**–13
peaceful assembly **142**–1 ♪ AWL
peaches **68**–10
peacock **220**–15
peak **214**–14 ♪
pearls **95**–39
pears **68**–4
peas **69**–21
pedal **163**–45, **163**–46
pedestrian **130**–14
  pedestrian crossing **158**–13
pediatrician **122**–4
peel 77–K
peeler **78**–15
peephole **51**–33
pelvis **107**–50
pen **7**–22 ♪
pencil **7**–20 ♪
  eyebrow pencil **109**–34
  pencil eraser **7**–21
  pencil sharpener **7**–23, **189**–26
penguin **220**–12
peninsula **214**–7
penny / 1 cent **26**–1 ♪
Pentagon **141**–23
PEOPLE **32** ♪
pepper **55**–13, **69**–7, **69**–29 ♪
percent ♪
  50 percent **17**–10 ♪
  100 percent **17**–8 ♪
  75 percent **17**–9 ♪
  10 percent **17**–12 ♪
  25 percent **17**–11 ♪
Percents **17** ♪
Percussion **244**
perfume **108**–6
perimeter **205**–43
period **202**–14 ♪ AWL
Period **208** ♪ AWL
periodic table **207**–26 ♪ AWL
periodicals **135**–4 AWL
perm 33–B
permanent marker **7**–24
peroxide **119**–10

perpendicular lines **205**–24
person ♪
  appliance repairperson **170**–4
  assemblyperson **140**–18
  bus person **193**–13
  businessperson **170**–12 ♪
  congressperson **140**–4
  councilperson **140**–22
  counterperson **79**–17
  delivery person **171**–21 ♪
  electronics repairperson **171**–24
  repairperson **62**–10
personal CD player **240**–7 ♪
PERSONAL HYGIENE **108**–**109**
PERSONAL INFORMATION **4** ♪
Personal Qualities **178** ♪
pesticide poisoning **224**–16
pests **62** ✦
pet ♪
  pet food **72**–6 ♪
  pet store **132**–6 ♪
petals **217**–8
petition **152**–5
petroleum **224**–6
Pets **221** ♪
pharmacist **114**–1
pharmacy **130**–4
PHARMACY **114**–**115**
Phases of the Moon **215** ♪ AWL
Phillips screwdriver **194**–31
phishing **147**–4
phlebotomist **123**–29
phone ♪
  automated phone system **14**–22 ♪ AWL
  cell phone **4**–13, **14**–8 ♪
  cell phone case **94**–15 ♪
  headphones **6**–8
  home phone **4**–12 ♪
  Internet phone call **14**–19 ♪
  lightweight headphones **240**–4
  microphone **191**–36, **240**–16
  pay phone **131**–23 ♪
  phone card **15**–23 ♪
  phone jack **14**–2
  phone line **14**–1 ♪
  phone number **4**–11, **15**–29 ♪
  smartphone **15**–25
Phone **14** ♪
Phone Bill **15** ♪
Phone Call **15** ♪
photo **58**–3, **138**–4 ♪
  digital photo album **241**–30 ♪
  funny photo **226**–2 ♪
  photo album **241**–29 ♪
  photocopier **189**–23
  serious photo **226**–3 ♪
photographer **226**–1 ♪
PHOTOGRAPHY **240**–**241** ♪
photosynthesis **206**–10
physical ♪ AWL
  physical education **201**–17 ♪
  physical therapist **117**–12
  physical therapy **117**–11

physically challenged **32**–10 ♪ AWL
physician assistant **172**–47
physicist **207**–33
Physics **207** ♪
pi (π) **205**–46
piano **244**–14 ♪
pick **108**–15
pick up 6–I, **11**–E, **38**–M ♪
  pick up a prescription **114** ✦
pickax **196**–21
picker **196**–5
pickle **80**–11
pickup truck **160**–12
picnic 230–D
picnic table **230**–8
picture ♪
  picture book **135**–12 ♪
  picture dictionary **7**–32 ♪
  picture frame **58**–4 ♪
pie **81**–35
  pie pan **78**–28
pier **231**–18
pierced
  pierced ear **32**–17
  pierced earrings **95**–36
pig **221**–2, **221**–14 ♪
pigeon **220**–16
pile **53**–25 ♪
pill **115**–21 ♪
pillow **56**–2, **58**–11
  pillowcase **58**–14
pilot **165**–11 ♪
pin **95**–38 ♪
  bobby pins **108**–21
  clothespin **101**–10
  pincushion **100**–13
  pushpin **189**–35
  rolling pin **78**–30
  safety pins **37**–9, **100**–14 ♪
  straight pin **100**–12 ♪
pine **216**–9
  pine cone **216**–11
pineapples **68**–23
pink **24**–7 ♪
pint **75**–3 ♪
pipe **162**–15, **195**–17 ♪
  pipe wrench **195**–47
pitch 236–A
pizza **79**–10
place **150**–1 ♪
  fireplace **56**–13
  place of birth **4**–15 ♪
  place setting **83**–17
  placemat **55**–11
PLACES TO GO **228**–**229** ♪
PLACES TO LIVE **52** ♪
plaid **96**–22
plain **97**–33 ♪
plains **214**–19
plan **198**–4 ♪
plan 150–A
plane **148**–3, **154**–8, **195**–57 ♪
Planets **215**

Planning and Goal Setting **174**–**175** 🔑
plant **186**–E, **187**–A, **225**–N
plants 🔑
  houseplant **56**–4, **217**–27
PLANTS **216** 🔑
Plants **216** 🔑
plaque **120**–13
plastic 🔑
  plastic storage bags **72**–25 🔑
  plastic utensils **79**–19
  plastic wrap **72**–24 🔑
plate **55**–1 🔑
  bread-and-butter plate **83**–19 🔑
  dinner plate **83**–18 🔑
  license plate **138**–12, **162**–12 🔑 AWL
  salad plate **83**–20 🔑
  vanity plate **138** ✦
platform **156**–7 🔑
platter **55**–20
platypus **223**–46
play **229**–8 🔑
  play area **132**–11 🔑 AWL
  playground **50**–3
play **241**–B
  play an instrument **244**–A 🔑
  play cards **239**–H 🔑
  play games **238**–B 🔑
  play with **36**–M 🔑
player **235**–5 🔑
  Blu-ray player **240**–9
  CD / cassette player **102**–8 🔑
  DVD player **240**–11 🔑
  personal CD player **240**–7 🔑
  video MP3 player **240**–2 🔑
  video player **213**–18 🔑
PLAYGROUND **230**
pliers **194**–7
plug **241**–25
  earplugs **197**–15
plumber **63**–20
plums **68**–13
plunger **195**–50
plywood **196**–18
p.m. **18**–5 🔑
pneumatic drill **196**–9
pneumonia **112**–10
PO box (post office box) **137**–9
poached eggs **76**–9
pocket **100**–7 🔑
podium **226**–5
poinsettia **217**–24
point **17**–7 🔑
  endpoint **205**–21
poison **118**–J 🔑
  poison ivy **216**–25
  poison oak **216**–24
  poison sumac **216**–23
poisoning **224**–16
poisonous fumes **197**–3 🔑
pole **232**–18, **237**–25 🔑
police 🔑
  police officer **144**–1, **172**–48 🔑
  police station **126**–6 🔑

policyholder / insured **121**–5
polish **61**–8, **109**–33 🔑
polish **60**–E, **109**–O
political 🔑
  political movement **209**–16 🔑
  political party **143** ✦🔑
polka-dotted **96**–21
polling booth / voting booth **143**–10
pollution **224**–11, **224**–14 🔑
Pollution **224** 🔑
polo **235**–16
  polo shirt **92**–14
poncho **90**–19
pond **214**–21
pool **51**–22, **192**–22, **234**–2 🔑
  pool service **192**–21 🔑
  pool table **50**–15 🔑
pop **73**–34, **243**–25 🔑
  pop-up ad **213**–17
porch light **53**–13
porcupine **222**–10
Pork **70**
pork chops **70**–10
porpoise **219**–32
port **190**–20 🔑
  airport **155**–10 🔑
portable charger **240**–16
positive **178**–2 🔑 AWL
positive integers **204**–2 🔑 AWL
post **136**–6 🔑
  post office **127**–11 🔑
  post office box (PO box) **137**–9
  post office lobby drop **137**–11 🔑
  postcard **136**–16
  postmark **136**–24
POST OFFICE **136**–**137** 🔑
postage **137** ✦🔑
postal **137**–10
  postal clerk **137**–7
  postal forms **136**–19
  postal scale **137**–8, **189**–27
  postal worker **173**–49
pot **54**–16, **78**–6 🔑
  potholders **78**–29
  teapot **55**–16
potatoes **69**–17 🔑
  baked potato **81**–25 🔑
  mashed potatoes **81**–23
  potato chips **73**–35 🔑
  potato salad **80**–19 🔑
  sweet potatoes **69**–18 🔑
potty seat **37**–15
pouch **223**–50
POULTRY **70**
Poultry **70, 76**
pound **75**–12 🔑
  pound key **14**–7 🔑
pour **82**–C 🔑
powder **37**–14, **108**–4, **109**–41 🔑
power **224**–2, **224**–5 🔑
  international power adapter
    241–26 🔑
  power cord **190**–10

power outlet **163**–42
power sander **194**–11
pox **112**–6
practical 🔑
  licensed practical nurse (LPN)
    122–11
prairie dog **221**–22
praise **36**–J
predators **147**–2
pregnant **32**–15 🔑
preheat **77**–A
premium **121**–7
preparation **193**–4 🔑
PREPARATION **76**–**77** 🔑
prepare **179**–A 🔑
PREPOSITIONS **25**
PREPOSITIONS OF MOTION **157**
preschool **200**–1
prescribe medication **114** ✦
prescription **114**–2
  pick up a prescription **114** ✦
  prescription label **114**–4
  prescription medication **114**–3
  prescription number **114**–5
present **94** ✦, **246**–3 🔑
presentation **188**–6 🔑
presentation program **191**–31
president **140**–8, **209**–5 🔑
  first president **208**–11 🔑
  Presidents' Day **22**–11
  vice president **140**–9
press **78**–11, **142**–4 🔑
press **15**–B
presser foot **98**–19
pressure 🔑
  blood pressure gauge **111**–9 🔑
  high blood pressure **113**–24
pretend **239**–G 🔑
Prewriting **203**
price **27**–2, **27**–3, **27**–7 🔑
  price tag **27**–1
prime minister **209**–7 🔑 AWL
principal **5**–4 AWL
print **96**–23
  fingerprint **138**–5
print **4**–C, **177**–I, **191**–E 🔑
printer **173**–50, **190**–21 🔑
  inkjet printer **189**–18
  laser printer **189**–19
Priority Mail® **136**–1
prism **207**–35
prisoner / convict **144**–15 🔑
private school **5** ✦🔑
probe / rover **215**–20
Problem **204** 🔑
problems **117**–1, **204**–11 🔑
PROBLEMS **62**–**63** 🔑
Problems **117, 120** 🔑
PROCEDURES **150**–**151** 🔑 AWL
Procedures **111, 119** 🔑 AWL
Process **203** 🔑 AWL
processor **54**–26
Processor **92**

produce section **72**–2 🔑
product **204**–9 🔑
Products **72, 73** 🔑
professional development **175**–7 🔑 AWL
program
   children's program **242**–9
   nature program **242**–7
   news program **242**–1
   open the program **210**–A
   presentation program **191**–31
   quit the program **210**–F
   shopping program **242**–10
   sports program **242**–11
   spreadsheet program **191**–30
   word processing program **191**–29
program 176–I
Programs **242**
projector **6**–5, **241**–27
promotion **175**–8 🔑 AWL
proof of insurance **138**–8 🔑
proofread 203–I
prosecuting attorney **144**–10 🔑
prospective tenant **51**–29 AWL
protect 146–D 🔑
Protect Children **147** 🔑
protector **190**–11
proton **207**–31
proud **43**–21 🔑
prunes **68**–26
pruning shears **186**–9
psychiatrist **122**–8
PUBLIC SAFETY **146** 🔑
public school 5 ✦🔑
PUBLIC TRANSPORTATION **156** 🔑 AWL
pull 120–F, **230**–A 🔑
puller **185**–10
pullover sweater **88**–3
pulse **124**–A
pumps **95**–26
Punctuation **202**
puppy **221**–12
purchase 94–A 🔑 AWL
purifier **115**–14
purple **24**–6 🔑
purses **94**–2, **94**–14
push 230–B 🔑
pushpin **189**–35
put 9–X, **49**–O, **164**–I 🔑
   put away 9–Z, **60**–G 🔑
   put down 6–J 🔑
   put in 161–I 🔑
   put on 87–B, **108**–D, **109**–P, **137**–C, **177**–N 🔑
puzzle **59**–17
pyramid **205**–39

quad **5**–1
quart **75**–4
quarter 🔑
   quarter / 25 cents **26**–4 🔑
   quarter after one **18**–9 🔑
   1/4 cup **75**–8 🔑

quarter moon **215**–11 🔑
quarter to two **18**–13 🔑
3/4 sleeved **96**–13 🔑
question **212**–1, **212**–C 🔑
   question mark **202**–15
Quick and Easy Cake **77** 🔑
quiet **23**–12 🔑
quill **222**–23
quilt **58**–16
   quilt block **238**–15
quilt 238–C
quit the program **210**–F
quotation **202**–10
   quotation marks **202**–18
quotient **204**–10

rabbit **221**–13
raccoon **222**–13
race 236–S
racing **234**–19 🔑
rack **98**–16
   dish rack **54**–5
   roasting rack **78**–14
   towel rack **57**–15
racket **237**–2
racquetball **234**–12
radiation **224**–15
radiator **162**–19
radio **102**–6, **197**–22 🔑
radioactive materials **197**–7
radiologist **122**–6
radishes **69**–4
radius **205**–35
rafting **232**–2
rags **61**–9
rail **59**–10 🔑
railroad crossing **158**–14
rain **13**–11 🔑
   acid rain **224**–13 🔑
   rain boots **90**–20 🔑
   rain forest **214**–1 🔑
   raincoat **90**–18
raise 6–A 🔑
raisins **68**–25
rake **186**–8
rake 186–C
rally **143**–7
RAM (random access memory) **190**–17
ranch **52**–10
Ranch Hand **92**
rancher **187**–22
RANCHING **187**
R&B **243**–28
range **214**–15 🔑 AWL
ranger **166**–1
rash **113**–14
raspberries **68**–15
rat **63**–27, **221**–17
rattle **37**–27
   rattlesnake **219**–45
raw **70**–24 🔑
ray **218**–11

razor **109**–27
   razor blade **109**–28
reaction **118**–E 🔑 AWL
read 🔑
   proofread 203–I
   read the card **137**–G 🔑
   read the definition **8**–B 🔑 AWL
   read the paper **39**–V 🔑
   read to **36**–N 🔑
Reading a Phone Bill **15** 🔑
reality show **242**–6 🔑
rearview mirror **163**–35 🔑
receipt **27**–6 🔑
receive 137–F 🔑
receiver **14**–4
reception area **188**–15 🔑 AWL
receptionist **111**–2, **173**–51, **182**–5, **188**–14
reclined seat **165**–27
record 207–D, **241**–A
records **172**–39 🔑
RECREATION **232**
Recreation Room **50**
recreational vehicle (RV) **160**–10
recruiter **174**–J
rectangle **205**–29
recycle 60–B, **225**–C
recycling bin **61**–2
red **24**–1 🔑
   red hair **33**–13 🔑
   redcoat **208**–9
   redwood **216**–18
redecorate 48 ✦
reduce 225–A 🔑
reenter 211–Q
referee **235**–6
reference librarian **135**–9
refresh button **213**–11
refrigerator **54**–9
refund 97 ✦
refuse 12–F 🔑
reggae **243**–31
register **27**–10, **73**–16 AWL
register 142–D, **161**–F 🔑 AWL
registered nurse (RN) **122**–10
Registering an Account **211** 🔑 AWL
registration AWL
   registration sticker **138**–13
   registration tag **138**–13
regular price **27**–2 🔑
regulations **182**–6 AWL
relatives **44**–6 🔑
relax 39–U 🔑 AWL
relieved **42**–15
reliever **115**–26
religious holiday **22**–7 🔑
remain 151–E 🔑
remarried **35**–24
remote **240**–10 🔑
remove 109–Q, **134**–F 🔑 AWL
remover **109**–42
renew a license **138** ✦

rental agreement / lease **51**–28
Rental Office **51**
Renting an Apartment **48** 🔑
repair **176**–J 🔑
repairperson **62**–10
   appliance repairperson **170**–4
   electronics repairperson **171**–24
REPAIRS **62**–**63** 🔑
repellent **232**–23
replace **161**–K 🔑
report **146**–J, **146**–K 🔑
reporter **144**–12, **173**–52 🔑
representative **140**–3, **171**–20 🔑
REPTILES **218**–**219**
Reptiles **219**
request **10**–F, **12** ✦🔑
Requirements **142** 🔑 AWL
rescue **149**–20 🔑
   rescue breathing **119**–17 🔑
research **212** ✦🔑 AWL
   research and development **184**–5 🔑 AWL
   research local companies **168**–D 🔑 AWL
   research question **212**–1 🔑 AWL
RESEARCH **212**–**213** 🔑 AWL
Research **212** 🔑 AWL
resident **180**–4 🔑 AWL
Resident Alien card **40**–2
Resources **225** 🔑 AWL
respirator **197**–13
respond **2**–C, **178**–H 🔑 AWL
Responding **203** 🔑 AWL
Responsibilities **142** 🔑
restaurant **127**–14, **130**–10 🔑
RESTAURANT **79**, **82**–**83** 🔑
Restaurant Dining **193**
Restaurant Kitchen **193** 🔑
restrooms **5**–9
results **143**–11, **212**–5, **212**–E 🔑
resuscitation **119**–18
retail clerk **173**–53
retire **41**–O 🔑
return 🔑
   return address **136**–21 🔑
return **27**–H, **135**–D 🔑
REUNION **44**–**45**
reuse **225**–B
revise **203**–J 🔑 AWL
Revising **203** 🔑 AWL
Revolutionary War **208**–8
revolving
   revolving door **192**–2
   revolving nosepiece **206**–15
rewind **241**–C
rewrite **203**–J
rhinoceros **223**–28
ribbon **99**–30
ribs **70**–5, **76**–2
   rib cage **107**–48
rice **67**–10, **81**–30, **187**–1 🔑
ride **131**–D 🔑
rider **156**–3 🔑
riding **232**–9 🔑

right **25**–3, **159**–B 🔑
   right angle **205**–26 🔑
   right turn only **158**–7 🔑
rights **208**–13 🔑
Rights **142** 🔑
ring **95**–40 🔑
   clip-on earrings **95**–37
   onion rings **79**–4
   pierced earrings **95**–36
   teething ring **37**–26
rinse **108**–F
ripe **68**–30
ripped **97**–41
ripper **100**–18
rise 🔑
   high-rise **129**–13
   sunrise **18**–14
river **159**–10, **214**–3 🔑
RN (registered nurse) **122**–10
roaches **63**–26
ROAD TRIP **166**–**167** 🔑
Road Worker **92** 🔑
roadwork **158**–16 🔑
roast **70**–1
   roast beef **71**–21
   roast chicken **81**–22
   roasted turkey **76**–4
   roasting pan **78**–13
   roasting rack **78**–14
robe **91**–28
robin **220**–17
rock **219**–38, **243**–23 🔑
rock **36**–D
rock concert **228**–5 🔑
rocking chair **37**–22 🔑
RODENTS **221**
Rodents **221**
roll **74**–23 🔑
rollers **33**–18, **195**–23
rolling pin **78**–30
rolls **74**–11, **80**–17 🔑
Roman Numerals **16**
romance **243**–16
roof **46**–2 🔑
   roof garden **50**–4 🔑
roofer **62**–8
room 🔑
   baby's room **47**–11 🔑
   ballroom **192**–26
   banquet room **193**–14
   bathroom **46**–5 🔑
   bedroom **46**–3 🔑
   classroom **5**–7 🔑
   conference room **188**–4 🔑 AWL
   courtroom **144**–7
   dining room **82**–1
   dining room chair **55**–8
   dining room table **55**–9
   dish room **83**–13 🔑
   guest room **192**–13 🔑
   kids' bedroom **47**–10 🔑
   living room **47**–13 🔑

meeting room **192**–25 🔑
restrooms **5**–9
room service **192**–17 🔑
roommates **64**–1
storeroom **193**–5
ROOM **56** 🔑
Room **50**, **111**, **123** 🔑
rooster **221**–7
root **216**–5, **217**–3 🔑
rope **230**–4, **232**–19 🔑
rose **217**–15 🔑
rotary
   rotary card file **189**–44 🔑
   rotary cutter **238**–16
rotten **68**–32
round trip **156**–17 🔑
route 🔑 AWL
   bus route **156**–1 🔑 AWL
   escape route **150**–3 🔑 AWL
   evacuation route **150**–5 🔑 AWL
   U.S. route **158**–17 🔑 AWL
router **191**–33, **194**–12
ROUTINES **38**–**39** 🔑
rover / probe **215**–20
rubber 🔑
   rubber band **189**–34 🔑
   rubber gloves **61**–4 🔑
   rubber mat **57**–5
ruffle **58**–17
rug **58**–22
ruler **17**–13 🔑
rules **64**–7 🔑
Rules **202** 🔑
run 🔑
   run across **157**–G 🔑
   run around **157**–H 🔑
   run for office **143**–J 🔑
   run out **166**–E 🔑
   run to class **11**–B 🔑
runner **193**–15
rural area **52**–4 🔑 AWL
RV (recreational vehicle) **160**–10
rye bread **71**–20

sad **43**–19 🔑
safety 🔑
   car safety seat **37**–20 🔑
   child safety seat **163**–53 🔑
   high visibility safety vest **92**–4
   safety boots **197**–20 🔑
   safety deposit box **134**–7 🔑
   safety glasses **92**–10, **197**–10 🔑
   safety goggles **197**–11
   safety pin **37**–9, **100**–14 🔑
   safety rail **59**–10 🔑
   safety regulations **182**–6 🔑 AWL
   safety visor **197**–12
SAFETY **76**–**77**, **146**, **147**, **197** 🔑
Safety **76** 🔑
Safety Equipment **197** 🔑 AWL
Safety Hazards and Hazardous
   Materials **197** 🔑

Safety Solutions **147** 🔑

sail 🔑
  sailboat **231**–2
  sailing **233**–8 🔑

sailor / seaman **141**–31 🔑

salad 🔑
  chef's salad **80**–14
  fruit salad **80**–21 🔑
  garden salad **80**–15 🔑
  house salad **80**–15 🔑
  pasta salad **80**–20
  potato salad **80**–19 🔑
  salad bar **79**–24 🔑
  salad fork **83**–27 🔑
  salad plate **83**–20 🔑
  spinach salad **80**–13

Salads **80** 🔑

salamander **218**–28

salami **71**–24

SALE **102**–**103** 🔑

sales **184**–7 🔑
  sale price **27**–3 🔑
  sales tax **27**–8 🔑
  salesclerk **94**–3 🔑

Salesperson **92**

salmon **71**–3
  salmon steak **71**–4

salon **132**–3, **133**–18

salt and pepper shakers **55**–13 🔑

same **23**–15 🔑

SAME AND DIFFERENT **28**–**29** 🔑

samples **84**–5 🔑

sand **231**–23 🔑
  sand dune **214**–5
  sandbox **230**–15
  sandcastle **231**–12
  sandpaper **195**–56

sandals **88**–9

sander **194**–11

sandwich **79**–5, **80**–10, **80**–12

sanitation worker **173**–54

sanitizing jar **33**–16

satellite **215**–19
  satellite dish **53**–5

satisfied **42**–6 🔑

Saturday **20**–14 🔑

Saturn **215**–6

saucepan **78**–25

saucer **83**–25

sausage **70**–12, **80**–2

saute **77**–E

save **225**–E 🔑
  save the document **210**–D 🔑 AWL

saving **19**–25 🔑
  lifesaving device **231**–20
  savings account number **134**–16 🔑

saw
  circular saw **194**–9
  hacksaw **194**–5
  handsaw **194**–4
  jigsaw **194**–10

saxophone **244**–5

say **2**–A, **3**–M, **4**–A 🔑

scaffolding **196**–4

scale **57**–27, **72**–3, **137**–8, **159**–7, **207**–41, **218**–3 🔑
  postal scale **189**–27

scallions **69**–20

scallops **71**–12, **218**–20

scan **177**–H

scanner **189**–20

scared / afraid **43**–23 🔑

scarf / scarves **95**–12
  winter scarf **90**–5

scenery **166**–4

schedule **156**–4 🔑 AWL

schedule **177**–J AWL

school **128**–9 🔑
  adult school **200**–8 🔑 AWL
  career and technical school **200**–5 🔑
  elementary school **200**–2
  high school **200**–4 🔑
  junior high school **200**–3 🔑
  middle school **200**–3 🔑
  nursery school **200**–1
  parochial school **5** ✦
  preschool **200**–1
  private school **5** ✦🔑
  public school **5** ✦🔑
  school bus **160**–21 🔑
  school crossing **158**–15 🔑
  vocational school **200**–5

SCHOOL **5, 10, 11** 🔑

SCHOOLS AND SUBJECTS **200**–**201** 🔑

science **201**–11 🔑

SCIENCE **206**–**207** 🔑

Science Lab **207** 🔑

scissors **100**–16 🔑

scoop neck **96**–10

score **10**–3, **235**–1 🔑

scorpion **220**–31

scrambled eggs **76**–7

scraper **195**–52

screen **6**–2, **241**–28 🔑
  big-screen TV **50**–14 🔑
  click on the screen **210**–G 🔑
  fire screen **56**–12 🔑
  flat-screen TV **240**–8 🔑
  screen door **53**–15 🔑
  screen **froze** **191**–B 🔑
  sunscreen **108**–7, **231**–10
  touch screen **163**–37 🔑

Screen **211** 🔑

screener **164**–5

screening area **164**–4

screw **194**–33 🔑
  machine screw **194**–32 🔑
  Phillips screwdriver **194**–31
  screwdriver **194**–30
  wood screw **194**–33 🔑

scroll **211**–M

scrub **60**–K

scrubs **93**–31
  scrub brush **61**–20
  surgical scrub cap **93**–35
  surgical scrubs **93**–38

scuba
  scuba diving **233**–12
  scuba tank **231**–6

sea 🔑
  sea anemone **218**–25
  sea lion **219**–35
  sea otter **219**–37
  sea urchin **218**–22
  seahorse **218**–13
  seashell **231**–24

Sea Animals **218** 🔑

Sea Mammals **219**

SEAFOOD AND DELI **71**

seal **219**–36

seam ripper **100**–18

seaman / sailor **141**–31 🔑

search 🔑
  apartment search tool **48**–1 🔑
  search and rescue team **149**–20 🔑 AWL
  search box **212**–3 🔑
  search engine **212**–2, **212**–A 🔑
  search results **212**–5 🔑

SEARCH **168**–**169** 🔑

SEASONAL CLOTHING **90**

Seasons **21** 🔑

seat 🔑
  back seat **163**–54 🔑
  booster car seat **37**–21 🔑
  car safety seat **37**–20 🔑
  child safety seat **163**–53 🔑
  front seat **163**–51 🔑
  love seat **56**–1 🔑
  potty seat **37**–15
  reclined seat **165**–27
  seat belt **163**–52 🔑
  upright seat **165**–28

seat **82**–B

seaweed **231** ✦

second **16** 🔑

Second Floor **50** 🔑

seconds **18**–3

Secretary of Defense **141**–24

section **72**–2 🔑 AWL

security **184**–13 🔑 AWL
  cybersecurity **190**–4
  security camera **50**–19 🔑 AWL
  security gate **50**–16 🔑 AWL
  security guard **134**–5, **173**–55 🔑 AWL
  security pants **93**–22 🔑 AWL
  security screener **164**–5
  security shirt **93**–20 🔑 AWL

Security Checkpoint **164** 🔑 AWL

Security Guard **93** 🔑 AWL

sedan **160** ✦

see **106**–A 🔑

seed **217**–1 🔑
  seedling **217**–4

seek **116**–A, **151**–H 🔑 AWL

select **212**–A 🔑 AWL

Selecting and Changing Text **210** 🔑 AWL

self-checkout **73**–10, **135**–10

sell **176**–K 🔑

semi / tractor-trailer **160**–15

semicolon **202**–21
Senate **140**–5 🔑
senator **140**–6 🔑
   state senator **140**–19 🔑
send 211–Z 🔑
Sending a Card **137** 🔑
Sending Email **211** 🔑
senior 🔑
   senior citizen **30**–5 🔑
   senior housing **52**–11 🔑
Senses **106** 🔑
sentence **202**–2 🔑
sentence 144–F 🔑
separate 76–B
September **21**–33 🔑
sequins **99**–33
serious photo **226**–3 🔑
serve 143–N, **236**–P 🔑
   serve on a jury **142**–E 🔑
   serve the meal **82**–F 🔑
Serve **76** 🔑
server **82**–8, **83**–9, **173**–56, **193**–8
service 🔑
   customer service **97** ✦, **184**–11 🔑
   customer service representative **171**–20 🔑
   guest services **132**–12 🔑
   pool service **192**–21 🔑
   room service **192**–17 🔑
SERVICE **140**–141, **193** 🔑
serving bowl **55**–21 🔑
set 10–A, **82**–A 🔑
   set a goal **168**–A 🔑 AWL
   set a long-term goal **174**–G 🔑 AWL
   set a short-term goal **174**–H 🔑 AWL
   set up an interview **169**–M 🔑
   sunset **18**–18
setting **83**–17
seven **16** 🔑
seventeen **16** 🔑
seventeenth **16**
seventh **16** 🔑
seventieth **16** 🔑
seventy **16** 🔑
   75 percent **17**–9 🔑
sew 98–A, **98**–B, **176**–L 🔑
sewing
   sewing machine **98**–13 🔑
   sewing machine operator **98**–14
Sewing Machine **98** 🔑
Sewing Supplies **100** 🔑
shade **231**–13 🔑
   lampshade **58**–26
shadow **109**–35 🔑
shake
   milkshake **79**–14
shake 3–K, **179**–I 🔑
shakers **55**–13
shampoo **108**–10
shanks **70**–13
shaper **91**–15
Shapes **205** 🔑
shapewear slip **91**–21
share 8–M 🔑

Sharing and Responding **203** 🔑 AWL
shark **218**–4
sharpener **7**–23, **189**–26
shave
   aftershave **109**–30
shave 109–M 🔑
shaver **109**–26
shaving cream **109**–29 🔑
shears **33**–17, **186**–9
sheep **221**–6 🔑
sheet 🔑
   answer sheet **10**–2
   cookie sheet **78**–27 🔑
   dryer sheets **101**–5
   fitted sheet **58**–12
   flat sheet **58**–13 🔑
shelf **54**–2 🔑
shell 🔑
   seashell **231**–24
Shellfish **71**
shelter **52**–13 🔑
shield
   windshield **162**–1
   windshield wipers **162**–2
shift **180**–6 🔑 AWL
   gearshift **163**–47
   stick shift **163**–50
shin **106**–21
   shin guards **237**–13
shingles **112**–8, **196**–20
ship 185–D
shipping clerk **185**–14
shirt **86**–1 🔑
   long-sleeved shirt **96**–14 🔑
   nightshirt **91**–27
   polo shirt **92**–14
   security shirt **93**–20 🔑 AWL
   short-sleeved shirt **96**–12 🔑
   sleeveless shirt **96**–11 🔑
   sport shirt **88**–4 🔑
   3/4-sleeved shirt **96**–13 🔑
   T-shirt **86**–4, **101**–15 🔑
   work shirt **92**–2 🔑
shock **118**–B, **118**–F 🔑
shoes **87**–13, **95**–32 🔑
   athletic shoes **94** ✦
   shoe department **95**–7 🔑
   shoe store **132**–10 🔑
   shoelaces **94**–24
SHOES AND ACCESSORIES **94**–95 🔑
shoot **217**–5
shoot 236–H 🔑
shop 🔑
   barbershop **131**–19
   beauty shop **132** ✦ 🔑
   coffee shop **128**–11 🔑
   donut shop **131**–17
   gift shop **132** ✦, **192**–5 🔑
   ice cream shop **133**–16 🔑
shop 28–A, **146**–H
SHOP **80**–81 🔑
Shop **100**
shoplifting **145**–8

shopping 🔑
   shopping bag **67**–13 🔑
   shopping basket **73**–9
   shopping list **67**–14 🔑
   shopping mall **128**–7 🔑
   shopping program **242**–10
SHOPPING **27** 🔑
shore **214**–12
short **32**–6, **96**–16 🔑
   short hair **33**–1 🔑
   short-order cook **193**–1 🔑
   short-sleeved **96**–12 🔑
shorten 100–B
shorts **89**–25, **91**–4
shoulder **105**–13 🔑
   shoulder bag **94**–17 🔑
   shoulder blade **107**–28 🔑
   shoulder pads **237**–20
   shoulder-length hair **33**–2
shovel **186**–7, **196**–22
show **242**–4, **242**–6, **242**–8
show 139–C, **164**–C 🔑
shower 🔑
   shower cap **108**–1 🔑
   shower curtain **57**–14 🔑
   shower gel **108**–2
   showerhead **57**–13
   stall shower **57** ✦
   take a shower **38**–C, **108**–A 🔑
shredder **189**–24
shrimp **71**–11, **218**–19
shut-off **150**–4 🔑
shuttle **156**–19
sick **42**–12 🔑
   homesick **43**–20
side 🔑
   sideburns **33**–7
   side-view mirror **162**–3
   sunny-side up **76**–10
Side Salads **80** 🔑
sidewalk **131**–24
sight impaired / blind **32**–11 🔑
sign 🔑
   street sign **131**–26 🔑
   vacancy sign **50**–7
   vital signs monitor **123**–26 🔑 AWL
sign 4–E, **48**–D
signal 🔑
   strong signal **14**–11 🔑
   turn signal **162**–6, **163**–34 🔑
   weak signal **14**–12 🔑
signature **4**–20 🔑
SIGNS **158** 🔑
silk **98**–5 🔑
simmer 77–P
sing 36–O, **244**–B 🔑
single 🔑
   single father **35**–23 🔑
   single mother **35**–22 🔑
sink **54**–4, **57**–25
Sirius **215** ✦
sister **34**–5 🔑
   half sister **35**–27 🔑

sister-in-law **34**–16
stepsister **35**–29
sit down **6**–F 🔑
sitcom (situation comedy) **242**–2 🔑
site **128**–2 🔑 AWL
sitter **170**–9
situation comedy (sitcom) **242**–2 🔑
six **16**
six-pack **74**–9, **74**–21
6-year-old boy **31**–9 🔑
sixteen **16**
sixteenth **16**
sixth **16**
sixtieth **16**
sixty **16**
Sizes **96** 🔑
skate **236**–U
skates **237**–9, **237**–10
skateboard **230**–7
skateboarding **234**–13
skating **233**–4, **233**–5, **234**–10
Skeleton **107**
ski **236**–V
skiing **233**–1, **233**–3
waterskiing **233**–7
SKILLS **176**–**179** 🔑
Skills **177**, **178** 🔑
skin **107**–31 🔑
skinless **70** ✦
skirt **87**–10 🔑
skis **237**–24
ski boots **237**–26
ski hat **90**–11
ski mask **90**–15
ski poles **237**–25
SKU number **27**–5
skull **107**–47
skunk **222**–12
sky **231**–4 🔑
skycap **164**–1
skyscraper **129**–13
slacks **87**–12
slaves **208**–4
sledding **233**–6
sledgehammer **196**–23
sleeper **91**–26
sleeping bag **232**–12 🔑
SLEEPWEAR **91**
Sleepwear **91**
sleepy **42**–3 🔑
sleeve **100**–6 🔑
long-sleeved **96**–14 🔑
short-sleeved **96**–12 🔑
sleeveless **96**–11
3/4 sleeved **96**–13 🔑
slender **32**–9
slice **77**–C
slide **206**–3, **230**–13
mudslide **148**–6
sliding glass door **53**–18 🔑
sling **115**–19
slip **91**–21, **91**–22, **134**–4
slippers **91**–25

slippery floor **197**–6 🔑
slow **23**–4 🔑
small **96**–1, **96**–2, **97**–37 🔑
small town **52**–3 🔑
smartphone **15**–25
smell **106**–C 🔑
smile **2**–E 🔑
smock **93**–26
smog **224**–11
smoggy **13**–16
smoke **116**–G
smoke detector **51**–30 🔑 AWL
smoked turkey **71**–25
Snack Foods **73**
snail **218**–23
snake 🔑
garter snake **219**–46
rattlesnake **219**–45
snap **99**–26
sneakers **86**–7
sneezing **113**–12
snorkeling **233**–11
snow **13**–12 🔑
snowboard **237**–23
snowboarding **233**–2
snowstorm **13**–24
soap **57**–4, **61**–5, **108**–3 🔑
soap dish **57**–3 🔑
soap opera **242**–5
sober **146** ✦
soccer **235**–13
soccer ball **237**–12
social 🔑
Social Security card **40**–5
Social Security number **4**–19
social worker **173**–57 🔑
social media links **213**–19 🔑 AWL
socks **86**–6 🔑
ankle socks **91**–7 🔑
crew socks **91**–8
dress socks **91**–9 🔑
low-cut socks **91**–10 🔑
Socks **91** 🔑
soda **73**–34, **79**–11
sofa **56**–18
sofa cushions **56** ✦
soft **23**–6 🔑
softball **235**–11
soft skills **174**–E 🔑
SOFT SKILLS **178** 🔑
softener **101**–6
software **171**–18 🔑
Software / Applications **191** 🔑
solar
solar eclipse **215**–16
solar energy **224**–1
Solar System and the Planets **215** 🔑
soldier **141**–29, **173**–58 🔑
sole **94**–21 AWL
solid **96**–19 🔑
Solids **205** 🔑
solution **204**–14 🔑
solve **176**–M, **178**–A 🔑

son **34**–15 🔑
grandson **34** ✦ 🔑
son-in-law **34** ✦
sore throat **110**–6 🔑
sort **101**–A
soul **243**–28 🔑
soup **72**–18, **80**–16 🔑
soup bowl **83**–21 🔑
soup spoon **83**–32 🔑
Soup **77** 🔑
sour **84**–4 🔑
sour cream **72**–21 🔑
source **202**–13, **213**–13
Sources **224** 🔑 AWL
sous-chef **193**–6
south **159**–3 🔑
soybeans **187**–3
space **50**–18, **130**–5 🔑
space station **215**–18 🔑
Space **215** 🔑
Space Exploration **215**
spades **239**–30
spaghetti **81**–26
spare tire **162**–23 🔑
sparrow **220**–8
spatula **78**–19
speak **174**–J, **176**–N 🔑
speaker **50**–5, **190**–28 🔑
guest speaker **226**–4 🔑
speakers **240**–14 🔑
Special **80**
Specialists **122** 🔑
speech **142**–2 🔑
speed limit **158**–4 🔑
speed skating **233** ✦
speedometer **163**–27
spell **4**–B 🔑
sphere **205**–42 AWL
spider **220**–30 🔑
spill **224**–17 🔑
spinach **69**–11
spinach salad **80**–13
spinal column **107**–49
spiral notebook **7**–30
splint **119**–15
sponge **61**–19
sponge mop **61**–6
spoon **55**–5, **78**–9 🔑
soup spoon **83**–32 🔑
tablespoon **75**–7
teaspoon **75**–6, **83**–31
spoon **77**–F
sports 🔑
sport coat **89**–14 🔑
sport jacket **89**–14 🔑
sport shirt **88**–4 🔑
sport utility vehicle (SUV) **160**–7
sports car **160**–4 🔑
sports program **242**–11
SPORTS **233**, **234**, **235** 🔑
SPORTS EQUIPMENT **237** 🔑 AWL
SPORTS VERBS **236**
sprained ankle **110**–14

spray **108**–12, **115**–32 🔑

  spray gun **195**–21 🔑

  spray starch **101**–12

spread 🔑

  bedspread **59**–11

  spreadsheet program **191**–30

spring **21**–37, **58**–19 🔑

sprinkler **53**–22

square **205**–30 🔑

squash **69**–24

squeegee **61**–15

squid **218**–7

squirrel **221**–21

stadium **128**–1

staff **180**–2 🔑

Staff **122** 🔑

stage **206**–17 🔑

  stage clips **206**–21

stain **195**–24

stained **97**–42

stairs **50**–10 🔑

  upstairs **51** ✦ 🔑

stairway **50**–10

stall shower **57** ✦

stamps **136**–18, **136**–23, **189**–47 🔑

stand **156**–18

  checkstand **73**–13

  newsstand **130**–12

  nightstand **58**–23

stand 144–D 🔑

  stand up 6–D 🔑

standard time **19**–26 🔑

staple 177–F

stapler **189**–28

staples **189**–29

star **215**–13 🔑

  star key **14**–6 🔑

  starfish **218**–17

starch **101**–12

stars **166**–3 🔑

start 12–A, **40**–B, **169**–P, **236**–R 🔑

state **4**–8, **150**–2 🔑

  state capital **140**–16

  state senator **140**–19 🔑

state 15–G, **207**–A

State Government **140** 🔑

statement **134**–17 🔑

station 🔑

  bus station **126**–7 🔑

  charging station / dock **240**–3 🔑

  fire station **127**–12 🔑

  gas station **127**–10 🔑

  lifeguard station **231**–21 🔑

  police station **126**–6 🔑

  space station **215**–18 🔑

  subway station **155**–11

Station **156** 🔑

stationery **189**–42

stay 🔑

  stay away 151–I 🔑

  stay fit **116**–E 🔑

  stay on the line **15**–H 🔑

  stay on well-lit streets **146**–B 🔑

Stay Well **116** 🔑

steak **70**–2, **81**–24

  broiled steak **76**–3

  halibut steak **71**–6

  salmon steak **71**–4

  steak knife **83**–29

steal 145 ✦ 🔑

steam 77–D

steamed vegetables **81**–32 🔑

steamer **78**–3

steel 🔑

  steel toe boots **92**–6 🔑

  steel-wool soap pads **61**–5

steering wheel **163**–26 🔑

stems **217**–9

step 🔑

  stepbrother **35**–30

  stepdaughter **35** ✦

  stepfather **35**–25

  stepladder **61**–13

  stepmother **35**–26

  steps **53**–3 🔑

  stepsister **35**–29

stereo system **56**–8

sterile

  sterile pad **119**–7

  sterile tape **119**–8

stethoscope **111**–10

stewing beef **70**–3

stick **237**–11, **238**–11 🔑

  drumsticks **70**–23

  lipstick **109**–38

  stick shift **163**–50 🔑

  yardstick **195**–16

sticker **102**–3, **138**–13

sticky notes **189**–39 🔑

stir 77–O 🔑

  stir-fried beef **76**–6 🔑

stitches **119**–16

stock clerk **173**–59 🔑

stocker **72**–5

stomach **107**–41 🔑

  stomachache **110**–4

stop **131**–16, **155**–13, **158**–1

stop 159–D 🔑

Stop **156**

stopped up **63**–19 🔑

storage **72**–25, **78**–4

  storage locker **50**–17

store 🔑

  bookstore **132**–4 🔑

  candy store **133**–17 🔑

  card store **132**–7 🔑

  convenience store **130**–3

  department store **133**–13 🔑

  electronics store **133**–20

  furniture store **128**–8 🔑

  hardware store **152**–4

  home improvement store **129**–20 🔑

  jewelry store **132**–2 🔑

  maternity store **133**–19

  men's store **132** ✦ 🔑

  music store **132**–1 🔑

office supply store **129**–21 🔑

pet store **132**–6 🔑

shoe store **132**–10 🔑

toy store **132**–5 🔑

used book store **131**–20 🔑

STORE **72**–73 🔑

Store **99** 🔑

storeroom **193**–5

storm **13**–20 🔑

  snowstorm **13**–24

  storm door **53**–10 🔑

  thunderstorm **13**–13

story 🔑

  action story **243**–19 🔑

  adventure story **243**–19 🔑

  horror story **243**–17 🔑

  science fiction story **243**–18 🔑

  two-story house **52** ✦ 🔑

stove **54**–18, **232**–16 🔑

stow 164–G

straight **159**–A 🔑

  straight hair **33**–9 🔑

  straight line **205**–22 🔑

  straight pin **100**–12 🔑

strainer **78**–22

straw **79**–18

  straw hat **90**–23

  strawberries **68**–14

stream / creek **214** ✦ 🔑

street **154**–5, **159**–8 🔑

  street address **4**–5 🔑

  street sign **131**–26 🔑

  street vendor **131**–29

  streetlight **152**–3

STREETS **128**–**129** 🔑

strep throat **112**–4

stress **117**–4 🔑 AWL

stretch 236–M 🔑

stretcher **123**–33

string 🔑

  string beans **69**–8

  string lights **245**–18 🔑

  string of pearls **95**–39

Strings **244** 🔑

striped **96**–20 🔑

stripper **195**–42

stroller **37**–18

strong signal **14**–11 🔑

stub **183**–11

stucco **196**–15

student **6**–6 🔑

study 10–D, **139**–A

STUDYING **8**–9 🔑

stuffed animals **59**–15 🔑

style 🔑 AWL

  in style **88** ✦ 🔑 AWL

  stylist **171**–31

Style Hair **33** 🔑 AWL

Styles **96** 🔑 AWL

SUBJECTS **200**–**201** 🔑

submit 10–P, **48**–C, **169**–L AWL

  click submit **211**–S 🔑 AWL

substitute **79**–20 🔑 AWL

281

subtract **204**–B
suburbs **52**–2
subway **155**–12
   subway car **156**–6
   subway station **155**–11
Subway Station **156**
Succeed **10** 🔑
SUCCEEDING IN SCHOOL **10** 🔑
suede **99**–8
sugar **73**–30 🔑
   sugar bowl **55**–14 🔑
   sugar substitute **79**–20 🔑
   sugar-free **124**–7
suit **87**–11 🔑
   bathing suit **90**–26
   business suit **88**–11 🔑
   jumpsuit **93**–24
   wetsuit **231**–5
suite **192**–16
sum **204**–7 🔑 AWL
sumac **216**–23
summer **21**–38 🔑
sun 🔑
   sunblock **108**–8, **231**–10
   sunburn **110**–13
   sunflower **217**–10
   sunglasses **90**–27
   sunrise **18**–14
   sunscreen **108**–7, **231**–10
   sunset **18**–18
Sunday **20**–8 🔑
sunny **13**–9, **76**–10
superintendent **50**–8
supermarket **129**–18 🔑
supervise **176**–O
supervisor **183**–8, **185**–4
SUPPLIES **61, 194–195** 🔑
Supplies **100, 189** 🔑
supply **129**–21 🔑
   supply cabinet **188**–1 🔑
support **197**–18 🔑
   support group **117**–15 🔑
supporter **91**–6 🔑
Supreme Court **140**–11
surface **76** ✦ 🔑
surfboard **231**–16
surfer **231**–15
surfing **233**–9, **233**–10
surge protector **190**–11
surgeon **123**–36
Surgeon **93**
surgical
   surgical cap **123**–37
   surgical gloves **123**–39
   surgical gown **93**–37, **123**–38
   surgical mask **93**–36
   surgical nurse **122**–9
   surgical scrub cap **93**–35
   surgical scrubs **93**–38
Surgical Assistant **93**
surprised **43**–30 🔑

suspenders **94**–1
suspense **243**–20
SUV (sport utility vehicle) **160**–7
swallow **118**–J 🔑
swap meet **228**–6
sweat 🔑
   sweatpants **89**–23
   sweatshirt **89**–22
sweater **28**–2, **87**–14 🔑
   cardigan sweater **88**–2
   crewneck sweater **96**–7
   pullover sweater **88**–3
   scoop neck sweater **96**–10
   turtleneck sweater **96**–9
   v-neck sweater **96**–8
sweep **60**–J 🔑
sweet potatoes **69**–18 🔑
sweets **84**–8
swelling **113**–16 🔑
swim **236**–L 🔑
   swimsuit **90**–26
swimming 🔑
   swimming pool **51**–22 🔑
   swimming trunks **90**–22
swing **236**–Q 🔑
swings **230**–11
Swiss cheese **71**–27
switch **58**–27 🔑
swollen finger **110**–16 🔑
swordfish **71**–5, **218**–10
symbol **159**–5 🔑 AWL
SYMPTOMS AND INJURIES **110** 🔑 AWL
synagogue **129**–16
synthetic materials **98** ✦
syringe **111**–12
syrup **115**–29
system 🔑
   fuel injection system **162**–17 🔑
   stereo system **56**–8
SYSTEM **144** 🔑

tab **213**–14
table 🔑
   bed table **123**–21 🔑
   changing table **59**–1 🔑
   coffee table **56**–19 🔑
   dining room table **55**–9
   end table **56**–14 🔑
   examination table **111**–7 🔑
   folding card table **102**–4 🔑
   night table **58**–23 🔑
   operating table **123**–40 🔑
   periodic table **207**–26 🔑 AWL
   picnic table **230**–8
   pool table **50**–15 🔑
   table tennis **234**–14
   tablecloth **55**–12
   tablespoon **75**–7
   tray table **165**–21
   turntable **240**–12
tablet **115**–22, **115**–27, **190**–6 🔑

tackle **236**–F 🔑
taco **79**–8
tag **92**–15, **138**–13
tail **222**–22 🔑
   taillight **162**–13
   tailpipe **162**–15
tailor **100**–3
take 🔑
   do not take with dairy products **114**–D 🔑
   take a bath **108**–B 🔑
   take a break **11**–H 🔑
   take a citizenship test **142**–I 🔑
   take a driver education course **139**–B 🔑
   take a driver's training course **139**–G 🔑
   take a message **177**–Q 🔑
   take a nap **53**–A
   take a picture **226**–A 🔑
   take a seat **6**–F 🔑
   take a shower **38**–C, **108**–A 🔑
   take a written test **139**–E 🔑
   take an interest inventory **174**–C 🔑
   take care of children **176**–P 🔑
   take cover **151**–J 🔑
   take in **100**–D 🔑
   take medicine **116**–D 🔑
   take notes **10**–C, **177**–K 🔑
   take off **109**–Q, **164**–J 🔑
   take one hour before eating **114**–B 🔑
   take out **9**–Y, **60**–Q 🔑
   take ownership **49**–K
   take temperature **111**–B 🔑
   take the bus to school **38**–H 🔑
   take the car to a mechanic **161**–C 🔑
   take the children to school **38**–G 🔑
   take the order **82**–E 🔑
   take with food or milk **114**–A 🔑
   take X-rays **120**–B
Taking a Flight **164** 🔑
Taking a Test **10** 🔑
Taking Care of Your Car **161** 🔑
TAKING CARE OF YOUR HEALTH **116–117** 🔑
talk
   talk show **242**–4
   talk therapy **117**–13
talk 🔑
   talk about **179**–L 🔑
   talk on the phone **15**–C 🔑
   talk to friends **168**–E 🔑
   talk to the teacher **6**–B 🔑
tall **32**–4 🔑
tambourine **244**–17
tan **24**–18
tangerines **68**–9
tank **162**–10, **231**–6 🔑
   tank top **89**–24
   tank truck **160**–20 🔑
tape 🔑 AWL
   clear tape **189**–30 🔑 AWL
   correction tape **189**–37
   duct tape **195**–49
   electrical tape **195**–43

masking tape **195**–53
packing tape **189**–32
sterile tape **119**–8
tape measure **100**–17, **195**–45
target **237**–7 🔑 AWL
taste 106–D
tattoo **32**–18
tax / taxes **27**–8 🔑
taxi **154**–3 🔑
   hail a taxi **156** ✦
   taxi driver **156**–21 🔑
   taxi license **156**–22 🔑 AWL
   taxi stand **156**–18
TB / tuberculosis **113**–23
TDD **15**–26
tea **79**–12, **81**–39, **81**–40 🔑
   teacup **55**–6
   teakettle **54**–17
   teapot **55**–16
   teaspoon **75**–6, **83**–31
teach 176–Q 🔑
teacher **5**–8, **6**–4, **22**–5 🔑
   teacher's aide **5**–16
team **149**–20, **235**–3 🔑 AWL
   cooperate with teammates
      178–F AWL
   team player **180**–3 🔑 AWL
TEAM SPORTS **235** 🔑 AWL
technical school **200**–5 🔑
technician
   computer technician **171**–19, **188**–12
   emergency medical technician (EMT)
      123–32 🔑
   medical records technician
      172–39 🔑
Technician **93**
teddy bear **37**–24
teen / teenager **31**–11
teeth / tooth **106**–7 🔑
   toothache **110**–2
   toothbrush **57**–23, **109**–22
   toothbrush holder **57**–24
   toothpaste **109**–23
teething ring **37**–26
telemarketer **173**–60
TELEPHONE **14**–**15** 🔑
Telephone Skills **177** 🔑
telescope **215**–23
television / TV **56**–6 🔑
   big-screen TV **50**–14 🔑
   flat-panel TV **240**–8 🔑
   flat-screen TV **240**–8 🔑
teller **134**–1
Teller **134**
Telling Time **18** 🔑
temperature **110**–7 🔑
   temperature control dial **163**–38 🔑
   temperature gauge **163**–30
Temperature **13** 🔑
ten **16**
   ten after one **18**–8 🔑

ten dollars **26**–9
10 percent **17**–12 🔑
ten thousand **16**
10-year-old girl **31**–10 🔑
tenant **50**–6, **51**–29
TENANT MEETING **64**–**65**
tennis **234**–15
   table tennis **234**–14
   tennis court **230**–6
   tennis racket **237**–2
   tennis shoes **95**–32
tent **232**–10 🔑
tenth **16**
term **143** ✦🔑
Terminal **164** AWL
termites **63**–22
Terms **209** 🔑
test **123**–30 🔑
   online test **10**–5 🔑
   test booklet **10**–1 🔑
   test tube **207**–42
   testing area **138**–2 🔑 AWL
Test **10** 🔑
text 🔑 AWL
   copy text **210**–K 🔑
   drag to select text **210**–J 🔑 AWL
   paste text **210**–L
   text message **14**–18 🔑
   textbook **7**–26
Text **210** 🔑
thank 12–D, **179**–N 🔑
Thanksgiving **22**–17
theater **128**–6, **129**–23 🔑
theft **145**–9
therapist **117**–12, **117**–14, **172**–45
therapy **117**–11, **117**–13
thermal undershirt **91**–2
thermometer **111**–11
thick **23**–7 🔑
thighs **70**–22, **106**–19
thimble **100**–15
thin **23**–8, **32**–9 🔑
THINGS **23** 🔑
think 🔑
   think about 203–E 🔑
   think critically **178**–B 🔑
third **16**
Third Floor **50**
thirsty **42**–2 🔑
thirteen **16**
   thirteen colonies **208**–1
thirteenth **16**
thirtieth **16**
thirty **16**
this week **20**–19 🔑
thorn **217**–29
thread **99**–23, **100**–11 🔑
three **16**
   three times a week **20**–24 🔑
   three-piece suit **88** ✦🔑
   3/4 sleeved **96**–13 🔑

3-ring binder **7**–28
throat **107**–35, **110**–6, **112**–4 🔑
   throat lozenges **115**–30
through **157**–K 🔑
throw 236–C 🔑
   throw away 11–N 🔑
   throw up 110–C
throw pillow **56**–2
thumb **106**–16 🔑
thumb drive / flash drive **190**–25
thunderstorm **13**–13
Thursday **20**–12 🔑
tick **220**–28
ticket **156**–15, **165**–19 🔑
   ticket agent **164**–3 🔑
   ticket window **156**–12 🔑
tidal wave **149**–17
tide **231** ✦
tie **88**–12, **89**–16, **92**–13
tie 86–A, **235** ✦🔑
tiger **223**–37
tight **97**–29 🔑
tights **91**–16, **91**–17
tile **57**–12, **196**–11, **196**–C
time 🔑
   Alaska time **19**–28
   arrival time **165** ✦🔑
   Atlantic time **19**–33
   Central time **19**–31
   daylight saving time **19**–25 🔑
   departure time **165** ✦🔑
   Eastern time **19**–32
   Hawaii-Aleutian time **19**–27
   manage time **178**–D 🔑
   Mountain time **19**–30
   Newfoundland time **19**–34
   on time **19**–23, **165**–29 🔑
   Pacific time **19**–29
   standard time **19**–26 🔑
   three times a week **20**–24 🔑
   time clock **182**–7 🔑
TIME **18**–**19** 🔑
Time **18** 🔑
Time Zones **19** 🔑
timer **78**–18
Times of Day **18** 🔑
tire **162**–5, **162**–23, **166**–C 🔑
tired **43**–32 🔑
title **135**–14, **202**–5 🔑
toad **218**–29
toast **80**–4
toaster **54**–11
   toaster oven **54**–15
today **20**–5 🔑
toddler **31**–8
toe **94**–23, **105**–10 🔑
   steel toe boots **92**–6 🔑
   toenail **106** ✦
Tofu **77**
toggle bolt **194**–38
to-go box **82**–5 🔑

toilet **57**–21
   toilet brush **57**–20
   toilet paper **57**–19, **150**–13
token **156**–10
tomatoes **69**–6
tomorrow **20**–6
tongs **78**–23, **207**–44
tongue **106**–8
too
   too big **97**–38
   too expensive **97**–44
   too small **97**–37
tool belt **92**–3
TOOLS AND BUILDING SUPPLIES **194**–**195**
tooth / teeth **106**–7
   pull a tooth **120**–F
   toothache **110**–2
   toothbrush **57**–23, **109**–22
   toothbrush holder **57**–24
   toothpaste **109**–23
top **88**–7, **89**–24
torn **97**–41
tornado **149**–15
torso **106** ✦
tortoise **219**–41
total **27**–9
tote bag **94**–19
touch **106**–E
touch screen / audio display **163**–37
tow truck **160**–14
towel
   bath towel **57**–16
   dish towel **61**–22
   hand towel **57**–17
   paper towels **54**–3
   towel rack **57**–15
towelettes **150**–12
tower **190**–7
town **52**–3
   town car **156**–20
   townhouse **52**–6
toy
   toy chest **59**–16
   toy store **132**–5
Toys and Games **59**
track **5**–21, **156**–14
   track and field **234**–18
track pad **190**–24
tractor **187**–9
   tractor-trailer **160**–15
traffic light **130**–8
TRAFFIC SIGNS **158**
tragedy **243**–14
trailer **160**–15, **160**–17
train **154**–7, **239**–27
Train Station **156**
training **175**–3, **175**–9, **175**–12
   training pants **37**–16
Training **175**
transcribe **177**–C
transfer **156**–5 AWL
transfer **177**–O AWL
translate **8**–C

translator **172**–35
Transmission **163** AWL
TRANSPORTATION **154**–**156** AWL
Transportation **156** AWL
trash
   trash bags **61**–24
   trash bin **51**–23
   trash chute **51**–26
travel **41**–P
travel agency **133**–14
tray **55**–17, **83**–10
   tray table **165**–21
Tree **216**
trees **245**–16
TREES AND PLANTS **216**
trench coat **90**–21
trial **142**–5
triangle **205**–32
tricycle **230**–12
trigonometry **204**–18
trim **186**–B
Trim **99**
trip **156**–16, **156**–17
tripe **70**–8
tripod **241**–20
trombone **244**–10
trout **71**–1
trowel **186**–10, **196**–13
truck **154**–6
   dump truck **160**–19
   fire truck **148**–10
   garbage truck **129**–22
   hand truck **185**–11
   pickup truck **160**–12
   tank truck **160**–20
   tow truck **160**–14
   truck driver **173**–61
TRUCKS **160**
trumpet **244**–11
trunk **162**–11, **216**–4, **223**–47
Trunk **162**
trunks
   swimming trunks **90**–22
try on **95**–C
TSA agent **164**–5
T-shirt **86**–4
tsunami **149**–17
tub
   bathtub **57**–2
tuba **244**–12
tube **74**–24, **207**–42
tuberculosis (TB) **113**–23
tubes **74**–12
Tuesday **20**–10
tulip **217**–11
tuna **71**–7, **72**–19, **218**–8
tuner **240**–13
turbulence **165**–22
turkey **70**–17, **245**–14
   roasted turkey **76**–4
   smoked turkey **71**–25
turn **158**–5, **158**–7, **158**–8
   turn signal **162**–6, **163**–34

turnstile **156**–8
turntable **240**–12
turn
   turn in **203**–M
   turn left **159**–C
   turn off **11**–P, **179**–G, **225**–G
   turn on **11**–D, **147**–A
   turn right **159**–B
turnips **69**–16
turquoise **24**–9
turtle **219**–42
   turtleneck **96**–9
tusk **223**–48
tuxedo **89**–17
TV / television **56**–6
   big-screen TV **50**–14
   flat-panel TV **240**–8
   flat-screen TV **240**–8
TV Programs **242**
tweezers **119**–5
twelfth **16**
twelve **16**
twentieth **16**
twenty **16**
   twenty after one **18**–10
   twenty dollars **26**–10
   twenty to two **18**–12
   twenty-first **16**
   twenty-five **16**
   25 percent **17**–11
   twenty-four **16**
   twenty-one **16**
   twenty-three **16**
   twenty-two **16**
twice a week **20**–23
twig **216**–1
twins **28**–1
two **16**
   2 x 4 (two by four) **195**–19
   two-story house **52** ✦
   two-way radio **197**–22
type **4**–D, **176**–R, **210**–C
   type a letter **177**–A
   type in a phrase **212**–B
   type in a question **212**–C
   type the password again **211**–Q
   type the subject **211**–V
   type the verification code **211**–R
Types of Charges **15**
Types of Health Problems **117**
Types of Material **98**–**99**
Types of Math **204**
Types of Medication **115**
Types of Movies **243**
Types of Music **243**
Types of Training **175**
Types of TV Programs **242**

ugly **23**–22
umbrella **90**–17, **231**–14
umpire **235** ✦
uncle **34**–8
uncomfortable **42**–9

unconscious **118**–A 🔑

under **25**–10, **157**–A 🔑
   long underwear **91**–3 🔑
   thermal undershirt **91**–2
   underexposed **241**–33
   underpants **91**–14
   undershirt **91**–1

Under the Hood **162**

underline **9**–S

Underwear **91** 🔑

UNDERWEAR AND SLEEPWEAR **91** 🔑

undress **36**–E

unfurnished apartment **48**–4 🔑

uniform **88**–10, **237**–16 🔑 AWL

Unisex Socks **91**

Unisex Underwear **91**

universal remote **240**–10

UNIVERSE **215** 🔑

university **200**–7 🔑

unload **101**–E 🔑

unpack **49**–N

unraveling **97**–43

unripe **68**–31

unscented **108** ✦

unscramble **9**–W

up 🔑
   buckle up **36**–L
   clean up **151**–M
   cut up **77**–I 🔑
   eggs sunny-side up **76**–10 🔑
   get up **38**–B 🔑
   hang up **15**–D, **101**–H 🔑
   look up **8**–A 🔑
   pick up **6**–I, **11**–E, **38**–M 🔑
   pop-up ad **213**–17 🔑
   set up an interview **169**–M 🔑
   stand up **6**–D 🔑
   stopped up **63**–19
   throw up **110**–C
   wake up **38**–A 🔑
   walk up **157**–C 🔑

update security software **147**–E 🔑 AWL

upright seat **165**–28

upset **43**–28 🔑

upstairs **51** ✦🔑

Uranus **215**–7

urban area **52**–1 🔑 AWL

urchin **218**–22

URL/website address **213**–10 🔑

urologists **122** ✦

U.S.
   U.S. Capitol **140**–1
   U.S. route **158**–17 🔑 AWL

U.S. HISTORY **208** 🔑

U.S. Military **141** 🔑 AWL

USB port **190**–20 🔑

use 🔑
   use a cash register **176**–S 🔑 AWL
   use a credit card **27**–B 🔑
   use a debit card **27**–C 🔑
   use a gift card **27**–E 🔑
   use deodorant **108**–C
   use encrypted / secure sites **147**–F

use energy-efficient bulbs **225**–H
use punctuation **202**–C
use the arrow keys **211**–N 🔑

Used Car **161** 🔑

used clothing **102**–2 🔑

utensils **79**–19

utility / utilities **48**–5, **160**–7 AWL

U-turn **158**–5

vacancy sign **50**–7

vacation **22**–6 🔑

vaccination **116** ✦

vacuum
   vacuum cleaner **61**–10
   vacuum cleaner attachments **61**–11
   vacuum cleaner bag **61**–12

vacuum **60**–H

valley **214**–18 🔑

valuables **134**–8 🔑

valve **150**–4

van **160**–13, **160**–18 🔑

vandalism **145**–1

vanity plate **138** ✦

variable **204**–12 AWL

vase **55**–23

vault **134**–6

VCR **102**–7

veal cutlets **70**–6

Vegetable **77** 🔑

vegetables **66**–8, **72**–27, **81**–32 🔑
   vegetable garden **53**–27, **187**–14 🔑
   vegetable peeler **78**–15

VEGETABLES **69** 🔑

vegetarian **70** ✦

vehicles **126**–4, **160**–2, **160**–7,
   160–10 🔑 AWL

vein **107**–37

velvet **99**–10

vending machine **156**–9

vendors **84**–7, **131**–29

ventilation mask **92**–7

Venus **215**–2

verdict **144**–14

verification code **211**–R

vertebrates **206**–12

vest **89**–15
   down vest **90**–14
   high visibility safety vest **92**–4 🔑 AWL
   life vest **165**–25, **232**–14

Veterans Day **22**–16

veterinarian **173**–62

vice president **140**–9

victim **145**–10 🔑

video 🔑
   can't stream video **191**–F
   video game console **238**–3
   video game controller **238**–4
   video MP3 player **240**–2 🔑
   video player **213**–18 🔑

videotape **246**–A

view 🔑
   rearview mirror **163**–35 🔑
   side-view mirror **162**–3 🔑

village **52**–3 🔑

vine **216**–22

vineyard **187**–16

violence **145**–4

violet **24**–8, **217**–23

violin **244**–6

virus alert **190**–5

vise **194**–26

vision 🔑 AWL
   vision exam **138**–6 🔑 AWL
   vision problems **117**–1 🔑 AWL

visit **174**–A 🔑

Visit **120**

visor **197**–12

vital signs monitor **123**–26 🔑 AWL

vitamins **115**–17

v-neck **96**–8

vocational
   vocational school **200**–5
   vocational training **175**–9

voice mail **14**–17 🔑

volcanic eruption **149**–16

volleyball **235**–15, **237**–3

Volume **75, 205** 🔑 AWL

volunteer **123**–17 AWL

volunteer **41**–Q AWL

vomit **110**–C

vote **142**–A

voting booth / polling booth **143**–10

waffles **80**–8

wages **183**–12 🔑

waist 🔑
   waist apron **93**–30
   waistband **100**–5

wait **94**–B 🔑

wait for **130**–B 🔑

wait on **176**–T 🔑

wait staff **193** ✦🔑

waiter **82**–8 🔑
   headwaiter **193**–12

waiting area **188**–16 🔑 AWL

Waiting Room **111** 🔑

waitress **83**–9 🔑

wake up **38**–A 🔑

walk **53**–2
   crosswalk **130**–15
   walk-in freezer **193**–3

walk 🔑
   walk a dog **131**–F 🔑
   walk down **157**–D 🔑
   walk to class **11**–A 🔑
   walk up **157**–C 🔑
   walk with a friend **146**–A 🔑

walker **115**–11

wall **56**–10 🔑
   cell wall **206**–5 🔑
   drywall **196**–19
   wallpaper **59**–8

wallet **94**–13

walrus **219**–34

war **209**–10 🔑
   Revolutionary War **208**–8

warehouse **184**–3, **185**–7
warm **13**–4 🔑
   warm clothes **150**–6 🔑
warning label **114**–8 🔑
Warnings **114** 🔑
wash
   mouthwash **109**–25
   washcloth **57**–6
wash 🔑
   wash clothes **225**–K 🔑
   wash hair **108**–E 🔑
   wash the dishes **60**–M 🔑
   wash the windows **60**–I 🔑
washer **50**–12, **101**–3, **194**–37
   dishwasher **54**–8, **83**–14, **193**–2
wasp **220**–18
waste **123**–31, **224**–12 🔑
   wastebasket **57**–26
watch **94**–16
watch **39**–X, **151**–C 🔑
water **219**–30, **231**–1 🔑
   body of water **214** ✦🔑
   bottled water **150**–11 🔑
   cold water **57**–10 🔑
   hot water **57**–9 🔑
   hot water bottle **115**–15 🔑
   water fountain **230**–9
   water glass **83**–22 🔑
   water pollution **224**–14 🔑
   water polo **235**–16
   watercolors **239**–21
   waterfall **214**–2
   watermelons **68**–18
   waterskiing **233**–7
water **186**–F
WATER SPORTS **233** 🔑
wave **149**–17, **231**–17 🔑
wave **2**–G
wavy hair **33**–10
way 🔑
   hallway **192**–18
   one way **158**–3 🔑
   one-way trip **156**–16 🔑
   two-way radio **197**–22 🔑
   wrong way **158**–2 🔑
Ways to Conserve Energy and
   Resources **225** 🔑 AWL
Ways to Get Well **116** 🔑
Ways to Pay **27** 🔑
Ways to Serve Eggs **76** 🔑
Ways to Serve Meat and Poultry **76** 🔑
Ways to Stay Well **116** 🔑
Ways to Succeed **10** 🔑
weak signal **14**–12 🔑
WEATHER **13** 🔑
Weather Conditions **13** 🔑
Weather Map **13** 🔑
Web Conferencing **191** 🔑 AWL
web page **213**–12 🔑
webcam **191**–37
website address **213**–10 🔑

wedding **22**–2 🔑
Wednesday **20**–11 🔑
weed
   seaweed **231** ✦
   weed eater **186**–12
   weed whacker **186**–12
weed **186**–G
week **20**–15 🔑
   last week **20**–18 🔑
   next week **20**–20 🔑
   once a week **20**–22 🔑
   this week **20**–19 🔑
   three times a week **20**–24 🔑
   twice a week **20**–23 🔑
   weekdays **20**–16
   weekend **20**–17 🔑
Week **20** 🔑
weigh **75**–B 🔑
weight **32**–8 🔑
Weight **32, 75** 🔑
weightlifting **234**–16
weights **237**–22 🔑
WEIGHTS AND MEASUREMENTS **75** 🔑
welder **173**–63
well **42**–14 🔑
Well **116** 🔑
west **159**–2 🔑
western **243**–15 🔑
wet **101**–17 🔑
   wetsuit **231**–5
whacker **186**–12
whale **219**–33
wheat **187**–2
   wheat bread **71**–19
wheel **163**–26 🔑
   wheel cover **162**–9 🔑
   wheelbarrow **186**–3
   wheelchair **115**–9
whisk **78**–21
whiskers **222**–18
white **24**–14 🔑
   white bread **71**–18 🔑
   White House **140**–7
   whiteboard **6**–1
whole salmon **71**–3
wide **97**–36 🔑
widow **41** ✦
widower **41** ✦
width **17**–19 🔑
wife **34**–12 🔑
   ex-wife **35** ✦
   former wife **35** ✦🔑
Wi-Fi connection **191**–32
wild **221** ✦🔑
wildlife **166**–2
willing to learn **178**–3 🔑
willow **216**–13
win **235** ✦🔑
wind 🔑
   wind power **224**–2 🔑
   windbreaker **90**–24

windshield **162**–1
windshield wipers **162**–2
windsurfing **233**–10
window **47**–12, **56**–17, **138**–7 🔑
   browser window **213**–7
   drive-thru window **130**–11
   ticket window **156**–12 🔑
   windowpane **196**–16
windy **13**–19
wine glass **83**–23 🔑
wing **70**–20, **220**–1 🔑
winter **21**–40 🔑
   winter scarf **90**–5
WINTER AND WATER SPORTS **233** 🔑
wipe **60**–O
wipers **162**–2
wipes **37**–12, **61**–23
wire **195**–13 🔑
   wire stripper **195**–42
wiring **198**–7
withdraw **134**–E 🔑
witness **144**–11 🔑
wolf **222**–5
woman **30**–2 🔑
women **30**–3 🔑
Women's Socks **91** 🔑
Women's Underwear **91** 🔑
wood **196**–17 🔑
   plywood **196**–18
   redwood **216**–18
   wood floor **58**–21 🔑
   wood screw **194**–33 🔑
   wood stain **195**–24
   woodpecker **220**–9
   woodworking kit **238**–14
wooden spoon **78**–9 🔑
Woodwinds **244**
wool **61**–5, **98**–3 🔑
word **202**–1 🔑
   delete a word **210**–I
   double-click to select a word **210**–H 🔑
   word problem **204**–11 🔑
   word processing program **191**–29 🔑
Words **8** 🔑
work 🔑
   blood work **123**–30 🔑
   roadwork **158**–16
   work gloves **92**–17, **197**–17 🔑
   work light **195**–44 🔑
   work pants **92**–5 🔑
   work shirt **92**–2 🔑
   workbook **7**–27
work **8**–I, **10**–J, **38**–K 🔑
WORK **188**–**189**, **198**–**199** 🔑
Work Clothes **88** 🔑
work out **236**–N 🔑
worker 🔑
   careful worker **197**–2 🔑
   careless worker **197**–1 🔑
   childcare worker **170**–16
   construction worker **196**–1 🔑 AWL

dock worker **171**–23
factory worker **185**–3 🔑
farmworker **187**–8
food preparation worker **193**–4 🔑
garment worker **171**–29
postal worker **173**–49
sanitation worker **173**–54
social worker **173**–57 🔑
Worker **92, 93** 🔑
working 🔑
    not working **62**–1 🔑
    woodworking kit **238**–14
Working with a Partner **8** 🔑 AWL
Working with Your Classmates **8** 🔑
WORKPLACE **182**–**183**
WORKPLACE CLOTHING **92**–**93**
workshop **175**–14
world 🔑
    world languages **201**–13 🔑
    world music **243**–32 🔑
WORLD HISTORY **209** 🔑
worm **218**–24
worried **42**–13 🔑
wrap **72**–24
wrap 246–F 🔑

wrench **162**–22
    adjustable wrench **195**–48
    pipe wrench **195**–47
wrestling **234**–17
wrinkled **101**–19
wrist **106**–14 🔑
    wristwatch **94**–16
write 🔑
    rewrite 203–J
    write a check **27**–D
    write a cover letter **169**–K 🔑
    write a final draft **203**–L 🔑 AWL
    write a first draft **203**–H 🔑 AWL
    write a note **137**–A 🔑
    write a resume **168**–B
    write a thank-you note **179**–O 🔑
    write back **137**–H 🔑
    write on the board **6**–E 🔑
writer **173**–64 🔑
Writing and Revising **203** 🔑 AWL
Writing Process **203** 🔑 AWL
Writing Rules **202** 🔑
wrong way **158**–2 🔑

xylophone **244**–15

yard **46**–1 🔑
    courtyard **51**–21
    yardstick **195**–16
YARD **53** 🔑
yarn **239**–22
year **20**–4, **31**–9, **31**–10 🔑
Year **21** 🔑
yell 180–A
yellow **24**–2 🔑
yesterday **20**–7 🔑
yield **158**–9
yoga **124**–4
yogurt **72**–22
young **32**–1 🔑
Your First License **139** 🔑 AWL
YOUR HEALTH **116**–**117** 🔑

zebra **223**–33
zero **16** 🔑
ZIP code **4**–9
zipper **99**–25
Zones **19**
zoo **228**–1
zoom lens **241**–19
zucchini **69**–25

Index   Índice

10 por ciento **17**–12
100 por ciento **17**–8
25 por ciento **17**–11
50 por ciento **17**–10
75 por ciento **17**–9
a cuadros **96**–24
a tiempo **19**–23, **165**–29
a. m. **18**–4
abadejo **218**–5
abalorios **95**–34
abdomen **107**–26
abedul **216**–7
abeja melífera **220**–26
abogado **172**–36
abogado defensor **144**–4
abonar las plantas **186**–D
aborde el avión **164**–E
abra el libro **6**–G
abra el programa **210**–A
abrace **2**–F
abrazadera en forma de C **194**–6
abrecosturas **100**–18
abrelatas **78**–1, **150**–8
abrelatas eléctrico **54**–14
abrigo **87**–14, **90**–2
abrigo cerrado **88**–3
abrigo de lana tejida **88**–2
abril **21**–28
abrir una cuenta **211**
abrocharle el cinturón **36**–L
abróchese el cinturón de
    seguridad **164**–H
abuela **34**–1
abuelo **34**–2
aburrido(a) **43**–25
acabe todo el medicamento **114**–C
acatar las leyes **142**–C
accesorios **195**–18
accesorios para aspiradora **61**–11
accidente aéreo **148**–3
accidente automovilístico **148**–2
acción **243**–19
acebo **216**–19
aceite **73**–31
acelerador **163**–46
acepte una disculpa **12**–H
acepte una invitación **12**–J
acera **131**–24
aclarar las instrucciones **178**–G
acolchar **238**–C
acomode los muebles **49**–Q
acondicionador **108**–11
acordeón **244**–19
acortar los pantalones **100**–B
acostarse **39**–Y
acta de nacimiento **40**–1
active los controles de padres **147**–A
activista **209**–17
actor **170**–2
actriz **170**–2
actualice el *software* de
    seguridad **147**–E
actuar **239**–G
acuarelas **239**–21

acuario **228**–7
acupuntura **124**–2
acusado **144**–5
adaptador de corriente
    internacional **241**–26
adjunte un archivo **211**–Y
administrador **50**–8
administradora **122**–13
administradores **5**
administrar el tiempo **178**–D
admirador **235**–4
adolescente **31**–11
adorno **245**–15
adornos **99**
aduana **165**
ADULTOS Y NIÑOS **30**–31
advertencias medicas **114**
aeromoza **165**–12
aeropuerto **155**–10
AEROPUERTO **164**–165
aerosol nasal **115**–32
afeitarse **109**–M
afueras **52**–2
agallas **218**–2
agarraollas **78**–29
agarrar **236**–D
agencia de viajes **133**–14
agente de aduana **165**–17
agente de la TSA **164**–5
agente de pasajes **164**–3
agosto **21**–32
agradézcale a alguien **12**–D
agradézcale al entrevistador **179**–N
agresión **145**–3
agria **84**–4
agricultor **187**–13
AGRICULTURA Y LA GANADERÍA **187**
agua **219**–30, **231**–1
agua caliente **57**–9
agua en botella **150**–11
agua fría **57**–10
agua oxigenada **119**–10
aguacates **84**–6
águila **220**–10
aguja **98**–17, **100**–10, **216**–10
agujas de tejer **239**–23
ahogarse **118**–I
ahorrar agua **225**–E
aislamiento **196**–14
ajedrez **238**–8
ajíes **69**–29
ajo **69**–30
ajustar el termostato **225**–J
ala **220**–1
alambre **195**–13
alargar los pantalones **100**–A
alas **70**–20
albañil **198**–8
albaricoques **68**–12
alberca **51**–22, **192**–22
albornoz **90**–25
álbum de fotos **241**–29
álbum de fotos digital **241**–30
alcachofas **69**–22

alcalde **140**–20
alcaldía **127**–8
alce **222**–1
aldea **52**–3
alegre **44**–5
alergias **112**–11
alerta antivirus **190**–5
aleta **218**–1
aletas **231**–8
ALFABETIZACIÓN DIGITAL **210**–211
alfabeto **7**–13
alfalfa **187**–5
alfiler **100**–12
alfiler de seguridad **100**–14
alfiletero **100**–13
alfombra **56**–24, **58**–22
alfombra de goma **57**–5
alfombrilla de baño **57**–28
álgebra **204**–16
algodón **98**–1, **187**–6
alguacil **144**–13
alicates **194**–7
alicates pelacables **195**–42
alimentador **98**–20
alimentar **187**–D
alimentarlo **36**–C
alimento para bebé **37**–4
alimentos congelados **72**
alimentos envasados **72**
alineador transparente **120**–7
aliviado(a) **42**–15
aliviador de dolor **115**–26
almacén **184**–3, **185**–7, **193**–5
almacén-congelador **193**–3
almejas **71**–15
almidón para rociar **101**–12
almirante **141**–26
almohada **58**–11
almohadilla de
    calentamiento **115**–13
almohadilla de tinta **189**–46
almohadilla para cambiar
    pañales **59**–2
alquiler de un apartamento **48**
alrededor del campus **5**
altavoz **190**–28
ALTERACIONES **100**
alteraciones **100**
alterado(a) **43**–28
alto(a) **32**–4
altura **17**–16
ama de casa **172**–33
amamantarlo **36**–B
amanecer **18**–14
amarillo **24**–2
amarrar **86**–A
ambulancia **118**–1, **123**–34
ampolla **110**–17
añada las legumbres y
    hortalizas **77**–N
añadir el detergente **101**–B
anafilaxis **113**–15
analgésico **115**–26
anaranjado **24**–4

ancho **17**–19
anciana **30**–5
anciano(a) **32**–3
andador **115**–11
andamiaje **196**–4
andar en bicicleta **131**–D
anémona de mar **218**–25
anestesiar la boca **120**–C
anestesiólogo **123**–35
anfibios **218**
anfitriona **82**–2
anguila **218**–12
ángulo agudo **205**–28
ángulo de 90° **205**–26
ángulo obtuso **205**–27
ángulo recto **205**–26
ángulos **205**
anillo **95**–40
anillo barato **23**–20
anillo caro **23**–19
anillo de dentición **37**–26
anillos de cebolla **79**–4
animales **112**
animales de granja **221**
animales de peluche **59**–15
ANIMALES DOMÉSTICOS Y
    ROEDORES **221**
aniversario **22**–3
año **20**–4
anochecer **18**–19
anote los resultados **207**–D
antebrazo **106**–13
antena parabólica **53**–5
anteojos **117**–7
anteojos de seguridad **92**–10
antes de una emergencia **150**
antiácido **115**–28
antifaz **245**–9
antiguas **209**–1
antílope **223**–35
antitranspirante **108**–5
anuncio de pancarta **44**–1
anuncios clasificados **48**–2
apagar las luces **225**–G
apague las luces **11**–P
apague su teléfono celular **179**–G
aparador con vitrina **55**–22
aparato para trepar **230**–14
aparcamiento **126**–1
apartado postal (PO box) **137**–7
apartamento amueblado **48**–3
APARTAMENTOS **50**–51
apartamentos no amueblados **48**–4
apellido **4**–4
apio **69**–9
aplaudir **152**–B
aplicaciones **191**
aplicarse **109**–P
apliques **99**–31
apósito estéril **119**–7
apóstrofe **202**–19
aprender a conducir **40**–E
aprender palabras nuevas **8**
aprendizaje **175**–10

araña **220**–30
arándanos **68**–16
arandela **194**–37
árbitro **235**–6
árbol de las pulgas **216**–24
árbol de Navidad **245**–16
ÁRBOLES Y PLANTAS **216**
arce **216**–12
archivero **188**–11
archivista **188**–10
archivo de tarjetas giratorio **189**–44
arco **237**–6
ardilla **221**–21
ardilla listada **221**–20
área de control de seguridad **164**–4
área de espera **188**–16
área de examen **138**–2
área de juegos **132**–11
área de recepción **188**–15
área del comedor **46**–8
área rural **52**–4
área urbana **52**–1
arena **231**–23
aretes de colgar **95**–36
aretes de presilla **95**–37
armadillo **222**–8
armar **185**–C
armario **5**–11, **55**–24
armario de almacenamiento **50**–17
armónica **244**–21
aro de baloncesto **235**–8
arquitecta **170**–5
arquitecto **170**–5
arranque **163**–33
arrastrar el cochecito **230**–A
arrastre el cursor para seleccionar
    el texto **210**–J
arreglar el cabello **33**
arreglar una caries **120**–E
arrendador **51**–27
arrendajo azul **220**–7
arrendatario **50**–6
arrestar a un sospechoso **144**–A
arrojar **236**–C
arroz **67**–10, **81**–30, **187**–1
arteria **107**–36
artes **201**–15
artes del lenguaje **201**–9
artes marciales **234**–11
artículos de costura **100**
ARTÍCULOS DE LIMPIEZA **61**
artículos de oficina **189**
artista **170**–6
artritis **113**–20
asado **70**–1
Asamblea Legislativa **140**–17
asambleísta **140**–18
ascender los peldaños **157**–C
ascenso **175**–8
ascensor **50**–9, **133**–21, **192**–9
asegurado **121**–5
asesinato **145**–12
asfixiarse **118**–L, **118**–N
asienta **12**–L

asiento de seguridad para
    el automóvil **37**–20
asiento delantero **163**–51
asiento elevador para el
    automóvil **37**–21
asiento en posición vertical **165**–28
asiento para niños **163**–53
asiento reclinado **165**–27
asiento trasero **163**–54
asista a una feria de empleos **174**–I
asistenta de atención de la salud
    a domicilio **171**–32
asistente **122**–16
asistente administrativa **170**–3
asistente administrativo **170**–3
asistente certificada de
    enfermería **122**–12
asistente de director **5**–5
asistente del médico **172**–47
asistente del profesor o
    maestro **5**–16
asistente dental **171**–22, **120**–2
asistir a un cliente **95**–D
asma **113**–18
aspecto **32**
aspiradora **61**–10
aspirar la alfombra **60**–H
astas **222**–16
astromóvil **215**–20
astronauta **215**–17
astrónomo **215**–22
asustado(a) **43**–23
atajar **236**–F
ataque **145**–11
atardecer **18**–18
ATENCIÓN DENTAL **120**
ATENCIÓN MÉDICA **111**–**112**
atender a los clientes **176**–T
atendiente en el mostrador **79**–17
aterriza **164**–K
atlas **135**–8
atletismo **234**–18
átomo **207**–28
atractivo(a) **32**–13
atragantarse **118**–L
atrapar **236**–D
atún **71**–7, **72**–19, **218**–8
audífono **14**–13, **117**–10, **191**–35
audífono Bluetooth **14**–14
audífonos **6**–8
audífonos intraurales **240**–5
audiolibro **135**–17
audiólogo **117**–9
audiopantalla **163**–37
auditorio **5**–18
auricular **14**–4
auriculares con cancelación
    de ruido **240**–6
auriculares livianos **240**–4
autobús **130**–9, **155**–14
autobús de servicio regular **156**–19
autobús puente **156**–19
automóvil **154**–1
automóvil con puerta trasera **160**–6

automóvil deportivo **160**–4
automóvil urbano **156**–20
AUTOMÓVILES Y CAMIONES **160**
autopago **73**–10
autopista **159**–9
autor **135**–15, **173**–64
autora **173**–64
autoservicio **135**–10
auxiliar de estacionamiento **192**–3
avalancha **149**–18
avanzar rápido **241**–D
aventar **236**–C
aventarse **236**–K
aventuras **243**–19
avergonzado(a) **43**–24
averiarse **166**–F
aviador **141**–33
avión **154**–8, **165**
aviso **102**–1
aviso de "se alquila" **50**–7
aviso emergente **213**–17
avispa **220**–18
ayer **20**–7
ayuda para los problemas
    de salud **117**
ayudante de la tienda **72**–4
ayudante de meseros **193**–13
ayudante del camarero **83**–12
ayudante del dentista **120**–2
ayudar a los pacientes **176**–B
ayude a las personas
    discapacitadas **151**–G
ayude a un compañero **8**–J
azadón de pico **196**–21
azafata **165**–12
azafrán **217**–17
azúcar **73**–30
azucarera **55**–14
azucena **217**–26
azul **24**–3
azul brillante **24**–12
azul claro **24**–11
azul marino **28**–5
azul oscuro **24**–10
azul turquesa **24**–9
azulejo **57**–12
babero **37**–5
bacalao **71**–8, **218**–5
bacinilla **37**–15, **123**–23
bádminton **234**–6
bagre **71**–2
bahía **214**–9
bailar **64**–A
bajarse del taxi **157**–F
bajo **244**–8
bajo cero **13**–7
bajo del ruedo **100**–9
bajo(a) **32**–6
balanza **57**–27, **72**–3, **207**–41
balcón **51**–20
balde **61**–7
baldosa **57**–12
baldosas **196**–11
ballena **219**–33

balompié **235**–13
balón de fútbol americano **237**–21
baloncesto **235**–9
bañarlo **36**–F
bañarse **108**–B
banca **230**–10
banco **126**–5
BANCO **134**
banda de cabeza **90**–3
bandeja **55**–17
bandeja de los postres **83**–10
bandeja de pintura **195**–51
bandeja para asar **78**–13
bandeja para galletas dulces **78**–27
bandera **245**–8
bañera **57**–2
baño **46**–5
BAÑO **57**
baños **5**–9
barba **33**–6
barbería **131**–19
barbilla **106**–1
barquillo de helado **79**–13
barra de ensaladas **79**–24
barra de menús **213**–7
barra de sujeción **57**–11
barras de chocolate **73**–37
barrena **194**–28
barrer el piso **60**–J
báscula **207**–41
base **14**–3, **109**–40, **205**–45, **206**–20
bastidor **98**–16
bastón **115**–16
bastones de esquí **237**–25
bastones dulces **245**–17
basura **152**–2
bata **91**–28
bata de hospital **123**–19
bata de playa **90**–25
bata la mezcla **77**–S
bata quirúrgica **123**–38
batatas **69**–18
bate de béisbol **237**–14
batería **162**–20
batidor **78**–21
batidor de huevos **78**–20
batidora eléctrica **54**–25
baúl **162**–11
baúl de los juguetes **59**–16
bayas **216**–20
bayas mixtas **81**–36
bazar **228**–6
beba **11**–J
beba líquidos **116**–C
bebé **31**–6
bebedero **230**–9
bebidas **73**
bebidas gaseosas **73**–34
beige **24**–18
béisbol **235**–10
berenjenas **69**–23
besarlo en la noche **36**–P
bese **3**–L
betabeles **69**–5

biblioteca **127**–15
BIBLIOTECA **135**
biblioteca **5**–17
bibliotecaria de referencias **135**–9
bibliotecario **135**–1
bicicleta **131**–22, **155**–15
bien **42**–14
bigote **33**–5
bigotes **222**–18
billar **234**–2
billete **156**–11, **156**–15
billete de transbordo **156**–5
billetera **94**–13
billetes **26**
bioenergía **224**–9
biografía **135**–13
biología **206**
biólogo **206**–2
birrete **226**–7
bisonte **222**–6
bistec **70**–2, **81**–24
blanco **24**–14, **237**–7
blanqueador **101**–7
blazer **92**–12
bloque de colcha **238**–15
bloque de pilas secas **241**–23
bloqueador solar **108**–8
bloquee los sitios
    inapropiados **147**–C
bloques **59**–19
blues **243**–22
blusa **87**–8
blusa bordada **88**–7
blusa lisa **97**–33
blusa vistosa **97**–34
blusón **93**–26
bobina **98**–21
boca **104**–7, **106**
boca de incendio **131**–27
bocina **163**–32
boda **22**–2
bodega **185**–7, **193**–5
bola **59**–12
bola de baloncesto **237**–4
bola de boliche **237**–5
bola de fútbol **237**–12
bola de voleibol **237**–3
bolas de carne **81**–27
boleto **156**–11, **156**–15
boliche **234**–3
bolígrafo **7**–22
bollo dulce **79**–16
bollo dulce inglés **80**–5
bollos con forma de rosquilla **73**–40
bolsa **94**–19, **223**–50
bolsa bandolera **94**–17
bolsa de aire **163**–43
bolsa de calentamiento **115**–13
bolsa de comestibles **67**–13
bolsa de compras **67**–13
bolsa de harina **74**–19
bolsa de hielo **119**–14
bolsa de la aspiradora **61**–12
bolsa de lechuga **69**–31

bolsas **74**–7
bolsas de basura **61**–24
bolsas de plástico para
    almacenar **72**–25
bolsillo **100**–7
bolso **87**–9
bolso de mano **89**–19
bolso para la cámara **241**–22
bombero **148**–9, **171**–26
bonito(a) **32**–14
bordado **239**–24
borde de la acera **131**–21
borrador **7**–19
borre el error **10**–M
bosque **214**–11
bosque húmedo **214**–1
botanas **73**
botas **95**–28
botas con punta de acero **92**–6
botas de esquí **237**–26
botas de seguridad **197**–20
botas para excursión **95**–31
botas para la lluvia **90**–20
botella **37**–1
botella de agua **74**–13
botella de agua caliente **115**–15
botellas **74**–1
botiquín **57**–22
botiquín de primeros
    auxilios **119**–1, **150**–18
botón **99**–24
botón actualizar **213**–11
botón de encendido del aire
    acondicionado **163**–40
botón de retorno **213**–9
botón para llamar **123**–28
botones **192**–7
bóveda **134**–6
boxeo **234**–4
brazalete de emergencia
    médica **119**–3
brazaletes **95**–9
brazo **105**–14, **206**–23
brazo, la mano y los dedos **106**
brigadas de búsqueda y
    rescate **149**–20
broca **194**–28
brocha **195**–22
broche **108**–20
brócoli **69**–13
brote **217**–5
buceo con escafandra **233**–12
buceo de superficie **233**–11
buenas noticias **23**–18
búfalo **222**–6
bufanda para el invierno **90**–5
bufandas **95**–12
bufé **193**–10
búho **220**–6
bulbo **217**–2
buldózer **196**–6
buriladora **194**–12
burrito **79**–9
burro **221**–3

buscando para comprar **28**–A
buscar avisos de "se solicita
    ayuda" **168**–G
buscar un libro **135**–B
busque la palabra **8**–A
busque refugio **151**–H
busque resguardo **151**–J
BÚSQUEDA DE CASA **48**–**49**
BÚSQUEDA EN INTERNET **212**–**213**
butaca **56**–22
buzón **53**–1, **130**–13, **137**–12
buzón del vestíbulo de la oficina
    de correos **137**–11
buzones **50**–11
caballete **239**–18
caballo **221**–4
caballo de mar **218**–13
cabecera **58**–10
cabello **104**–2
cabello a la altura de
    los hombros **33**–2
cabello castaño **33**–15
cabello corto **33**–1
cabello largo **33**–3
cabello liso **33**–9
cabello negro **33**–12
cabello ondulado **33**–10
cabello rizado **33**–11
cabello rubio **33**–14
cabestrillo **115**–19
cabeza **104**–1
cabeza de lechuga **69**–32
cabezal de la ducha **57**–13
cabina **160**–16
cabina de votación **143**–10
cabina del piloto **165**–10
cabina electoral **143**–10
cable **190**–12
cable de alimentación **190**–10
cable de carga **14**–9
cable desgastado **197**–5
cable elástico **195**–15
cableado **198**–7
cables para pasar corriente **162**–21
cables puente **162**–21
cabra **221**–5
cacahuate **112**
cacerola **54**–16, **78**–6
cacerola a vapor **78**–3
cacerola doble **78**–8
cachemir **98**–4
cachete **106**–3
cacillo **78**–25
cactus **216**–21
cadena **95**–33, **194**–41
cadena para puerta **51**–34
cadera **107**–27
caerse **118**–O
café **24**–17, **73**–33, **81**–37
café descafeinado **81**–38
cafetera **54**–6
cafetería **5**–14, **128**–11
caimán **219**–39
caja **73**–13, **164**–6, **190**–7

caja de arena **230**–15
caja de cereal **74**–18
caja de fusibles **62**–13
caja de seguridad **134**–7
caja liviana **23**–14
caja para llevar **82**–5
caja pesada **23**–13
caja registradora **27**–10, **73**–16
caja toráxica **107**–48
cajas **74**–6
cajas de cartón **74**–4
cajera **73**–14, **170**–15
cajero **134**–1, **170**–15
cajero automático **134**
cajón **54**–23, **58**–2
calabacín **69**–25
calabacita **69**–25
calabaza **69**–24
calamar **218**–7
calcetines **86**–6
calcetines al tobillo **91**–7
calcetines cortos **91**–11
calcetines de mujer **91**
calcetines de tobillo **91**–10
calcetines de trabajo **91**–8
calcetines de vestir **91**–9
calcetines hasta la rodilla **91**–12
calcetines unisex **91**
calculadora **17**–6, **189**–25
calcule **17**–B
cálculo **204**–19
caldera está estropeada **63**–15
CALENDARIO **20**–**21**
CALENDARIO DE EVENTOS **22**
calentador de agua no
    funciona **62**–1
cálido **13**–3
caliente **13**–3
calificaciones **10**–4
calle **154**–5, **159**–8
calle sin salida **158**–6
callejón **51**–24
callejón sin salida **158**–6
CALLES DE LA CIUDAD **128**–**129**
calvo **33**–24
calzoncillos **91**–5
calzoncillos tipo bóxer **91**–4
calzoncitos de entrenamiento **37**–16
calzones **91**–14
calzones (bikinis) **91**–13
cama **58**–9
cama de hospital **123**–22
cama de resortes **58**–19
cama *king-size* **192**–15
cama matrimonial **192**–14
cámara congeladora **193**–3
Cámara de Representantes **140**–3
cámara de seguridad **50**–19
cámara de video y audio **241**–21
cámara digital **241**–17
cámara web **191**–37
camarera **83**–9, **173**–56, **193**–8
camarero **82**–8
camarón **71**–11, **218**–19

cambiar **27**–1, **152**–C
cambiar las sábanas **60**–P
cambiar un cheque de viajero **27**–F
cambiarle el pañal **36**–G
cambie los servicios públicos a
    su nombre **49**–O
camello **223**–38
camilla **123**–33
camillero **122**–16
caminata **232**–7
camine a la clase **11**–A
camine con un amigo **146**–A
caminito **53**–2
camino para bicicletas **230**–3
camión **130**–9
camión de bomberos **148**–10
camión de la basura **129**–22
camión de mudanza **160**–18
camión semirremolque **160**–15
camión tanque **160**–20
camión volquete **160**–19
camionero **173**–61
camioneta **154**–6, **160**–12
camisa **86**–1
camisa arrugada **101**–19
camisa con mangas cortas **96**–12
camisa de dormir **91**–27
camisa de manga de 3/4 **96**–13
camisa de manga larga **96**–14
camisa de seguridad **93**–20
camisa de trabajo **92**–2
camisa deportiva **88**–4
camisa húmeda **101**–17
camisa planchada **101**–20
camisa seca **101**–18
camisa sin mangas **96**–11
camisa tipo polo **92**–14
camiseta **86**–4, **89**–24, **91**–1
camiseta limpia **101**–16
camiseta sucia **101**–15
camiseta térmica **91**–2
camisola **91**–20
camisón **91**–24, **93**–38
camisón de cirugía **93**–37
camotes **69**–18
campamento **232**–5
camper **160**–9
campo **5**–2, **52**–4, **187**–7
campo de béisbol **230**–1
campo de búsqueda **212**–3
campus **5**
caña **79**–18
caña de pescar **232**–18
canal **53**–6
canalón **53**–6
canas **33**–23
canasta **73**–9
cáncer **113**–17
cancha de baloncesto **235**–7
cancha de tenis **230**–6
canciones de cuna **37**–23
candidato **143**–6
cangrejo **71**–9, **218**–21
canguro **223**–44

canilla **106**–21
cañón **214**–17
cansado(a) **43**–32
cantar una canción **244**–B
cantarle una canción de cuna **36**–O
cantimplora **232**–24
capacitación **175**–3
capacitación en el trabajo **175**–12
capacitación profesional y
    técnica **175**–9
capacitación vocacional **175**–9
capital del estado **140**–16
capitán de botones **192**–6
capitán de meseros **193**–12
capitolio de EE. UU. **140**–1
capó **162**–4
capota **162**–4
cápsula **115**–23
capullo **217**–7
cara **106**
caracol **218**–23
carbón **224**–4
cardenal **110**–11
cárdigan **88**–2
cardiólogo **122**–3
careta **245**–9
careta antigás **197**–13
careta de buzo **231**–7
careta del receptor **237**–15
cargador **240**–3
cargador de pilas **241**–24
cargador para bebé **37**–17
cargador portátil **240**–15
cargar la lavadora **101**–C
cargos adicionales **15**–32
cargos mensuales **15**–31
caries **120**–8
carne **66**–2
carne de aves de corral **70**
carne de cerdo **70**
carne de cordero **70**
carne de pavo cocida **70**–25
carne de pavo cruda **70**–24
carne de res **70**
carne de res sofrita **76**–6
carne en conserva **71**–22
carne molida **70**–4
carne para guisar **70**–3
CARNE Y AVES DE CORRAL **70**
carnicero **170**–13
carpa de campaña **232**–10
carpa dorada **221**–16
carpeta de 3 anillos **7**–28
carpeta de archivo **189**–50
carpintero **62**–12, **170**–14
carrera de caballos **234**–19
carretilla **186**–3
carretilla de mano **185**–11
carrito **37**–18, **73**–12, **131**–28
carrito de la limpieza **192**–19
carrito de maletas **192**–8
carroza **245**–2
carrusel de equipajes **165**–23
carta **136**–13

cartelera **7**–14
carteras **94**–2
cartero **136**–20
cartón de huevos **74**–16
cartucho de tinta **189**–45
Casa Blanca **140**–7
casa de muñecas **59**–18
casa móvil **52**–7
casa rodante **52**–7
CASA Y EL JARDÍN **53**
casacas rojas **208**–9
casados nuevamente **35**–24
casarse **41**–K
cascada **214**–2
casco **93**–23
casco de fútbol americano **237**–19
casco de protección **92**–9
casco de protección para la
    cabeza **92**–1
casco protector **197**–9
castillo de arena **231**–12
castor **222**–9
catálogo en línea **135**–11
catarata **214**–2
catarinita **220**–27
catorce **16**
cazo **78**–7
cebollas **69**–19
cebollas verdes **69**–20
cebollitas **69**–20
cebra **223**–33
cecina en conserva **71**–22
ceda el paso **158**–9
ceja **106**–9
celebrar **226**–C
célula **206**–4
cementerio **129**–15
cemento **196**–10
cenar la cena **39**–S
centavo **26**–1
centésimo **16**
centígrados **13**–2
centímetro [cm] **17**–14
centralita telefónica **188**–13
centro comercial **128**–7
CENTRO COMERCIAL **132**–**133**
centro de convenciones **129**–24
centro de enseñanza
    preescolar **200**–1
centro de entretenimiento **56**–5
centro de fotocopiado **131**–18
CENTRO DE LA CIUDAD **126**–**127**
centro postal automático
    (CPA) **137**–10
cepillarse…el cabello **108**–I
cepillarse…los dientes **109**–J
cepillo **33**–20, **108**–14, **195**–57
cepillo de dientes **57**–23, **109**–22
cepillo de fregar **61**–20
cepillo para el inodoro **57**–20
cera para muebles **61**–8
cerca **187**–19
cerdo **221**–2
cereal caliente **80**–9

cerebro **107**–34
ceremonia **226**–6
cerezas **68**–11
cerezo silvestre **216**–15
cerillas **150**–16, **232**–21
cero **16**
cerradura está estropeada **62**–6
cerrajero **62**–11
cerrojo de seguridad **51**–35
certificado de defunción **41**–11
certificado de nacimiento **40**–1
certificado de naturalización **40**–6
Certified Mail™ (el correo
    certificado) **136**–4
césped **53**–26
cesta **56**–3
cesta de la ropa sucia **57**–1
cesta para el pan **83**–11
cesto para la ropa sucia **101**–2
cesto para pañales **37**–7
chaleco **89**–15
chaleco de seguridad de alta
    visibilidad **92**–4
chaleco relleno con plumas **90**–14
chaleco salvavidas **165**–25, **232**–14
champú **108**–10
chaqueta **90**–8
chaqueta de chef **93**–29
chaqueta de cuero **90**–4
chaqueta deportiva **89**–14
chaqueta gruesa **97**–27
chaqueta liviana **97**–28
chaqueta rellena con plumas **90**–16
charca **214**–21
charle **12**–B
charola **55**–17
chef **83**–16
chef de partida **193**–6
chef ejecutivo **193**–7
chef principal **193**–7
cheque **134**–14
cheque de pago **183**–14
chequera **134**–13
chícharos **69**–21
chiles **69**–29
chimenea **53**–4, **56**–13
chimpancé **223**–27
chinches **63**–24
chofer de taxi **156**–21
chuletas de cerdo **70**–10
chuletas de cordero **70**–15
chuletas de ternera **70**–6
chupete **37**–25
chupón **37**–2, **37**–25, **195**–50
ciberacoso **147**–1
ciberseguridad **190**–4
ciclismo **234**–5
ciclismo de montañas **232**–8
ciclista **230**–2
ciego(a) **32**–11
cielo **231**–4
cien **16**
cien dólares **26**–12
cien mil **16**

ciencia-ficción **243**–18
ciencias **201**–11
CIENCIAS **206–207**
ciento uno **16**
cierre **99**–25
cierre el documento **210**–E
cierre el libro **6**–H
cierre está estropeado **97**–39
cierre las puertas con llave **146**–E
cierres **99**
cilindro **205**–41
cilindro graduado **207**–38
cima de la montaña **214**–14
cincel **195**–55
cinco **16**
cinco centavos **26**–2
cinco dólares **26**–8
cincuenta **16**
cincuenta dólares **26**–11
cine **128**–6, **228**–2
cinta **99**–30
cinta adhesiva para
    conductos **195**–49
cinta adhesiva para empacar **189**–32
cinta adhesiva protectora **195**–53
cinta adhesiva transparente **189**–30
cinta aislante **195**–43
cinta correctora **189**–37
cinta de aislar **195**–43
cinta de enganche **99**–29
cinta de medir **100**–17
cinta de medir **195**–45
cinta estéril **119**–8
cinta transportadora **185**–9
cinturón de seguridad **163**–52
círculo **205**–34
circunferencia **205**–36
ciruelas **68**–13
ciruelas pasas **68**–26
cirujano **123**–36
cita **22**–4, **111**–1, **202**–10
cite las fuentes **212**–I
citoplasma **206**–9
ciudad **4**–7, **52**–1
civilizaciones **209**
clarinete **244**–2
clásica **243**–21
clave **159**–6
clavel **217**–20
clavelón **217**–13
clavo **194**–34
claxon **163**–32
clienta **94**–4
cliente **72**–1, **82**–6, **134**–2,
    182–2, **193**–9
clínica **198**–2
clip **189**–31
cloro **101**–7
clóset **58**–5
club nocturno **229**–12
club sándwich **80**–12
cobija **58**–15, **91**–26
cobijas **150**–7
cobra **219**–44

cobre un cheque **134**–A
cochecito **37**–19
cochino **221**–2
cociente **204**–10
cocina **46**–6
COCINA **54**
cocina **54**–18, **83**–15
cocina de campamento **232**–16
cocina de restaurante **193**
cocinar **76**–C, **176**–C
cocine a fuego lento **77**–P
cocine el brócoli al vapor **77**–D
cocinero de platos rápidos **193**–1
cocodrilo **219**–40
cocos **68**–24
código de área **4**–10, **15**–28
código de barras **27**–4
código postal **4**–9
codo **106**–12
coja el lápiz **6**–I
cojín **56**–2
col **69**–2
cola **73**–11, **222**–22
coladera **78**–22
colcha **58**–16, **59**–11
colchón **58**–20
colchoneta de gomaespuma **232**–13
coleccionar objetos **238**–A
colgar la ropa **101**–H
colibrí **220**–11
coliflor **69**–14
colinas **214**–16
collar de perlas **95**–39
collares **95**–10
colmillo **223**–48
colocar ladrillos **196**–B
colonia **108**–6
colonos **208**–2
color crema **24**–16
color marfil **24**–16
COLORES **24**
colores básicos **24**
colores diferentes **23**–16
colores neutros **24**
columna vertebral **107**–49
columpios **230**–11
coma **11**–I
coma **202**–17
coma una dieta saludable **116**–F
comadreja **222**–4
comedia **243**–13
comedia de situación **242**–2
COMEDOR **55**
comedor **82**–1
comejenes **63**–22
comenzar **236**–R
comer en un restaurante **193**
comer la cena **39**–S
cometa **215**–24
cometa **231**–3
comida enlatada **150**–9
comida envasada **150**–10
comida para mascotas **72**–6
comidas congeladas **72**–28

comillas **202**–18
comisaría **126**–6
cómo llenar un formulario **4**
CÓMO TENER ÉXITO EN LA
    ESCUELA **10**
cómo tomar una prueba **10**
cómoda **58**–1
cómoda **59**–6
compaginar papeles **177**–E
compañera **180**–5
compañeras de habitación **64**–1
compañeros de habitación **64**–1
comparación de la ropa **97**
comparar planes **121**–A
comparecer ante el tribunal **144**–C
comparta un libro **8**–M
compartimiento **82**–4
compartimiento de guantes **163**–44
compartimiento para el equipaje
    de mano **165**–13
compartir el vehículo **225**–I
competir en una carrera **236**–S
comportarse mal **44**–B
composición **202**–4
composición **209**–15
COMPOSICIÓN EN INGLÉS **202–203**
compositor **209**–14
compra de un automóvil usado **161**
COMPRA Y MANTENIMIENTO DE
    UN AUTOMÓVIL **161**
comprar **27**–G, **94**–A
comprar productos reciclados **225**–D
comprar una casa **41**–M
cómprese un bocadito **11**–K
comprobante de depósito **134**–4
comprometerse para casarse **41**–J
computadora **7**–15, **189**–17
computadora central **190**–1
computadora de escritorio **190**–9
computadora no enciende **191**–A
computadora portátil **190**–22
comunicarse claramente **178**–E
comunicarse con los contactos para
    referencias **168**–C
con esmog **13**–16
con flores **96**–25
con lunares **96**–21
con problemas auditivos **32**–12
con rayas **96**–20
con trenzas tejidas en el
    cabello **33**–22
con viento **13**–19
concejal **140**–22
concentrador USB **190**–26
concertar una entrevista **169**–M
concesionario **162**
concesionario de autos **128**–4
concha de mar **231**–24
concierto de música clásica **229**–14
concierto de música *rock* **228**–5
conclusión **202**–9
condenado **144**–15
condenar al acusado **144**–E
condensador **206**–18

condiciones del tiempo **13**
condo **52**–5
condominio **52**–5
conducir a través del túnel **157**–K
conducir al trabajo **38**–I
conducir un camión **176**–E
conducto para basura **51**–26
conductor **156**–13
conejillo de indias **221**–14
conejo **221**–13
conexión a Internet **191**
conexión wifi **191**–32
CONFECCIÓN DE ROPA **98–99**
conferencia de padres y
    maestros **22**–5
conferencia web **191**
confeti **245**–3
confundido(a) **43**–26
congelador **54**–10
congestión nasal **113**–13
congresista **140**–4
Congreso **140**–2
cono **205**–40, **216**–11
conozca a sus vecinos **49**–R
conseguir empleo **40**–F
conseguir un trabajo **169**–O
consejera **5**–6
consejero **5**–6
Consejo Municipal **140**–21
conserje **192**–4
consola de videojuegos **238**–3
consolarlo **36**–I
constelación **215**–14
Constitución **208**–12
CONSTRUCCIÓN **196**
consulte con un orientador de
    carrera **174**–F
contabilidad **184**–9
contactos fuera del estado **150**–2
contador **170**–1
contadora **170**–1
contaminación **224**
contaminación del agua **224**–14
contaminación del aire **224**–11
contar **84**–A
contenedor de queso fresco **74**–17
contenedores **74**–5
CONTENEDORES Y ENVASES **74**
contenido **213**–16
contento(a) **43**–31
conteste una pregunta **8**–L
contorneador **194**–12
contrachapada **196**–18
contramuslos **70**–22
contrapuerta **53**–10
contratar a un abogado **144**–B
contratista **198**–5
contrato de alquiler **51**–28
control de la cama **123**–27
control del juego de video **238**–4
control remoto universal **240**–10
convergir **158**–10
CONVERSACIÓN DIARIA **12**
converse con alguien **11**–L

converse con un reclutador **174**–J

convertible **160**–5

convertir en abono las sobras de
alimentos **225**–M

convertirse en abuelo(a) **41**–N

convertirse en ciudadano **40**–G

convierta **17**–D

convierta las medidas **75**–C

cooperar con los compañeros de
equipo **178**–F

copa de vino **83**–23

copago **121**–8

copias de documentos
importantes **150**–20

copias de las tarjetas de identificación
y de crédito **150**–19

copie el texto **210**–K

copie la palabra **8**–E

coral **218**–16

corazón **107**–38, **245**–6

corazones **239**–31

corbata **88**–12, **92**–13

corbata ancha **97**–36

corbata de lazo **89**–16

corbata de moño **89**–16

corbata estrecha **97**–35

cordillera **214**–15

cordón del zapato **94**–24

cordón prolongador **195**–14

cornejo **216**–15

corno **244**–11

corno francés **244**–13

corona **120**–10

corra a la clase **11**–B

corral **187**–17

correa de herramientas **92**–3

correa de soporte para la
espalda **197**–18

correas **94**–6

correo aéreo **136**–5

correr alrededor de la esquina **157**–H

corrija el error **10**–N

corríjalo **203**–I

cortador **186**–12

cortador rotatorio **238**–16

cortadora de césped **186**–6

cortadora de papel **189**–22

cortar el cabello **33**–A

cortar el césped **186**–A

cortarse…las uñas **109**–N

cortaúñas **109**–31

cortaviento **90**–24

corte **110**–12

corte el apio en trocitos **77**–J

corte el pollo **77**–I

corte las cebollas **77**–L

Corte Suprema **140**–11

cortina **56**–16

cortina de la ducha **57**–14

cortinas **58**–7

cosechar **187**–B

coser a mano **98**–B

coser a máquina **98**–A

coser ropa **176**–L

costillas a la parrilla **76**–2

costillas de res **70**–5

costo **27**–7

costurera **100**–1

country **243**–27

coyote **222**–3

CPR (la resucitación
cardiopulmonar) **119**–18

CPU **190**–16

cráneo **107**–47

crayones **59**–14

creación de un documento **210**

cree contraseñas seguras **147**–D

cree un documento nuevo **210**–B

cree un nombre de usuario **211**–O

cree una contraseña **211**–P

crema **81**–41, **115**–25

crema agria **72**–21

crema antihistamínica **119**–11

crema de afeitar **109**–29

crema humectante **108**–9

crema para el cuerpo **108**–9

CRIANZA Y CUIDADO DE LOS
NIÑOS **36–37**

crin **223**–49

crisantemo **217**–21

croché **239**–25

cromosoma **206**–8

cronómetro de cocina **78**–18

cruce del ferrocarril **158**–14

cruce escolar **158**–15

cruce peatonal **130**–15, **158**–13

cruzar corriendo la calle **157**–G

cruzar imprudentemente una
calle **130**–C

cruzar la calle **130**–A

cuaderno de papel de tamaño
oficio **189**–38

cuaderno de trabajo **7**–27

cuadrado **205**–30

cuadragésimo **16**

cuadro **56**–9

cualidades personales **178**

cuarenta **16**

cuarto **16**, **17**–4

cuarto de galón de leche **75**–4

cuarto de lavado **83**–13

cuarto de taza de azúcar
morena **75**–8

cuarto menguante **215**–11

cuarto para las dos **18**–13

cuatro **16**

Cuatro de Julio **22**–13

cubeta **61**–7

cubículo **188**–7

cubierto **83**–17

cubo **61**–7, **205**–38

cubo de basura **53**–24

cubrecama **58**–16, **59**–11

cucarachas **63**–26

cuchara **55**–5

cuchara de madera **78**–9

cuchara para sopa **83**–32

cucharada de azúcar **75**–7

cucharadita de sal **75**–6

cucharita **83**–31

cucharón **78**–7

cuchilla **194**–27

cuchilla de afeitar **109**–28

cuchillo **55**–4, **83**–30

cuchillo de pelar **78**–16

cuchillo de trinchar **78**–12

cuchillo multiusos **232**–20

cuchillo para carne **83**–29

cuelgue **15**–D

cuello **100**–4, **104**–3

cuenta conjunta **134**–10

cuentas **95**–34, **99**–32

cuentas bancarias **134**

cuerda **101**–9, **232**–19

cuerda para saltar **230**–4

cuerno **222**–21

cuero **98**–6

CUERPO **104–105**

cuerpo **202**–8

cuidado de su automóvil **161**

CUIDADO DE SU SALUD **116–117**

cuidar niños **176**–P

culebra americana no
venenosa **219**–46

culebrilla **112**–8

cultivador **187**–13

cumpla con las indicaciones
médicas **116**–J

cumpleaños **22**–1

cuna **59**–3

cuna mecedora **59**–20

cuñada **34**–16

cuñado **34**–17

cupones **67**–15

curso en línea **175**–13

cuy **221**–14

dados **238**–6

damas **238**–7

dar instrucciones **180**–C

dar un discurso **152**–A

dar una clase **124**–B

dátiles **68**–28

datos **15**–36, **190**–3

dé su nombre **15**–F

dé un apretón de manos **3**–K

DE VUELTA DEL MERCADO **66–67**

DEA **119**–4

debajo del capó **162**

debatir **143**–L

décimo **16**

decimoctavo **16**

decimocuarto **16**

decimonoveno **16**

decimoquinto **16**

decimoséptimo **16**

decimosexto **16**

decimotercero **16**

declaración de aduana **165**–16

Declaración de Derechos **208**–13

Declaración de
Independencia **208**–5

decoraciones **99**–31, **246**–1

dedal **100**–15

dedo **105**–16

dedo del pie **105**–10

dedo hinchado **110**–16

deducciones **183**–13

defensa **162**–8

dejar a los niños **38**–G

dejar un mensaje **177**–P

dejar una propina **82**–J

del oeste **243**–15

delantal **93**–38

delantal de laboratorio **93**–33

deletree su nombre **4**–B

delfín **219**–31

delgado(a) **32**–9

DELINCUENCIA **145**

delineador (de ojos) **109**–36

delitos a través de Internet **147**

demasiado caro **97**–44

demasiado grande **97**–38

demasiado pequeña **97**–37

demencia **113**–19

demostración **124**–6

denominador **204**–6

dentadura postiza **120**–11

dentista **120**–1

dentro de la maletera **162**

DENTRO DE UNA EMPRESA **184**

dentro del automóvil **163**

dentro del botiquín **119**

DENTRO Y FUERA DEL
CUERPO **106–107**

denuncie los delitos a la
policía **146**–K

denuncie los paquetes
sospechosos **146**–J

departamento de calzado **95**–7

departamento de joyería **95**–8

DEPARTAMENTO DE VEHÍCULOS
MOTORIZADOS (DMV) **138–139**

Departamento de Vehículos
Motorizados **126**–4

dependiente de la tienda
minorista **173**–53

dependiente encargado del
despacho de mercadería **185**–14

dependientes **121**–6

DEPORTES DE INVIERNO Y
ACUÁTICOS **233**

DEPORTES EN EQUIPO **235**

DEPORTES INDIVIDUALES **234**

depósito **134**–3

depósito de almacenamiento **50**–17

depósito de basura **51**–23

depósito inicial **134**–11

depredadores cibernéticos **147**–2

depresión **117**–5

derechos **142**

derrame de petróleo **224**–17

derrumbe **148**–6

desagüe **57**–7

desarrollo profesional **175**–7

desatascador **195**–50

desayunar **38**–E

descansar **39**–U
descanse en la cama **116**–B
descargar la secadora **101**–E
descender los peldaños **157**–D
descifre las palabras **9**–W
descongelador **163**–41
DESCRIPCIÓN DE LA ROPA **96–97**
DESCRIPCIÓN DE LAS PERSONAS **32**
DESCRIPCIÓN DE LOS OBJETOS **23**
descripción de prestaciones **121**–11
DESCRIPCIÓN DEL CABELLO **33**
desechos peligrosos **224**–12
desempaque **49**–N
desenfocada **241**–31
desfibrilador externo
     automático **119**–4
desfile **245**–1
desierto **214**–4
desilusionada **28**–4
desmaquillador **109**–42
desodorante **108**–5
desorden **64**–8
despachar **185**–D
despega **164**–J
despejado **13**–9
despertarse **38**–A
desplace la imagen **211**–M
desplantador **186**–10
destino **166**–6
destornillador **194**–30
destornillador de estrella **194**–31
destornillador Phillips **194**–31
DESTREZAS DE ENTREVISTA **170–171**
destrezas de liderazgo **178**
DESTREZAS DE OFICINA **177**
destrezas de oficina **177**
destrezas interpersonales **178**
DESTREZAS LABORALES **176**
DESTREZAS NO TÉCNICAS **178**
destrezas telefónicas **177**
desván **47**–9
desvestirlo **36**–E
detector de humo **51**–30
detenerse **158**–1
deténgase en la esquina **159**–D
detergente para ropa **101**–8
devolver **27**–H
devolver un libro **135**–D
día **20**–2
Día de Acción de Gracias **22**–17
Día de Año Nuevo **22**–9
Día de Colón **22**–15
día de fiesta oficial **22**–8
Día de la Independencia **22**–13
Día de la Recordación **22**–12
Día de los Presidentes **22**–11
Día de los Veteranos **22**–16
Día de Martin Luther King Jr. **22**–10
Día del Trabajo **22**–14
DÍA EN LA ESCUELA **11**
día feriado legal **22**–8
diabetes **113**–26
diagonal **205**–31
diamantes **239**–29

diámetro **205**–37
diariamente **20**–21
días de la semana **20**, **20**–16
DÍAS FERIADOS **245**
días feriados legales **22**
dibujos animados **242**–3
diccionario gráfico **7**–32
diccionario para estudiantes de
     lengua extranjera **7**–31
diciembre **21**–36
dictador **209**–6
dicte una oración **8**–N
diecinueve **16**
dieciocho **16**
dieciséis **16**
diecisiete **16**
dientes **106**–7
dietista **122**–15
diez **16**
diez centavos **26**–3
diez dólares **26**–9
diez mil **16**
diferencia **204**–8
diga cuál es la emergencia **15**–G
diga su nombre **4**–A
diga: "Hasta luego" **3**–M
diga: "Hola" **2**–A
dimensiones **17**
DINERO **26**
diploma **40**–3
diploma universitario **41**–7, **175**–5
dirección de un sitio web **213**–10
dirección del destinatario **136**–22
dirección postal **4**–5
direcciones **159**
DIRECCIONES Y MAPAS **159**
director **5**–4
directora **5**–4
directorio **133**–24
dirigir una orquesta **244**–C
disc-jockey **64**–4
discapacidades **32**
disciplinarlo **36**–K
disco duro **190**–19
disco duro externo **190**–27
disco volador **237**–27
discúlpese **12**–G
discuta un problema **8**
diseñador **185**–2
diseñador gráfico **171**–30
diseñadora **185**–2
diseñadora paisajista **186**–5
diseñar **185**–A
disfraz **245**–11
disienta **12**–M
disparar **236**–H
dispositivo salvavidas **231**–20
dispuesta a aprender **178**–3
divida **17**–A
dividir **204**–D
dobladillo **100**–8
doblar la ropa **101**–F
doblarse **236**–O
doce **16**

doctor **111**–5
doctor en veterinaria **173**–62
doctora **111**–5
doctora en veterinaria **173**–62
documentales sobre la
     naturaleza **242**–7
dólar **26**–7
dolor **117**–3
dolor de cabeza **110**–1
dolor de espalda **110**–5
dolor de estómago **110**–4
dolor de garganta **110**–6
dolor de muelas **110**–2
dolor de oído **110**–3
domingo **20**–8
dormirse **39**–Z
dormitorio **46**–3
DORMITORIO **58**
dormitorio de los niños **47**–10
DORMITORIO DE LOS NIÑOS **59**
dos **16**
dos puntos **202**–20
dos veces por semana **20**–23
dosis **114**–6
driblar **236**–J
drogas ilegales **145**–6
ducharse **108**–A
dueña de negocios **170**–11
dueño **51**–27
dueño de la fábrica **185**–1
dueño de negocios **170**–11
dulcería **133**–17
dulces **84**–8, **245**–12
duna **214**–5
duodécimo **16**
durante una emergencia **151**
duraznos **68**–10
DVD **135**–19
échele salsa encima con una
     cuchara **77**–F
eclipse solar **215**–16
ecuación **204**–13
edad **32**
edificio de apartamentos **50**–1
edificio de oficinas **126**–2
edítelo **203**–I
educación básica **175**–1
educación física **201**–17
educación permanente **175**–7
efectivo y las monedas **150**–17
ejecutiva **188**–5
ejecutivo **188**–5
ejercicio aeróbico **124**–5
ejército **141**–28, **209**–11
ejotes **69**–8
elabore respuestas **8**–H
elabore soluciones **8**–H
elección **143**
electricista **62**–9
electrón **207**–30
ELECTRÓNICA Y
     FOTOGRAFÍA **240–241**
elefante **223**–42
elevador **50**–9, **133**–21, **192**–9

elevador de carga **185**–12
elimine los correos electrónicos
     sospechosos **147**–G
elimine una palabra **210**–I
elogiarlo **36**–J
elogie a alguien **12**–C
embarazada **32**–15
embrague **163**–49
embudo **207**–40
EMERGENCIAS MÉDICAS **118**
EMERGENCIAS Y DESASTRES
     NATURALES **148–149**
emocionado(a) **43**–22
empacador **185**–8
empacadora **185**–8
empacar **166**–A
empaque **49**–M
empareje los objetos **9**–T
empaste **120**–9
emperador **209**–3
empezar a ir al colegio **40**–B
empezar a trabajar **169**–P
empleada **5**–13
empleada de correos **173**–49
empleada de una fábrica
     de ropa **171**–29
empleado **5**–13, **183**–9, **188**–2
empleado de almacén **173**–59
empleado de correos **137**–7, **173**–49
empleado de servicios de la higiene
     pública **173**–54
empleado de una casa de
     mudanzas **172**–42
empleado de una fábrica
     de ropa **171**–29
empleado del DMV **138**–3
empleadora **182**–4
EMPLEOS Y PROFESIONES **170–173**
empresa aseguradora **121**–1
empresa de telefonía **15**–27
empujar el columpio **230**–B
EN BUSCA DE TRABAJO **168–169**
en punto **18**–6
enagua reductora **91**–21
enamorado(a) **42**–18
enamorarse **40**–H
encaje **99**–9
encargada del servicio de comida y
     bebidas **193**–16
encargado de admisiones **122**–14
encargado de nómina **183**–10
encargado de pedidos **185**–10
enchufe **58**–28, **241**–25
enchufe de carga **14**–10
enchufe del teléfono **14**–2
encías **106**–6
encienda las luces **11**–D
encierre en un círculo la
     respuesta **9**–Q
encintado **131**–21
encuentre su asiento **164**–F
endulzante artificial **79**–20
energía de biomasas **224**–9
energía de fusión **224**–10

energía eólica **224**–2
energía geotérmica **224**–7
energía hidroeléctrica **224**–5
energía nuclear **224**–8
energía solar **224**–1
ENERGÍA Y EL MEDIO
    AMBIENTE **224–225**
enero **21**–25
enfermedad de las encías **120**–12
enfermedades cardíacas **113**–28
enfermedades comunes **112**
ENFERMEDADES Y AFECCIONES
    MÉDICAS **112–113**
enfermera **111**–8, **172**–44
enfermera quirúrgica **122**–9
enfermera registrada **122**–10
enfermero **111**–8
enfermero con licencia
    práctica **122**–11
enfermero de urgencias **118**–2
enfermo(a) **42**–12
engrapadora **189**–28
engrapar **177**–F
engrase una cazuela para
    hornear **77**–B
enjuagarse…el cabello **108**–F
enjuague bucal **109**–25
enlaces **212**–6
enlaces a redes sociales **213**–29
ennegrezca el espacio
    correspondiente a la
    respuesta **10**–K
enojado(a) **43**–29
enredadera **216**–22
enrutador **191**–33
ensalada de col **80**–18
ensalada de espinaca **80**–13
ensalada de frutas **80**–21
ensalada de la casa **80**–15
ensalada de papas **80**–19
ensalada de pasta **80**–20
ensalada del chef **80**–14
ensalada verde **80**–15
ensamblador **170**–7
ensambladora **170**–7
ensamblar **185**–C
ensamblar componentes **176**–A
ensayo **202**–4
enseñanza de inglés **201**–14
enseñar **176**–Q
entarimado **246**–2
enterito **93**–24
entero **17**–1
entrada **182**–1
entrada **50**
entrada de la sala de
    emergencias **123**
entrada del apartamento **51**
entrada del garaje **53**–8
entrar en la autopista **157**–I
entregue la prueba **10**–O
entregue la tarjeta **137**–E
entregue los libros **11**–G
entregue su composición **203**–M

entrenador **5**–20, **235**–2
entrenar **236**–N
ENTRETENIMIENTO **242–243**
entusiasta **235**–4
enumere sus destrezas no
    técnicas **174**–E
envase con tapa **78**–4
envase especial para remitir objetos
    por correo **189**–40
envenenamiento con
    insecticidas **224**–16
envenenarse **118**–J
enviar correo electrónico **211**
enviar un documento por fax **177**–G
enviar una tarjeta **137**
envíe el correo electrónico **211**–Z
envíe la prueba **10**–P
envíe la tarjeta **137**–D
envío por vía terrestre **136**–6
envolver **246**–F
equipaje **165**–18
equipo **235**–3
equipo averiado o roto **197**–4
equipo de seguridad **197**
EQUIPO DEPORTIVO **237**
equipo para trabajar en el
    campo **187**–12
equipos de oficina **189**
equitación **232**–9
erizo de mar **218**–22
erupción **113**–14
erupción volcánica **149**–16
escala **159**–7
escalera **196**–2
escalera automática **133**–23
escaleras **50**–10
escalerilla **61**–13
escalofríos **110**–8
escalones **53**–3
escalones están rotos **62**–7
escamas **218**–3
escanear un documento **177**–H
escáner **189**–20
escape **162**–15
escarabajo **220**–19
esclavos **208**–4
escoba **61**–16
escocesa **96**–22
escoja la respuesta correcta **9**–P
esconderse **246**–D
escorpión **220**–31
escriba el borrador final **203**–L
escriba el mensaje **211**–W
escriba en la pizarra **6**–E
escriba en letra de imprenta
    su nombre **4**–C
escriba la dirección del destinatario
    del correo electrónico **211**–U
escriba la dirección en
    el sobre **137**–B
escriba un mensaje en
    la tarjeta **137**–A
escriba un primer borrador **203**–H

escríbale una nota de
    agradecimiento **179**–O
escribiente **144**–12
escribir en mayúsculas la inicial de los
    nombres **202**–A
escribir en mayúsculas la primera
    letra de una oración **202**–B
escribir un cheque (personal) **27**–D
escribir un currículum **168**–B
escribir una carta de
    presentación **169**–K
escritor **173**–64
escritora **173**–64
escritorio **6**–7, **188**–9
escritorio de distribución **135**–2
escritura del terreno **41**–9
escucharle el corazón **111**–C
escuche cuidadosamente **179**–K
escuche una grabación **6**–C
escuela **128**–9
ESCUELA **5**
escuela de párvulos **200**–1
escuela intermedia **200**–3
escuela para adultos **200**–8
escuela primaria **200**–2
escuela profesional y técnica **200**–5
escuela secundaria **200**–4
ESCUELAS Y MATERIAS **200–201**
escurridor **61**–15, **78**–17
esfera **205**–42
esgrima **234**–7
esmalte de uñas **109**–33
esmog **224**–11
esmoquin **89**–17
espacio de estacionamiento **50**–18
espadas **239**–30
espagueti **81**–26
espalda **104**–5
espárragos **69**–26
espátula **78**–19, **195**–52
especialista en operaciones
    informáticas **190**–2
especialistas médicos **122**
espejo **57**–18
espejo largo **58**–6
espejo lateral **162**–3
espejo retrovisor **163**–35
esperar a que cambie el
    semáforo **130**–B
esperar en cola **94**–B
esperar en fila **94**–B
espina **217**–29
espinaca **69**–11
espinilla **106**–21
espinilleras **237**–13
esponja **61**–19
esponjas de lana de acero **61**–5
esposa **34**–12
esposas **144**–2
esposo **34**–13
esquí acuático **233**–7
esquí de descenso **233**–1
esquí de fondo **233**–3
esquiar **236**–V

esquíes **237**–24
esquina **130**–7
está descosido **97**–41
está manchado **97**–42
está rasgado **97**–41
esta semana **20**–19
establezca una hipótesis **207**–A
estación de autobuses **126**–7
estación de bomberos **127**–12
estación de metro **156**
estación de policía **126**–6
estación de recarga **240**–3
estación de recarga de vehículos
    eléctricos **160**–3
estación de tren **156**
estación de tren subterráneo **156**
estación del metro **155**–11
estación del salvavidas **231**–21
estación espacial **215**–18
estacionamiento **126**–1
estacionamiento para
    minusválidos **130**–6, **158**–12
estacionar el auto **131**–E
estacionar el coche **131**–E
estaciones **21**
estadio **128**–1
estado **4**–8
estado de cuenta **134**–17
ESTADOS DE ÁNIMO Y
    SENTIMIENTOS **42–43**
estampado **96**–23
estampado búlgaro **96**–26
estampado de cachemir **96**–26
estampilla **136**–23
estanque **214**–21
estante **54**–2
estar de servicio activo **141**–B
estar en choque **118**–B
estar en clase **38**–J
estar en la reserva **141**–C
estar en *shock* **118**–B
estar herido **118**–C
estar inconsciente **118**–A
estar informado **142**–F
estar lesionado **118**–C
estar perdidos **166**–B
estatura **32**
estatura promedio **32**–5
este **159**–4
esté bien arreglado **179**–C
esté pendiente de los informes del
    tiempo **151**–C
esté pendiente de sus
    alrededores **146**–I
estéreo portátil **240**–1
estetoscopio **111**–10
estibador **171**–23
estilos **96**
estirarse **236**–M
estofado de verduras, hortalizas y
    tofu con queso **77**
estómago **107**–41
estornudo **113**–12
estréchense las manos **179**–I

estrella **215**–13
estrella de mar **218**–17
estrellas **166**–3
estrés **117**–4
estuche para la cámara **241**–22
estuche para teléfono celular **94**–15
estuco **196**–15
estudiante **6**–6
ESTUDIAR **8–9**
estudie el manual **139**–A
estudie en la casa **10**–D
estufa **54**–18
etapas del día **18**
etiqueta **102**–3
etiqueta de advertencia **114**–8
etiqueta de identificación **92**–15
etiqueta de la receta **114**–4
etiqueta de nutrición **124**–8
etiqueta de registro **138**–13
etiqueta del precio **27**–1
etiqueta engomada de dirección
    postal **189**–41
evacue el área **151**–K
evidencia **144**–9
examen de bajo costo **124**–1
examen de sangre **123**–30
examen de visión **138**–6
examinarle…la garganta **111**–E
examinarle…los ojos **111**–D
excursión **232**–7
expediente médico **123**–24
experimento **207**
explique algo **12**–N
exploración **209**–8
explorador **209**–9
explore opciones
    profesionales **174**–B
explosión **148**–4
Express Mail® (el correo
    expreso) **136**–2
extender los pantalones **100**–C
extensión **195**–14
exterminador **63**–21
extinguidor de incendios **197**–21
extintor de incendios **197**–21
extraer un diente **120**–F
extraer una muela **120**–F
extragrande **96**–5
extrapequeño **96**–1
fábrica **128**–3
fábrica de ropa **98**
FABRICACIÓN **185**
fabricar **185**–B
fagot **244**–4
Fahrenheit **13**–1
faja **91**–15
falda **87**–10
falda a media pierna **96**–17
falda corta **96**–16
falda larga **96**–18
falta un botón **97**–40
FAMILIAS **34–35**
farmaceuta **114**–1
farmacéutico **114**–1

FARMACIA **114–115**
farmacia **130**–4
fármacos **112**
fauna marina **218**
fauna silvestre **166**–2
fax **189**–21
febrero **21**–26
fecha **20**–1, **213**–20
fecha de nacimiento **4**–14
fecha de vacunación **112**
fecha de vencimiento **114**–7, **138**–10
feliz **28**–6
femenino **4**–18
feria de comida rápida **133**–15
FERIA DE SALUD **124–125**
feria del condado **229**–13
ferretería **152**–4
fertilizar las plantas **186**–D
festín **245**–13
ficha **156**–10
fichero **188**–11
fiebre **110**–7
fiesta **64**–2
FIESTA DE CUMPLEAÑOS **246–247**
fiesta religiosa **22**–7
figurilla **238**–1
fijarse una meta **168**–A
fije metas **10**–A
fíjese un objetivo de
    corto plazo **174**–H
fíjese un objetivo de
    largo plazo **174**–G
fila **73**–11
filete **70**–2, **81**–24
filete de halibut **71**–6
filete de res asado a la brasa **76**–3
filete de salmón **71**–4
fin de semana **20**–17
finalice la llamada **15**–D
firma **4**–20
firme el contrato de alquiler **48**–D
firme el contrato de renta **48**–D
firme su nombre **4**–E
fiscal **144**–10
física **207**
físico **207**–33
fisioterapeuta **117**–12
flaco(a) **32**–9
flauta **244**–1
flebotomista **123**–29
flechas **237**–8
fleco **33**–8, **99**–34
flequillo **33**–8
flor de Nochebuena **217**–24
flor de Pascua **217**–24
florería **132**–8
florero **55**–23
FLORES **217**
florista **171**–27
floristería **132**–8
foca **219**–36
foco **206**–19
fogata **232**–11
folclórica **243**–29

folleto de prueba **10**–1
fondo reductor **91**–21
formas **205**
formas de conservar la energía y los
    recursos **225**
formas de pagar **27**
formas de proteger a los niños **147**
formas para tener éxito **10**
fórmese ideas **203**–F
fórmula **37**–3, **207**–34
formulario de historial médico **111**–4
formularios de correo **136**–19
fósforos **150**–16, **232**–21
foto chistosa **226**–2
foto seria **226**–3
fotocopiadora **189**–23
fotografía **138**–4
fotografías **58**–3
fotógrafo **226**–1
fotos **58**–3
fotosíntesis **206**–10
fracciones **204**
fracciones y decimales **17**
fracturarse un hueso **118**–P
frambuesas **68**–15
frasco de mermelada **74**–14
frascos **74**–2
fraude electrónico **147**–4
frecuencia **20**
fregadero **54**–4
fregar el lavamanos **60**–K
fregona con esponja **61**–6
frenillos **120**–6
freno de mano **163**–48
frenos **120**–6
frente **106**–2
fresas **68**–14
fresco **13**–5
frijoles **72**–17
frijoles de soya **187**–3
frío **13**–6
frustrado(a) **43**–27
frutas **67**–9
FRUTAS **68**
frutos secos **73**–36
fuegos artificiales **245**–7
fuente **202**–13, **213**–13, **230**–5
fuente de agua para beber **230**–9
fuente de alimentación **190**–14
fuente de la cita **202**–11
fuentes de energía **224**
fuera de foco **241**–31
Fuerza Aérea **141**–32
Fuerzas Armadas de EE. UU. **141**
fumigador **63**–21
funcionario electo **143**–12
funda de la almohada **58**–14
fundadores **208**–7
furgón de carga **160**–13
furgoneta **160**–8
fútbol **235**–13
fútbol americano **235**–12
gabardina **90**–18
Gabinete **140**–10

gabinete **54**–1
gabinete de artículos de
    oficina **188**–1
gabinete de baño **57**–22
gafas de seguridad **92**–10, **197**–10
gafas de sol **90**–27
gafas protectoras **197**–11
galaxia **215**–15
galletas dulces **73**–38
gallina **221**–8
gallo **221**–7
galón de agua **75**–5
gamuza **99**–8
ganadero **187**–22
ganado **187**–15, **187**–21, **221**
ganchillo **239**–25
gancho **101**–11, **194**–39
gancho de ojo **194**–40
gancho para el cabello **108**–19
gancho y ojal **99**–27
ganso **220**–14
garaje **47**–15
gardenia **217**–18
garganta **107**–35
garra **220**–2, **222**–20
garrapata **220**–28
gas natural **224**–3
gasa **119**–9
gases venenosos **197**–3
gasolinera **127**–10
gatito **221**–10
gato **221**–9
gato hidráulico **162**–24
gaveta **54**–23, **58**–2
gavetero **59**–6
gel de cabello **108**–16
gel de ducha **108**–2
general **141**–25
GEOGRAFÍA Y LOS HÁBITATS **214**
geometría **204**–17
gerente **72**–8
gerente de cuentas **134**–9
gerente de oficina **188**–8
gimnasia **234**–9
gimnasio **5**–19, **128**–10, **192**–24
girar **236**–Q
girasol **217**–10
gire a la derecha **159**–B
gire a la izquierda **159**–C
gis **7**–18
globos **44**–4
gobernador **140**–14
Gobierno estatal **140**
Gobierno federal **140**
Gobierno municipal **140**
GOBIERNO Y EL SERVICIO
    MILITAR **140–141**
golf **234**–8
goma **189**–33
goma de borrar **7**–21
gorila **223**–29
gorra de baño **108**–1
gorra de béisbol **86**–5
gorra de cirugía **93**–35

gorrión **220**–8
gorrito **88**–1
gorro **90**–1
gorro de chef **93**–28
gorro de cirugía **93**–35
gorro de vaquero **92**–18
gorro para esquiar **90**–11
gorro quirúrgico **123**–37
gorros **95**–11
góspel **243**–30
gotas para los ojos **115**–31
goteo intravenoso **123**–25
gotero **207**–45
GPS (sistema de posicionamiento global) **159**–11
grabadora de videocasete **102**–7
grabar **241**–A
grabar en video **246**–A
gradas **5**–3, **13**–8
GRADUACIÓN **226**–**227**
graduarse **40**–D
gráfica **204**–15
grafiti **152**–1
grajo azul **220**–7
grande **96**–4
granizo **13**–22
granja **52**–9, **187**–11
grapadora **189**–28
grapas **189**–29
grifo **57**–8
grifo gotea **63**–17
grillo **220**–24
gripe **112**–2
gris **24**–15
gritar **180**–A
grúa **160**–14, **196**–7
grúa alzacarro **196**–5
grupo de apoyo **117**–15
guante **237**–17
guantera **163**–44
guantes **90**–6
guantes de goma **61**–4
guantes de trabajo **92**–17, **197**–17
guantes desechables **93**–27
guantes médicos **93**–34
guantes quirúrgicos **123**–39
guardabosque **166**–1
guardacostas **141**–37
guardaparques **166**–1
guardar los juguetes **60**–G
guarde el documento **210**–D
guarde su equipaje de mano **164**–G
guarde sus libros **9**–Z
guardería infantil **131**–30
guardia **144**–3
Guardia Costera **141**–36
guardia de seguridad **134**–5
guardia de seguridad **173**–55
Guardia Nacional **141**–38
guardia nacional **141**–39
guerra **209**–10
guerra de la Independencia de EE. UU. **208**–8
guillotina **189**–22

guion **202**–23
guisantes **69**–21
guitarra **244**–9
gusano **218**–24
habichuelas **72**–17
habitación del bebé **47**–11
habitación en el hospital **123**
habitación para huésped **192**–13
hábitat **206**–11
hablar con los amigos **168**–E
hablar otro idioma **176**–N
hable con la maestra **6**–B
hable por teléfono **15**–C
hable sobre su experiencia **179**–L
hacer artesanías **238**–D
hacer campaña **143**–K
hacer copias **177**–D
hacer creer **239**–G
hacer ejercicios **39**–P, **236**–N
hacer gárgaras **109**–L
hacer la cama **60**–F
hacer la cena **39**–Q
HACER LA COLADA **101**
hacer la permanente **33**–B
hacer la tarea **39**–T
hacer labores manuales **176**–D
hacer mechas **33**–C
hacer muebles **176**–G
hacer una comida campestre **230**–D
hacer una limpieza dental **120**–A
hacer una llamada de emergencia **15**
hacha **194**–3
hacienda **52**–10
haga clic en el icono de buscar **212**–D
haga clic en el icono de búsqueda **212**–D
haga clic en enviar **211**–S
haga clic en la pantalla **210**–G
haga clic en un enlace **212**–F
haga compras en sitios Web seguros **146**–H
haga contacto visual **179**–J
haga doble clic para seleccionar una palabra **210**–H
haga preguntas **179**–M
haga un depósito **134**–B
haga un dibujo **8**–F
haga un experimento **207**–B
haga un pago de hipoteca **49**–L
haga una oferta **49**–I
haga una pregunta **8**–K
haga una reverencia **3**–I
hágase exámenes médicos regularmente **116**–H
hágase inmunizar **116**–I
hamaca **53**–23
hambre epidémica **149**–12
hamburguesa **79**–1
hamburguesa con queso **79**–3
harina **73**–29
hebilla **99**–28
hebilla del cinturón **94**–20
heladería **133**–16

helado **13**–23, **72**–26
helicóptero **155**–9
hemorragia nasal **110**–15
heno **187**–18
hepatitis **112**–9
hermana **34**–5
hermanastra **35**–29
hermanastro **35**–30
hermano **34**–6
herramienta de búsqueda de apartamentos **48**–1
HERRAMIENTAS Y MATERIALES DE CONSTRUCCIÓN **194**–**195**
hibisco **217**–12
híbrido **160**–1
hiedra venenosa **216**–25
hielera **231**–9
hiena **223**–30
hierbas **84**–9
hierva el pollo **77**–M
hígado **70**–7, **107**–40
HIGIENE PERSONAL **108**–**109**
higienista dental **120**–3
higos **68**–27
hija **34**–14
hijo **34**–15
hilo **98**–2, **100**–11, **239**–22
hilo dental **109**–24
hilos **99**–23
hip hop **243**–26
hipertensión **113**–24
hipopótamo **223**–43
historia **201**–12
HISTORIA DE EE. UU. **208**
HISTORIA UNIVERSAL **209**
hockey sobre hielo **235**–14
HOGAR **46**–**47**
hogar **56**–13
hogar de ancianos **52**–12
hogaza de pan **74**–22
hogazas **74**–10
hoguera **232**–11
hoja **109**–28, **216**–6
hoja de ingreso **134**–4
hoja de respuestas **10**–2
hoja de vidrio **196**–16
hojas **217**–6
hombre **30**–1
hombreras **237**–20
hombres **30**–4
hombro **105**–13
hongos **69**–27
honrado **178**–4
hora **18**–1
HORA **18**–**19**
hora de Alaska **19**–28
hora de Hawai-Aleutianas **19**–27
hora de la montaña **19**–30
hora de Terranova **19**–34
hora de verano **19**–25
hora del Atlántico **19**–33
hora del centro **19**–31
hora del este **19**–32
hora del Pacífico **19**–29

hora estándar **19**–26
horario **156**–4
hormigas **63**–23
hornee **77**–H
hornee la mezcla en el horno microondas durante 5 minutos **77**–T
hornilla **54**–19
horno **54**–20
horno microondas **54**–13
horno tostador **54**–15
horquillas **108**–21
horror **243**–17
HOSPITAL **122**–**123**
hospital **127**–9, **158**–18
hotel **126**–3
HOTEL **192**
hoy **20**–5
huella digital **138**–5
huerta **53**–27, **187**–10
huerta de verduras y hortalizas **187**–14
huerto **53**–27
huerto de verduras y hortalizas **187**–14
hueso **107**–33
huésped **192**–10
huevos **66**–7
huevos duros **76**–8
huevos escalfados **76**–9
huevos fritos **76**–10
huevos fritos, con una vuelta **76**–11
huevos revueltos **76**–7
húmedo **13**–17
humidificador **115**–12
huracán **13**–18, **149**–14
hurtos en comercios **145**–8
identifique la imagen **9**–V
identifique sus destrezas técnicas **174**–D
idiomas del mundo **201**–13
iglesia **129**–14
ignición **163**–33
IGUAL Y DIFERENTE **28**–**29**
iguales **28**–3
imán **207**–36
impedido(a) físico **32**–10
impedido(a) visual **32**–11
imperdible **100**–14
impermeable **90**–18
impresor **173**–50
impresora **190**–21
impresora de chorro de tinta **189**–18
impresora láser **189**–19
imprimir un documento **177**–I
impuesto de ventas **27**–8
incendio **148**–8
incendio forestal **148**–7
incendio provocado **145**–7
incómodo(a) **42**–9
indicador de aceite **163**–29
indicador de gasolina **163**–31
indicador de temperatura **163**–30
indígenas norteamericanos **208**–3

infante de marina **141**–35
Infantes de Marina **141**–34
infección de la garganta **112**–4
infección de oído **112**–3
inflamación **113**–16
infle los neumáticos **161**–L
INFORMACIÓN PERSONAL **4**
informe de accidente **110**–18
ingeniero **171**–25
ingeniero de *software* de
   computadoras **171**–18
ingrese al salón **11**–C
inhalador **115**–33
inicial del segundo nombre **4**–3
inicie sesión en su cuenta **211**–T
inicie una conversación **12**–A
inmigración **209**–12
inmigrante **209**–13
inmigrar **40**–C
inodoro **57**–21
inodoro está atorado **63**–19
inquilino **50**–6
inscribirse en el servicio selectivo
   del ejército **142**–D
insectos y los arácnidos **220**
inserte la tarjeta de cajero
   automático **134**–C
insignia **93**–21
inspector de seguridad **164**–5
instalaciones **180**–1
instalar losas **196**–C
instalar un sistema de
   rociador **186**–H
instituto de capacitación
   vocacional **200**–5
instituto de enseñanza
   superior **129**–17, **200**–6
instructora **6**–4
instrumentos de bronce
   o metales **244**
instrumentos de cuerda **244**
instrumentos de percusión **244**
instrumentos de viento
   de madera **244**
instrumentos dentales **120**–4
insuficiencia renal **113**–27
intercomunicador **50**–5
internista **122**–1
interno **180**–4
intérprete **172**–35
interrogante de la
   investigación **212**–1
interruptor de la luz **58**–27
INTERSECCIÓN **130**–**131**
intestinos **107**–42
intrauriculares **240**–5
introducción **202**–6
introducir datos **177**–B
introduzca su clave en el
   teclado **134**–D
inundación **149**–19
invención **209**–19
inventor **209**–18
invertebrados **206**–13

investigación y desarrollo **184**–5
investigar las empresas
   locales **168**–D
invierno **21**–40
invitación **64**–9
invite a alguien **12**–I
ir a la cárcel **144**–G
ir a la tienda de comestibles **38**–L
ir a la universidad **41**–I
ir a prisión **144**–G
ir a una agencia de empleos **168**–F
ir a una entrevista **169**–N
ir al trabajo **38**–I
ir de campamento **232**–6
IR DE COMPRAS **27**
ir debajo del puente **157**–A
ir sobre el puente **157**–B
irritado **64**–6
isla **214**–8
jabón **57**–4, **108**–3
jabonera **57**–3
jamón **70**–9
jamón hervido **76**–5
jarabe para la tos **115**–29
jardín aéreo **50**–4
jardín botánico **228**–3
jardín de verduras y hortalizas **53**–27
jardín delantero y la casa **53**
jardín posterior **53**
jardinero **171**–28
jarretes de cordero **70**–13
jazmín **217**–22
jazz **243**–24
jefa **182**–4
jefa de comedor **82**–2
jefe de comedor **193**–11
jefe del personal de jardinería **186**–4
jeringa **111**–12
jirafa **223**–32
joroba **223**–51
joven **32**–1
joyería **132**–2
jubilarse **41**–O
judías verdes **69**–8
jueces **140**–12
juego de artesanía en
   madera **238**–14
juego de béisbol **44**–2
juego de mesa **238**–5
juego para construir modelos a
   escala **238**–9
jueves **20**–12
juez **144**–6
jugador **235**–5
jugar a los naipes **239**–H
jugar con él **36**–M
jugo de manzana **73**–32
juguetería **132**–5
juguetes y juegos **59**
juicio justo **142**–5
julio **21**–31
junio **21**–30
Júpiter **215**–5
jurado **144**–8

kétchup **79**–21
kiwis **68**–22
koala **223**–45
labio **106**–5
laboratorio **123**
laboratorio de ciencias **207**
laboratorio de computadoras **5**–15
laca **108**–12
lado **205**–44
ladrillos **196**–12
lagartija **219**–43
lago **214**–13
laguna **214**–21
lámpara **55**–18, **58**–25
lámpara de mano **150**–14
lámpara de pie **56**–15
lana **98**–3
langosta **71**–10
lanzar **236**–A
lápiz **7**–20
lápiz de cejas **109**–34
lápiz de labios **109**–38
lastimado(a) **42**–16
lata de frijoles **74**–15
latas **74**–3
lavadora **50**–12, **101**–3
lavamanos **57**–25
lavamanos se desborda **63**–18
lavandería **130**–1
lavaplatos **54**–8, **83**–14, **193**–2
LAVAR LA ROPA **101**
lavar la ropa en agua fría **225**–K
lavar las ventanas **60**–I
lavar los platos **60**–M
lavarse…el cabello **108**–E
lea la definición **8**–B
lea la tarjeta **137**–G
leche **66**–5
leche baja en grasa **81**–42
lechera **55**–15
lecho de flores **53**–20
lechuga **69**–1
lechuza **220**–6
lectura de la factura telefónica **15**
leer el periódico **39**–V
leerle **36**–N
leggings **90**–12
lejía **101**–7
lengua **106**–8
lenguado **218**–15
lentejuelas **99**–33
lentes de contacto **117**–8
león **223**–36
león marino **219**–35
leopardo **223**–34
letrero **131**–26
levantamiento de pesas **234**–16
levantarse **38**–B
levante la mano **6**–A
levante los libros **11**–E
libertad de expresión **142**–2
libertad de prensa **142**–4
libertad de religión **142**–3
libra de rosbif **75**–12

librería **132**–4
librería de libros usados **131**–20
librero **7**–10
libreta **7**–28
libreta de citas **189**–48
libreta de espiral **7**–30
libro de dibujos **135**–12
libro de estampillas **136**–18
libro de pintar **59**–13
libro de texto **7**–26
libro delgado **23**–8
libro digital **135**–18
libro grueso **23**–7
libro hablado **135**–17
licencia de conducir **40**–4
licencia de manejar **138**–9
licencia de matrimonio **41**–8
licencia del taxi **156**–22
licuadora **54**–12
lienzo **239**–17
liga elástica **189**–34
lijadora eléctrica **194**–11
lima **109**–32
limas **68**–8
límite de velocidad **158**–4
limonada **84**–3
limones **68**–7
limones verdes **68**–8
limpiador **188**–3
limpiador de hornos **61**–3
limpiador de vidrios **61**–14
limpiador multiuso **61**–18
limpiadora **172**–34, **192**–20
limpiaparabrisas **162**–2
limpiar **76**–A
limpiar el filtro de pelusas **101**–D
limpiar el horno **60**–C
limpiar el piso **60**–D
limpiar el tope **60**–O
limpiar la casa **39**–O
limpiar la encimera **60**–O
limpiarse **109**–Q
limpie los escombros **151**–M
limpie su escritorio **10**–I
LIMPIEZA COMUNITARIA **152**–**153**
limusina **160**–11
línea curva **205**–23
línea de ensamblaje **185**–6
línea de montaje **185**–6
línea de teléfono **14**–1
línea recta **205**–22
líneas **205**
líneas paralelas **205**–25
líneas perpendiculares **205**–24
linterna **150**–14, **232**–22
linterna hecha de calabaza **245**–10
líquido corrector **189**–36
líquido lavaplatos **61**–21
líquidos inflamables **197**–8
lirio **217**–16, **217**–26
lista de compra **67**–14
lista de contactos **14**–15
litera **59**–9
llama **223**–25

llamada de larga distancia **15**–34
llamada internacional **15**–35
llamada local **15**–33
llamada perdida **14**–16
llamada telefónica por
　Internet **14**–19
llamar para avisar que uno
　está enfermo **198**–A
llamar por teléfono **15**
llame a sus contactos fuera
　del estado **151**–L
llame al administrador **48**–A
llana de albañil **196**–13
llano **214**–19
llanta **162**–5
llanta de repuesto **162**–23
llanura **214**–19
llave **51**–31, **57**–8
llave ajustable **195**–48
llave corrediza **195**–47
llave de tuerca **162**–22
llave gotea **63**–17
llave inglesa para tubos **195**–47
llave USB **190**–25
llega **164**–K
llegar a la casa **39**–R
llenar la lavadora **101**–C
llenar una solicitud **169**–J
llene el espacio en blanco **9**–O
llene el tanque con gasolina **161**–G
llevar a cabo una investigación **212**
llevar a los niños al colegio **38**–G
llevar la bandeja **82**–H
lleve el automóvil a un
　mecánico **161**–C
lleve los libros **11**–F
lleve su currículum y su
　identificación **179**–D
lleve un registro de las
　fuentes **212**–H
llorar **226**–B
lluvia **13**–11
lluvia ácida **224**–13
lobo **222**–5
loción para bebé **37**–13
loción para después de
　afeitarse **109**–30
logística **184**–8
lombriz **218**–24
longitud **17**–17
losa **57**–12
losa está rota **62**–4
losas **196**–11
luces de peligro **163**–36
luces navideñas **245**–18
lucha **234**–17
luego de una emergencia **151**
lugar de encuentro **150**–1
lugar de nacimiento **4**–15
LUGAR DE TRABAJO **182–183**
lugar para estacionar **130**–5
LUGARES A DONDE IR **228–229**
LUGARES DIFERENTES PARA VIVIR **52**
luna llena **215**–12

luna nueva **215**–9
lunar **32**–16
lunes **20**–9
luz de freno **162**–14
luz de la calle **152**–3
luz de noche **37**–28
luz de trabajo **195**–44
luz del porche **53**–13
luz delantera **162**–7
luz direccional **162**–6
luz trasera **162**–13
madera **196**–17
madera de 2 x 4
　(dos por cuatro) **195**–19
madera terciada **196**–18
madero **196**–17
madrastra **35**–26
madre **34**–3
madre soltera **35**–22
maestra **6**–4
maestro **5**–8
magnolia **216**–8
maíz **69**–12, **187**–4
MAL DÍA EN EL TRABAJO **198–199**
malas noticias **23**–17
maletera **162**–11
maletero **164**–1
maletín **88**–13
malla para el cabello **93**–25
mallas **90**–12
malteada **79**–14
mamadera **37**–2
MAMÍFEROS **222–223**
mamíferos marinos **219**
mañana **18**–15, **20**–6
mandarinas **68**–9
mandil **92**–11
mandil de cintura **93**–30
mandril **223**–31
manejar en estado de
　embriaguez **145**–5
maneras de recuperarse **116**
maneras de servir las carnes de res y
　de ave **76**
maneras de servir los huevos **76**
maneras para mantenerse sano **116**
manga **100**–6
mangos **68**–21
manguera **53**–21
maní **112**
manicurista **172**–38
maniobra de Heimlich **119**–19
maniquí de la costurera **100**–2
mano **105**–15
mano grande **23**–2
mano pequeña **23**–1
manta **58**–15, **231**–11
mantas **150**–7
mantel **55**–12
mantel individual **55**–11
manténgase alejado de las
　ventanas **151**–I
manténgase en buena condición
　física **116**–E

mantenimiento **192**–23
mantenimiento de
　instalaciones **184**–12
mantequilla **66**–6
manual de primeros auxilios **119**–2
manual del DMV **138**–1
manzanas **68**–1
mapa **7**–12
mapa del tiempo **13**
mapa Internet **159**–12
mapache **222**–13
mapas **159**
maquillaje **109**
máquina de coser **98**–13
máquina de fax **189**–21
máquina expendedora **156**–9
máquina franqueadora **137**–8
máquina franqueadora **189**–27
maravilla **217**–13
marbete de registro **138**–13
marcador **235**–1
marcador borrable en seco **7**–17
marcador de autopista **158**–17
marcador de tiempo **182**–7
marcador indeleble **7**–24
marco de foto **58**–4
marco de la cama **58**–18
maremoto **149**–17
margarina **72**–20
margarita **217**–14
Marina **141**–30
marina **141**–31
marinera **141**–31
mariposa **220**–20
mariposa nocturna **220**–22
mariquita **220**–27
MARISCOS Y COMESTIBLES
　PREPARADOS **71**
marmota de las praderas **221**–22
marque 911 **15**–E
marque como favorito
　un sitio **212**–G
marque el número de teléfono **15**–A
marque las casillas correctas **9**–U
marrón **24**–17
marsopa **219**–32
Marte **215**–4
martes **20**–10
martillar **196**–D
martillo **194**–1
martillo perforador **196**–9
marzo **21**–27
máscara **245**–9
máscara de cirugía **93**–36
máscara de esquí **90**–15
máscara de oxígeno **165**–24
máscara de ventilación **92**–7
máscara facial **93**–32
mascarilla **197**–14
mascotas **221**
masculino **4**–17
matasellos **136**–24
matemáticas **201**–10
MATEMÁTICAS **204–205**

material inapropiado **147**–3
materiales radioactivos **197**–7
mayo **21**–29
mayonesa **79**–23
mazo **194**–2, **196**–23
mecánico de automóviles **170**–8
mecanografiar **176**–R
mecanografiar una carta **177**–A
mecanografíe **210**–C
mecerlo **36**–D
media enagua **91**–22
media hermana **35**–27
media luna **215**–10
Media Mail® (el correo de otros
　medios de información) **136**–3
media taza de pasas **75**–9
mediana edad **32**–2
mediano **96**–3
medianoche **18**–21
medias **86**–6
medias de malla **91**–16
medias de malla hasta los
　talones **91**–17
medias panti **91**–18
médica externa a la red **121**–10
medicamento **123**–20
medicamento prescrito **114**–3
medicamento sin receta **115**–18
medicamentos sin receta **115**
medición del área y el volumen **205**
médico **111**–5
médico de la red **121**–9
MEDIDAS **17**
medidas **17**
medidas de seguridad **147**
medidas para líquidos **75**
medidas secas **75**
medidor de aceite **163**–29
medidor de gas **62**–14
medidor de gasolina **163**–31
medidor de presión
　sanguínea **111**–9
medidor de temperatura **163**–30
medio **17**–2
medio dólar **26**–5
medio hermano **35**–28
mediodía **18**–16
medusa **218**–14
mejilla **106**–3
mejillón **218**–18
mejillones **71**–13
melena **223**–49
mellizas **28**–1
melocotones **68**–10
melones **68**–19
membrana de la célula **206**–6
memoria *flash* **190**–25
memoria RAM (memoria de acceso
　aleatorio) **190**–17
mensaje de texto **14**–18
mensaje de voz **14**–17
mensajero **172**–40
menú **82**–7
MENÚ DE UN CAFÉ **80–81**

menú desplegable **213**–15
mercadeo **184**–6
MERCADO DE AGRICULTORES **84–85**
mercado de pulgas **228**–6
Mercurio **215**–1
meriendas **73**
mes **20**–3
mesa de billar **50**–15
mesa de cama **123**–21
mesa de centro **56**–19
mesa de examen **111**–7
mesa del comedor **55**–9
mesa para cambiar pañales **59**–1
mesa para comidas
    campestres **230**–8
mesa plegable **102**–4
mesa quirúrgica **123**–40
mesera **83**–9, **193**–8
mesero **82**–8
meses del año **21**
mesita **165**–21
mesita auxiliar **56**–14
mesita de noche **58**–23
metro subterráneo **155**–12
mezcle los ingredientes **77**–R
mezquita **128**–5
micrófono **191**–36, **240**–16
microprocesador **190**–16
microscopio **206**
mida **17**–C
mida los ingredientes **75**–A
miércoles **20**–11
mil **16**
mil millones **16**
milésimo **16**
milicianos **208**–10
millón **16**
minifalda **96**–15
minipersianas **58**–8
ministro de Defensa **141**–24
miniván **160**–8
minutos **18**–2
mirar **102**–B
mire los anuncios de
    automóviles **161**–A
mirilla **51**–33
mismo color **23**–15
misterio **243**–20
mitones **90**–10
mocasines **95**–30
mochila **94**–18, **232**–15
modelo **99**–22, **172**–41
módem **191**–34
modernas **209**–2
módulo de información **132**–12
mofeta **222**–12
molde para pastel **78**–28
molde para torta **78**–26
molde refractario **78**–10
molécula **207**–27
molinete **156**–8
mollete **79**–16
moluscos y crustáceos **71**, **112**
monarca **209**–4

mondongo **70**–8
moneda de un dólar **26**–6
monedas **26**
monedero **94**–14
monitor **190**–8
monitor de signos vitales **123**–26
monitor para bebés **59**–7
monitores de salidas y
    llegadas **165**–7
mono **93**–24, **223**–26
mono de trabajo **92**–8
monopatín **230**–7
monopatinaje **234**–13
montar **185**–C
montar en trineo **233**–6
morado **24**–6, **110**–11
moras **68**–17
moreno **24**–18
moretón **110**–11
morir **41**–R
morsa **219**–34
mosca **220**–29
mosquito **220**–23
mostaza **79**–22
mostrador **54**–22
motel **128**–12
motocicleta **154**–4
motor **162**–18
motor de búsqueda **212**–2
moverse por la pantalla **211**
móvil **59**–5
movimiento político **209**–16
mozo de campo **187**–20
mudanza **49**
múdese al apartamento **48**–F
mueblería **128**–8
muebles del patio **53**–19
muebles y accesorios **59**
muelle **231**–18
muelle de carga **185**–15
muestras **84**–5
muestre su identificación **139**–C
muestre su tarjeta de embarque y
    su identificación **164**–C
mujer **30**–2
mujeres **30**–3
muletas **115**–10
multiplicar **204**–C
muñeca **59**–21, **106**–14
muñecas **239**–28
muñeco de acción **239**–26
murciélago **222**–7
músculo **107**–32
museo de arte **229**–9
MÚSICA **244**
música **64**–3, **201**–16
música en vivo **84**–1
música internacional **243**–32
músico **172**–43
muslo **106**–19
muslos **70**–23
muy frío **13**–7
nabos **69**–16
nacer **40**–A

nachos **79**–7
nadar **236**–L
nalgas **107**–30
naranjas **68**–5
narciso atrompetado **217**–25
nariz **104**–6
Navidad **22**–18
neblinoso **13**–21
negocie un precio **161**–D
negro **24**–13
Neptuno **215**–8
nervioso(a) **42**–10
neumático **162**–5
neumático de repuesto **162**–23
neutrón **207**–32
nevera **54**–9
nevera de playa **231**–9
nido **220**–5
nieve **13**–12
nilón **99**–12
niña de 10 años **31**–10
niña pequeña **31**–8
niñera **170**–9
niñez y las enfermedades
    infecciosas **112**
niño **31**–7
niño de 6 años **31**–9
niño perdido **148**–1
niños ruidosos **23**–11
niños tranquilos **23**–12
nivel **194**–29
no abra la puerta a extraños **146**–F
no beba alcohol **114**–F
no entrar **158**–2
no estacionarse **158**–11
no fume **116**–G
no hay electricidad **62**–2
no imprime **191**–E
no llegue tarde **179**–E
no lo tome con productos
    lácteos **114**–D
no maneje en estado de
    embriaguez **146**–G
no maneje ni opere maquinaria
    pesada **114**–E
no poder respirar **118**–N
no se permite girar a la
    izquierda **158**–8
no tirar basura **225**–L
noche **18**–20
nombre **4**–1
nonagésimo **16**
normas **64**–7
norte **159**–1
nostálgico(a) **43**–20
nota al pie de la página **202**–12
novela **135**–16
noveno **16**
noventa **16**
noviembre **21**–35
nublado **13**–10
núcleo **206**–7, **207**–29
nudillo **106**–17

nueve **16**
numerador **204**–5
número de acceso **15**–24
número de apartamento **4**–6
número de cuenta corriente **134**–15
número de cuenta de ahorro **134**–16
número de la receta **114**–5
número de licencia de
    conductor **138**–11
número de teléfono **4**–11, **15**–29
número del Seguro Social **4**–19
número SKU **27**–5
NÚMEROS **16**
números adicionales **4**
números cardinales **16**
números enteros **204**
números enteros negativos **204**–1
números enteros positivos **204**–2
números impares **204**–3
números ordinales **16**
números pares **204**–4
números romanos **16**
nutria marina **219**–37
obedecer las leyes **142**–C
obeso(a) **32**–7
objetivo **206**–16
objetos valiosos **134**–8
oboe **244**–3
obra **128**–2
obra teatral **229**–8
obrero **185**–3
obrero de construcción **196**–1
observatorio **215**–21
observe **207**–C
obstetra **122**–2
obtener cambio **26**–A
obtener una tarjeta para uso de
    la biblioteca **135**–A
obtenga atención médica **116**–A
obtenga buenas notas **10**–H
obtenga el título del
    vendedor **161**–E
obtenga su licencia **139**–I
obtenga un permiso de
    aprendiz **139**–F
obtenga un préstamo **49**–J
obteniendo su primera licencia **139**
océano **214**–6, **231**–1
ochenta **16**
ocho **16**
octavo **16**, **17**–5
octogésimo **16**
octubre **21**–34
ocular **206**–14
odómetro **163**–28
odontología **120**
oeste **159**–2
oficial **141**–27, **235**–6
oficial de policía **144**–1, **172**–48
oficina **182**–3
oficina de alquiler **51**
oficina de correos **127**–11
OFICINA DE CORREOS **136–137**
oficina principal **5**–12

oficinas corporativas **184**–1
ofrezca algo **12**–E
oftalmólogo **122**–7
oír **106**–B
ojo **105**–11, **106**
ojo mágico **51**–33
ola **231**–17
ola de calor **13**–15
oler **106**–C
olla **54**–16, **78**–6, **78**–25
olla a vapor **78**–3
olmo **216**–16
ómnibus escolar **160**–21
omóplato **107**–28
once **16**
oncóloga **122**–5
onza de queso **75**–11
onza líquida de leche **75**–1
ópera **229**–11
operaciones matemáticas **204**
operador **14**–20
operador de maquinaria **172**–37
operadora de la máquina de
    coser **98**–14
operadora de maquinaria **172**–37
operar maquinaria pesada **176**–H
opinión **44**–3
oponente **143**–8
oprima "hablar" **15**–B
óptica **132**–9
optómetra **117**–6
optometrista **117**–6
oración **202**–2
orador invitado **226**–4
orangután **223**–39
ordeñar **187**–C
oreja **105**–12
oreja perforada **32**–17
orejeras **90**–13, **197**–16
organice las ideas **203**–G
organismos **206**–1
organizador **189**–49
organizar materiales **177**–L
órgano **244**–20
orgulloso(a) **43**–21
orilla **214**–12
ornitorrinco **223**–46
orquídea **217**–19
ortodoncia **120**
ortodoncista **120**–5
oruga **220**–21
osito de peluche **37**–24
oso **222**–11
oso hormiguero **223**–24
ostras **71**–14
otomana **56**–23
otoño **21**–39
otros instrumentos **244**
otros productos **72**
oveja **221**–6
overol **88**–6, **92**–8
p. m. **18**–5
paciente **111**–6, **123**–18, **178**–1
padecimientos **113**

padrastro **35**–25
padre **34**–4
padre soltero **35**–23
pagar **27**–G
pagar el dinero prestado **26**–D
pagar en efectivo **27**–A
pagar impuestos **142**–B
pagar la cuenta **82**–I
pagar una multa **135**–E
pagar una reclamación **121**–B
página web **213**–12
pague el alquiler del primer y del
    último mes **48**–E
pague la renta del primer y del
    último mes **48**–E
pague los costos de solicitud **139**–D
paisaje **166**–4
PAISAJISMO Y JARDINERÍA **186**
pájaro carpintero **220**–9
PÁJAROS, INSECTOS Y
    ARÁCNIDOS **220**
pala **61**–17, **186**–7, **196**–22
palabra **202**–1
palabras clave **212**–4
palacio municipal **127**–8
palanca de cambio de
    velocidad **163**–47
palanca de luz direccional **163**–34
palanca de velocidades **163**–50
paleta **185**–13
palma **106**–15, **216**–14
palo de golf **237**–1
palo de *hockey* **237**–11
paloma **220**–16
paltas **84**–6
paludismo **113**–22
pan **67**–11
pan blanco **71**–18
pan con ajo **81**–28
pan de centeno **71**–20
pan de trigo **71**–19
pana **99**–11
panadera **170**–10
panadería **129**–19
panadero **170**–10
pañal de tela **37**–8
pañal desechable **37**–10
pañalera **37**–11
páncreas **107**–45
panda **223**–41
pandereta **244**–17
pandero **244**–17
pandillismo **145**–4
panecillos **80**–6, **80**–17
panel táctil **190**–24
paño de calentamiento **115**–13
panqueques **80**–7
pantaletas **91**–14
pantalla **6**–2, **241**–28
pantalla de la lámpara **58**–26
pantalla de protección **56**–12
pantalla se congeló **191**–B
pantalla táctil **163**–37
pantalón capri **88**–8

pantalones **87**–12
pantalones apretados **97**–29
pantalones ceñidos **97**–29
pantalones cortos **89**–25
pantalones de ejercicio **89**–23
pantalones de seguridad **93**–22
pantalones de trabajo **92**–5
pantalones flojos **97**–30
pantalones holgados **97**–30
pantalones *jeans* **86**–2, **92**–19
pantera **223**–40
pantimedias **91**–18
pantorrilla **106**–22
pantuflas **91**–25
pañuelo de cabeza **90**–7, **92**–16
papa al horno **81**–25
papa asada **81**–25
papas **69**–17
papas fritas **79**–2
papas fritas de bolsa **73**–35
papayas **68**–20
papel de aluminio **72**–23
papel de construcción **238**–13
papel de escribir **189**–42
papel de lija **195**–56
papel de notas adhesivo **189**–39
papel higiénico **57**–19, **150**–13
papel membreteado **189**–42
papel para libreta **7**–29
papel tapiz **59**–8
papelera **57**–26, **143**–9
paperas **112**–7
papitas doradas **80**–3
paquete **136**–17
paquete de galletas dulces **74**–20
paquete de seis bebidas
    gaseosas **74**–21
paquetes **74**–8
paquetes de seis **74**–9
par de tijeras **100**–16
parabrisas **162**–1
parachoques **162**–8
parada de autobús **131**–16,
    155–13, **156**
parada de taxis **156**–18
paraguas **90**–17
paralelogramo **205**–33
paramédico **118**–2
pararse **158**–1
parásitos intestinales **113**–25
pared **56**–19
pared celular **206**–5
pared de yeso **196**–19
pareja **245**–4
pareja casada **35**–20
pareja divorciada **35**–21
paréntesis **202**–22
parientes **44**–6
parka **90**–9
parlantes **240**–14
párpado **106**–10
parque **50**–3
parque de atracciones **229**–10
PARQUE Y EL PATIO DE RECREO **230**

parquímetro **131**–25
párrafo **202**–3
parrilla **53**–17, **54**–21
parrilla al aire libre **230**–16
parrilla para asar **78**–14
parte inferior de la espalda **107**–29
PARTES DE UN AUTOMÓVIL **162**–**163**
partes de un ensayo **202**
partes de una flor **217**
partes de una máquina de coser **98**
PARTICIPACIÓN
    CIUDADANA **142**–**143**
participar en juegos **238**–B
participe en la clase **10**–B
partida de nacimiento **40**–1
pasadores **108**–21
pasaje **156**–2
pasaje electrónico **165**–19
pasajero **154**–2, **156**–3, **165**–15
pasantía **175**–11
pasaporte **41**–10
pasar **236**–G
pasas **68**–25
PASATIEMPOS Y JUEGOS **238**–**239**
pase **159**–E
pase por el área de seguridad **164**–D
pase una prueba **10**–E
pase una prueba de manejo **139**–H
pasear el perro **131**–F
paseo a caballo **232**–9
paseo en balsa **232**–2
paseo en bote **232**–1
pasillo **5**–10, **51**, **72**–7, **192**–18
pasta **67**–12
pasta de dientes **109**–23
pastel **81**–35
pastillas para el resfriado **115**–27
pastillas para la garganta **115**–30
pastrami **71**–23
pata de cordero **70**–14
patas **70**–21
patear **236**–E
patillas **33**–7
patinaje artístico de figuras **233**–5
patinaje sobre hielo **233**–4
patinaje sobre ruedas **234**–10
patinar **236**–C
patines de hielo **237**–9
patines de rueda **237**–10
patio **46**–1, **51**–21, **53**–16
patio interior **5**–1
pato **70**–18, **220**–13
patrón **99**–22
patrones **96**
pausar **241**–E
pavo **70**–17, **245**–14
pavo ahumado **71**–25
pavo al horno **76**–4
pavo real **220**–15
peatona **130**–14
pecho **104**–4, **107**–25
pechugas **70**–19
pedal de freno **163**–45
pedal de gasolina **163**–46

pediatra **122**–4
pedir del menú **82**–D
pedir prestado dinero **26**–B
pedir un deseo **246**–B
pega **189**–33
pegamento **238**–11
pegar **236**–B
pegatina **102**–3
pegue el texto **210**–L
peinarse…el cabello **108**–G
peine **33**–19, **108**–13
peineta **108**–15
peinilla **33**–19, **108**–13
pelador de verduras y
    hortalizas **78**–15
pelaje **222**–19
peldaños **53**–3
pele las zanahorias **77**–K
peligro eléctrico **198**–6
peligros de seguridad y materiales
    peligrosos **197**
peligroso **198**–1
pelirrojo(a) **33**–13
pelo **104**–2
pelota de béisbol **237**–18
peluquera **171**–31
peluquería **133**–18
pelvis **107**–50
península **214**–7
pensar de manera crítica **178**–B
Pentágono **141**–23
peón de labranza **187**–20
pepinillo en vinagre **80**–11
pepinos **69**–10
pequeño **96**–2
peras **68**–4
percha **101**–11, **218**–6
pérdida de la audición **117**–2
perejil **69**–28
perfume **108**–6
perilla de la puerta **53**–12
perímetro **205**–43
periódico **135**–6
período colonial **208**
período de facturación **15**–30
periquito **221**–15
permanezca en calles bien
    iluminadas **146**–B
permanezca en la línea **15**–H
permanezca tranquilo **151**–E
perno **194**–35
peróxido de hidrógeno **119**–10
perrito **221**–12
perro **221**–11
perro caliente **79**–6
persona de negocios **170**–12
persona que empaca la
    compra **73**–15
persona que realiza ventas por
    teléfono **173**–60
personal **180**–2
personal de enfermería **122**
personal de jardinería **186**–1
personal del hospital **122**

pesado(a) **32**–7
pesas **237**–22
pesca **232**–4
pescado **66**–1, **71**
pescado a la parrilla **81**–29
pescado congelado **71**–17
pescado fresco **71**–16
pescador comercial **171**–17
pese la comida **75**–B
peso **32**, **75**
peso promedio **32**–8
PESOS Y MEDIDAS **75**
pestaña **213**–14
pestañas **106**–11
pétalos **217**–8
petición **152**–5
petirrojo **220**–17
petróleo **224**–6
pez espada **71**–5, **218**–10
pezuñas **222**–17
pi **205**–46
piano **244**–14
picadura de insecto **110**–10
picaduras **120**–8
picaflor **220**–11
pickup **160**–12
pico **220**–3
pico de la montaña **214**–14
pida ayuda **10**–F
pie **104**–8
pie prensatelas **98**–19
piel **107**–31, **222**–19
piense sobre la tarea **203**–E
pierna **105**–9
pierna y el pie **106**
piezas **185**–5
pijama **91**–23
pila de abono **53**–25
pilas **150**–15
píldora **115**–21
piloto **165**–11
pimentones **69**–7
pimientos **69**–7
pimpollo **217**–4
piña **216**–11
piñas **68**–23
pincel **239**–20
pingüino **220**–12
pino **216**–9
pinta de yogur congelado **75**–3
pintar **196**–A, **239**–E
pintarse…las uñas **109**–O
pinte **49**–P
pintor (de casas) **172**–46
pintura **195**–25
pintura de acrílico **238**–10
pintura de óleo **239**–19
pintura de uñas **109**–33
pinza para colgar la ropa **101**–10
pinza para el cabello **108**–19
pinzas **78**–23, **119**–5, **206**–21
piragüismo **232**–3
pirámide **205**–39
piratería informática **147**–5

piscina **51**–22, **192**–22
piso **46**–7
piso de madera **58**–21
piso resbaloso **197**–6
pista **5**–21
pista de boliche **228**–4
pistola **145**–13
pistola de pegamento **238**–12
pistola rociadora **195**–21
piyama **91**–23
pizarra **6**–3
pizarra para rotuladores **6**–1
pizza **79**–10
placa **138**–12, **162**–12
placa de la aguja **98**–18
plancha **101**–13
planchar la ropa **101**–G
planes de seguro **121**–2
PLANIFICACIÓN DE
    CARRERAS **174**–**175**
planificación y el establecimiento
    de objetivos **174**
planifique para una
    emergencia **150**–A
planta **198**–4
planta de interiores **217**–27
planta interior **56**–4
plantar un árbol **186**–E, **225**–N
plántula **217**–4
plástico para envolver **72**–24
plataforma **156**–7
plátano maduro **68**–30
plátano pasado **68**–32
plátano podrido **68**–32
plátano verde **68**–31
plátanos **68**–2
platillo **83**–25
platina **206**–17
platito **83**–25
plato **55**–1, **83**–18
plato grande **55**–20
plato hondo **55**–2
plato hondo de servir **55**–21
plato para el pan y la
    mantequilla **83**–19
plato para ensalada **83**–20
platón **55**–20
playa **214**–10
PLAYA **231**
plomero **63**–20
pluma **7**–22, **220**–4
plumero **61**–1
podar los setos **186**–B
podio **226**–5
policía **144**–1
polilla **220**–22
póliza de seguro **121**–4
pollo **66**–3, **70**–16
pollo asado **81**–22
pollo frito **76**–1
polo acuático **235**–16
polución **224**
polvo facial **109**–41
pomada **115**–24

poncho **90**–19
poner en espera al que llama **177**–N
poner la mesa **82**–A
ponerse **109**–P
ponerse protector solar **108**–D
ponérselo **87**–B
ponga las oraciones en orden **9**–X
ponga su teléfono celular en
    modo avión **164**–I
póngale la estampilla **137**–C
póngale refrigerante **161**–I
póngase de pie **6**–D
pop **243**–25
porcentajes **17**
porche frontal **53**
portacepillos **57**–24
portaobjetos **206**–3
portavelas **56**–21
portero **192**–1
posible inquilino **51**–29
positiva **178**–2
postal **136**–16
postularse para un cargo **143**–J
prácticas **175**–11
pradera **214**–20
prado **214**–20
precaliente el horno **77**–A
precio **27**–7
precio de oferta **27**–3
precio normal **27**–2
pregunte: "¿Cómo está usted?" **2**–B
pregúntele al vendedor sobre el
    automóvil **161**–B
pregúntele sobre las
    características **48**–B
prendedor **95**–38
prendedores de seguridad **37**–9
prensa de tornillo **194**–26
prensa para ajo **78**–11
preocupado(a) **42**–13
PREPARACIÓN Y SEGURIDAD DE
    LOS ALIMENTOS **76**–**77**
preparador de comidas **193**–4
preparar el almuerzo **38**–F
preparar la cena **39**–Q
prepare un equipo de suministros en
    caso de desastres **150**–B
prepárese para la entrevista **179**–A
PREPOSICIONES **25**
PREPOSICIONES DE
    MOVIMIENTO **157**
prescripción **114**–2
presentación **188**–6
presentar una solicitud **169**–L
presente **246**–3
presente a un amigo **3**–J
presente su composición **203**–M
presente una solicitud **48**–C
preséntese **2**–D
presidente **140**–8, **209**–5
presidente de la Corte
    Suprema **140**–13
presilla **99**–26
presión arterial alta **113**–24

preso **144**–15
prestaciones **121**–3
prestar dinero **26**–C
preste atención a las
    advertencias **151**–D
presupuesto **198**–3
pretina **100**–5
prima **34**–9, **121**–7
primavera **21**–37
primer congreso continental **208**–6
PRIMER DÍA DE TRABAJO **180–181**
primer ministro **209**–7
primer nombre **4**–2
primer presidente **208**–11
primero **16**
PRIMEROS AUXILIOS **119**
primeros auxilios **119**
primo **34**–9
Priority Mail® (el correo
    prioritario) **136**–1
prisma **207**–35
probarse zapatos **95**–C
problema difícil **23**–25
problema expresado con
    palabras **204**–11
problema fácil **23**–23
problema matemático **204**
problemas con la ropa **97**
problemas de visión **117**–1
problemas dentales **120**
PROBLEMAS Y REPARACIONES
    DOMÉSTICAS **62–63**
PROCEDIMIENTOS DE
    EMERGENCIA **150–151**
procedimientos de primeros
    auxilios **119**
procedimientos médicos **111**
procesador de alimentos **54**–26
procesador de textos **191**–29
proceso de escritura **203**
producto **204**–9
productos de pastelería **73**
productos lácteos **72**
productos orgánicos **84**–2
productos para pastelerías **73**
profesor **5**–8
profesora **6**–4
profundidad **17**–18
programa de hojas de
    cálculo **191**–30
programa de presentaciones **191**–31
programar computadoras **176**–I
programar una reunión **177**–J
programas de entrevistas **242**–4
programas de juegos **242**–8
programas de noticias **242**–1
programas de preguntas **242**–8
programas de telerrealidad **242**–6
programas de ventas por
    televisión **242**–10
programas deportivos **242**–11
programas dramáticos **242**–12
programas para niños **242**–9
progrese **10**–G

protector **59**–4
protector de sobretensión **190**–11
protector solar **108**–7, **231**–10
proteja el bolso o la billetera **146**–D
proteja el bolso o la cartera **146**–D
protón **207**–31
proyector LCD **6**–5, **241**–27
prueba **202**–7
prueba de seguro **138**–8
prueba en línea **10**–5
pruebas **144**–9
púa **222**–23
publicaciones periódicas **135**–4
pueblo pequeño **52**–3
puerco **221**–2
puerco espín **222**–10
puerta **46**–4, **53**–9, **165**, **165**–8
puerta de seguridad **50**–16
puerta de vidrio deslizante **53**–18
puerta del garaje **53**–7
puerta giratoria **192**–2
puerta mosquitero **53**–15
puerta principal **53**–11
puerto USB **190**–20
puesta del sol **18**–18
puesto de periódicos **130**–12
pulgada [in] **17**–15
pulgar **106**–16
pulgas **63**–25
pulir los muebles **60**–E
pulmón **107**–39
pulmonía **112**–10
pulóver **88**–3
pulpo **218**–9
pulsera de emergencia
    médica **119**–3
puma **222**–2
punta **94**–23
puntaje **10**–3
punto **202**–14
punto de inspección de
    seguridad **164**
punto extremo **205**–21
punto o la coma decimal **17**–7
punto y coma **202**–21
puntos **119**–16
puntuación **202**
puré de papas **81**–23
purificador de aire **115**–14
quedarse con **28**–B
quedarse sin gasolina **166**–E
QUEHACERES DOMÉSTICOS **60**
quejarse **180**–B
quemador Bunsen **207**–37
quemadura de sol **110**–13
quemar(se) **118**–H
quemarse por el frío **118**–G
queso **66**–4
queso americano **71**–26
queso cheddar **71**–28
queso mozzarella **71**–29
queso suizo **71**–27
quijada **106**–4
química **207**

químico **207**–25
quince **16**
quincuagésimo **16**
quinto **16**
quiosco **124**–3, **133**–22
quiosco para registrarse **164**–2
quirófano **123**
quitar la maleza de las flores **186**–G
quitarse **109**–Q
R&B **243**–28
rábanos **69**–4
racimo de plátanos **68**–29
radiación **224**–15
radiador **162**–19
radio **205**–35
radio bidireccional **197**–22
radio-reloj **102**–6
radiólogo **122**–6
raíces **217**–3
raíz **216**–5
rallador **78**–2
ralle el queso **77**–G
rama **216**–2
rama ejecutiva **140**
rama judicial **140**
rama legislativa **140**
rama secundaria **216**–3
ramas de las Fuerzas Armadas **141**
ramas de las matemáticas **204**
ramillete **217**–28
ramita **216**–1
ramo **217**–28
rana **218**–26
rancho **52**–10
raqueta de tenis **237**–2
ráquetbol **234**–12
rascacielos **129**–13
raspador **195**–52
rastrillar las hojas **186**–C
rastrillo **186**–8
rasuradora **109**–27
rasuradora eléctrica **109**–26
rata **221**–17
ratas **63**–27
ratón **190**–13, **221**–18
ratones **63**–28
raya **33**–4, **218**–11
reacciones alérgicas **113**
rebane el tofu **77**–C
rebobinar **241**–C
rebotar **236**–J
recamarera **172**–34, **192**–20
recepción **192**–12
recepcionista **111**–2, **173**–51, **182**–5,
    188–14, **192**–11
receptor **14**–4
receta **114**–2
rechace una invitación **12**–K
rechace una oferta **12**–F
reciba comentarios **203**–K
reciba la tarjeta **137**–F
recibir una boleta de
    infracción **166**–D
recibir una descarga eléctrica **118**–F

recibo **27**–6
reciclar **225**–C
reciclar los periódicos **60**–B
recipiente de desinfección **33**–16
recipiente de reciclaje **61**–2
recipiente para desechos
    médicos **123**–31
recipiente refractario **78**–10
reclame su equipaje **164**–L
recogedor **61**–17
recoger a los niños **38**–M
recoger los pantalones **100**–D
recoger los platos **82**–G
recoja los libros **11**–E
recortador **186**–12
RECREACIÓN AL AIRE LIBRE **232**
rectángulo **205**–29
recursos humanos **184**–4
red de pescar **232**–17
redacte el mensaje **211**–W
reducir la basura **225**–A
reemplace los
    limpiaparabrisas **161**–K
reescríbalo **203**–J
refresco **79**–11
refrigerador **54**–9
refrigerar **76**–D
refugio **52**–13
regalo **246**–3
regar las plantas **186**–F
regatear **102**–A, **236**–J
reggae **243**–31
registre el automóvil **161**–F
registre su equipaje **164**–B
regístrese electrónicamente **164**–A
regla **17**–13, **195**–16
reglamentos de seguridad **182**–6
reglas de escritura **202**
regrese a la clase **11**–M
reír **44**–A
reja de seguridad **50**–16
relacionarse con otros **168**–E
relámpagos **13**–14
relicario **95**–35
reloj **7**–9
reloj (de pulsera) **94**–16
reloj despertador **58**–24
reloj registrador **182**–7
remitente **136**–21
remolachas **69**–5
remolque **160**–17
reparador **62**–10
reparador de techos **62**–8
reparar electrodomésticos **176**–J
reparar los grifos con goteras **225**–F
repartidor **171**–21
repartir **180**–D
repelente de insectos **232**–23
repisa de la chimenea **56**–11
repollo chino **69**–15
reponedor **72**–5
reportera **173**–52
reportero **173**–52

representante de servicio al cliente **171**–20
reproducir **241**–B
reproductor de Blu-ray **240**–9
reproductor de casete y CD **102**–8
reproductor de DVD **240**–11
reproductor de video **213**–18
reproductor de video y MP3 **240**–2
reproductor personal de CD **240**–7
reptiles **219**
requisitos de ciudadanía **142**
resaltador **7**–25
resfrío **112**–1
resguarde su clave **146**–C
residencia universitaria **52**–8
residencia urbana **52**–6
resolver problemas **178**–A
resolver problemas matemáticos **176**–M
respiración de boca a boca **119**–17
responda **137**–H
responda un cuestionario de intereses **174**–C
responda: "Bien, gracias" **2**–C
responder bien a los comentarios **178**–H
responsabilidades **142**
restar **204**–B
restaurante **127**–14
RESTAURANTE **82–83**
restaurante de comida rápida **130**–10
RESTAURANTE DE COMIDA RÁPIDA **79**
resultados de la búsqueda **212**–5
resultados de las elecciones **143**–11
retire el efectivo **134**–E
retire la tarjeta **134**–F
retrasado **165**–30
retroexcavadora **196**–8
reúnase con un agente inmobiliario **49**–G
REUNIÓN DE LOS INQUILINOS **64–65**
REUNIÓN FAMILIAR **44–45**
reunión pacífica **142**–1
reunirse en apoyo a un candidato **143**–7
REUNIRSE Y SALUDAR **2–3**
revisar el correo electrónico **39**–W
revisar los mensajes **177**–R
revisar los sitios web de empleo **168**–H
revisarle…la presión sanguínea **111**–A
revise el aceite **161**–H
revise la ortografía **211**–X
revise los resultados **212**–E
revise los servicios básicos **151**–N
revise su trabajo **10**–L
revíselo **203**–J
revisor de seguridad **164**–5
revista **135**–5
revólver **206**–15
revuelva **77**–O

riel de seguridad **59**–10
riesgos de Internet para los niños **147**
rímel **109**–39
rinoceronte **223**–28
riñón **107**–43
río **159**–10, **214**–3
rizador **108**–17
rizadores **33**–18
róbalo **218**–6
roble **216**–17
robo **145**–2
roca **219**–38
rociador **53**–22
rock **243**–23
rodilla **106**–20
rodilleras **197**–19
rodillo **78**–30
rodillo de pintar **195**–23
roedores **221**
rojo **24**–1
rollo de carne **81**–31
rollo de tela **98**–15
rollo de toallas de papel **74**–23
rollos **74**–11
románticas **243**–16
rompa 2 huevos en un tazón para horno microonda **77**–Q
rompecabezas **59**–17
ropa casual **88**
ROPA CASUAL, DE TRABAJO Y FORMAL **88–89**
ropa de dormir **91**
ropa de la enfermera **93**–31
ROPA DE TEMPORADA **90**
ropa de trabajo **88**
ROPA DE TRABAJO **92–93**
ROPA DIARIA **86–87**
ropa formal **89**
ropa interior de hombre **91**
ropa interior de invierno **91**–3
ropa interior de mujer **91**
ropa interior unisex **91**
ROPA INTERIOR Y ROPA DE DORMIR **91**
ropa para hacer ejercicio **89**
ropa sucia **101**–1
ropa usada **102**–2
rosa **217**–15
rosado **24**–7
rosbif **71**–21
rosquilla **79**–15
rubor **109**–37
ruedo **100**–8
ruido **64**–5
ruta de autobús **156**–1
ruta de EE. UU. **158**–17
ruta de escape **150**–3
ruta de evacuación **150**–5
RUTINAS DIARIAS **38–39**
RV (vehículo recreacional) **160**–10
sábado **20**–14
sábana **58**–13
sábana esquinera **58**–12

saber la hora **18**
saborear **106**–D
sacapuntas **7**–23
sacapuntas eléctrico **189**–26
sacar la basura **60**–Q
sacar un diente **120**–F
sacar un libro en préstamo **135**–C
sacar una muela **120**–F
sacarle…sangre **111**–F
saco para dormir **232**–12
sacudir los muebles **60**–A
sala **47**–13
SALA **56**
sala de banquetes **193**–14
sala de conferencias **188**–4, **192**–25
sala de espera **111**
sala de examen **111**
sala de operaciones **123**
sala del tribunal **144**–7
salamandra **218**–28
salamandra acuática **218**–27
salami **71**–24
saldo **134**–18
salero y el pimentero **55**–13
salga del programa **210**–F
salga del salón **11**–O
salida de emergencia **51**–25, **165**–14
salida de incendios **50**–2
salida del sol **18**–14
salir de la autopista **157**–J
salir del trabajo **38**–N
salir en libertad **144**–H
salmón entero **71**–3
salón de bailes **192**–26
salón de clase **5**–7
SALÓN DE CLASE **6–7**
salón de uñas **132**–3
saltamontes **220**–25
saltar **236**–I
saltee las setas **77**–E
saltee los hongos **77**–E
salto de agua **214**–2
saludar al que llama **177**–M
salude a la gente **3**–H
salude al entrevistador **179**–H
salude con la mano **2**–G
salvavidas **231**–19
sandalias **88**–9
sandías **68**–18
sándwich de pollo **79**–5
sándwich de queso a la plancha **80**–10
sangrar **118**–M
sangrar la primera oración de un párrafo **202**–D
sanguíneo **123**–30
sapo **218**–29
saque una conclusión **207**–E
saque una hoja de papel **9**–Y
sarampión **112**–5
sarpullido **113**–14
sarro **120**–13
sartén **54**–24, **78**–5

sastre **100**–3
satélite **215**–19
Saturno **215**–6
sauce **216**–13
saxofón **244**–5
se está descosiendo **97**–43
se va **164**–J
sea puntual **179**–F
secador **33**–21
secador de cabello **108**–18
secador de vajilla **54**–5
secadora **50**–13, **101**–4
secaplatos **54**–5
secar los platos **60**–N
secarse…el cabello **108**–H
sección de verduras, hortalizas y frutas **72**–2
secoya **216**–18
secretario **144**–12
seda **98**–5
sede central **184**–1
segmento de línea **205**–20
seguir las instrucciones **9**
segundo **16**
segundos **18**–3
seguridad **184**–13
SEGURIDAD CIBERNÉTICA **147**
seguridad de los alimentos **76**
SEGURIDAD EN EL LUGAR DE TRABAJO **197**
SEGURIDAD PÚBLICA **146**
seguro de puerta **163**–25
SEGURO MÉDICO **121**
seis **16**
seleccionar y modificar texto **210**
seleccione un motor de búsqueda **212**–A
selector de control de temperatura **163**–38
sello **189**–47
selva tropical húmeda **214**–1
semáforo **130**–8
semana **20**–15
semana pasada **20**–18
semana próxima **20**–20
sembrar **187**–A
semilla **217**–1
Senado **140**–5
senador **140**–6
senador del estado **140**–19
señal débil **14**–12
señal fuerte **14**–11
SEÑALES DE TRÁFICO **158**
seno **107**–25
sentar al cliente **82**–B
sentenciar al acusado **144**–F
sentido contrario **158**–2
sentidos **106**
sentir dolor **42**–11
sentir náuseas **110**–B
sentirse asqueada **42**–7
sentirse mareado **110**–A
sentirse satisfecho(a) **42**–6
separar **76**–B

separar la ropa **101**–A
septiembre **21**–33
séptimo **16**
septuagésimo **16**
sequía **149**–11
ser contratado **169**–O
ser electo **143**–M
ser juzgado **144**–D
ser miembro de una banda
    de *rock* **244**–D
ser recluta **141**–A
ser veterano **141**–D
serpiente de cascabel **219**–45
serrucho **194**–4
servicio al cliente **184**–11
SERVICIO DE COMIDAS **193**
servicio de directorio **14**–21
servicio en la alberca **192**–21
servicio en la habitación **192**–17
servicio en la piscina **192**–21
servicio militar **141**
servicio para automovilistas **130**–11
servicios públicos **48**–5
servidor de comida **193**–15
servilleta **55**–10, **83**–26
servir **143**–N, **236**–P
servir el agua **82**–C
servir en un jurado **142**–E
servir la comida **82**–F
sesenta **16**
setas **69**–27
setenta **16**
sexagésimo **16**
sexo **4**–16
sexto **16**
SIDA **113**–21
siembras **187**
siéntese **6**–F
sierra **214**–15
sierra alternativa vertical **194**–10
sierra circular **194**–9
sierra de arco **194**–5
siete **16**
siga las instrucciones **151**–F
signo de admiración **202**–16
signo de interrogación **202**–15
silenciador **162**–16
silla **7**–11
silla alta **37**–6
silla alta **82**–3
silla blanda **23**–6
silla de playa **231**–22
silla de ruedas **115**–9
silla del comedor **55**–8
silla dura **23**–5
silla mecedora **37**–22
silla plegable **102**–5
sillón **56**–22
símbolo **159**–5
sin azúcar **124**–7
sinagoga **129**–16
SÍNTOMAS Y LAS LESIONES **110**
sintonizador **240**–13
siquiatra **122**–8

sistema estereofónico **56**–8
sistema inyector de
    combustible **162**–17
SISTEMA LEGAL **144**
sistema solar y los planetas **215**
sistema telefónico
    automatizado **14**–22
snowboard **233**–2
sobre **136**–14
sobre **189**–43
sobreexpuesta **241**–32
sobretodo **90**–2
sobrina **34**–18
sobrino **34**–19
sofá **56**–18
sofá para dos **56**–1
sófbol **235**–11
software **191**
soldado **141**–29
soldado **173**–58
soldador **173**–63
soleado **13**–9
solicitar un trabajo **169**–I
solicite ayuda **10**–F
sólido **96**–19
sólidos geométricos **205**
solo giro a la derecha **158**–7
solo sentido **158**–3
solo(a) **42**–17
solución **204**–14
sombra **109**–35, **231**–13
sombrero de paja **90**–23
sombrilla de playa **231**–14
somier tapizado **58**–19
sonaja **37**–27
sonajero **37**–27
sonría **2**–E
sopa **72**–18, **80**–16
sopa de pollo fácil **77**
soplador de hojas **186**–2
soplar las velas **246**–C
soporte atlético **91**–6
sorbeto **79**–18
sordo(a) **32**–12
sorprendido(a) **43**–30
sostén **91**–19
sostenerlo **36**–A
sótano **47**–14, **50**
soul **243**–28
suavizador **101**–6
suavizante **101**–6
subchef **193**–6
subexpuesta **241**–33
subirse al taxi **157**–E
subraye la palabra **9**–S
suburbios **52**–2
SUCESOS DE LA VIDA Y
    DOCUMENTOS **40**–**41**
sucursales **184**–2
sudadera **89**–22
suegra **34**–10
suegro **34**–11
suela **94**–21
sueldos **183**–12

suelte el lápiz **6**–J
suéter **28**–2, **87**–14
suéter anaranjado está sobre el
    suéter gris **25**–11
suéter azul turquesa está dentro
    de la caja **25**–6
suéter blanco está en frente del
    suéter negro **25**–7
suéter con cuello de cisne **96**–7
suéter con cuello de tortuga **96**–9
suéter con cuello en V **96**–8
suéter con cuello redondo **96**–10
suéter gris está debajo del suéter
    anaranjado **25**–10
suéter negro está detrás del suéter
    blanco **25**–8
suéter verde está entre los
    suéteres rosados **25**–12
suéter violeta está al lado del
    suéter gris **25**–9
suéteres amarillos están a la
    izquierda **25**–1
suéteres azules están debajo de
    los suéteres rojos **25**–5
suéteres marrones están a
    la derecha **25**–3
suéteres morados están en
    medio **25**–2
suéteres rojos están encima de
    los suéteres azules **25**–4
suite **192**–16
sujetapapeles **189**–31
suma **204**–7
sumar **204**–A
superación profesional **175**–6
superintendente **50**–8
supermercado **129**–18
supervisar a las personas **176**–O
supervise el uso que hacen los niños
    de Internet **147**–B
supervisor **183**–8
supervisor de la cadena **185**–4
supervisor de línea **185**–4
sur **159**–3
surf **233**–9
surfista **231**–15
suspenso **243**–20
suspensor **91**–6
sustancias ilegales **145**–6
SUV (vehículo deportivo
    utilitario) **160**–7
tabla de cortar **54**–27
tabla de partículas **195**–20
tabla de picar **54**–27
tabla de *snowboard* **237**–23
tabla hawaiana **231**–16
tabla para planchar **101**–14
tabla periódica **207**–26
tablero y el panel de
    instrumentos **163**
tableta **115**–22, **190**–6
tablilla **119**–15, **138**–12, **162**–12
tache la palabra **9**–R
tachuela **189**–35

taco **79**–8
tacón **94**–22
tacones altos **89**–21 , **95**–25, **97**–32
tacones bajos **97**–31
taladrar un diente **120**–D
taladrar una muela **120**–D
taladro eléctrico **194**–8
taladro neumático **196**–9
talco **108**–4
talco para bebé **37**–14
talla universal **96**–6
tallas **96**
taller **175**–14
taller del mecánico **162**
tallos **217**–9
talón **106**–24
talón de pago **183**–11
tambores **244**–16
tanque de buceo **231**–6
tanque de gasolina **162**–10
tanteo **235**–1
tapa **78**–24
tapa de rueda **162**–9
tapa del tomacorriente **195**–46
tapacubos **162**–9
tapete de hule **57**–5
tapones para el oído **197**–15
tarde **18**–17, **19**–24
tarjeta **245**–5
tarjeta de cajero automático **134**–12
tarjeta de embarque móvil **165**–20
tarjeta de emergencia **165**–26
tarjeta de felicitación **136**–15
tarjeta de memoria **241**–18
tarjeta de residente
    permanente **40**–2
tarjeta de seguro médico **111**–3
tarjeta del club de
    conductores **166**–5
tarjeta del seguro social **40**–5
tarjeta madre **190**–18
tarjeta telefónica **15**–23
tarjetas de béisbol **238**–2
tatuaje **32**–18
taxi **154**–3
taxímetro **156**–23
taza **83**–24
taza de aceite **75**–2
taza de azúcar **55**–14
taza de harina **75**–10
taza de té **55**–6
taza grande de café **55**–7
tazón **55**–2
tazón de sopa **83**–21
tazón para batir **54**–28
tazón para mezclar **54**–28, **78**–31
TDD **15**–26
té **81**–39
té de hierbas **81**–40
té helado **79**–12
teatro **129**–23
techo **46**–2
techo gotea **62**–3
tecla estrella **14**–6

tecla numérica **14**–7

teclado **14**–5, **190**–23

teclado electrónico **244**–18

teclee **210**–C

teclee el asunto **211**–V

teclee el código de
verificación **211**–R

teclee la contraseña de nuevo **211**–Q

teclee su nombre **4**–D

teclee una frase **212**–B

teclee una pregunta **212**–C

técnica de registros médicos **172**–39

técnico de
computadoras **171**–19, **188**–12

técnico de reparación de aparatos
electrodomésticos **170**–4

técnico de reparación
electrónica **171**–24

técnico médico de
emergencias **123**–32

TECNOLOGÍA DE LA INFORMACIÓN
(TI) **190**–**191**

tecnología de la información **184**–10

tejas de madera **196**–20

tejer **239**–F

tela de *jeans* **99**–7

tela vaquera **99**–7

TELÉFONO **14**–**15**

teléfono celular **4**–13, **14**–8

teléfono de trabajo **4**

teléfono inteligente **15**–25

teléfono público **131**–23

teléfono residencial **4**–12

telenovelas **242**–5

teleobjetivo **241**–19

telescopio **215**–23

televisor **56**–6

televisor de pantalla grande **50**–14

televisor de pantalla plana **240**–8

temeroso(a) **43**–23

temperatura **13**

templado **13**–5

temprano **19**–22

tenazas **78**–23, **207**–43

tenazas de crisol **207**–44

tendedero **101**–9

tenedor **55**–3, **83**–28

tenedor para ensalada **83**–27

tener 18 o más años de edad **142**–G

tener calor **42**–1

tener frío **42**–4

tener hambre **42**–5

tener náuseas **110**–B

tener sed **42**–2

tener sueño **42**–3

tener un ataque al corazón **118**–D

tener un bebé **41**–L

tener un neumático
reventado **166**–C

tener una reacción alérgica **118**–E

teñir el cabello **33**–D

tenis **86**–7, **234**–15

tenis de mesa **234**–14

terapeuta **117**–14

terapia del habla **117**–13

terapia física **117**–11

terapista ocupacional **172**–45

tercero **16**

tercio **17**–3

terciopelo **99**–10

terminal de la línea aérea **164**

terminar **236**–T

términos históricos **209**

termitas **63**–22

termómetro **111**–11

terno **87**–11

terremoto **148**–5

testigo **144**–11

tetera **54**–17

tetera **55**–16

TI **184**–10

tía **34**–7

tibio **13**–4

tiburón **218**–4

TIEMPO **13**

tienda de alteraciones **100**

tienda de aparatos
electrónicos **133**–20

tienda de artículos de oficina **129**–21

tienda de campaña **232**–10

TIENDA DE COMESTIBLES **72**–**73**

tienda de conveniencia **130**–3

tienda de mascotas **132**–6

tienda de mejoras para el
hogar **129**–20

tienda de música **132**–1

tienda de regalos **192**–5

tienda de ropa de
maternidad **133**–19

tienda de rosquillas **131**–17

tienda de tarjetas **132**–7

tienda de telas **99**

tienda por departamentos **133**–13

Tierra **215**–3

tigre **223**–37

tijeras **33**–17

tijeras de podar **186**–9

tijeras para setos **186**–11

timbre **51**–32, **53**–14

timón **163**–26

tintorería **130**–2

tintura para madera **195**–24

tío **34**–8

tipos de capacitación **175**

tipos de cargos **15**

tipos de material **98**, **99**

tipos de medicamento **115**

tipos de música **243**

tipos de películas **243**

tipos de problemas de salud **117**

tipos de programas de televisión **242**

tirantes **94**–1

tirar **236**–H

tirarse **236**–K

tire la basura **11**–N

tiro con arco **234**–1

titular **135**–7

titular de la póliza **121**–5

título **135**–14, **202**–5

tiza **7**–18

toalla de baño **57**–16

toalla de manos **57**–17

toalla de playa **231**–11

toalla para platos **61**–22

toallas de papel **54**–3

toallita para la cara **57**–6

toallitas húmedas **37**–12, **150**–12

toallitas húmedas
desinfectantes **61**–23

toallitas para la secadora **101**–5

tobillo **106**–23

tobillo torcido **110**–14

tobogán **230**–13

tocadiscos **240**–12

tocar **106**–E

tocar un instrumento **244**–A

tocino **70**–11, **80**–1

todos los días **20**–21

toga **226**–8

tomacorriente **58**–28, **163**–42

tomar apuntes **177**–K

tomar decisiones **178**–C

tomar el autobús para ir al
colegio **38**–H

tomar la orden **82**–E

tomar un baño **108**–B

tomar un examen de
ciudadanía **142**–I

tomar un mensaje **177**–Q

tomar un vuelo **164**

tomar una ducha **38**–C, **108**–A

tomar una foto **226**–A

tomar una radiografía **120**–B

tomar una siesta **53**–A

tomar una sobredosis de
drogas **118**–K

tomarle…la temperatura **111**–B

tomates **69**–6

tome asiento **6**–F

tome notas **10**–C

tome posesión **49**–K

tome un curso de capacitación para
conductores **139**–G

tome un curso de manejo **139**–B

tome un descanso **11**–H

tome un medicamento **116**–D

tome una prueba escrita **139**–E

tómelo con alimentos o leche **114**–A

tómelo una hora antes de
comer **114**–B

tope **54**–22

tormenta **13**–13

tormenta de nieve **13**–24

tormenta de polvo **13**–20

tornado **149**–15

tornillo articulado **194**–38

tornillo de banco **194**–26

tornillo macrométrico **206**–24

tornillo micrométrico **206**–22

tornillo para madera **194**–33

tornillo para máquina **194**–32

toronjas **68**–6

torre **190**–7

torta **73**–39

torta de capas **81**–33

torta de queso **81**–34

torta fácil y rápida **77**

tortilla de huevos **76**–12

tortuga **219**–42

tortuga de tierra **219**–41

tos **110**–9

tostada **80**–4

tostadora **54**–11

total **27**–9

trabajador agrícola **187**–8

trabajador cuidadoso **197**–2

trabajador descuidado **197**–1

trabajador en equipo **180**–3

trabajador portuario **171**–23

trabajadora de cuidado
de niños **170**–16

trabajadora social **173**–57

trabajar **38**–K

trabajar como voluntario **41**–Q

trabajar con sus compañeros
de clase **8**

trabajar en el jardín **53**–B

trabaje en grupo **8**–I

trabaje por sí solo **10**–J

trabajo de nivel de entrada **175**–2

TRABAJO DE OFICINA **188**–**189**

trabajo nuevo **175**–4

trabajos en carretera **158**–16

tractor **187**–9

tractor nivelador **196**–6

tradicional **243**–29

traductor **172**–35

traduzca la palabra **8**–C

traer **246**–E

tragedia **243**–14

tráiler **160**–15

traje **87**–11

traje de baño **90**–22, **90**–26

traje de buzo **231**–5

traje de calle **88**–11

traje formal **88**–11

tranquilo(a) **42**–8

transcribir notas **177**–C

transferir la llamada **177**–O

transmisión automática **163**

transmisión manual **163**

TRANSPORTE BÁSICO **154**–**155**

transporte para ir y volver
del aeropuerto **156**

TRANSPORTE PÚBLICO **156**

trapear el piso **60**–D

trapo para cubrir **195**–54

trapos de limpieza **61**–9

trayectoria de carrera **175**

tréboles **239**–32

trece **16**

trece colonias **208**–1

treinta **16**

tren **154**–7

tren a escala **239**–27

tren subterráneo **155**–12
trepar las barras **230**–C
tres **16**
tres veces por semana **20**–24
triángulo **205**–32
tribunal **127**–13
triciclo **230**–12
trigésimo **16**
trigo **187**–2
trigonometría **204**–18
trinchera **90**–21
tripa **70**–8
trípode **241**–20
triste **43**–19
tritón **218**–27
triturador de desperdicios **54**–7
trituradora de papel **189**–24
trombón **244**–10
trompa **223**–47
trompeta **244**–11
trompón **217**–25
tronco **216**–4
trucha **71**–1
tuba **244**–12
tuberculosis **113**–23
tuberías están congeladas **63**–16
tubo **195**–17
tubo de pasta de dientes **74**–24
tubo de pruebas **207**–42
tubos **74**–12
tuerca **194**–36
tulipán **217**–11
tumbar **236**–F
turbulencia **165**–22
turno **180**–6
tuza **221**–19
TV **56**–6
uña **106**–18
una y cinco **18**–7
una y cuarenta **18**–12
una y cuarenta y cinco **18**–13
una y cuarto **18**–9
una y diez **18**–8
una y media **18**–11
una y quince **18**–9
una y treinta **18**–11
una y veinte **18**–10
únase al grupo de vigilancia
     del vecindario **146**–L
undécimo **16**
ungüento **115**–24
ungüento antibacteriano **119**–12
unidad de DVD y CD-ROM **190**–15
uniforme **88**–10, **237**–16
universidad **200**–7
UNIVERSO **215**
uno **16**
Urano **215**–7
URL **213**–10
usar bulbos de bajo consumo
     energético **225**–H
usar desodorante **108**–C
usar hilo dental **109**–K
usar la puntuación **202**–C

usar una caja registradora **176**–S
usar una tarjeta de crédito **27**–B
usar una tarjeta de débito **27**–C
usar una tarjeta de regalo **27**–E
use las teclas de flecha **211**–N
use sitios cifrados **147**–F
use sitios seguros **147**–F
usuario de la biblioteca **135**–3
usurpación de identidad **145**–9
UTENSILIOS DE COCINA **78**
utensilios de plástico **79**–19
uvas **68**–3
vaca **221**–1
vacaciones **22**–6
vaciar la basura **60**–L
vaciar la secadora **101**–E
vagón del tren subterráneo **156**–6
vale **156**–10
vales **67**–15
valle **214**–18
válvula de cierre del gas **150**–4
vandalismo **145**–1
vaqueros **86**–2, **92**–19
variable **204**–12
varicela **112**–6
vaso de agua **83**–22
vaso de laboratorio **207**–39
vaso lleno **23**–9
vaso vacío **23**–10
vaya directo **159**–A
vaya para que le hagan a su
     automóvil una inspección
     de seguridad y control de
     emisiones **161**–J
vaya una cuadra **159**–F
vea casas **49**–H
vehículo de doble tracción **160**–7
vehículo de exploración
     espacial **215**–20
vehículo eléctrico **160**–2
veinte **16**
veinte dólares **26**–10
veinte para las dos **18**–12
veinticinco **16**
veinticinco centavos **26**–4
veinticuatro **16**
veintidós **16**
veintitrés **16**
veintiuno **16**
vejiga **107**–46
vela **56**–20
velerismo **233**–8
velero **231**–2
velocidad alta **23**–3
velocidad baja **23**–4
velocidad del ventilador **163**–39
velocímetro **163**–27
vena **107**–37
venado **222**–14
venda adhesiva **119**–6
vendaje elástico **119**–13
vendedor ambulante **131**–29
vendedora **94**–3
vendedores **84**–7

vender automóviles **176**–K
venir a la casa **39**–R
VENTA DE GARAJE **102**–**103**
ventana **47**–12, **56**–17
ventana del navegador **213**–8
ventana está rota **62**–5
ventanilla **138**–7
ventanilla de billetes **156**–12
ventanilla de boletos **156**–12
ventas **184**–7
ventilador **55**–19
ventisca **13**–24, **149**–13
Venus **215**–2
ver **106**–A
ver televisión **39**–X
verano **21**–38
VERBOS UTILIZADOS EN LOS
     DEPORTES **236**
verde **24**–5
verduras congeladas **72**–27
verduras y hortalizas **66**–8
VERDURAS Y HORTALIZAS **69**
verduras y hortalizas al vapor **81**–32
vereda **53**–2
veredicto **144**–14
verificar…el pulso **124**–A
verifique la pronunciación **8**–D
verifique lo que oye **12**–O
vertebrados **206**–12
vesícula biliar **107**–44
vestíbulo **50**
vestido **86**–3
vestido de cóctel **89**–20
vestido de maternidad **88**–5
vestido de noche **89**–18
vestimentas calientes **150**–6
vestirlo **36**–H
vestirse **38**–D
vez por semana **20**–22
vía férrea **156**–14
viajar **41**–P
viaje de ida **156**–16
viaje de ida y vuelta **156**–17
VIAJE POR CARRETERA **166**–**167**
vicegobernador **140**–15
vicepresidente **140**–9
víctima **145**–10
VIDA MARINA, ANFIBIOS Y
     REPTILES **218**–**219**
videograbadora digital **56**–7
vieira **218**–20
vieiras **71**–12
viernes **20**–13
viga I **196**–3
viga maestra **196**–3
vigésimo **16**
vigesimoprimero **16**
VIH **113**–21
viña **187**–16
violeta **24**–8, **217**–23
violín **244**–6
violoncelo **244**–7
visera de seguridad **197**–12
visita a la oficina del dentista **120**

visite un centro de planificación
     profesional **174**–A
vista fea **23**–22
vista hermosa **23**–21
vístase con ropa adecuada **179**–B
visualizador digital **7**–16
vitaminas **115**–17
vitrina **94**–5
viviendas para ancianos **52**–11
vivir en EE. UU. por cinco años **142**–H
volante **58**–17, **102**–1, **163**–26
volar un avión **176**–F
voleibol **235**–15
voluntaria **123**–17
voluntario **123**–17
volver a usar las bolsas de
     compra **225**–B
vomitar **110**–C
votar **142**–A
vuelta en U permitida **158**–5
vuelva a ingresar la
     contraseña **211**–Q
waffles **80**–8
windsurf **233**–10
xilófono **244**–15
yeso **115**–20
yo no puedo iniciar sesión **191**–D
yo no puedo instalar la
     actualización **191**–C
yo no puedo ver la transmisión
     del video **191**–F
yoga **124**–4
yogur **72**–22
zanahorias **69**–3
zapatería **132**–10
zapatillas de tenis **95**–32
zapatos **87**–13
zapatos de salón **95**–26
zapatos de tacón bajo **95**–27
zapatos Oxford **95**–29
ZAPATOS Y ACCESORIOS **94**–**95**
zarigüeya **222**–4
zarpa **222**–20
zarzamoras **68**–17
zona de embarque **165**–9
zonas horarias **19**
zoológico **228**–1
zoom **241**–19
zorrillo **222**–12
zorro **222**–15
zumaque venenoso **216**–23

Research Bibliography

The authors and publisher wish to acknowledge the contribution of the following educators for their research on vocabulary development, which has helped inform the principles underlying *OPD*.

Burt, M., J. K. Peyton, and R. Adams. *Reading and Adult English Language Learners: A Review of the Research.* Washington, DC: Center for Applied Linguistics, 2003.

Coady, J. "Research on ESL/EFL Vocabulary Acquisition: Putting it in Context." In *Second Language Reading and Vocabulary Learning,* edited by T. Huckin, M. Haynes, and J. Coady. Norwood, NJ: Ablex, 1993.

de la Fuente, M. J. "Negotiation and Oral Acquisition of L2 Vocabulary: The Roles of Input and Output in the Receptive and Productive Acquisition of Words." *Studies in Second Language Acquisition* 24 (2002): 81–112.

DeCarrico, J. "Vocabulary learning and teaching." In *Teaching English as a Second or Foreign Language,* edited by M. Celcia-Murcia. 3rd ed. Boston: Heinle & Heinle, 2001.

Ellis, R. *The Study of Second Language Acquisition.* Oxford: Oxford University Press, 1994.

Folse, K. *Vocabulary Myths: Applying Second Language Research to Classroom Teaching.* Ann Arbor, MI: University of Michigan Press, 2004.

Gairns, R. and S. Redman. *Working with Words: A Guide to Teaching and Learning Vocabulary.* Cambridge: Cambridge University Press, 1986.

Gass, S. M. and M. J. A. Torres. "Attention When?: An Investigation of the Ordering Effect of Input and Interaction." *Studies in Second Language Acquisition* 27 (Mar 2005): 1–31.

Henriksen, Birgit. "Three Dimensions of Vocabulary Development." *Studies in Second Language Acquisition* 21 (1999): 303–317.

Koprowski, Mark. "Investigating the Usefulness of Lexical Phrases in Contemporary Coursebooks." *Oxford ELT Journal* 59(4) (2005): 322–332.

McCrostie, James. "Examining Learner Vocabulary Notebooks." *Oxford ELT Journal* 61 (July 2007): 246–255.

Nation, P. *Learning Vocabulary in Another Language.* Cambridge: Cambridge University Press, 2001.

National Center for ESL Literacy Education Staff. *Adult English Language Instruction in the 21st Century.* Washington, DC: Center for Applied Linguistics, 2003.

National Reading Panel. *Teaching Children to Read: An Evidenced-Based Assessment of the Scientific Research Literature on Reading and its Implications on Reading Instruction.* 2000. https://www.nichd.nih.gov/publications/pubs/nrp/documents/report.pdf.

Newton, J. "Options for Vocabulary Learning through Communication Tasks." *Oxford ELT Journal* 55(1) (2001): 30–37.

Prince, P. "Second Language Vocabulary Learning: The Role of Context Versus Translations as a Function of Proficiency." *Modern Language Journal* 80(4) (1996): 478–493.

Savage, K. L., ed. *Teacher Training Through Video - ESL Techniques: Early Production.* White Plains, NY: Longman Publishing Group, 1992.

Schmitt, N. *Vocabulary in Language Teaching.* Cambridge: Cambridge University Press, 2000.

Smith, C. B. *Vocabulary Instruction and Reading Comprehension.* Bloomington, IN: ERIC Clearinghouse on Reading English and Communication, 1997.

Wood, K. and J. Josefina Tinajero. "Using Pictures to Teach Content to Second Language Learners." *Middle School Journal* 33 (2002): 47–51.